SOURCES

Notable Selections in *Race and Ethnicity*

SECOND EDITION

1.1, 5.2, 1.2, 13

About the Editors

ADALBERTO AGUIRRE, JR., received his bachelor's degree from the University of California, Santa Cruz, and a master's degree and a doctorate in sociology and linguistics from Stanford University. He is a professor of sociology at the University of California, Riverside. His research interests are in sociolinguistics, the sociology of education, and race and ethnic relations. Professor Aguirre has written extensively for such professional journals as *Social Problems, Social Science Journal, Social Science Quarterly, International Journal of Sociology of Language,* and *La Revue Roumaine de Linguistique.* He is the author or coauthor of *An Experimental Sociolinguistic Investigation of Chicano Bilingualism; Intelligence Testing, Education and Chicanos; Language in the Chicano Speech Community; American Ethnicity: The Dynamics and Consequences of Discrimination;* and *Chicanos in Higher Education: Issues and Dilemmas for the Twenty-First Century.*

DAVID V. BAKER received his bachelor's degree in political science from California State University, Northridge, and a master's degree and a doctorate in sociology from the University of California, Riverside. He is an associate professor of sociology in the Department of Behavioral Sciences at Riverside Community College in Riverside, California. His research and teaching interests are in race and ethnic relations and racism in the American criminal justice system. He has contributed works to several professional journals, including *Ethnic Studies, Social Justice,* the *Justice Professional, Criminal Justice Abstracts,* and the *Social Science Journal.* Professor Baker is also an associate editor for the *Justice Professional.*

Professors Aguirre and Baker are coauthors of *Race, Racism and the Death Penalty in the United States; Perspectives on Race and Ethnicity in American Criminal Justice;* and *Structured Inequality in American Society: Critical Discussions on the Continuing Significance of Race, Ethnicity, Gender, and Class.*

SOURCES

Notable Selections in
Race and Ethnicity

SECOND EDITION

Edited by

ADALBERTO AGUIRRE, JR.
University of California, Riverside

DAVID V. BAKER
Riverside Community College

Dushkin/McGraw-Hill

A Division of The McGraw-Hill Companies

This book is dedicated to the loving memory of a father and a brother, Adalberto Aguirre, Sr., and Forrest S. Baker, Jr.

Manufactured in the United States of America

Second Edition

10 9 8 7 6 5 4 3 2 1

Library of Congress Cataloging-in-Publication Data
  Main entry under title:
    Sources: notable selections in race and ethnicity/edited by Adalberto Aguirre, Jr. and David V. Baker.—2nd ed.
    Includes bibliographical references and index.
    1. United States—Race relations. 2. United States—Ethnic relations. 3. Minorities—United States. 4. Racism—United States. 5. Ethnicity—United States I. Aguirre, Adalberto, Jr., *comp.* II. Baker, David V., *comp.*

305.800973—dc20

0-697-34332-4

ISSN: 1098-5433

Preface

Although the study of racial and ethnic groups and relations has long been integral to the social sciences, in the United States this field has witnessed revived and renewed attention in recent years. It is a dynamic, challenging, and changing field that captures the attention and passion of sociologists, educators, political scientists, psychologists, policymakers, and social commentators. However, this field of study is not remote from our everyday experiences. Issues related to race and ethnic relations confront all of us personally and are a topic of concern everywhere in our society.

Sources: Notable Selections in Race and Ethnicity is an introductory-level college text anthology that contains 35 carefully edited selections that have shaped the study of race and ethnicity and our contemporary understanding of it. Included here are the works of a wide range of distinguished observers, past and present, and each selection contains essential ideas or has served as a touchstone for other scholars. These selections offer findings from a variety of disciplines and are well suited to courses that attempt to examine in some depth topics related to race and ethnicity. Each selection is preceded by a headnote that establishes the relevance of the selection. There is also a volume introduction, which contains some provocative recommendations for studying racial and ethnic relations in the United States.

The selections are organized topically around the major areas of study in race and ethnic relations in the social sciences: the selections in Part 1 introduce the basic concepts; Part 2, theoretical orientations to the study of race and ethnicity in the United States; Part 3, race and ethnicity in American institutions; Part 4, race and ethnicity in popular culture and community; and Part 5, the future of race and ethnic relations in the United States.

Changes to this edition. This edition of *Sources: Notable Selections in Race and Ethnicity* represents a considerable revision from the first edition. Of the 35 classic readings, 9 are new. The greatest changes are reflected in chapter 6, "The Educational Institution," and chapter 9, "The Legal Institution," as well as in chapter 11, "The Race and Ethnic Community," which is itself a brand new chapter. Many of these revisions are directly attributable to feedback from the users of the first edition.

A word to the instructor. An *Instructor's Manual With Test Questions* (multiple-choice and essay) is available through the publisher for the instructor using *Sources* in the classroom.

Sources: Notable Selections in Race and Ethnicity is only one title in the Sources series. If you are interested in seeing the table of contents for any of the other titles, please visit the Sources Web site at http://www.dushkin.com/ sources/.

Acknowledgments.   Thanks go to those who reviewed the first edition of *Sources* and responded with specific suggestions for the second edition:

Peter Adler
University of Denver

Cliff Brown
University of New Hampshire

Georgine E. Dickens
Morgan Community College

Steven Smith
Rutgers University

We welcome your comments and observations about the selections in this volume and encourage you to write to us with suggestions for other selections to include or changes to consider. Please send your remarks to us in care of SOURCES, Dushkin/McGraw Hill, Sluice Dock, Guilford, CT 06437.

Adalberto Aguirre, Jr.
University of California, Riverside

David V. Baker
Riverside Community College

Contents

CHAPTER 8   The Economic Institution   248

vii

*Notable
Selections in
Race and
Ethnicity*

Introduction: Studying Race and Ethnic Relations

Adalberto Aguirre, Jr., and David V. Baker

Many people assume that inequality does not exist in the United States. Others believe that if inequality does exist, then it is rooted in individual short-comings. This view suggests that it is easier to blame the victims of bias for their unequal status than to acknowledge the existence of social processes in society that promote and maintain inequality. Given this kind of thinking, it is not surprising that discussions of inequality in the United States are usually both technical and passionate. Such discussions become technical when distinctions begin to be made between *equality* and *equal rights*. They become passionate when the topic of *victims* and *victimizers* is introduced into the discussion.

We think that inequality is the foundation upon which equality is promoted in U.S. society. Implicit in this premise is the idea that equality is a relative measure of one's quality of life. That is, to be equal someone has to be unequal. Secondly, equality is a comparative social activity. That is, one compares oneself with others to evaluate one's level of equality. Interestingly, status characteristics, such as sex, race, or ethnicity, are crucial determinants in shaping social perceptions for equality and inequality. The collection of selections in this book will provide the reader with a variety of notable examples illustrating the social context in which status characteristics shape perceptions of equality and inequality.

The Sociological Context for the Study of Inequality

In this book we also look at the patterns and contexts of structured social inequality for racial and ethnic groups. *Social inequality* is both the means and ends of social stratification. Social stratification establishes a graded hierarchy of superior and inferior ranks in society. The resources and opportunities available in society are distributed according to a person's placement in the social hierarchy. For example, those at the top of the social hierarchy have access to a larger share of social opportunity and resources than those near the bottom of the social hierarchy. The resources that are valued in a society are usually those things that count in any society—namely, material wealth, social status or social prestige, and political power.

The dynamics of a stratified social system are rooted in a disproportionate distribution of valued resources and results in two culturally distinct groups of people: a culturally dominant group and a culturally subordinate group. The dominant group maintains its social position by controlling the production of valued resources, which they are able to do because they have better access to a larger share of opportunities and resources. For example, by means of property ownership, the dominant group can decide who will have access to valued resources—jobs, home mortgages, etc. In contrast, members of the subordinate group are unable to improve their rank within the social hierarchy because they lack access to the necessary resources.

Structured Social Inequality

The term *structured social inequality* defines a social arrangement patterned socially and historically, which is rooted in an ideological framework that legitimates and justifies the subordination of particular groups of people. In other words, social inequality is *institutionalized*. For example, one can find a record of consistent patterns of institutionalized discrimination in U.S. society that reflect a racial ideology that has resulted in members of particular racial and ethnic groups being systematically denied full and equal participation in major social institutions—education, employment, politics, etc. The discrimination and segregation experienced by African Americans, Hispanic Americans, Native Americans, and Asian Americans in the U.S. educational system have resulted in a pattern of limited occupational and economic growth for each group. Thus, the dynamics of discrimination and segregation have confined the African American, Hispanic, and Native American populations to a subordinate position in U.S. society. Yet participation in these institutions is essential for social mobility—the transition from one social position to another in the stratified system. In a sense, the subordinate position of racial and ethnic groups in U.S. society amounts to a caste system. The structured social relationship of racial and ethnic groups to U.S. society is characterized by closure and rigidity of rank, and institutionalization and acceptance of rigid ranks. Several selections in this book illustrate the extent to which racial and ethnic stratification in the United States is institutionalized.

Structured Discrimination

Racial and ethnic groups in U.S. society are victims of *structured discrimination*. Where social inequality reflects the procedural nature of unequal access to resources in society, structured discrimination identifies the existence of racial and ethnic prejudice. Together, social inequality and structural discrimination define the sociocultural relationship of racial and ethnic groups to society. For example, the limited access of racial and ethnic groups to valued resources constrains their ability to alter their social position in society. Secondly, since their social position is a subordinate one, racial and ethnic minorities are unable to promote their interests as either a group of individuals or as a class of individuals. As a result, racial and ethnic groups are ignored by social institutions that control access to valued resources because the groups do not possess the required resources for legitimate participation within those social institutions. In the end, racial and ethnic minorities become the victims of racial ideologies that serve as the basis for an unequal distribution of and access to valued resources. Thus, another purpose of this book is to examine the context of structured discrimination for racial and ethnic groups in U.S. society.

Racial and Ethnic Oppression

The intersection between racial ideology, racial prejudice, and structured racial inequality is *racial oppression*. Racial oppression is the cumulative product of discriminatory acts built into social structures and legitimated or sanctioned by cultural beliefs and legal codes. Racial oppression takes on two dimensions: a *structural* dimension, in which the structural arrangements of social institutions act to physically control members of a perceived inferior group through discriminatory actions; and a *sociocultural* dimension, by which the cultural (prejudicial) beliefs and the statutory (legal) requirements act to legitimate or sanction these physical controls of subordinate groups. A purpose of this book is to provide observations regarding the existence of racial oppression.

The Persistence of Inequality

Racism and its racist ideologies remain pervasive in contemporary society because they are deeply ingrained in U.S. culture. One social critic notes that "racial ideologies become embodied in the thought of future generations who have no conception of the exact context in which they originated, and are thus transformed into broad-based racial prejudice even among people whose interests are not served by it."[1]

Another social critic adds to this viewpoint by arguing that racial prejudice has become part of our cultural heritage and that "as such both exploiter and exploited for the most part are born heirs to it."[2]

Still another critic noted that racism in American society remains pervasive because "new civil rights laws have failed to diminish the violence of poverty, to reallocate resources, to redistribute wealth and income and to penetrate the corporate boardrooms and federal bureaucracies."[3]

These observations reinforce the idea that racial prejudice and the ideology of racism in contemporary American society are irrational, ingrained racial folklore at work.

Despite the intention of the framers of the Constitution to ensure equal rights to every person, social differences between persons developed during the historical maturation of the United States. These social differences matured as forms of social, political, educational, and economic inequality. The persistence of racial and ethnic inequality in a society committed to individual rights is, therefore, a direct challenge to the historical romanticism surrounding the arrival of immigrants to the United States seeking freedom and opportunity. Race and ethnicity have played a significant historical role in determining the individual rights of certain racial and ethnic immigrant groups in U.S. society. To borrow an observation from C. Wright Mills in *The Sociological Imagination:* the study of racial and ethnic inequality in the United States is the sociologist's quest for an introspective understanding of equality in American society. Thus, we have selected the contributions in this text in hopes of enlightening our readers to this theme. We have selected critical and important discussions on race and ethnic inequality that uncover the social consequences of structured inequality.

Organization of the Book

In our shared teaching experience, we have come to see that a preponderance of American college students presumes that the aims of the civil rights campaigns of the 1960s alleviated the gross social inequities suffered by racial and ethnic minorities in U.S. society. Many students believe that members of racial and ethnic minority groups are no longer systematically denied equal participation in the major social institutions of U.S. society. We think this misconception has been encouraged, in part, by the continued debate regarding the liabilities of affirmative action programs and whether or not majority White group members are the *new* victims of "reverse discrimination." Our purpose in this book, then, is to introduce students to some of the notable discourse regarding consistent patterns of institutionalized discrimination and forms of racial ideology in U.S. society. The selections in Part 1 introduce students to some basic sociological ideas underlying race and ethnic relations in the United States; namely, race, ethnicity, prejudice, discrimination, and racism. Discussions in Part 2 concern theoretical orientations to the study of race and ethnic relations in the United States. Part 3 focuses on the institutional consequences of race and ethnic inequality in U.S. society. Part 4 discusses the relationship between race and popular culture and explores the ethnic community. And Part 5 involves arguments centering on the future of race and ethnic relations in U.S. society.

Notes

1. M. Barrera, *Race and Class in the Southwest* (Notre Dame, IL: University of Notre Dame Press, 1979), p. 198.
2. O. Cox, *Caste, Class and Race* (London, England: Modern Reader, 1948).
3. L. Litwark, "Professor Seeks Revolution of Values." *The University of California Clip Sheet* (May 1987), p. 21.

PART ONE

Basic Concepts

On the Internet . . .

Sites appropriate to Part One

The American Civil Liberties Union (ACLU) is the foremost
advocate of individual rights in the United States, litigating,
legislating, and educating the public on a broad array of issues
affecting individual freedom. This page includes links to racial
equality, women's rights, criminal justice, and immigrants'
rights.

    http://www.aclu.org/

Established in 1957, the Civil Rights Division of the
Department of Justice is the primary institution within the
federal government responsible for enforcing federal statutes
prohibiting discrimination on the basis of race, sex, handicap,
religion, and national origin. The site includes links to special
issues and the full text of select cases and speeches.

    http://www.usdoj.gov/crt/

The U.S. Commission on Civil Rights is an independent,
bipartisan agency first established by Congress to investigate
complaints, research information, and appraise federal laws
relating to discrimination.

    http://www.usccr.gov/

The primary purpose of the Institute on Race and Ethnicity is
to conduct and encourage a variety of activities designed to
enhance conceptual, theoretical, and empirical inquiry into the
phenomena of race and ethnicity.

    http://www.uwm.edu/Dept/IRE/

CHAPTER 1 # Race and Ethnicity

1.1 MICHAEL OMI AND HOWARD WINANT

Racial Formations

For social scientists, one decisive aspect of race is that it is a sociopolitical construct. The maxim that racial distinctions are socially defined is clearly illustrated throughout the sociopolitical history of the United States: Black Africans were easily identified as slaves by the color of their skin, while Whites were always associated with freedom. Mob violence and vigilantism were directed toward the Chinese "coolies," who could easily be identified by their "slanted" eyelids. The U.S. government's extermination policy of American Indians was possible because Indians were easily identified by their skin color and by their hair color and texture. The U.S. repatriation policy toward Haitian political refugees has been identified by many in Congress as racially biased against Blacks. In other words, the biological attributes of race have served as the basis of racial oppression in American history. These historical examples illustrate that beyond its biological importance, race is a political arrangement.

In the present selection, Michael Omi, a professor in the Department of Ethnic Studies at the University of California, Berkeley, and Howard Winant, a professor of sociology at Temple University, refer to the sociohistorical development of race as the *racialization* of American society. They argue that because race is arbitrarily constructed, the meaning and use of race follows economic and political changes in U.S. society.

Key Concept: the social significance of race in U.S. society

*I*n 1982–83, Susie Guillory Phipps unsuccessfully sued the Louisiana Bureau of Vital Records to change her racial classification from black to white. The descendant of an eighteenth-century white planter and a black slave, Phipps was designated "black" in her birth certificate in accordance with a 1970 state law which declared anyone with at least one-thirty-second "Negro blood" to be black. The legal battle raised intriguing questions about the concept of race, its meaning in contemporary society, and its use (and abuse) in public policy. Assistant Attorney General Ron Davis defended the law by pointing out that some type of racial classification was necessary to comply with federal record-keeping requirements and to facilitate programs for the prevention of genetic diseases. Phipps's attorney, Brian Begue, argued that the assignment of racial categories on birth certificates was unconstitutional and that the one-thirty-second designation was inaccurate. He called on a retired Tulane University professor who cited research indicating that most whites have one-twentieth "Negro" ancestry. In the end, Phipps lost. The court upheld a state law which quantified racial identity, and in so doing affirmed the legality of assigning individuals to specific racial groupings.[1]

The Phipps case illustrates the continuing dilemma of defining race and establishing its meaning in institutional life. Today, to assert that variations in human physiognomy are racially based is to enter a constant and intense debate. *Scientific* interpretations of race have not been alone in sparking heated controversy; *religious* perspectives have done so as well.[2] Most centrally, of course, race has been a matter of *political* contention. This has been particularly true in the United States, where the concept of race has varied enormously over time without ever leaving the center stage of US history.

WHAT IS RACE?

Race consciousness, and its articulation in theories of race, is largely a modern phenomenon. When European explorers in the New World "discovered" people who looked different than themselves, these "natives" challenged then existing conceptions of the origins of the human species, and raised disturbing questions as to whether *all* could be considered in the same "family of man."[3] Religious debates flared over the attempt to reconcile the Bible with the existence of "racially distinct" people. Arguments took place over creation itself, as theories of polygenesis questioned whether God had made only one species of humanity ("monogenesis"). Europeans wondered if the natives of the New World were indeed human beings with redeemable souls. At stake were not only the prospects for conversion, but the types of treatment to be accorded them. The expropriation of property, the denial of political rights, the introduction of slavery and other forms of coercive labor, as well as outright extermination, all presupposed a worldview which distinguished Europeans—children of God, human beings, etc.—from "others." Such a worldview was needed to explain why some should be "free" and others enslaved, why some had rights to land and property while others did not. Race, and the interpretation of racial differences, was a central factor in that worldview.

In the colonial epoch science was no less a field of controversy than religion in attempts to comprehend the concept of race and its meaning. Spurred on by the classificatory scheme of living organisms devised by Linnaeus in *Systema Naturae*, many scholars in the eighteenth and nineteenth centuries dedicated themselves to the identification and ranking of variations in humankind. Race was thought of as a *biological* concept, yet its precise definition was the subject of debates which, as we have noted, continue to rage today. Despite efforts ranging from Dr. Samuel Morton's studies of cranial capacity[4] to contemporary attempts to base racial classification on shared gene pools,[5] the concept of race has defied biological definition. . . .

Attempts to discern the *scientific meaning* of race continue to the present day. Although most physical anthropologists and biologists have abandoned the quest for a scientific basis to determine racial categories, controversies have recently flared in the area of genetics and educational psychology. For instance, an essay by Arthur Jensen which argued that hereditary factors shape intelligence not only revived the "nature or nurture" controversy, but raised highly volatile questions about racial equality itself.[6] Clearly the attempt to establish a *biological* basis of race has not been swept into the dustbin of history, but is being resurrected in various scientific arenas. All such attempts seek to remove the concept of race from fundamental social, political, or economic determination. They suggest instead that the truth of race lies in the terrain of innate characteristics, of which skin color and other physical attributes provide only the most obvious, and in some respects most superficial, indicators.

RACE AS A SOCIAL CONCEPT

The social sciences have come to reject biologistic notions of race in favor of an approach which regards race as a *social* concept. Beginning in the eighteenth century, this trend has been slow and uneven, but its direction clear. In the nineteenth century Max Weber discounted biological explanations for racial conflict and instead highlighted the social and political factors which engendered such conflict.[7] The work of pioneering cultural anthropologist Franz Boas was crucial in refuting the scientific racism of the early twentieth century by rejecting the connection between race and culture, and the assumption of a continuum of "higher" and "lower" cultural groups. Within the contemporary social science literature, race is assumed to be a variable which is shaped by broader societal forces.

Race is indeed a pre-eminently *sociohistorical* concept. Racial categories and the meaning of race are given concrete expression by the specific social relations and historical context in which they are embedded. Racial meanings have varied tremendously over time and between different societies.

In the United States, the black/white color line has historically been rigidly defined and enforced. White is seen as a "pure" category. Any racial intermixture makes one "nonwhite." In the movie *Raintree County*, Elizabeth Taylor describes the worst of fates to befall whites as "havin' a little Negra blood in ya'—just one little teeny drop and a person's all Negra."[8] This thinking flows from what Marvin Harris has characterized as the principle of *hypo-descent*:

> By what ingenious computation is the genetic tracery of a million years of evolution unraveled and each man [sic] assigned his proper social box? In the United States, the mechanism employed is the rule of hypo-descent. This descent rule requires Americans to believe that anyone who is known to have had a Negro ancestor is a Negro. We admit nothing in between.... "Hypo-descent" means affiliation with the subordinate rather than the superordinate group in order to avoid the ambiguity of intermediate identity.... The rule of hypo-descent is, therefore, an invention, which we in the United States have made in order to keep biological facts from intruding into our collective racist fantasies.[9]

The Susie Guillory Phipps case merely represents the contemporary expression of this racial logic.

By contrast, a striking feature of race relations in the lowland areas of Latin America since the abolition of slavery has been the relative absence of sharply defined racial groupings. No such rigid descent rule characterizes racial identity in many Latin American societies. Brazil, for example, has historically had less rigid conceptions of race, and thus a variety of "intermediate" racial categories exist. Indeed, as Harris notes, "One of the most striking consequences of the Brazilian system of racial identification is that parents and children and even brothers and sisters are frequently accepted as representatives of quite opposite racial types."[10] Such a possibility is incomprehensible within the logic of racial categories in the US.

To suggest another example: the notion of "passing" takes on new meaning if we compare various American cultures' means of assigning racial identity. In the United States, individuals who are actually "black" by the logic of hypo-descent have attempted to skirt the discriminatory barriers imposed by law and custom by attempting to "pass" for white.[11] Ironically, these same individuals would not be able to pass for "black" in many Latin American societies.

Consideration of the term "black" illustrates the diversity of racial meanings which can be found among different societies and historically within a given society. In contemporary British politics the term "black" is used to refer to all nonwhites. Interestingly this designation has not arisen through the racist discourse of groups such as the National Front. Rather, in political and cultural movements, Asian as well as Afro-Caribbean youth are adopting the term as an expression of self-identity.[12] The wide-ranging meanings of "black" illustrate the manner in which racial categories are shaped politically.[13]

The meaning of race is defined and congested throughout society, in both collective action and personal practice. In the process, racial categories themselves are formed, transformed, destroyed and reformed. We use the term *racial formation* to refer to the process by which social, economic and political forces determine the content and importance of racial categories, and by which they are in turn shaped by racial meanings. Crucial to this formulation is the treatment of race as a *central axis* of social relations which cannot be subsumed under or reduced to some broader category or conception.

*Michael Omi
and Howard
Winant*

RACIAL IDEOLOGY AND RACIAL IDENTITY

The seemingly obvious, "natural" and "common sense" qualities which the existing racial order exhibits themselves testify to the effectiveness of the racial formation process in constructing racial meanings and racial identities.

One of the first things we notice about people when we meet them (along with their sex) is their race. We utilize race to provide clues about *who* a person is. This fact is made painfully obvious when we encounter someone whom we cannot conveniently racially categorize—someone who is, for example, racially "mixed" or of an ethnic/racial group with which we are not familiar. Such an encounter becomes a source of discomfort and momentarily a crisis of racial meaning. Without a racial identity, one is in danger of having no identity.

Our compass for navigating race relations depends on preconceived notions of what each specific racial group looks like. Comments such as, "Funny, you don't look black," betray an underlying image of what black should be. We also become disoriented when people do not act "black," "Latino," or indeed "white." The content of such stereotypes reveals a series of unsubstantiated beliefs about who these groups are and what "they" are like.[14]

In US society, then, a kind of "racial etiquette" exists, a set of interpretative codes and racial meanings which operate in the interactions of daily life. Rules shaped by our perception of race in a comprehensively racial society determine the "presentation of self,"[15] distinctions of status, and appropriate modes of conduct. "Etiquette" is not mere universal adherence to the dominant group's rules, but a more dynamic combination of these rules with the values and beliefs of subordinated groupings. This racial "subjection" is quintessentially ideological. Everybody learns some combination, some version, of the rules of racial classification, and of their own racial identity, often without obvious teaching or conscious inculcation. Race becomes "common sense"—a way of comprehending, explaining and acting in the world.

Racial beliefs operate as an "amateur biology," a way of explaining the variations in "human nature."[16] Differences in skin color and other obvious physical characteristics supposedly provide visible clues to differences lurking underneath. Temperament, sexuality, intelligence, athletic ability, aesthetic preferences and so on are presumed to be fixed and discernible from the palpable mark of race. Such diverse questions as our confidence and trust in others (for example, clerks or salespeople, media figures, neighbors), our sexual preferences and romantic images, our tastes in music, films, dance, or sports, and our very ways of talking, walking, eating and dreaming are ineluctably shaped by notions of race. Skin color "differences" are thought to explain perceived differences in intellectual, physical and artistic temperaments, and to justify distinct treatment of racially identified individuals and groups.

The continuing persistence of racial ideology suggests that these racial myths and stereotypes cannot be exposed as such in the popular imagination. They are, we think, too essential, too integral, to the maintenance of the US social order. Of course, particular meanings, stereotypes and myths can change, but the presence of a *system* of racial meanings and stereotypes, of racial ideology, seems to be a permanent feature of US culture.

Film and television, for example, have been notorious in disseminating images of racial minorities which establish for audiences what people from these groups look like, how they behave, and "who they are."[17] The power of the media lies not only in their ability to reflect the dominant racial ideology, but in their capacity to shape that ideology in the first place. D. W. Griffith's epic *Birth of a Nation*, a sympathetic treatment of the rise of the Ku Klux Klan during Reconstruction, helped to generate, consolidate and "nationalize" images of blacks which had been more disparate (more regionally specific, for example) prior to the film's appearance.[18] In US television, the necessity to define characters in the briefest and most condensed manner has led to the perpetuation of racial caricatures, as racial stereotypes serve as shorthand for scriptwriters, directors and actors, in commercials, etc. Television's tendency to address the "lowest common denominator" in order to render programs "familiar" to an enormous and diverse audience leads it regularly to assign and reassign racial characteristics to particular groups, both minority and majority.

These and innumerable other examples show that we tend to view race as something fixed and immutable—something rooted in "nature." Thus we mask the historical construction of racial categories, the shifting meaning of race, and the crucial role of politics and ideology in shaping race relations. Races do not emerge full-blown. They are the results of diverse historical practices and are continually subject to challenge over their definition and meaning.

RACIALIZATION: THE HISTORICAL DEVELOPMENT OF RACE

In the United States, the racial category of "black" evolved with the consolidation of racial slavery. By the end of the seventeenth century, Africans whose specific identity was Ibo, Yoruba, Fulani, etc., were rendered "black" by an ideology of exploitation based on racial logic—the establishment and maintenance of a "color line." This of course did not occur overnight. A period of indentured servitude which was not rooted in racial logic preceded the consolidation of racial slavery. With slavery, however, a racially based understanding of society was set in motion which resulted in the shaping of a specific *racial* identity not only for the slaves but for the European settlers as well. Winthrop Jordan has observed: "From the initially common term *Christian*, at mid-century there was a marked shift toward the terms *English* and *free*. After about 1680, taking the colonies as a whole, a new term of self-identification appeared—*white*."[19]

We employ the term *racialization* to signify the extension of racial meaning to a previously racially unclassified relationship, social practice or group.

Racialization is an ideological process, an historically specific one. Racial ideology is constructed from pre-existing conceptual (or, if one prefers, "discursive") elements and emerges from the struggles of competing political projects and ideas seeking to articulate similar elements differently. An account of racialization processes that avoids the pitfalls of US ethnic history[20] remains to be written.

Particularly during the nineteenth century, the category of "white" was subject to challenges brought about by the influx of diverse groups who were not of the same Anglo-Saxon stock as the founding immigrants. In the nineteenth century, political and ideological struggles emerged over the classification of Southern Europeans, the Irish and Jews, among other "nonwhite" categories.[21] Nativism was only effectively curbed by the institutionalization of a racial order that drew the color line *around*, rather than *within*, Europe.

By stopping short of racializing immigrants from Europe after the Civil War, and by subsequently allowing their assimilation, the American racial order was reconsolidated in the wake of the tremendous challenge placed before it by the abolition of racial slavery.[22] With the end of Reconstruction in 1877, an effective program for limiting the emergent class struggles of the later nineteenth century was forged: the definition of the working class *in racial terms*— as "white." This was not accomplished by any legislative decree or capitalist maneuvering to divide the working class, but rather by white workers themselves. Many of them were recent immigrants, who organized on racial lines as much as on traditionally defined class lines.[23] The Irish on the West Coast, for example, engaged in vicious anti-Chinese race-baiting and committed many pogrom-type assaults on Chinese in the course of consolidating the trade union movement in California.

Thus the very political organization of the working class was in important ways a racial project. The legacy of racial conflicts and arrangements shaped the definition of interests and in turn led to the consolidation of institutional patterns (e.g., segregated unions, dual labor markets, exclusionary legislation) which perpetuated the color line *within* the working class. Selig Perlman, whose study of the development of the labor movement is fairly sympathetic to this process, notes that:

> The political issue after 1877 was racial, not financial, and the weapon was not merely the ballot, but also "direct action"—violence. The anti-Chinese agitation in California, culminating as it did in the Exclusion Law passed by Congress in 1882, was doubtless the most important single factor in the history of American labor, for without it the entire country might have been overrun by Mongolian [sic] labor and *the labor movement might have become a conflict of races instead of one of classes*.[24]

More recent economic transformations in the US have also altered interpretations of racial identities and meanings. The automation of southern agriculture and the augmented labor demand of the postwar boom transformed blacks from a largely rural, impoverished labor force to a largely urban, working-class group by 1970.[25] When boom became bust and liberal welfare statism moved rightwards, the majority of blacks came to be seen, increasingly, as part of the "underclass," as state "dependents." Thus the particularly deleterious effects on blacks of global and national economic shifts (generally rising unemployment rates, changes in the employment structure away from reliance on labor intensive work, etc.) were explained once again in the late 1970s and 1980s (as they had been in the 1940s and mid-1960s) as the result of defective black cultural norms, of familial disorganization, etc.[26] In this way new racial attributions, new racial myths, are affixed to "blacks."[27] Similar changes in racial identity are presently affecting Asians and Latinos, as such economic forces as increasing Third World impoverishment and indebtedness fuel immigration and high interest rates, Japanese competition spurs resentments, and US jobs seem to fly away to Korea and Singapore.[28] ...

Once we understand that race overflows the boundaries of skin color, super-exploitation, social stratification, discrimination and prejudice, cultural domination and cultural resistance, state policy (or of any other particular social relationship we list), once we recognize the racial dimension present to some degree in *every* identity, institution and social practice in the United States—once we have done this, it becomes possible to speak of *racial formation*. This recognition is hard-won; there is a continuous temptation to think of race as an *essence*, as something fixed, concrete and objective, as (for example) one of the categories just enumerated. And there is also an opposite temptation: to see it as a mere illusion, which an ideal social order would eliminate.

In our view it is crucial to break with these habits of thought. The effort must be made to understand race as *an unstable and "decentered" complex of social meanings constantly being transformed by political struggle.*

NOTES

1. *San Francisco Chronicle,* 14 September 1982, 19 May 1983. Ironically, the 1970 Louisiana law was enacted to supersede an old Jim Crow statute which relied on the idea of "common report" in determining an infant's race. Following Phipps's unsuccessful attempt to change her classification and have the law declared unconstitutional, a legislative effort arose which culminated in the repeal of the law. See *San Francisco Chronicle,* 23 June 1983.

2. The Mormon church, for example, has been heavily criticized for its doctrine of black inferiority.

3. Thomas F. Gossett notes:

   Race theory ... had up until fairly modern times no firm hold on European thought. On the other hand, race theory and race prejudice were by no means unknown at the time when the English colonists came to North America. Undoubtedly, the age of exploration led many to speculate on race differences at a period when neither Europeans nor Englishmen were prepared to make allowances for vast cultural diversities. Even though race theories had not then secured wide acceptance or even sophisticate formulation, the first contacts of the Spanish with the Indians in the Americas can now be recognized as the beginning of a struggle between conceptions of the nature of primitive peoples which has not yet been wholly settled. (Thomas F. Gossett, Race: The History of an Idea in America (New York: Schocken Books, 1965), p. 16)

Winthrop Jordan provides a detailed account of early European colonialists' attitudes about color and race in *White Over Black: American Attitudes Toward the Negro, 1550–1812* (New York: Norton, 1977 [1968]), pp. 3–43.

4. Pro-slavery physician Samuel George Morton (1799–1851) compiled a collection of 800 crania from all parts of the world which formed the sample for his studies of race. Assuming that the larger the size of the cranium translated into greater intelligence, Morton established a relationship between race and skull capacity. Gossett reports that:

In 1849, one of his studies included the following results: The English skulls in his collection proved to be the largest, with an average cranial capacity of 96 cubic inches. The Americans and Germans were rather poor seconds, both with cranial capacities of 90 cubic inches. At the bottom of the list were the Negroes with 83 cubic inches, the Chinese with 82, and the Indians with 79. (Ibid., p. 74)

On Morton's methods, see Stephen J. Gould, "The Finagle Factor," *Human Nature* (July 1978).

5. Definitions of race founded upon a common pool of genes have not held up when confronted by scientific research which suggests that the differences *within* a given human population are greater than those between populations. See L. L. Cavalli-Sforza, "The Genetics of Human Populations," *Scientific American* (September 1974), pp. 81–9.

6. Arthur Jensen, "How Much Can We Boost IQ and Scholastic Achievement?", *Harvard Educational Review*, vol. 39 (1969), pp. 1–123.

7. Ernst Moritz Manasse, "Max Weber on Race," *Social Research*, vol. 14 (1947), pp. 191–221.

8. Quoted in Edward D.C. Campbell, Jr, *The Celluloid South: Hollywood and the Southern Myth* (Knoxville: University of Tennessee Press, 1981), pp. 168–70.

9. Marvin Harris, *Patterns of Race in the Americas* (New York: Norton, 1964), p. 56.

10. Ibid., p. 57.

11. After James Meredith had been admitted as the first black student at the University of Mississippi, Harry S. Murphy announced that he, and not Meredith, was the first black student to attend "Ole Miss." Murphy described himself as black but was able to pass for white and spent nine months at the institution without attracting any notice (ibid., p. 56).

12. A. Sivanandan, "From Resistance to Rebellion: Asian and Afro-Caribbean Struggles in Britain," *Race and Class*, vol. 23, nos. 2–3 (Autumn–Winter 1981).

13. Consider the contradictions in racial status which abound in the country with the most rigidly defined racial categories—South Africa. There a race classification agency is employed to adjudicate claims for upgrading of official racial identity. This is particularly necessary for the "coloured" category. The apartheid system considers Chinese as "Asians" while the Japanese are accorded the status of "honorary whites." This logic nearly detaches race from any grounding in skin color and other physical attributes and nakedly exposes race as a juridicial category subject to economic, social and political influences. (We are indebted to Steve Talbot for clarification of some of these points.)

14. Gordon W. Allport, *The Nature of Prejudice* (Garden City, New York: Doubleday, 1958), pp. 184–200.

15. We wish to use this phrase loosely, without committing ourselves to a particular position on such social psychological approaches as symbolic interactionism, which are outside the scope of this study. An interesting study on this subject is S. M. Lyman

and W. A. Douglass, "Ethnicity: Strategies of Individual and Collective Impression Management," *Social Research*, vol. 40, no. 2 (1973).

16. Michael Billig, "Patterns of Racism: Interviews with National Front Members," *Race and Class*, vol. 20, no. 2 (Autumn 1978), pp. 161–79.

17. "Miss San Antonio USA Lisa Fernandez and other Hispanics auditioning for a role in a television soap-opera did not fit the Hollywood image of real Mexicans and had to darken their faces before filming." Model Aurora Garza said that their faces were bronzed with powder because they looked too white. " 'I'm a real Mexican [Garza said] and very dark anyway. I'm even darker right now because I have a tan. But they kept wanting me to make my face darker and darker' " (*San Francisco Chronicle*, 21 September 1984). A similar dilemma faces Asian American actors who feel that Asian character lead roles inevitably go to white actors who make themselves up to be Asian. Scores of Charlie Chan films, for example, have been made with white leads (the last one was the 1981 *Charlie Chan and the Curse of the Dragon Queen*). Roland Winters, who played in six Chan features, was asked by playwright Frank Chin to explain the logic of casting a white man in the role of Charlie Chan: " 'The only thing I can think of is, if you want to cast a homosexual in a show, and get a homosexual, it'll be awful. It won't be funny ... and maybe there's something there ...' " (Frank Chin, "Confessions of the Chinatown Cowboy," *Bulletin of Concerned Asian Scholars*, vol 4. no. 3 [Fall 1972]).

18. Melanie Martindale-Sikes, "Nationalizing 'Nigger' Imagery Through 'Birth of a Nation'," paper prepared for the 73rd Annual Meeting of the American Sociological Association, 4–8 September 1978 in San Francisco.

19. Winthrop D. Jordan, op. cit., p. 95; emphasis added.

20. Historical focus has been placed either on particular racially defined groups or on immigration and the "incorporation" of ethnic groups. In the former case the characteristic ethnicity theory pitfalls and apologetics such as functionalism and cultural pluralism may be avoided, but only by sacrificing much of the focus on race. In the latter case, race is considered a manifestation of ethnicity.

21. The degree of antipathy for these groups should not be minimized. A northern commentator observed in the 1850s: "An Irish Catholic seldom attempts to rise to a higher condition than that in which he is placed, while the Negro often makes the attempt with success." Quoted in Gossett, op. cit., p. 288.

22. This analysis, as will perhaps be obvious, is essentially DuBoisian. Its main source will be found in the monumental (and still largely unappreciated) *Black Reconstruction in the United States, 1860–1880* (New York: Atheneum, 1977 [1935]).

23. Alexander Saxton argues that:

North Americans of European background have experienced three great racial confrontations: with the Indian, with the African, and with the Oriental. Central to each transaction has been a totally one-sided preponderance of power, exerted for the exploitation of nonwhites by the dominant white society. In each case (but especially in the two that began with systems of enforced labor), white workingmen have played a crucial, yet ambivalent, role. They have been both exploited and exploiters. On the one hand, thrown into competition with nonwhites as enslaved or "cheap" labor they suffered economically; on the other hand, being white, they benefited by that very exploitation which was compelling the nonwhites to work for low wages or for nothing. Ideologically they were drawn in opposite directions. *Racial identification cut at right angles to class consciousness.* (Alexander Saxton, *The Indispensable Enemy: Labor and the Anti-Chinese Movement in California* (Berkeley and Los Angeles: University of California Press, 1971), p. 1, emphasis added.)

24. Selig Perlman, *The History of Trade Unionism in the United States* (New York: Augustus Kelley, 1950), p. 52; emphasis added.

25. Whether southern blacks were "peasants" or rural workers is unimportant in this context. Some time during the 1960s blacks attained a higher degree of urbanization than whites. Before World War II most blacks had been rural dwellers and nearly 80 percent lived in the South.

26. See George Gilder, *Wealth and Poverty* (New York: Basic Books, 1981); Charles Murray, *Losing Ground* (New York: Basic Books, 1984).

27. A brilliant study of the racialization process in Britain, focused on the rise of "mugging" as a popular fear in the 1970s, is Stuart Hall *et al.*, *Policing the Crisis* (London: Macmillan, 1978).

28. The case of Vincent Chin, a Chinese American man beaten to death in 1982 by a laid-off Detroit auto worker and his stepson who mistook him for Japanese and blamed him for the loss of their jobs, has been widely publicized in Asian American communities. On immigration conflicts and pressures, see Michael Omi, "New Wave Dread: Immigration and Intra-Third World Conflict," *Socialist Review*, no. 60 (November–December 1981).

1.2 BETH B. HESS, ELIZABETH W. MARKSON, AND PETER J. STEIN

Racial and Ethnic Minorities: An Overview

Through historical patterns of immigration and colonialism the United States has become a multiracial and multiethnic society. Equal status in U.S. society, however, is denied to various racial and ethnic groups. As a result, U.S. society stratifies people into dominant and subordinate groups defined by race and ethnicity. Subordinate group status is thus synonymous with minority group status. A *minority group* refers to a category of people who (a) share a distinctive racial or ethnic identity that sets them apart from members of a dominant group, and (b) suffer differential or unequal treatment at the hands of the dominant group because of their racial or ethnic characteristics.

In the following selection, sociologists Beth B. Hess, Elizabeth W. Markson, and Peter J. Stein provide an overview of racial and ethnic minorities in the United States and the forms of mistreatment suffered by these groups throughout American history.

Key Concept: racial and ethnic minorities

RACIAL MINORITIES

Native Americans

Estimates of the size of the Native American population prior to the invasion of Europeans in North America vary; a conservative estimate is 5 million when Columbus discovered America. It was not long after the arrival of Europeans that Native American tribes were reduced to a racial and ethnic group "inferior" to the "more civilized" white newcomers. Because Europeans viewed their own cultures as superior, the physical characteristics of Native Americans were taken as evidence of biological inferiority. All Native Americans were categorized as "Indians" and their widely varying cultures destroyed. Disease was a major factor in reducing the Native American population; frequently, entire communities became ill, halting everyday life and enabling conquest by white settlers. Remarkably, Native Americans had previously been almost free of infectious diseases such as smallpox and measles, and they lacked any biological defenses against epidemics (Thornton, 1987) brought by Europeans.

Because Native Americans were not considered to be entitled to equal status with whites, treaties with the "Indians" were ignored. During the 1800s, whole tribes were resettled forcibly into reservations distant from centers of population and business. The complex interaction of relocation, war, and forced culture change combined with disease to reduce the Native American population to its low point of roughly 250,000 people in 1900 (Thornton, 1987). By the early 1980s, about 53 million acres, or 2.4 percent, of U.S. land was managed in trust by the Bureau of Indian Affairs. These reservations became notorious for their lack of economic opportunities. Moreover, most tribes own only a small part of their reservations.

Native Americans remain the poorest and the most disadvantaged of all racial or ethnic groups in the United States. Contrary to popular belief, only slightly more than half of all Native Americans live on reservations. Many live in metropolitan areas such as Los Angeles, Chicago, Seattle, and Minneapolis–St. Paul. Others are farmers and migrant laborers in the Southwest and north central regions, and many live in New York State and New England. The earnings of metropolitan Native Americans are higher than those of nonmetropolitan Native Americans. Better jobs and higher levels of education of metropolitan Native Americans account for these differences (Snipp and Sandefur, 1988)....

Self-determination and economic self-sufficiency cannot be achieved easily when the most basic needs, such as adequate education, housing, and health care, have not yet been met. Death rates from a range of diseases are greater than among the U.S. population as a whole. Mortality from alcohol-related causes among Native Americans remains about 22 times higher than the national average, and the suicide rate is twice the national average. Housing is substandard, and nearly half the hospitals built by the Indian Health Service were built before 1940 and are both understaffed and in need of repairs.

Far from being on the verge of extinction, however, the Native American population is growing faster than the U.S. population as a whole. According to Government statistics, there are around 1.5 million Native Americans, most heavily concentrated in California, Oklahoma, Arizona, New Mexico, and North Carolina. It is difficult, however, to know the precise size of the current Native American population, as the Federal government uses a variety of criteria to count "Indians." Although the birthrate among Native Americans accounts for a small proportion of the increase in their numbers, it seems likely that many people who identified themselves as belonging to some other race or ethnicity in earlier censuses now identify themselves as Native Americans, reflecting a new militancy.

Demonstrations and lawsuits have called attention to the treaties broken by the U.S. government and the unmet needs of Native Americans. Several lawsuits have resulted in a return of native lands and/or reparation payments in the millions. But despite the rising tide of political activity illustrated by the American Indian Movement (AIM), it has been difficult for Native Americans to create a unified political front. The variety among tribes is great, and there is no typical Native American, no one Indian culture, language, religion, or physical type.

AFRICAN-AMERICANS AND STRATIFICATION HIERARCHIES   In 1989, 30 million African-Americans accounted for almost 13 percent of the total population of the United States. To what extent have African-Americans moved into and up the stratification system?

Although all legal barriers to voting have been removed, African-Americans are less likely to vote than whites, partly because of difficulties encountered in registering and voting in the South but primarily as a result of lower income and less education, which, in turn, are associated with lower voter turnout in general. Also, feelings of powerlessness and alienation reduce the motivation to vote ("What good would it do?"). Although African-Americans constitute about 12 percent of the country's voting-age population, it will not be until 1998 that they achieve parity in voting in congressional elections (National Urban League, 1989).

The number of African-American state legislators rose from about 168 in 1970 to over 400 today. Other elected officials increased, and an African-American political elite has begun to emerge. But the rate of increase of elected African-American officials has declined and is about only one-third of what it was from 1970 to 1976. At the moment, elected African-American officials represent considerably fewer than the almost 13 percent that would reflect their percentage in the American population. . . .

In the arenas of employment, occupation, income, and wealth, African-Americans remain disadvantaged compared to whites. . . . The average income for white families was 78 percent higher than for African-American families in 1987 dollars. Economic disparity between the two racial groups has increased since 1978 (Urban League, 1989). Indeed, analysis of trend data show that the income gap between African-Americans and white men has not lowered since 1948 (Farley and Allen, 1987). About one African-American in three lives below the poverty line today compared to about one in ten whites (U.S. Bureau of the Census, Series P-20, No. 442). At the current rate of progress of African-Americans, parity with whites will not be achieved in individual poverty rates until the year 2148 for individuals and 2158 for families (National Urban League, 1989). The rate of unemployment for young African-American men is three times that of young white men—a disparity increasing since 1948. Among young central-city African-Americans men, unemployment rates (excluding "discouraged workers") are as high as 50 percent (Farley and Allen, 1987). Although African-American women fare somewhat better, their higher income in comparison to white females is primarily due to lower earnings of women regardless of race or ethnicity. In 1980, more than a century after the abolition of slavery, there were still more African-American women employed as domestics than there were African-American women professionals (Farley and Allen, 1987). . . .

High unemployment, poverty, and economic tension have taken their toll among African-Americans. An African-American male teenager is six times as likely as a white male teenager to be a victim of homicide (National Urban League, 1989). African-Americans suffer from higher rates of almost all cancers and are 33 percent more likely to develop diabetes. Higher rates of heart disease and stroke among African-American women account for nearly half of the black-white difference in their life expectancy: cancer, homicide, and strokes account for 50 percent of the six-year difference between African-American and white men (Farley and Allen, 1987). Nearly 40 percent of all African-American mothers receive no prenatal care in the first trimester of pregnancy. One in eight African-American infants is born at a low birth weight, and the infant mortality rate is twice that of white infants. The infant mortality rate for whites ranks with Britain and West Germany; for African-Americans it ranks with Cuba. African-American children are more likely to drop out of elementary or high school and less likely to attend college.

Much has been written about the increasing numbers of African-American families that have moved into the middle class (Wilson, 1980, 1981), but they still work harder for equal rewards. At the same level of education and occupation, African-American wages are lower than those of whites.

Given the political, income, and occupational data just presented, it is evident that sources of personal and social prestige are systematically denied to African-Americans. In one area of most rapid gains, education, advancement may be more apparent than real....

African-Americans have made occupational gains since 1960, but they have not been as significant as those of whites, particularly white males. In football, for example, although 57 percent of total members of the NFL were African-American by 1987, only 6.5 percent of the administrative posts were held by African-Americans. Even African-Americans in positions that pay well and sound prestigious have complained that they have been placed in high-visibility dead-end jobs.

The evidence supports the caste model of stratification in the United States today, although debates over the relative importance of class and race continue. Some analysts (Wilson, 1978, 1986) claim that race itself is less important than the overwhelming effects of poverty. Others cite continuing racism as a major factor in perpetuating the cycle of poverty. That African-Americans have fared poorly in our economic system seems evident. Although African-Americans have achieved higher levels of education and have greater opportunities for political activity, they remain outside the mainstream stratification system. And their disadvantages have been built into the social structure. For generations, despite their familiarity with American customs and language, African-Americans were systematically denied the right to vote, to be on juries, and even to be promoted in the military long after newer immigrant groups had achieved these goals (Lieberson, 1981).

Comparative studies of African-American and white ethnic immigrants indicate that the greater success of whites in achieving middle-class status has been aided by "a set of bootstraps that must be government issued ... a system of protection that takes the civil rights of groups to acquire property and to pursue a wide range of economic opportunities" (Smith, 1987, p. 168). African-Americans have not been issued similar bootstraps enabling collective entry into the middle class....

Like European-Americans, Asian-Americans come from different cultures and religious backgrounds and speak different languages. Yet, a tendency to classify all Asians together has dominated both immigration policy and popular attitudes....

The Asian-American population increased by 142 percent between 1970 and 1980. Despite the growing importance of Asians, the decennial census is the only source of detailed information currently available. Unlike Latinos, on whom data are collected by the federal government each year, Asians are still too small a category to be captured in sample surveys.... Those people described by the Bureau of the Census as Asian are diverse, representing different languages, religions, cultural traditions, time of immigration, and poverty level.... The only other source of national data on Asians comes from the Immigration and Naturalization Service, which collects annual information on immigrants. Immigration data indicate that the three largest groups of Asian immigrants during the past few years have been Chinese, Filipino, and Korean. These three groups make up more than 20 percent of the total number of legal immigrants coming to the United States.

CHINESE   In the mid-nineteenth century, young Chinese males were imported to work on the transcontinental railroad. Unable to bring a wife with them or to send for a woman to marry, those who remained in the United States formed an almost exclusively male community, concentrated in a few occupations (Siu, 1987). Chinese men were victims of extreme prejudice, discrimination, and open violence until the outbreak of World War II, when suddenly they became the "good" Asians compared to the "evil" Japanese. Restrictive immigration laws ended in the 1960s, and ... 63.3 percent of Chinese-Americans in 1980 were foreign born.

The majority of Chinese live in seven states, with California having the highest concentration (40 percent), followed by New York, Hawaii, Illinois, Texas, Massachusetts, and New Jersey. As older immigrant groups have left the garment industry, an increasing number of immigrant Chinese entrepreneurs in New York have opened small manufacturing plants that do not require large initial capital investments; they have also recruited workers through kin and friendship networks (Waldinger, 1987).

As barriers to discrimination were lifted, Chinese-Americans entered colleges and universities in growing numbers.... A high proportion of both American- and foreign-born Chinese in the labor force held jobs as managers, professionals, or executives in 1980, and this percentage is growing. Although residential discrimination still exists in some areas, it has been less difficult for Chinese than for African-Americans to assimilate culturally or to amalgamate.

JAPANESE   According to one social scientist (Kitano, 1976), Japanese immigrants "came to the wrong country and the wrong state (California) at the wrong time (immediately after the Chinese) with the wrong race and skin color, with the wrong religion, and from the wrong country" (p. 31). After the outbreak of World War II, the Japanese in North America were forcibly moved from their homes and "relocated." Inasmuch as hostility toward Japan was high in the United States during World War II, Japanese-Americans provided visible targets for its expression. Their appearance, language, and culture were interpreted as indications of disloyalty to the United States. More than 100,000 West Coast Japanese-Americans were placed in detention camps, with guard towers and barbed-wire fences. Their property was confiscated, sold, or stolen. Among the long-term effects of relocation were a reduction in the relative power of men over women in the family, a weakening of control over offspring, and reinforcement of a sense of ethnic identity.

Has the pattern of Japanese-Americans assimilation been similar to that of other minority... groups, or are they still excluded from the majority society, as their relocation during World War II dramatically illustrated? In the history of U.S. race relations, few nonwhite minorities have established as secure an economic position as whites. The Japanese-Americans in California are a notable exception and have been upwardly mobile in part because of their economic ethnic hegemony. *Ethnic hegemony* refers to the power exerted by one ethnic group over another. Japanese-Americans achieved economic control over produce agriculture, thereby dominating an important economic area that permitted them to interact from a position of power with the majority culture (Jiobu, 1988).

Greater mobility, in turn, has been associated with a shift from jobs in the ethnic community to employment in the corporate economy, and to greater assimilation. For example, third-generation Japanese-Americans have a higher percentage of non-Japanese friends than do first- or second-generation Japanese-Americans. They are also more likely to have non-Japanese spouses, to live in a non-Japanese neighborhood, and to profess non-Japanese religious beliefs (Montero, 1981). Moreover, the Japanese are the only Asian-American group to have a higher proportion of childless couples than do whites (Robey, 1985). In short, as occupational and financial mobility has occurred, greater cultural, structural, and marital assimilation has taken place.

Can the Japanese-American community remain intact or will it be amalgamated into the majority society? The answer will depend on whether Japanese-Americans develop a broader identity as Asian-Americans. But the most highly educated and most successful Japanese-Americans have become the most cut off from their ethnic background; for example, 40 percent have non-Japanese spouses. The irony of this trend toward amalgamation is that the Japanese may lose their roots in the tradition that gave rise to their upward mobility.

THE INDOCHINESE   Indochina is a region in southeast Asia that includes Vietnam, Cambodia, Thailand, and Laos. In 1960, a total of only 59 immigrants were admitted to the United States from Vietnam, Laos, and Cambodia combined; all but 3 of these came from Vietnam. However, in the decade following the end of the Vietnam War, about 842,000 Indochinese immigrants, primarily refugees, arrived in the United States. In 1987 alone, more than 50,000 Indochinese immigrated to the United States (*Statistical Abstract, 1989*). Indochinese now represent more than one Asian-American in five.

Within the Indochinese population, there are marked cultural and linguistic variations. Only about one-sixth came as part of the largely elite first wave of South Vietnamese who brought with them money and skills. In contrast, recent arrivals have been both more numerous and more diverse: Vietnamese "boat people," lowland Laotians, almost all of the Hmong or Laotian hill tribes, and Cambodians. Many of these people came from rural backgrounds, had little education or transferable occupational skills, no knowledge of English, and had spent long periods in refugee camps overseas prior to coming to the United States. Moreover, their arrival coincided with inflation, recession, and growing fears of displacement among the native-born population (Rumbaut, 1986). Despite government policies that attempted to settle these new refugees throughout the United States, about 40 percent of Indochinese immigrants live in California, and 8 percent in Texas. Vietnamese also cluster in Washington, Pennsylvania, New York, Louisiana, and the District of Columbia. Laotians can be found in places as diverse as Minnesota, Rhode Island, and Oregon, with a large concentration of Hmong in agricultural central California.

OTHER ASIANS In 1980, there were about 1.7 million people of other Asian ethnicities in the United States. Filipinos accounted for 45 percent, followed by Asian Indians and Koreans. Koreans showed the most remarkable growth, increasing from 69,999 in 1970 to 357,000 by 1980. The welcome given to the arrival of Asian-Americans, like that of most new immigrants who are not of northern European origin, has been mixed. However, Asians, whether from Korea, India, or elsewhere, may be the achievers of the future. An incredible 52 percent of adult Asian Indians and more than one-third of Filipinos are college graduates. (It is important to note that most Asian Indians admitted to this country already had a good educational background upon arrival.)

ETHNIC MINORITIES

The great variety of nationalities is a defining characteristic of American society. To illustrate general themes in the immigrant experiences and to introduce you to the fastest growing ethnic minorities in the United States, our discussion will focus on two recent entrants: Latinos and Middle-Easterners.

Latinos

Latino is a category made up of many separate cultural and racial subgroups bound together by a common language, Spanish (although even language patterns vary by country of origin). In 1989, about 21 million Spanish-speaking people were officially recorded as residing in the United States, and several million others are believed to have entered without official documents. Because of their generally younger ages and high birthrates, it is likely that Spanish-speaking Americans will soon outnumber African-Americans as the single largest minority group in the United States.

In 1989, the four major ethnic subdivisions within the Spanish-speaking population were Mexican-Americans; Puerto Ricans; Cubans; and people from

Central and South American countries, particularly the Dominican Republic, Colombia, and El Salvador.... The remainder were from other Spanish-speaking nations.... Differences within the Spanish-speaking minority are striking, especially in terms of education and income. Each ethnic group has its own immigration history, cultural patterns, and its own internal diversity.

There is a stratification system within the Latino population, based not only on indicators of socioeconomic status but also on skin color. Race and ethnicity combine to determine the relative status of Spanish-speaking Americans, both within the stratification system of the wider society and within the hierarchy of the Latino subculture. These divisions reduce the likelihood of the development of shared interests necessary to build a unified Latino power base.

MEXICAN-AMERICANS   When the United States conquered Mexico in 1848 the Southwest had already been settled by Mexicans. A gradual pattern of economic and social subordination of the Mexicans, as well as Native Americans, developed as white Americans ("Anglos") migrated into the Southwest.

Like many other ethnic groups that have not been accepted by the majority group, Mexican-Americans tend ... to live in particular geographic areas, such as southern California, south Texas, and New Mexico.... Although the stereotype of the Mexican farm laborer persists, relatively few Mexican-Americans today work on farms, in contrast to the employment pattern of their parents. This change reflects the increasing industrialization of agriculture rather than gains in job status or income. The occupational mobility of Mexican-Americans has been horizontal rather than vertical. That is, the present generation has moved from farm labor into other unskilled jobs, such as work in canning factories. Relatively few have moved into semiskilled or higher-status occupations. Many undocumented workers from Mexico have been employed in low-wage service and manufacturing jobs to keep labor costs low and to prevent unionization.

On various measures of social mobility, Mexican-Americans rank below the average for the population as a whole. In general they have less education than do non-Latinos or African-Americans. The traditional Mexican family is an extended one, with the kinship group being both the main focus of obligation and the source of emotional and social support. Birthrates are relatively high, especially among first-generation and poorly educated women (Bean and Swicegood, 1985). Within the family, gender roles are well defined. Both mothers and daughters are expected to be protected and submissive and to dedicate themselves to caring for the males of the family. For the Mexican male, *machismo,* or the demonstration of physical and sexual prowess, is basic to self-respect.

These traditional patterns protect Mexican-Americans against the effects of prejudice and discrimination, but they also reinforce isolation from the majority culture. An upwardly mobile Mexican-American must often choose between remaining locked into a semi-isolated ethnic world or becoming alienated from family, friends, and ethnic roots (Arce, 198).

PUERTO RICANS   Technically U.S. citizens since the United States took the island after the Spanish-American War in 1898, Puerto Ricans began to arrive on the mainland in large numbers in the 1950s because of the collapse of the sugar industry on their island. One-third of the world's Puerto Ricans now reside in the mainland United States. Of the 2.3 million mainland Puerto Ricans, 80 percent live in six states: New York, New Jersey, Connecticut, Illinois, Pennsylvania, and Massachusetts. Although almost two-fifths of the Puerto Ricans in the continental United States have incomes below the poverty level, their expectations of success are higher than the expectations of those who have remained in Puerto Rico.

Although Puerto Ricans are often grouped with Mexican-Americans, the two populations are very different in history, culture, and racial composition. Puerto Rico's culture is a blend of African and Spanish influences, with a heavy dose of American patterns. In Mexico, both Spanish and Native American elements combine.

The Puerto Rican experience on the mainland has included a continuing struggle for stability and achievement in education, politics, the arts, and community control. Puerto Ricans have been elected to the U.S. Congress, to state legislatures, and to city councils. Growing numbers of Puerto Ricans have moved from the inner city to middle-income, homeowner suburbs, and young Puerto Ricans are entering the fields of law, business, medicine, and teaching.... Others continue to have difficulty on standardized English and math tests, to drop out of school, and to face unemployment. About 43 percent of Puerto Rican families are likely to be headed by a woman with no husband present.

CUBANS   Cuban immigration to the United States began in large numbers when Fidel Castro came to power in the mid-1950s. Between 1954 and 1978, more than 325,000 Cubans were admitted as permanent residents in the United States, especially in the Miami, Florida, area. In early 1980, an additional 115,000 refugees entered the country in a sudden, somewhat chaotic exodus from Cuba. Although it is too early to determine how these new Cuban immigrants will fare in the United States, many earlier immigrants have achieved success operating businesses within Cuban communities... and a Cuban-American woman from Florida was elected to Congress.

Of all Spanish-speaking subgroups in the U.S. the Cubans are older and better educated; are more likely to live in metropolitan areas, though not the central city; and have the highest median income. Much of their success, however, can be attributed to the educational and occupational characteristics with which they entered America. Theirs was an upper- and middle-class emigration in contrast to that of the Cuban newcomers of 1980, who were, on the average, younger, less educated, and less skilled. Recent Cuban immigrants have also been received with greater hostility and fear, and they are experiencing barriers to mobility within the established Cuban communities as well as outside.

Middle Easterners

In recent years, a new group of immigrants from the Middle East has begun to emerge as a visible urban minority. The number of immigrants from Middle Eastern countries has averaged more than 18,000 annually since 1970.

Yet, little is known about them.... They have come from a number of different countries such as Egypt, Syria, Lebanon, Iran, and Jordan, and they speak a number of languages. Their religious affiliations include Muslim, Coptic Christian, and Melkite Catholic, and they bring with them diverse cultural norms. Many would not describe themselves as "Arabs." They do not speak Arabic or identify with Arabic history and culture. The one common denominator of these different ethnic groups is their Middle Eastern origin. The socioeconomic position of the various ethnic groups also varies: the Lebanese, the Syrians, and the Iranians are primarily middle class, whereas other groups are mostly working class....

In the Detroit area, which now has the largest concentration of Arabic-speaking people outside the Middle East—more than 200,000 Lebanese, Palestinians, Yemenis, and Iraqi-Chaldeans—there has been conflict between Middle Easterners and other ethnic groups. From the limited information available, however, there seems to be little racial tension, juvenile delinquency, or crime within Near Eastern immigrant communities. Tensions are caused by drinking, dating, and language, as younger people become acculturated to the norms of the dominant society and reject traditional values and behavior. As with most other immigrant groups, length of residence in the United States is an important factor both in acculturation and in socioeconomic status.

Ethnicity in American Life: The Historical Perspective

Ethnicity refers to an affiliation of people who share similar cultural characteristics. Members of ethnic groups share common languages, religious beliefs, cultural traditions and customs, value systems, and normative orientations. They also share a similar worldview, an ethnic consciousness —a peoplehood. Ethnicity is a sociopolitical construct that emerges from collective experiences in a society. That is, ethnic consciousness is a consequence of or a response to the social conditions minority populations encounter once they migrate to a foreign country. Centuries of persecution in the United States have produced an ethnic consciousness of "us" and "them." The Anglo ideology of domination has defined the history of Chicanos, for example, as a collective experience of military conquest, labor exploitation, political oppression, and social conflict based upon their common ethnic heritage in the United States.

In the following selection, historian John Hope Franklin traces the history of ethnic exclusion suffered by immigrants in the United States. Franklin is the James B. Duke Professor Emeritus at Duke University as well as a professor of legal history at Duke University Law School. Professor Franklin has published extensively on the history of racial equality in American society. Among his published works are *From Slavery to Freedom: A History of Negro Americans* (Alfred A. Knopf, 1988), coauthored with Alfred A. Moss, Jr., and *Racial Equality in America* (University of Missouri Press, 1976).

Key Concept: ethnic exclusion in U.S. society

*T*he United States is unique in the ethnic composition of its population. No other country in the world can point to such a variety of cultural, racial, religious, and national backgrounds in its population. It was one of the salient features in the early history of this country; and it would continue to be so down into the twentieth century. From virtually every corner of the globe they came— some enthusiastically and some quite reluctantly. Britain and every part of the continent of Europe provided prospective Americans by the millions. Africa and Asia gave up great throngs. Other areas of the New World saw inhabitants desert their own lands to seek their fortunes in the colossus to the North. Those who came voluntarily were attracted by the prospect of freedom of religion, freedom from want, and freedom from various forms of oppression. Those who were forced to come were offered the consolation that if they were white they would some day inherit the earth, and if they were black they would some day gather their reward in the Christian heaven.

One of the interesting and significant features of this coming together of peoples of many tongues and races and cultures was that the backgrounds out of which they came would soon be minimized and that the process by which they evolved into Americans would be of paramount importance. Hector St. Jean de Crevecoeur sought to describe this process in 1782 when he answered his own question, "What, then, is the American, this new man?" He said, "He is either an European, or the descendant of an European, hence that strange mixture of blood, which you will find in no other country.... He is an American, who, leaving behind him all his ancient prejudices and manners, receives new ones from the new mode of life he has embraced, the new government he obeys, and the new rank he holds. He becomes an American by being received in the broad lap of our great *Alma Mater.* Here individuals of all nations are melted into a new race of men, whose labours and posterity will one day cause great changes in the world."

This was one of the earliest expressions of the notion that the process of Americanization involved the creation of an entirely new mode of life that would replace the ethnic backgrounds of those who were a part of the process. It contained some imprecisions and inaccuracies that would, in time, become a part of the lore or myth of the vaunted melting pot and would grossly misrepresent the crucial factor of ethnicity in American life. It ignored the tenacity with which the Pennsylvania Dutch held onto their language, religion, and way of life. It overlooked the way in which the Swedes of New Jersey remained Swedes and the manner in which the French Huguenots of New York and Charleston held onto their own past as though it was the source of all light and life. It described a process that in a distant day would gag at the notion that Irish Catholics could be assimilated on the broad lap of Alma Mater or that Asians could be seated on the basis of equality at the table of the Great American Feast.

By suggesting that only Europeans were involved in the process of becoming Americans, Crevecoeur pointedly ruled out three quarters of a million blacks already in the country who, along with their progeny, would be regarded as ineligible to become Americans for at least another two centuries. To be sure, the number of persons of African descent would increase enormously, but the view of their ineligibility for Americanization would be very slow to change. And when such a change occurred, even if it merely granted freedom from bondage, the change would be made most reluctantly and without any suggestion that freedom qualified one for equality on the broad lap of Alma Mater. It was beyond the conception of Crevecoeur, as it was indeed beyond the conception of the founding fathers, that Negroes, slave or free, could become true Americans, enjoying that fellowship in a common enterprise about which Crevecoeur spoke so warmly. It was as though Crevecoeur was arguing that ethnicity, where persons of African descent were concerned, was either so powerful or so unattractive as to make their assimilation entirely impossible or so insignificant as to make it entirely undesirable. In any case Americanization in the late eighteenth century was a precious commodity to be cherished and enjoyed only by a select group of persons of European descent.

One must admit, therefore, that at the time of the birth of the new nation there was no clear-cut disposition to welcome into the American family persons of any and all ethnic backgrounds. Only Europeans were invited to fight for independence. And when the patriots at long last relented and gave persons of African descent a chance to fight, the concession was made with great reluctance and after much equivocation and soul-searching. Only Europeans were regarded as full citizens in the new states and in the new nation. And when the founding fathers wrote the Constitution of the United States, they did not seem troubled by the distinctions on the basis of ethnic differences that the Constitution implied.

If the principle of ethnic exclusiveness was propounded so early and so successfully in the history of the United States, it is not surprising that it would, in time, become the basis for questioning the ethnic backgrounds of large numbers of prospective Americans, even Europeans. Thus, in 1819, a Jewish immigrant was chilled to hear a bystander refer to him and his companion as "more damned emigrants." A decade later there began a most scathing and multifaceted attack on the Catholic church. On two counts the church was a bad influence. First, its principal recruits were the Irish, the "very dregs" of the Old World social order; and secondly, its doctrine of papal supremacy ran counter to the idea of the political and religious independence of the United States. Roman Catholics, Protestant Americans warned, were engaged in a widespread conspiracy to subvert American institutions, through parochial schools, the Catholic press, immoral convents, and a sinister design to control the West by flooding it with Catholic settlers. The burning of convents and churches and the killing of Catholics themselves were indications of how deeply many Americans felt about religious and cultural differences for which they had a distaste and suspicion that bordered on paranoia.

Soon the distaste for the foreign-born became almost universal, with Roman Catholics themselves sharing in the hostility to those who followed them to the new Republic. Some expressed fear of the poverty and criminality that accompanied each wave of immigrants. Some felt that those newly arrived from abroad were a threat to republican freedom. Some saw in the ethnic differences of the newcomers an immediate danger to the moral standards of Puritan America. Some feared the competition that newcomers posed in the labor market. Some became convinced that the ideal of a national homogeneity would disappear with the influx of so many unassimilable elements. Soon, nativist societies sprang up all across the land, and they found national expression in 1850 in a new organization called the Order of the Star Spangled Banner. With its slogan, "America for Americans," the order, which became the organizational basis for the Know-Nothing party, engendered a fear through its preachments that caused many an American to conclude that his country was being hopelessly subverted by the radical un-Americanism of the great variety of ethnic strains that were present in the United States.

If there was some ambivalence regarding the ethnic diversity of white immigrants before the Civil War, it was dispelled by the view that prevailed regarding immigrants in the post–Civil War years. The "old" immigrants, so the argument went, were at least assimilable and had "entered practically every line of activity in nearly every part of the country." Even those who had been non-English speaking had mingled freely with native Americans and had therefore been quickly assimilated. Not so with the "new" immigrants who came after 1880. They "congregated together in sections apart from native Americans and the older immigrants to such an extent that assimilation had been slow." Small wonder that they were different. Small wonder that they were barely assimilable. They came from Austro-Hungary, Italy, Russia, Greece, Rumania, and Turkey. They dressed differently, spoke in unfamiliar tongues, and clung to strange, if not exotic customs. It did not matter that Bohemians, Moravians, and Finns had lower percentages of illiteracy than had the Irish and Germans or that Jews had a higher percentage of skilled laborers than any group except the Scots. Nor did it matter that, in fact, the process of assimilation for the so-called "new" group was about as rapid as that of the so-called "old" group.

What did matter was that the new nativism was stronger and more virulent than any anti-immigration forces or groups of the early nineteenth century and that these groups were determined either to drive from the shores those who were different or to isolate them so that they could not contaminate American society. Old-stock Americans began to organize to preserve American institutions and the American way of life. Those who had been here for five years or a decade designated themselves as old-stock Americans and joined in the attack on those recently arrived. If the cult of Anglo-Saxon superiority was all but pervasive, those who were not born into the cult regarded themselves as honorary members. Thus, they could celebrate with as much feeling as any the virtues of Anglo-Saxon institutions and could condemn as vehemently as any those ideas and practices that were not strictly Anglo-Saxon. Whenever possible they joined the American Protective Association and the Immigrant Restriction League; and in so doing they sold their own ethnicity for the obscurity that a pseudoassimilation brought. But in the end, they would be less than successful. The arrogance and presumption of the Anglo-Saxon complex was not broad enough to embrace the Jews of eastern Europe or the Bohemians of central Europe or the Turks of the Middle East. The power and drive of the Anglo-Saxon forces would prevail; and those who did not belong would be compelled to console themselves by extolling the virtues of cultural pluralism.

By that time—near the end of the nineteenth century—the United States had articulated quite clearly its exalted standards of ethnicity. They were standards that accepted Anglo-Saxons as the norm, placed other whites on what may be called "ethnic probation," and excluded from serious consideration the Japanese, Chinese, and Negroes. It was not difficult to deal harshly with the Chinese and Japanese when they began to enter the United States in considerable numbers in the post–Civil War years. They simply did not meet the standards that the arbiters of American ethnicity had promulgated. They were different in race, religion, language, and public and private morality. They had to be excluded; and eventually they were.

The presence of persons of African descent, almost from the beginning, had helped whites to define ethnicity and to establish and maintain the conditions by which it could be controlled. If their color and race, their condition of servitude, and their generally degraded position did not set them apart, the laws and customs surrounding them more than accomplished that feat. Whether in Puritan Massachusetts or cosmopolitan New York or Anglican South Carolina, the colonists declared that Negroes, slave or free, did not and could not belong to the society of equal human beings. Thus, the newly arrived Crevecoeur could be as blind to the essential humanity of Negroes as the patriots who tried to keep them out of the Continental Army. They were not a part of America, these new men. And in succeeding years their presence would do more to define ethnicity than the advent of several scores of millions of Europeans.

It was not enough for Americans, already somewhat guilt-ridden for maintaining slavery in a free society, to exclude blacks from American society on the basis of race and condition of servitude. They proceeded from that point to argue that Negroes were inferior morally, intellectually, and physically. Even as he reviewed the remarkable accomplishments of Benjamin Banneker, surveyor, almanacker, mathematician, and clock-maker, Thomas Jefferson had serious doubts about the mental capabilities of Africans, and he expressed these doubts to his European friends. What Jefferson speculated about at the end of the eighteenth century became indisputable dogma within a decade after his death.

In the South every intellectual, legal, and religious resource was employed in the task of describing the condition of Negroes in such a way as to make them the least attractive human beings on the face of the earth. Slavery was not only the natural lot of blacks, the slaveowners argued, but it was in accordance with God's will that they should be kept in slavery. As one sanctimonious divine put it, "We feel that the souls of our slaves are a solemn trust and we shall strive to present them faultless and complete before the presence of God. . . . However the world may judge us in connection with our institution of slavery, we conscientiously believe it to be a great missionary institution—one arranged by God, as He arranges all moral and religious influences of the world so that the good may be brought out of seeming evil, and a blessing wrung out of every form of the curse." It was a difficult task that the owners of slaves set for themselves. Slaves had brought with them only heathenism, immorality, profligacy, and irresponsibility. They possessed neither the mental capacity nor the moral impulse to improve themselves. Only if their sponsors—those to whom were entrusted not only their souls but their bodies—were fully committed to their improvement could they take even the slightest, halting steps toward civilization.

What began as a relatively moderate justification for slavery soon became a vigorous, aggressive defense of the institution. Slavery, to the latter-day defenders, was the cornerstone of the republican edifice. To a governor of South Carolina, it was the greatest of all the great blessings which a kind Providence had bestowed upon the glorious region of the South. It was, indeed, one of the remarkable coincidences of history that such a favored institution had found such a favored creature as the African to give slavery the high value that was placed on it. A childlike race, prone to docility and manageable in every respect, the African was the ideal subject for the slave role. Slaveholders had to work hard to be worthy of this great Providential blessing.

Nothing that Negroes could do or say could change or seriously affect this view. They might graduate from college, as John Russwurm did in 1826, or they might write a most scathing attack against slavery, as David Walker did in 1829. It made no difference. They might teach in an all-white college, as Charles B. Reason did in New York in the 1850s, or publish a newspaper, as Frederick Douglass did during that same decade. Their racial and cultural backgrounds disqualified them from becoming American citizens. They could even argue in favor of their capacities and potentialities, as Henry Highland Garnet did, or they might argue their right to fight for union and freedom, as 186,000 did in the Civil War. Still, it made no sense for white Americans to give serious consideration to their arguments and their actions. They were beyond the veil, as the Jews had been beyond the veil in the barbaric and bigoted communities of eastern Europe.

The views regarding Negroes that had been so carefully developed to justify and defend slavery would not disappear with emancipation....

In time the Irish, Germans, and other Europeans made it and were accepted on the broad lap of Alma Mater. But not the free Negroes, who continued to suffer disabilities even in the North in the years just before the Civil War. Was this the key to the solution of postwar problems? Perhaps it was. After all, Negroes had always been a group apart in Boston, New York, Philadelphia, and other northern cities. They all lived together in one part of the city—especially if they could find no other place to live. They had their own churches—after the whites drove them out of theirs. They had their own schools—after they were excluded from the schools attended by whites. They had their own social organizations—after the whites barred them from theirs.

If Negroes possessed so many ethnic characteristics such as living in the same community, having their own churches, schools, and social clubs, and perhaps other agencies of cohesion, that was all very well. They even seemed "happier with their own kind," some patronizing observers remarked. They were like the Germans or the Irish or the Italians or the Jews. They had so much in common and so much to preserve. There was one significant difference, however. For Europeans, the ethnic factors that brought a particular group together actually eased the task of assimilation and, in many ways, facilitated the process of assimilation, particularly as hostile elements sought to disorient them in their drive toward full citizenship. And, in time, they achieved it.

For Negroes, however, such was not the case. They had been huddled together in northern ghettoes since the eighteenth century. They had had their own churches since 1792 and their own schools since 1800. And this separateness, this ostracism, was supported and enforced by the full majesty of the law, state and federal, just to make certain that Negroes did, indeed, preserve their ethnicity! And as they preserved their ethnicity—all too frequently as they looked down the barrel of a policeman's pistol or a militiaman's shotgun—full citizenship seemed many light years away. They saw other ethnic groups pass them by, one by one, and take their places in the sacred Order of the Star Spangled Banner, the American Protective Association, the Knights of the Ku Klux Klan—not always fully assimilated but vehemently opposed to the assimilation of Negroes. The ethnic grouping that was a way station, a temporary resting place for Europeans as they became Americans, proved to be a terminal point for blacks who found it virtually impossible to become Americans in any real sense.

There was an explanation or at least a justification for this. The federal government and the state governments had tried to force Negroes into full citizenship and had tried to legislate them into equality with the whites. This was not natural and could not possibly succeed. Negroes had not made it because they were not fit, the social Darwinists[1] said. Negroes were beasts, Charles Carroll declared somewhat inelegantly. "Stateways cannot change folkways," William Graham Sumner, the distinguished scholar, philosophized. The first forty years of Negro freedom had been a failure, said John R. Commons, one of the nation's leading economists. This so-called failure was widely acknowledged in the country as northerners of every rank and description acquiesced, virtually without a murmur of objection, to the southern settlement of the race problem characterized by disfranchisement, segregation, and discrimination.

Here was a new and exotic form of ethnicity. It was to be seen in the badges of inferiority and the symbols of racial degradation that sprang up in every sector of American life—in the exclusion from the polling places with its specious justification that Negroes were unfit to participate in the sacred rite of voting; the back stairway or the freight elevator to public places; the separate, miserable railway car, the separate and hopelessly inferior school; and even the Jim Crow[2] cemetery. Ethnic considerations had never been so important in the shaping of public policy. They had never before been used by the American government to define the role and place of other groups in American society. The United States had labored hard to create order out of its chaotic and diverse ethnic backgrounds. Having begun by meekly suggesting the difficulty in assimilating all groups into one great society, it had acknowledged failure by ruling out one group altogether, quite categorically, and frequently by law, solely on the basis of race.

It could not achieve this without doing irreparable harm to the early notions of the essential unity of America and Americans. The sentiments that promoted the disfranchisement and segregation of Negroes also encouraged the infinite varieties of discrimination against Jews, Armenians, Turks, Japanese, and Chinese. The conscious effort to degrade a particular ethnic group reflects a corrosive quality that dulls the sensitivities of both the perpetrators and the victims. It calls forth venomous hatreds and crude distinctions in high places as well as low places. It can affect the quality of mind of even the most cultivated scholar and place him in a position scarcely distinguishable from the Klansman or worse. It was nothing out of the ordinary, therefore, that at a dinner in honor of the winner of one of Harvard's most coveted prizes, Professor Barrett Wendell warned that if a Negro or a Jew ever won the prize the dinner would have to be canceled.

By the time that the Statue of Liberty was dedicated in 1886 the words of Emma Lazarus on the base of it had a somewhat hollow ring. Could anyone seriously believe that the poor, tired, huddled masses "yearning to breathe free," were really welcome here? This was a land where millions of black human beings whose ancestors had been here for centuries were consistently treated as pariahs and untouchables! What interpretation could anyone place on the sentiments expressed on the statue except that the country had no real interest in or sympathy for the down-trodden unless they were white and preferably Anglo-Saxon? It was a disillusioning experience for some newcomers to discover that their own ethnic background was a barrier to success in their adopted land. It was a searing and shattering experience for Negroes to discover over and over again that three centuries of toil and loyalty were nullified by the misfortune of their own degraded ethnic background.

In the fullness of time—in the twentieth century—the nation would confront the moment of truth regarding ethnicity as a factor in its own historical development. Crevecoeur's words would have no real significance. The words of the Declaration of Independence would have no real meaning. The words of Emma Lazarus would not ring true. All such sentiments would be put to the severe test of public policy and private deeds and would be found wanting. The Ku Klux Klan would challenge the moral and human dignity of Jews, Catholics, and Negroes. The quotas of the new immigration laws would define ethnic values in terms of race and national origin. The restrictive covenants[3] would arrogate to a select group of bigots the power of determining what races or ethnic groups should live in certain houses or whether, indeed, they should have any houses at all in which to live. If some groups finally made it through the escape hatch and arrived at the point of acceptance, it was on the basis of race, now defined with sufficient breadth to include all or most peoples who were not of African descent.

By that time ethnicity in American life would come to have a special, clearly definable meaning. Its meaning would be descriptive of that group of people vaguely defined in the federal census returns as "others" or "nonwhites." It would have something in common with that magnificent term "cultural pluralism," the consolation prize for those who were not and could not be assimilated. It would signify the same groping for respectability that describes that group of people who live in what is euphemistically called "the inner city." It would represent a rather earnest search for a hidden meaning that would make it seem a bit more palatable and surely more sophisticated than something merely racial. But in 1969 even a little child would know what ethnicity had come to mean.

In its history, ethnicity, in its true sense, has extended and continues to extend beyond race. At times it has meant language, customs, religion, national origin. It has also meant race; and, to some, it has always meant only race. It had already begun to have a racial connotation in the eighteenth century. In the nineteenth century, it had a larger racial component, even as other factors continued to loom large. In the present century, as these other factors have receded in importance, racial considerations have come to have even greater significance. If the history of ethnicity has meant anything at all during the last three centuries, it has meant the gradual but steady retreat from the broad and healthy regard for cultural and racial differences to a narrow, counter-productive concept of differences in terms of whim, intolerance, and racial prejudice. We have come full circle. The really acceptable American is still that person whom Crevecoeur described almost two hundred years ago. But the true American, acceptable or not, is that person who seeks to act out his role in terms of his regard for human qualities irrespective of race. One of the great tragedies of American life at the beginning was that ethnicity was defined too narrowly. One of the great tragedies of today is that this continues to be the case. One can only hope that the nation and its people will all some day soon come to reassess ethnicity in terms of the integrity of the man rather than in terms of the integrity of the race.

NOTES

1. SOCIAL DARWINISM: The theory that applied Darwin's theory of evolution, "survival of the fittest," to society; it assumed that upper classes were naturally superior, and the failure of the lower classes was the result of their natural inferiority, not of social policies and practices.
2. JIM CROW: Laws and practices, especially in the South, that separated blacks and whites and enforced the subordination of blacks.
3. RESTRICTIVE COVENANTS: Codes prohibiting members of some groups—often blacks, Jews, and Asians—from buying real estate in certain areas.

CHAPTER 2 Prejudice and Discrimination

2.1 ROBERT K. MERTON

Discrimination and the American Creed

Prejudice can be defined as the disapproving attitudes that people hold toward an entire category of people. Prejudicial beliefs are based upon preconceived notions about people, called *stereotypes*. Stereotypes have been constructed for almost every racial and ethnic minority in U.S. society and are deeply rooted in its culture. *Discrimination*, on the other hand, occurs when categories of people are treated unfairly. Prejudice and discrimination are often seen as occurring together, but prejudice and discrimination can take place independently of each other. For example, a person may hold negative attitudes about other persons but not treat them unfairly, or a person may be unprejudiced yet discriminatory in his or her actions.

The importance of this distinction, according to Robert K. Merton, in the selection that follows, is that it has far-reaching consequences for U.S. social policies directed at repressing racial and ethnic malevolence—particularly in a society that reveres the absolute right of all people to "equitable access to justice, freedom and opportunity, irrespective of race or religion or ethnic origin."

Merton, an eminent sociological theorist and a well-known defender of sociology as a genuine science, is an adjunct professor at Rockefeller University, a resident scholar at the Russel Sage Foundation, and a professor emeritus at Columbia University, all located in New York City. His publications include *On the Shoulders of Giants: A Shandean Postscript*

(Free Press, 1965) and *The Sociology of Science: Theoretical and Empirical Investigations* (University of Chicago Press, 1973).

Key Concept: prejudice and discrimination

*T*he primary function of the sociologist is to search out the determinants and consequences of diverse forms of social behavior. To the extent that he succeeds in fulfilling this role, he clarifies the alternatives of organized social action in a given situation and of the probable outcome of each. To this extent, there is no sharp distinction between pure research and applied research. Rather, the difference is one between research with direct implications for particular problems of social action and research which is remote from these problems. Not infrequently, basic research which has succeeded only in clearing up previously confused concepts may have an immediate bearing upon the problems of men in society to a degree not approximated by applied research oriented exclusively to these problems. At least, this is the assumption underlying the present paper: clarification of apparently unclear and confused concepts in the sphere of race and ethnic relations is a step necessarily prior to the devising of effective programs for reducing intergroup conflict and for promoting equitable access to economic and social opportunities....

THE AMERICAN CREED: AS CULTURAL IDEAL, PERSONAL BELIEF AND PRACTICE

The American creed as set forth in the Declaration of Independence, the preamble of the Constitution and the Bill of Rights has often been misstated. This part of the cultural heritage does *not* include the patently false assertion that all men are created equal in capacity or endowment. It does *not* imply that an Einstein and a moron are equal in intellectual capacity or that Joe Louis and a small, frail Columbia professor (or a Mississippian Congressman) are equally endowed with brawny arms harboring muscles as strong as iron bands. It does *not* proclaim universal equality of innate intellectual or physical endowment.

Instead, the creed asserts the indefeasible principle of the human right to full equity—the right of equitable access to justice, freedom and opportunity, irrespective of race or religion or ethnic origin. It proclaims further the universalist doctrine of the dignity of the individual, irrespective of the groups of which he is a part. It is a creed announcing full moral equities for all, not an absurd myth affirming the equality of intellectual and physical capacity of all men everywhere. And it goes on to say that though men differ in innate endowment, they do so as individuals, not by virtue of their group memberships.

Viewed sociologically, the creed is a set of values and precepts embedded in American culture, to which Americans are expected to conform. It is a complex of affirmations, rooted in the historical past and ceremonially celebrated in the present, partly enacted in the laws of the land and partly not. Like all creeds, it is a profession of faith, a part of cultural tradition sanctified by the larger traditions of which it is a part.

It would be a mistaken sociological assertion, however, to suggest that the creed is a fixed and static cultural constant, unmodified in the course of time, just as it would be an error to imply that as an integral part of culture, it evenly blankets all subcultures of the national society. It is indeed dynamic, subject to change and in turn promoting change in other spheres of culture and society. It is, moreover, unevenly distributed throughout the society, being institution-alized as an integral part of local culture in some regions of the society and rejected in others.

... Learned men and men in high public positions have repeatedly ob-served and deplored the disparity between ethos and behavior in the sphere of race and ethnic relations. In his magisterial volumes on the American Negro, for example, Gunnar Myrdal called this gulf between creed and conduct "an American dilemma," and centered his attention on the prospect of narrowing or closing the gap. The President's Committee on Civil Rights, in their report to the nation, and ... President [Truman] himself, in a message to Congress, have called public attention to this "serious gap between our ideals and some of our practices."

But as valid as these observations may be, they tend so to simplify the relations between creed and conduct as to be seriously misleading both for social policy and for social science. All these high authorities notwithstanding, the problems of racial and ethnic inequities are not expressible as a discrepancy between high cultural principles and low social conduct. It is a relation not between two variables, official creed and private practice, but between three: first, the cultural creed honored in cultural tradition and partly enacted into law; second, the beliefs and attitudes of individuals regarding the principles of the creed; and third, the actual practices of individuals with reference to it.

Once we substitute these three variables of cultural ideal, belief and ac-tual practice for the customary distinction between the two variables of cul-tural ideals and actual practices, the entire formulation of the problem becomes changed. We escape from the virtuous but ineffectual impasse of deploring the alleged hypocrisy of many Americans into the more difficult but potentially effectual realm of analyzing the problem in hand.

To describe the problem and to proceed to its analysis, it is necessary to consider the official creed, individuals' beliefs and attitudes concerning the creed, and their actual behavior. Once stated, the distinctions are readily appli-cable. Individuals may *recognize* the creed as part of a cultural tradition, *without having any private conviction of its moral validity or its binding quality.* Thus, so far as the beliefs of individuals are concerned, we can identify two types: those who genuinely believe in the creed and those who do not (although some of these may, on public or ceremonial occasions, profess adherence to its principles). Similarly, with respect to actual practices: conduct may or may not conform to the creed. But, and this is the salient consideration: *conduct may or may not conform with individuals' own beliefs concerning the moral claims of all men to equal opportunity.*

Stated in formal sociological terms, this asserts that attitudes and overt behavior vary independently. *Prejudicial attitudes need not coincide with discrimi-*

natory behavior. The implications of this statement can be drawn out in terms of a logical syntax whereby the variables are diversely combined, as can be seen in the following typology.

By exploring the interrelations between prejudice and discrimination, we can identify four major types in terms of their attitudes toward the creed and their behavior with respect to it. Each type is found in every region and social class, though in varying numbers. By examining each type, we shall be better prepared to understand their interdependence and the appropriate types of action for curbing ethnic discrimination. The folklabels for each type are intended to aid in their prompt recognition.

Type I: The Unprejudiced Non-Discriminator or All-Weather Liberal

These are the racial and ethnic liberals who adhere to the creed in both belief and practice. They are neither prejudiced nor given to discrimination. Their orientation toward the creed is fixed and stable. Whatever the environing situation, they are likely to abide by their beliefs: hence, the *all-weather* liberal.

This is, of course, the strategic group which *can* act as the spearhead for the progressive extension of the creed into effective practice. They represent the solid foundation both for the measure of ethnic equities which now exist and for the future enlargement of these equities. Integrated with the creed in both belief and practice, they would seem most motivated to influence others toward the same democratic outlook. They represent a reservoir of culturally legitimatized goodwill which can be channeled into an active program for extending belief in the creed and conformity with it in practice.

Most important, as we shall see presently, the all-weather liberals comprise the group which can so reward others for conforming with the creed, as to transform deviants into conformists. They alone can provide the positive social environment for the other types who will no longer find it expedient or rewarding to retain their prejudices or discriminatory practices.

But though the ethnic liberal is a *potential* force for the successive extension of the American creed, he does not fully realize this potentiality in actual fact, for a variety of reasons. Among the limitations on effective action are several fallacies to which the ethnic liberal seems peculiarly subject. First among these is the *fallacy of group soliloquies.* Ethnic liberals are busily engaged in talking to themselves. Repeatedly, the same groups of like-minded liberals seek each other out, hold periodic meetings in which they engage in mutual exhortation and thus lend social and psychological support to one another. But however much these unwittingly self-selected audiences may reinforce the creed among themselves, they do not thus appreciably diffuse the creed in belief or practice to groups which depart from it in one respect or the other.

More, these group soliloquies in which there is typically wholehearted agreement among fellow-liberals tend to promote another fallacy limiting effective action. This is the *fallacy of unanimity.* Continued association with like-minded individuals tends to produce the illusion that a large measure of consensus has been achieved in the community at large. The unanimity regarding essential cultural axioms which obtains in these small groups provokes an overestimation of the strength of the movement and of its effective inroads upon the larger population which does not necessarily share these creedal axioms. Many also mistake participation in the groups of like-minded individuals for effective action. Discussion accordingly takes the place of action. The reinforcement of the creed for oneself is mistaken for the extension of the creed among those outside the limited circle of ethnic liberals.

Arising from adherence to the creed is a third limitation upon effective action, the *fallacy of privatized solutions* to the problem. The ethnic liberal, precisely because he is at one with the American creed, may rest content with his own individual behavior and thus see no need to do anything about the problem at large. Since his own spiritual house is in order, he is not motivated by guilt or shame to work on a collective problem. The very freedom of the liberal from guilt thus prompts him to secede from any *collective* effort to set the national house in order. He essays a *private* solution to a *social* problem. He assumes that numerous individual adjustments will serve in place of a collective adjustment. His outlook, compounded of good moral philosophy but poor sociology, holds that each individual must put his own house in order and fails to recognize that privatized solutions cannot be effected for problems which are essentially social in nature. For clearly, if each person *were* motivated to abide by the American creed, the problem would not be likely to exist in the first place. It is only when a social environment is established by conformists to the creed that deviants can in due course be brought to modify their behavior in the direction of conformity. But this "environment" can be constituted only through collective effort and not through private adherence to a public creed. Thus we have the paradox that the clear conscience of many ethnic liberals may promote the very social situation which permits deviations from the creed to continue unchecked. Privatized liberalism invites social inaction. Accordingly, there appears the phenomenon of the inactive or passive liberal, himself at spiritual ease, neither prejudiced nor discriminatory, but in a measure tending to contribute to the persistence of prejudice and discrimination through his very inaction.

The fallacies of group soliloquy, unanimity and privatized solutions thus operate to make the potential strength of the ethnic liberals unrealized in practice.

It is only by first recognizing these limitations that the liberal can hope to overcome them. With some hesitancy, one may suggest initial policies for curbing the scope of the three fallacies. The fallacy of group soliloquies can be removed only by having ethnic liberals enter into organized groups not comprised merely by fellow-liberals. This exacts a heavy price of the liberal. It means that he faces initial opposition and resistance rather than prompt consensus. It entails giving up the gratifications of consistent group support.

The fallacy of unanimity can in turn be reduced by coming to see that American society often provides large rewards for those who express their ethnic prejudice in discrimination. Only if the balance of rewards, material and psychological, is modified will behavior be modified. Sheer exhortation and propaganda are not enough. Exhortation verges on a belief in magic if it is not supported by appropriate changes in the social environment to make conformity with the exhortation rewarding.

Finally, the fallacy of privatized solutions requires the militant liberal to motivate the passive liberal to collective effort, possibly by inducing in him a sense of guilt for his unwitting contribution to the problems of ethnic inequities through his own systematic inaction.

One may suggest a unifying theme for the ethnic liberal: goodwill is not enough to modify social reality. It is only when this goodwill is harnessed to social-psychological realism that it can be used to reach cultural objectives.

Type II: The Unprejudiced Discriminator or Fair-Weather Liberal

The fair-weather liberal is the man of expediency who, despite his own freedom from prejudice, supports discriminatory practices when it is the easier or more profitable course. His expediency may take the form of holding his silence and thus implicitly acquiescing in expressions of ethnic prejudice by others or in the practice of discrimination by others. This is the expediency of the timid: the liberal who hesitates to speak up against discrimination for fear he might lose status or be otherwise penalized by his prejudiced associates. Or his expediency may take the form of grasping at advantages in social and economic competition deriving solely from the ethnic status of competitors. This is the expediency of the self-assertive: the employer, himself not an anti-Semite or Negrophobe, who refuses to hire Jewish or Negro workers because "it might hurt business"; the trade union leader who expediently advocates racial discrimination in order not to lose the support of powerful Negrophobes in his union.

In varying degrees, the fair-weather liberal suffers from guilt and shame for departing from his own effective beliefs in the American creed. Each deviation through which he derives a limited reward from passively acquiescing in or actively supporting discrimination contributes cumulatively to this fund of guilt. He is, therefore, peculiarly vulnerable to the efforts of the all-weather liberal who would help him bring his conduct into accord with his beliefs, thus removing this source of guilt. He is the most amenable to cure, because basically he wants to be cured. His is a split conscience which motivates him to cooperate actively with those who will help remove the source of internal conflict. He thus represents the strategic group promising the largest returns for the least effort. Persistent re-affirmation of the creed will only intensify his conflict; but a long regimen in a favorable social climate can be expected to transform the fair-weather liberal into an all-weather liberal.

Type III: The Prejudiced Non-Discriminator or Fair-Weather Illiberal

The fair-weather illiberal is the reluctant conformist to the creed, the man of prejudice who does not believe in the creed but conforms to it in practice through fear of sanctions which might otherwise be visited upon him. You know him well: the prejudiced employer who discriminates against racial or ethnic groups until a Fair Employment Practice Commission, able and willing to enforce the law, puts the fear of punishment into him; the trade union leader, himself deeply prejudiced, who does away with Jim Crow in his union because the rank-and-file demands that it be done away with; the businessman who foregoes his own prejudices when he finds a profitable market among the very people he hates, fears or despises; the timid bigot who will not express his prejudices when he is in the presence of powerful men who vigorously and effectively affirm their belief in the American creed.

It should be clear that the fair-weather illiberal is the precise counterpart of the fair-weather liberal. Both are men of expediency, to be sure, but expediency dictates different courses of behavior in the two cases. The timid bigot conforms to the creed only when there is danger or loss in deviations, just as the timid liberal deviates from the creed when there is danger or loss in conforming. *Superficial similarity in behavior of the two in the same situation should not be permitted to cloak a basic difference in the meaning of this outwardly similar behavior,* a difference which is as important for social policy as it is for social science. Whereas the timid bigot is under strain when he conforms to the creed, the timid liberal is under strain when he deviates. For ethnic prejudice has deep roots in the character structure of the fair-weather bigot, and this will find overt expression unless there are powerful countervailing forces, institutional, legal and interpersonal. He does not accept the moral legitimacy of the creed; he conforms because he must, and will cease to conform when the pressure is removed. The fair-weather liberal, on the other hand, is effectively committed to the creed and does not require strong institutional pressure to conform; continuing interpersonal relations with all-weather liberals may be sufficient.

This is the one critical point at which the traditional formulation of the problem of ethnic discrimination as a departure from the creed can lead to serious errors of theory and practice. Overt behavioral deviation (or conformity) may signify importantly different situations, depending upon the underlying motivations. Knowing simply that ethnic discrimination is rife in a community does not, therefore, point to appropriate lines of social policy. It is necessary to know also the distribution of ethnic prejudices and basic motivations for these prejudices as well. Communities with the same amount of overt discrimination may represent vastly different types of problems, dependent on whether the population is comprised by a large nucleus of fair-weather liberals ready to abandon their discriminatory practices under slight interpersonal pressure or a large nucleus of fair-weather illiberals who will abandon discrimination only if major changes in the local institutional setting can be effected. Any statement of the problem as a gulf between creedal ideals and prevailing practice is thus seen to be overly-simplified in the precise sense of masking this decisive difference between the type of discrimination exhibited by the fair-weather liberal and by the fair-weather illiberal. That the gulf-between-ideal-and-practice does not adequately describe the nature of the ethnic problem will become more apparent as we turn to the fourth type in our inventory of prejudice and discrimination.

Type IV: The Prejudiced Discriminator or the All-Weather Illiberal

This type, too, is not unknown to you. He is the confirmed illiberal, the bigot pure and unashamed, the man of prejudice consistent in his departure from the American creed. In some measure, he is found everywhere in the land, though in varying numbers. He derives large social and psychological gains from his conviction that "any white man (including the village idiot) is 'better' than any nigger (including George Washington Carver)." He considers differential treatment of Negro and white not as "discrimination," in the sense of unfair treatment, but as "discriminating," in the sense of showing acute discernment. For him, it is as clear that one "ought" to accord a Negro and a white different treatment in a wide diversity of situations, as it is clear to the population at large that one "ought" to accord a child and an adult different treatment in many situations.

This illustrates anew my reason for questioning the applicability of the unusual formula of the American dilemma as a gap between lofty creed and low conduct. For the confirmed illiberal, ethnic discrimination does *not* represent a discrepancy between *his* ideals and *his* behavior. His ideals proclaim the right, even the duty, of discrimination. Accordingly, his behavior does not entail a sense of social deviation, with the resultant strains which this would involve. The ethnic illiberal is as much a conformist as the ethnic liberal. He is merely conforming to a different cultural and institutional pattern which is centered, not about the creed, but about a doctrine of essential inequality of status ascribed to those of diverse ethnic and racial origins. To overlook this is to overlook the well-known *fact* that our national culture is divided into a number of local subcultures which are not consistent among themselves in all respects. And again, to fail to take this fact of different subcultures into account is to open the door for all manner of errors of social policy in attempting to control the problems of racial and ethnic discrimination.

This view of the all-weather illiberal has one immediate implication with wide bearing upon social policies and sociological theory oriented toward the problem of discrimination. The extreme importance of the social surroundings of the confirmed illiberal at once becomes apparent. For as these surroundings vary, so, in some measure, does the problem of the consistent illiberal. The illiberal, living in those cultural regions where the American creed is widely repudiated and is no effective part of the subculture, has his private ethnic attitudes and practices supported by the local mores, the local institutions and the local power-structure. The illiberal in cultural areas dominated by a large measure of adherence to the American creed is in a social environment where he is isolated and receives small social support for his beliefs and practices. In both instances, the *individual* is an illiberal, to be sure, but he represents two significantly different *sociological types*. In the first instance, he is a *social conformist*, with strong moral and institutional reinforcement, whereas in the second, he is a *social deviant*, lacking strong social corroboration. In the one case, his discrimination involves him in further integration with his network of social relations; in the other, it threatens to cut him off from sustaining interpersonal ties. In the first cultural context, personal change in his ethnic behavior involves alienating himself from people significant to him; in the second context, this change of personal outlook may mean fuller incorporation in groups meaningful to him. In the first situation, modification of his ethnic views requires him to take the path of greatest resistance whereas in the second, it may mean the path of least resistance. From all this, we may surmise that any social policy aimed at changing the behavior and perhaps the attitudes of the all-weather illiberal will have to take into account the cultural and social structure of the area in which he lives....

IMPLICATIONS OF THE TYPOLOGY FOR SOCIAL POLICY

... In approaching problems of policy, two things are plain. First, these should be considered from the standpoint of the militant ethnic liberal, for he alone is sufficiently motivated to engage in positive action for the reduction of ethnic discrimination. And second, the fair-weather liberal, the fair-weather illiberal and the all-weather illiberal represent types differing sufficiently to require diverse kinds of treatment.

Treatment of the Fair-Weather Liberal

The fair-weather liberal, it will be remembered, discriminates only when it appears expedient to do so, and experiences some measure of guilt for deviating from his own belief in the American creed. He suffers from this conflict between conscience and conduct. Accordingly, he is a relatively easy target for the all-weather liberal. He represents the strategic group promising the largest immediate returns for the least effort. Recognition of this type defines the first task for the militant liberal who would enter into a collective effort to make the creed a viable and effective set of social norms rather than a ceremonial myth....

Since the fair-weather liberal discriminates only when it seems rewarding to do so, the crucial need is so to change social situations that there are few occasions in which discrimination proves rewarding and many in which it does not. This would suggest that ethnic liberals self-consciously and deliberately seek to draw into the social groups where they constitute a comfortable majority a number of the "expedient discriminators." This would serve to counteract the dangers of self-selection through which liberals come to associate primarily with like-minded individuals. It would, further, provide an interpersonal and social environment for the fair-weather liberal in which he would find substantial social and psychological gains from abiding by his own beliefs, gains which would more than offset the rewards attendant upon occasional discrimination. It appears that men do not long persist in behavior which lacks social corroboration.

We have much to learn about the role of numbers and proportions in determining the behavior of members of a group. But it seems that individuals generally act differently when they are numbered among a minority rather than the majority. This is not to say that minorities abdicate their practices in the face of a contrary-acting majority, but only that the same people are subjected to different strains and pressures according to whether they are included in the majority or the minority. And the fair-weather liberal who finds himself associated with militant ethnic liberals may be expected to forego his occasional deviations into discrimination; he may move from category II into category

I; this at least is suggested by the Columbia-Lavanburg researches on ethnic relations in the planned community. . . .

Treatment of the Fair-Weather Illiberal

Because his *beliefs* correspond to those of the full-fledged liberal, the fair-weather liberal can rather readily be drawn into an interpersonal environment constituted by those of a comparable turn of mind. This would be more difficult for the fair-weather illiberal, whose beliefs are so fully at odds with those of ethnic liberals that he may, at first, only be alienated by association with them. If the initial tactic for the fair-weather liberal, therefore, is a change in interpersonal environment, the seemingly most appropriate tactic for the fair-weather illiberal is a change in the institutional and legal environment. It is, indeed, probably this type which liberals implicitly have in mind when they expect significant changes in behavior to result from the introduction of controls on ethnic discrimination into the legal machinery of our society.

For this type—and it is a major limitation for planning policies of control that we do not know his numbers or his distribution in the country—it would seem that the most effective tactic is the institution of legal controls administered with strict efficiency. This would presumably reduce the amount of *discrimination* practiced by the fair-weather illiberal, though it might *initially* enhance rather than reduce his *prejudices*. . . .

A second prevalent tactic for modifying the prejudice of the fair-weather illiberal is that of seeking to draw him into interethnic groups explicitly formed for the promotion of tolerance. This, too, seems largely ineffectual, since the deeply prejudiced individual will not enter into such groups of his own volition. As a consequence of this process of self-selection, these tolerance groups soon come to be comprised by the very ethnic liberals who initiated the enterprise.

This barrier of self-selection can be partially hurdled only if the ethnic illiberals are brought into continued association with militant liberals in groups devoted to significant common values, quite remote from objectives of ethnic equity as such. Thus, as our Columbia-Lavanburg researches have found, many fair-weather illiberals *will* live in interracial housing projects in order to enjoy the rewards of superior housing at a given rental. And some of the illiberals thus brought into personal contact with various ethnic groups under the auspices of prestigeful militant liberals come to modify their prejudices. It is, apparently, only through interethnic collaboration, initially enforced by pressures of the situation, for immediate and significant objectives (other than tolerance) that the self-insulation of the fair-weather illiberal from rewarding interethnic contacts can be removed.

But however difficult it may presently be to affect the *prejudicial sentiments* of the fair-weather illiberal, his *discriminatory practices* can be lessened by the uniform, prompt and prestigeful use of legal and institutional sanctions. The critical problem is to ascertain the proportions of fair-weather and all-weather illiberals in a given local population in order to have some clue to the probable effectiveness or ineffectiveness of anti-discrimination legislation.

*Robert K.
Merton*

It is, of course, the hitherto confirmed illiberal, persistently translating his prejudices into active discrimination, who represents the most difficult problem. But though he requires longer and more careful treatment, it is possible that he is not beyond change. In every instance, his social surroundings must be assiduously taken into account. It makes a peculiarly large difference whether he is in a cultural region of bigotry or in a predominantly "liberal" area, given over to verbal adherence to the American creed, at the very least. As this cultural climate varies, so must the prescription for his cure and the prognosis for a relatively quick or long delayed recovery.

In an unfavorable cultural climate—and this does not necessarily exclude the benign regions of the Far South—the immediate resort will probably have to be that of working through legal and administrative federal controls over extreme discrimination, with full recognition that, in all probability, these regulations will be systematically evaded from some time to come. In such cultural regions, we may expect nullification of the law as the common practice, perhaps as common as was the case in the nation at large with respect to the Eighteenth Amendment, often with the connivance of local officers of the law. The large gap between the new law and local mores will not *at once* produce significant change of prevailing practices; token punishments of violations will probably be more common than effective control. At best, one may assume that significant change will be fitful, and excruciatingly slow. But secular changes in the economy may in due course lend support to the new legal framework of control over discrimination. As the economic shoe pinches because the illiberals do not fully mobilize the resources of industrial manpower nor extend their local markets through equitable wage-payments, they may slowly abandon some discriminatory practices as they come to find that these do not always pay—even the discriminator. So far as discrimination is concerned, organized counteraction is possible and some small results may be expected. But it would seem that wishes father thoughts, when one expects basic changes in the immediate future in these regions of institutionalized discrimination.

The situation is somewhat different with regard to the scattered, rather than aggregated, ethnic illiberals found here and there throughout the country. Here the mores and a social organization oriented toward the American creed still have some measure of prestige and the resources of a majority of liberals can be mobilized to isolate the illiberal. In these surroundings, it is possible to move the all-weather illiberal toward Type III—he can be brought to conform with institutional regulations, even though he does not surrender his prejudices. And once he has entered upon this role of the dissident but conforming individual, the remedial program designed for the fair-weather illiberal would be in order.

The Declining Significance of Race

For decades, the idea of the *underclass* has been the subject of considerable debate in the social sciences. In short, the underclass refers to individuals who are outside the occupational structure of U.S. society. Often called the *inner-city (ghetto) poor*, their communities are plagued by extreme poverty, perpetual joblessness, drug addiction, street violence, high rates of out-of-wedlock childbirths, and transgenerational welfare dependency. Some commentators argue that the underclass constitutes a culturally deprived segment of the American population that is caught in a tangle of social pathology.

William Julius Wilson is the Lucy Flower Distinguished Service Professor of Sociology and Public Policy at the University of Chicago's Center for the Study of Urban Inequality, where he is currently directing a $2.8 million study on poverty, joblessness, and family structure in the inner city. His publications include *The Declining Significance of Race: Blacks and Changing American Institutions* (University of Chicago Press, 1978).

In the present article, Wilson traces the social history of the underclass and contends that, since World War II, class position has become more significant than race in defining the underclass. That is, the forces of post-war industrialization have diminished the effects of racial discrimination, and through occupational advancement a significant Black middle class has been created.

Key Concept: the underclass

Race relations in the United States have undergone fundamental changes in recent years, so much so that now the life chances of individual blacks have more to do with their economic class position than with their day-to-day encounters with whites. In earlier years the systematic efforts of whites to suppress blacks were obvious to even the most insensitive observer. Blacks were denied access to valued and scarce resources through various ingenious schemes of racial exploitation, discrimination, and segregation, schemes that were reinforced by elaborate ideologies of racism.

But the situation has changed. However determinative such practices were in the previous efforts of the black population to achieve racial equality, and however significant they were in the creation of poverty-stricken ghettos and a vast underclass of black proletarians—that massive population at the very bottom of the social class ladder plagued by poor education and low-paying, unstable jobs—they do not provide a meaningful explanation of the life chances of black Americans today. The traditional patterns of interaction between blacks and whites, particularly in the labor market, have been fundamentally altered.

NEW AND TRADITIONAL BARRIERS

In the pre-Civil War period, and in the latter half of the nineteenth through the first half of the twentieth century, the continuous and explicit efforts of whites to construct racial barriers profoundly affected the lives of black Americans. Racial oppression was designed, overt, and easily documented. As the nation has entered the latter half of the twentieth century, however, many of the traditional barriers have crumbled under the weight of the political, social, and economic changes of the civil rights era. A new set of obstacles has emerged from basic structural shifts in the economy.

These obstacles are therefore impersonal, but may prove to be even more formidable for certain segments of the black population. Specifically, whereas the previous barriers were usually designed to control and restrict the entire black population, the new barriers create hardships essentially for the black underclass; whereas the old barriers were based explicitly on the racial motivations derived from intergroup contact, the new barriers have racial significance only in their consequences, not in their origins. In short, whereas the old barriers portrayed the pervasive features of racial oppression, the new barriers indicate an important and emerging form of class subordination.

It would be shortsighted to view the traditional forms of racial segregation and discrimination as having essentially disappeared in contemporary America; the presence of blacks is still firmly resisted in various institutions and social arrangements, for example, residential areas and private social clubs. However, in the economic sphere class has become more important than race in determining black access to privilege and power. It is clearly evident in this connection that many talented and educated blacks are now entering positions of prestige and influence at a rate comparable to or, in some situations, exceeding that of whites with equivalent qualifications. It is equally clear that the black underclass is in a hopeless state of economic stagnation, falling further and further behind the rest of society.

THREE STAGES OF AMERICAN RACE RELATIONS

American society has experienced three major stages of black-white contact, and each stage embodies a different form of racial stratification structured by the particular arrangement of both the economy and the polity. Stage one coincides with antebellum slavery and the early postbellum era and may be designated the period of *plantation economy and racial-caste oppression*. Stage two begins in the last quarter of the nineteenth century and ends at roughly the New Deal era, and may be identified as the period of *industrial expansion, class conflict, and racial oppression*. Finally, stage three is associated with the modern, industrial, post-World War II era which really began to crystallize during the 1960s and 1970s, and may be characterized as the period of *progressive transition from race inequalities to class inequalities*. The different periods can be identified as the preindustrial, industrial, and modern industrial stages of American race relations, respectively.

Although this abbreviated designation of the periods of American race relations seems to relate racial change to fundamental economic changes rather directly, it bears repeating that the different stages of race relations are structured by the unique arrangements and interaction of the economy and polity. More specifically, although there was an economic basis of structured racial inequality in the preindustrial and industrial periods of race relations, the polity more or less interacted with the economy either to reinforce patterns of racial stratification or to mediate various forms of racial conflict. Moreover, in the modern industrial period race relations have bene shaped as much by important economic changes as by important political changes. Indeed, it would not be possible to understand fully the subtle and manifest changes in race relations in the modern industrial period without recognizing the dual and often reciprocal influence of structural changes in the economy and political changes in the state. Thus different systems of production and/or different arrangements of the polity have imposed different constraints on the way in which racial groups have interacted in the United States, constraints that have structured the relations between racial groups and that have produced dissimilar contexts not only for the manifestation of racial antagonisms, but also for racial group access to rewards and privileges.

In contrast to the modern industrial period in which fundamental economic and political changes have made the economic class position of blacks the determining factor in their prospects for occupational advancement, the preindustrial and industrial periods of black-white relations have one central feature in common: overt efforts of whites to solidify economic racial domination (ranging from the manipulation of black labor to the neutralization or elimination of black economic competition) through various forms of judicial, political, and social discrimination. Since racial problems during these two periods were principally related to group struggles over economic resources, they readily lend themselves to the economic class theories of racial antagonisms that associate racial antipathy with class conflict.

Although racial oppression, when viewed from the broad perspective of historical change in American society, was a salient and important feature during the preindustrial and industrial periods of race relations in the United

States, the problems of subordination for certain segments of the black population and the experience of social advancement for others are more directly associated with economic class in the modern industrial period. Economic and political changes have gradually shaped a black class structure, making it increasingly difficult to speak of a single or uniform black experience. Although a small elite population of free, propertied blacks did in fact exist during the pre-Civil War period, the interaction between race and economic class only assumed real importance in the latter phases of the industrial period of race relations; and the significance of this relationship has grown as the nation has entered the modern industrial period.

Each of the major periods of American race relations has been shaped in different measure both by the systems of production and by the laws and policies of the state. However, the relationships between the economy and the state have varied in each period, and therefore the roles of both institutions in shaping race relations have differed over time.

ANTEBELLUM SOUTH

In the preindustrial period the slave-based plantation economy of the South allowed a relatively small, elite group of planters to develop enormous regional power. The hegemony of the southern ruling elite was based on a system of production that required little horizontal or vertical mobility and therefore could be managed very efficiently with a simple division of labor that virtually excluded free white labor. As long as free white workers were not central to the process of reproducing the labor supply in the southern plantation economy, slavery as a mode of production facilitated the slaveholder's concentration and consolidation of economic power. And the slaveholders successfully transferred their control of the economic system to the political and legal systems in order to protect their class interest in slavery. In effect, the polity in the South regulated and reinforced the system of racial caste oppression, depriving both blacks and nonslaveholding whites of any meaningful influence in the way that slavery was used in the economic life of the South.

In short, the economy provided the basis for the development of the system of slavery, and the policy reinforced and perpetuated that system. Furthermore, the economy enabled the slaveholders to develop a regional center of power, and the polity was used to legitimate that power. Since nonslaveholding whites were virtually powerless both economically and politically, they had very little effect on the developing patterns of race relations. The meaningful forms of black-white contact were between slaves and slaveholders, and southern race relations consequently assumed a paternalistic quality involving the elaboration and specification of duties, norms, rights, and obligations as they pertained to the use of slave labor and the system of indefinite servitude.

In short, the pattern of race relations in the antebellum South was shaped first and foremost by the system of production. The very nature of the social relations of production meant that the exclusive control of the planters would be derived from their position in the production process, which ultimately led to the creation of a juridicial system that reflected and protected their class interests, including their investment in slavery.

WORKERS' EMERGING POWER

However, in the nineteenth century antebellum North the form of racial oppression was anything but paternalistic. Here a more industrial system of production enabled white workers to become more organized and physically concentrated than their southern counterparts. Following the abolition of slavery in the North, they used their superior resources to generate legal and informal practices of segregation that effectively prevented blacks from becoming serious economic competitors.

As the South gradually moved from a plantation to an industrial economy in the last quarter of the nineteenth century, landless whites were finally able to effect changes in the racial stratification system. Their efforts to eliminate black competition helped to produce an elaborate system of Jim Crow segregation. Poor whites were aided not only by their numbers but also by the development of political resources which accompanied their greater involvement in the South's economy.

Once again, however, the system of production was the major basis for this change in race relations, and once again the political system was used to reinforce patterns of race emanating from structural shifts in the economy. If the racial laws in the antebellum South protected the class interests of the planters and reflected their overwhelming power, the Jim Crow segregation laws of the late nineteenth century reflected the rising power of the white laborers; and if the political power of the planters was grounded in the system of producing in a plantation economy, the emerging political power of the workers grew out of the new division of labor that accompanied industrialization.

CLASS AND RACE RELATIONS

Except for the brief period of fluid race relations in the North between 1870 and 1890 and in the South during the Reconstruction era, racial oppression is the single best term to characterize the black experience prior to the twentieth century. In the antebellum South both slaves and free blacks occupied what could be best described as a caste position, in the sense that realistic chances for occupational mobility simply did not exist. In the antebellum North a few free blacks were able to acquire some property and improve their socioeconomic position, and a few were even able to make use of educational opportunities. However, the overwhelming majority of free northern Negroes were trapped in menial positions and were victimized by lower-class white antagonism, including the racial hostilities of European immigrant ethnics (who successfully curbed black economic competition). In the postbellum South the system of Jim Crow segregation wiped out the small gains blacks had achieved during Reconstruction, and blacks were rapidly pushed out of the more skilled jobs they had held since slavery. Accordingly, there was very little black occupational differentiation in the South at the turn of the century.

Just as the shift from a plantation economy to an industrializing economy transformed the class and race relations in the postbellum South, so too did industrialization in the North change the context for race-class interaction and confrontation there. On the one hand, the conflicts associated with the increased black-white contacts in the early twentieth century North resembled the forms of antagonism that soured the relations between the races in the postbellum South. Racial conflicts between blacks and whites in both situations were closely tied to class conflicts among whites. On the other hand, there were some fundamental differences. The collapse of the paternalistic bond between blacks and the southern business elite cleared the path for the almost total subjugation of blacks in the South and resulted in what amounted to a united white racial movement that solidified the system of Jim Crow segregation.

However, a united white movement against blacks never really developed in the North. In the first quarter of the twentieth century, management attempted to undercut white labor by using blacks as strikebreakers and, in some situations, as permanent replacements for white workers who periodically demanded higher wages and more fringe benefits. Indeed, the determination of industrialists to ignore racial norms of exclusion and to hire black workers was one of the main reasons why the industrywide unions reversed their racial policies and actively recruited black workers during the New Deal era. Prior to this period the overwhelming majority of unskilled and semiskilled blacks were nonunionized and were available as lower-paid labor or as strikebreakers. The more management used blacks to undercut white labor, the greater were the racial antagonisms between white and black labor.

Moreover, racial tension in the industrial sector often reinforced and sometimes produced racial tension in the social order. The growth of the black urban population created a housing shortage during the early twentieth century which frequently produced black "invasions" or ghetto "spillovers" into adjacent poor white neighborhoods. The racial tensions emanating from labor strife seemed to heighten the added pressures of racial competition for housing, neighborhoods, and recreational areas. Indeed, it was this combination of racial friction in both the economic sector and the social order that produced the bloody riots in East Saint Louis in 1917 and in Chicago and several other cities in 1919.

In addition to the fact that a united white movement against blacks never really developed in the North during the industrial period, it was also the case that the state's role in shaping race relations was much more autonomous, much less directly related to developments in the economic sector. Thus, in the brief period of fluid race relations in the North from 1870 to 1890, civil rights laws were passed barring discrimination in public places and in public institutions. This legislation did not have any real significance to the white masses at that time because, unlike in the pre-Civil War North and the post-Civil War South, white workers did not perceive blacks as major economic competitors. Blacks constituted only a small percentage of the total population in northern cities; they had not yet been used in any significant numbers as cheap labor in industry or as strikebreakers; and their earlier antebellum competitors in low-status jobs (the Irish and German immigrants) had improved their economic status in the trades and municipal employment.

POLITY AND RACIAL OPPRESSION

For all these reasons liberal whites and black professionals, urged on by the spirit of racial reform that had developed during the Civil War and Reconstruction, could pursue civil rights programs without firm resistance; for all these reasons racial developments on the political front were not directly related to the economic motivations and interests of workers and management. In the early twentieth century the independent effect of the political system was displayed in an entirely different way. The process of industrialization had significantly altered the pattern of racial interaction, giving rise to various manifestations of racial antagonism.

Although discrimination and lack of training prevented blacks from seeking higher-paying jobs, they did compete with lower-class whites for unskilled and semiskilled factory jobs, and they were used by management to undercut the white workers' union movement. Despite the growing importance of race in the dynamics of the labor market, the political system did not intervene either to mediate the racial conflicts or to reinforce the pattern of labor-market racial interaction generated by the system of production. This was the case despite the salience of a racial ideology system that justified and prescribed unequal treatment for Afro-Americans. (Industrialists will more likely challenge societal racial norms in situations where adherence to them results in economic losses.)

If nothing else, the absence of political influence on the labor market probably reflected the power struggles between management and workers. Thus legislation to protect the rights of black workers to compete openly for jobs would have conflicted with the interests of white workers, whereas legislation to deny black participation in any kind of industrial work would have conflicted with the interest of management. To repeat, unlike in the South, a united white movement resulting in the almost total segregation of the work force never really developed in the North.

But the state's lack of influence in the industrial sector of private industries did not mean that it had no significant impact on racial stratification in the early twentieth century North. The urban political machines, controlled in large measure by working-class ethnics who were often in direct competition with blacks in the private industrial sector, systematically gerrymandered black neighborhoods and excluded the urban black masses from meaningful political participation throughout the early twentieth century. Control by the white ethnics of the various urban political machines was so complete that blacks were never really in a position to compete for the more important municipal political rewards, such as patronage jobs or government contracts and services. Thus the lack of racial competition for municipal political rewards did not provide the basis for racial tension and conflict in the urban political system. This political racial oppression had no direct connection with or influence on race relations in the private industrial sector.

In sum, whether one focuses on the way race relations were structured by the system of production or the polity or both, racial oppression (ranging from the exploitation of black labor by the business class to the elimination of black competition for economic, social, and political resources by the white masses) was a characteristic and important phenomenon in both the preindustrial and industrial periods of American race relations. Nonetheless, and despite the prevalence of various forms of racial oppression, the change from a preindustrial to an industrial system of production did enable blacks to increase their political and economic resources. The proliferation of jobs created by industrial expansion helped generate and sustain the continuous mass migration of blacks from the rural South to the cities of the North and West. As the black urban population grew and became more segregated, institutions and organizations in the black community also developed, together with a business and professional class affiliated with these institutions. Still, it was not until after World War II (the modern industrial period) that the black class structure started to take on some of the characteristics of the white class structure.

CLASS AND BLACK LIFE CHANCES

Class has also become more important than race in determining black life chances in the modern industrial period. Moreover, the center of racial conflict has shifted from the industrial sector to the sociopolitical order. Although these changes can be related to the more fundamental changes in the system of production and in the laws and policies of the state, the relations between the economy and the polity in the modern industrial period have differed from those in previous periods. In the preindustrial and industrial periods the basis of structured racial inequality was primarily economic, and in most situations the state was merely an instrument to reinforce patterns of race relations that grew directly out of the social relations of production.

Except for the brief period of fluid race relations in the North from 1870 to 1890, the state was a major instrument of racial oppression. State intervention in the modern industrial period has been designed to promote racial equality, and the relationship between the polity and the economy has been much more reciprocal, so much so that it is difficult to determine which one has been more important in shaping race relations since World War II. It was the expansion of the economy that facilitated black movement from the rural areas to the industrial centers and that created job opportunities leading to greater occupational differentiation in the black community (in the sense that an increasing percentage of blacks moved into white-collar positions); and it was the intervention of the state (responding to the pressures of increased black political resources and to the racial protest movement) that removed many artificial discrimination barriers by municipal, state, and federal civil rights legislation, and that contributed to the more liberal racial policies of the nation's labor unions by protective union legislation. And these combined political and economic changes created a pattern of black occupational upgrading that resulted, for example, in a substantial drop in the percentage of black males in the low-paying service, unskilled laborer, and farm jobs.

However despite the greater occupational differentiation within the black community, there are now signs that the effect of some aspects of structural economic change has been the closer association between black occupational mobility and class affiliation. Access to the means of production is increasingly based on educational criteria (a situation which distinguishes the modern industrial from the earlier industrial system of production) and thus threatens to solidify the position of the black underclass. In other words, a consequence of the rapid growth of the corporate and government sectors has been the gradual creation of a segmented labor market that currently provides vastly different mobility opportunities for different segments of the black population.

On the one hand, poorly trained and educationally limited blacks of the inner city, including that growing number of black teenagers and young adults, see their job prospects increasingly restricted to the low-wage sector, their unemployment rates soaring to record levels (which remain high despite swings in the business cycle), their labor force participation rates declining, their movement out of poverty slowing, and their welfare roles increasing. On the other hand, talented and educated blacks are experiencing unprecedented job opportunities in the growing government and corporate sectors, opportunities that are at least comparable to those of whites with equivalent qualifications. The improved job situation for the more privileged blacks in the corporate and government sectors is related both to the expansion of salaried white-collar positions and to the pressures of state affirmative action programs.

In view of these developments, it would be difficult to argue that the plight of the black underclass is solely a consequence of racial oppression, that is, the explicit and overt efforts of whites to keep blacks subjugated, in the same way that it would be difficult to explain the rapid economic improvement of the more privileged blacks by arguing that the traditional forms of racial segregation and discrimination still characterize the labor market in American industries. The recent mobility patterns of blacks lend strong support to the view that economic class is clearly more important than race in predetermining job placement and occupational mobility. In the economic realm, then, the black experience has moved historically from economic racial oppression experienced by virtually all blacks to economic subordination for the black underclass. And as we begin the last quarter of the twentieth century, a deepening economic schism seems to be developing in the black community, with the black poor falling further and further behind middle- and upper-income blacks.

SHIFT IN RACIAL CONFLICT

If race is declining in significance in the economic sector, explanations of racial antagonism based on labor-market conflicts, such as those advanced by economic class theories of race, also have less significance in the period of modern industrial race relations. Neither the low-wage sector nor the corporate and government sectors provide the basis for the kind of interracial job competition and conflict that plagued the economic order in previous periods. With the absorption of blacks into industrywide labor unions, protective union legislation, and equal employment legislation, it is no longer feasible for management to undercut white labor by using black workers. The traditional racial struggles for power and privilege have shifted away from the economic sector and are now concentrated in the sociopolitical order. Although poor blacks and poor whites are still the main actors in the present manifestations of racial strife, the immediate source of the tension has more to do with racial competition for public schools, municipal political systems, and residential areas than with the competition for jobs.

To say that race is declining in significance, therefore, is not only to argue that the life chances of blacks have less to do with race than with economic class affiliation, but also to maintain that racial conflict and competition in the economic sector—the most important historical factors in the subjugation of blacks—have been substantially reduced. However, it would be argued that the firm white resistance to public school desegregation, residential integration, and black control of central cities all indicate the unyielding importance of race in the United States. The argument could even be entertained that the impressive occupational gains of the black middle class are only temporary, and that as soon as affirmative action pressures are relieved, or as soon as the economy experiences a prolonged recession, industries will return to their old racial practices.

Both of these arguments are compelling if not altogether persuasive. Taking the latter contention first, there is little available evidence to suggest that the economic gains of privileged blacks will be reversed. Despite the fact that the recession of the early 1970s decreased job prospects for all educated workers, the more educated blacks continued to experience a faster rate of job advancement than their white counterparts. And although it is always possible that an economic disaster could produce racial competition for higher-paying jobs and white efforts to exclude talented blacks, it is difficult to entertain this idea as a real possibility in the face of the powerful political and social movement against job discrimination. At this point there is every reason to believe that talented and educated blacks, like talented and educated whites, will continue to enjoy the advantages and privileges of their class status.

My response to the first argument is not to deny the current racial antagonism in the sociopolitical order, but to suggest that such antagonism has far less effect on individual or group access to those opportunities and resources that are centrally important for life survival than antagonism in the economic sector. The factors that most severely affected black life chances in previous years were the racial oppression and antagonism in the economic sector. As race declined in importance in the economic sector, the Negro class structure became more differentiated and black life chances became increasingly a consequence of class affiliation.

Furthermore, it is even difficult to identify the form of racial contact in the sociopolitical order as the source of the current manifestations of conflict between lower-income blacks and whites, because neither the degree of racial competition between the have-nots, nor their structural relations in urban communities, nor their patterns of interaction constitute the ultimate source of present racial antagonism. The ultimate basis for current racial tension is the deleterious effect of basic structural changes in the modern American economy on black and white lower-income groups, changes that include uneven economic growth, increasing technology and automation, industry relocation, and labor market segmentation.

FIGHTING CLASS SUBORDINATION

The situation of marginality and redundancy created by the modern industrial society deleteriously affects all the poor, regardless of race. Underclass whites, Hispano Americans, and Native Americans all are victims, to a greater or lesser degree, of class subordination under advanced capitalism. It is true that blacks are disproportionately represented in the underclass population and that about one-third of the entire black population is in the underclass. But the significance of these facts has more to do with the historical consequences of racial oppression than with the current effects of race.

Although the percentage of blacks below the low-income level dropped steadily throughout the 1960s, one of the legacies of the racial oppression in previous years is the continued disproportionate black representation in the underclass. And since 1970 both poor whites and nonwhites have evidenced very little progress in their elevation from the ranks of the underclass. In the final analysis, therefore, the challenge of economic dislocation in modern industrial society calls for public policy programs to attack inequality on a broad class front, policy programs—in other words—that go beyond the limits of ethnic and racial discrimination by directly confronting the pervasive and destructive features of class subordination.

2.3 JOE R. FEAGIN

The Continuing Significance of Race: Antiblack Discrimination in Public Places

To dispel the commonly held belief that racial and ethnic discrimination have been effectively eliminated from society, social scientists have documented the life experiences of minority groups. To this end, Joe R. Feagin, a sociology professor at the University of Florida and the author of *Racial and Ethnic Relations,* 3rd ed. (Prentice Hall, 1989), has drawn on several in-depth interviews with members of the Black middle class to ascertain the sites and character of discriminatory actions and the range of coping mechanisms Blacks draw upon to deal with discriminatory actions. His findings show that "deprivation and discrimination in public accommodations persist."

Key Concept: the continuing significance of race

*T*itle II of the 1964 Civil Rights Act stipulates that "all persons shall be entitled to the full and equal enjoyment of the goods, services, facilities, privileges, advantages, and accommodations of any place of public accommodation... without discrimination or segregation on the ground of race, color, religion, or national origin." The public places emphasized in the act are restaurants, hotels, and motels, although racial discrimination occurs in many other public places. Those black Americans who would make the greatest use of these public accommodations and certain other public places would be middle-class, i.e., those with the requisite resources....

ASPECTS OF DISCRIMINATION

Discrimination can be defined in social-contextual terms as "actions or practices carried out by members of dominant racial or ethnic groups that have a differential and negative impact on members of subordinate racial and ethnic groups" (Feagin and Eckberg 1980, pp. 1–2). This differential treatment ranges from the blatant to the subtle (Feagin and Feagin 1986). Here I focus primarily on blatant discrimination by white Americans targeting middle-class blacks. Historically, discrimination against blacks has been one of the most serious forms of racial/ethnic discrimination in the United States and one of the most difficult to overcome, in part because of the institutionalized character of color coding. I focus on three important aspects of discrimination: (1) the variation in sites of discrimination; (2) the range of discriminatory actions; and (3) the range of responses by blacks to discrimination.

Sites of Discrimination

There is a spatial dimension to discrimination. The probability of experiencing racial hostility varies from the most private to the most public sites. If a black person is in a relatively protected site, such as with friends at home, the probability of experiencing hostility and discrimination is low. The probability increases as one moves from friendship settings to such outside sites as the workplace, where a black person typically has contacts with both acquaintances and strangers, providing an interactive context with greater potential for discrimination.

In most workplaces, middle-class status and its organizational resources provide some protection against certain categories of discrimination. This protection probably weakens as a black person moves from those work and school settings where he or she is well-known into public accommodations such as large stores and city restaurants where contacts are mainly with white strangers. On public streets blacks have the greatest public exposure to strangers and the least protection against overt discriminatory behavior, including violence. A key feature of these more public settings is that they often involve contacts with white strangers who react primarily on the basis of one ascribed characteristic. The study of the micro-life of interaction between strangers in public was pioneered by Goffman (1963: 1971) and his students, but few of their analyses have treated hostile discriminatory interaction in public places. A rare exception is the research by Gardner (1980: see also Gardner 1988), who documented the character and danger of passing remarks by men directed against women in unprotected public places. Gardner writes of women (and blacks) as "open persons," i.e. particularly vulnerable targets for harassment that violates the rules of public courtesy.

The Range of Discriminatory Actions

In his classic study, *The Nature of Prejudice*, Allport (1958, pp. 14–5) noted that prejudice can be expressed in a series of progressively more serious actions, ranging from antilocution to avoidance, exclusion, physical attack, and extermination. Allport's work suggests a continuum of actions from avoidance, to exclusion or rejection, to attack. In his travels in the South in the 1950s a white journalist who changed his skin color to black encountered discrimination in each of these categories (Griffin 1961). In my data, discrimination against middle-class blacks still ranges across this continuum: (1) avoidance actions, such as a white couple crossing the street when a black male approaches; (2) rejection actions, such as poor service in public accommodations; (3) verbal attacks, such as shouting racial epithets in the street; (4) physical threats and harassment by white police officers; and (5) physical threats and attacks by other whites, such as attacks by white supremacists in the street. Changing relations between blacks and whites in recent decades have expanded the repertoire of discrimination to include more subtle forms and to encompass discrimination in arenas from which blacks were formerly excluded such as formerly all-white public accommodations.

Black Responses to Discrimination

Prior to societal desegregation in the 1960s much traditional discrimination, especially in the South, took the form of an asymmetrical "deference ritual" in which blacks were typically expected to respond to discriminating whites with great deference.... Such rituals can be seen in the obsequious words and gestures—the etiquette of race relations—that many blacks, including middle-class blacks, were forced to utilize to survive the rigors of segregation (Doyle 1937). However, not all responses in this period were deferential. From the late 1800s to the 1950s, numerous lynchings and other violence targeted blacks whose behavior was defined as too aggressive (Raper 1933), Blauner's (1989) respondents reported acquaintances reacting aggressively to discrimination prior to the 1960s.

Deference rituals can still be found today between some lower-income blacks and their white employers. In her northeastern study Rollins (1985, p. 157) found black maids regularly deferring to white employers. Today, most discriminatory interaction no longer involves much asymmetrical deference, at least for middle-class blacks. Even where whites expect substantial deference, most middle-class blacks do not oblige. For middle-class blacks contemporary discrimination has evolved beyond the asymmetrical deference rituals and "No Negroes served" type of exclusion to patterns of black-contested discrimination....

Some white observers have suggested that many middle-class blacks are paranoid about white discrimination and rush too quickly to charges of racism (Wieseltier 1989, June 5; for male views of female "paranoia" see Gardner 1988). But the daily reality may be just the opposite, as middle-class black Americans often evaluate a situation carefully before judging it discriminatory and taking additional action. This careful evaluation, based on past experiences (real or vicarious), not only prevents jumping to conclusions, but also reflects the hope that white behavior is not based on race, because an act not based on race is easier to endure. After evaluation one strategy is to leave the site of

TABLE 1

*Percentage Distribution of Discriminatory Actions By Type and Site:
Middle-Class Blacks in Selected Cities, 1988–1990*

Type of Discriminatory Action	Site of Discriminatory Action	
	Public Accommodations	Street
Avoidance	3	7
Rejection/poor service	79	4
Verbal epithets	12	25
Police threats/harassment	3	46
Other threats/harassment	3	18
Total	100	100
Number of actions	34	28

discrimination rather than to create a disturbance. Another is to ignore the discrimination and continue with the interaction, a "blocking" strategy similar to that Gardner (1980, p. 345) reported for women dealing with street remarks. In many situations resigned acceptance is the only realistic response. More confrontational responses to white actions include verbal reprimands and sarcasm, physical counterattacks, and filing lawsuits. Several strategies may be tried in any given discriminatory situation. In crafting these strategies middle-class blacks, in comparison with less privileged blacks, may draw on middle-class resources to fight discrimination.

THE RESEARCH STUDY

To examine discrimination, I draw primarily on 37 in-depth interviews from a larger study of 135 middle-class black Americans in Boston, Buffalo, Baltimore, Washington, D.C., Detroit, Houston, Dallas, Austin, San Antonio, Marshall, Las Vegas, and Los Angeles....

Although all types of mistreatment are reported, there is a strong relationship between type of discrimination and site, with rejection/poor-service discrimination being most common in public accommodations and verbal or physical threat discrimination by white citizens or police officers most likely in the street....

The most common black responses to racial hostility in the street are withdrawal or a verbal reply. In many avoidance situations (e.g., a white couple crossing a street to avoid walking past a black college student) or attack situations (e.g., whites throwing beer cans from a passing car), a verbal response is difficult because of the danger or the fleeting character of the hostility. A black victim often withdraws, endures this treatment with resigned acceptance,

TABLE 2

59

Percentage Distribution of Primary Responses to Discriminatory Incidents by Type and Site: Middle-Class Blacks in Selected Cities, 1988–1990

Joe R. Feagin

	Site of Discriminatory Incident	
Response to Discriminatory Incident	*Public Accommodations*	*Street*
Withdrawal/exit	4	22
Resigned acceptance	23	7
Verbal response	69	59
Physical counterattack	4	7
Response unclear	–	4
Total	100	99
Number of responses	26	27

or replies with a quick verbal retort. In the case of police harassment, the response is limited by the danger, and resigned acceptance or mild verbal protests are likely responses. Rejection (poor service) in public accommodations provides an opportunity to fight back verbally—the most common responses to public accommodations discrimination are verbal counterattacks or resigned acceptance. Some black victims correct whites quietly, while others respond aggressively and lecture the assailant about the discrimination or threaten court action. A few retaliate physically. Examining materials in these 37 interviews . . . we will see that the depth and complexity of contemporary black middle-class responses to white discrimination accents the changing character of white-black interaction and the necessity of continual negotiation of the terms of that interaction.

RESPONSES TO DISCRIMINATION: PUBLIC ACCOMMODATIONS

Two Fundamental Strategies: Verbal Confrontation and Withdrawal

In the following account, a black news director at a major television station shows the interwoven character of discriminatory action and black response. The discrimination took the form of poor restaurant service, and the responses included both suggested withdrawal and verbal counterattack.

He [her boyfriend] was waiting to be seated. . . . He said, "You go to the bathroom and I'll get the table. . . . " He was standing there when I came back; he continued to stand there. The restaurant was almost empty. There were waiters, waitresses, and no one seated. And when I got back to him, he was ready to leave, and said, "Let's go," I said, "What happened to our table?" He wasn't seated. So I said, "No, we're not leaving, please." And he said, "No, "I'm leaving." So we went outside and we talked about it. And what I said to him was, you have to be aware of the possibilities that this is not the first time that this has happened at this restaurant or at other restaurants, but this is the first time it has happened to a black news director here or someone who could make an issue of it, or someone who is prepared to make an issue of it.

So we went back inside after I talked him into it and, to make a long story short, I had the manager come. I made most of the people who were there (while conducting myself professionally the whole time) aware that I was incensed at being treated this way.... I said, "Why do you think we weren't seated?" And the manager said, "Well, I don't really know." And I said, "Guess." He said, "Well I don't know, because you're black?" I said, "Bingo. Now isn't it funny that you didn't guess that I didn't have any money" (and I opened up my purse) and I said, "because I certainly have money. And isn't it odd that you didn't guess that it's because I couldn't pay for it because I've got two American Express cards and a Master Card right here. I think it's just funny that you would have assumed that it's because I'm black."... And then I took out my card and gave it to him and said, "If this happens again, or if I hear of this happening again, I will bring the full wrath of an entire news department down on this restaurant." And he just kind of looked at me. "Not [just] because I am personally offended. I am. But because you have no right to do what you did, and as a people we have lived a long time with having our rights abridged...." There were probably three or four sets of diners in the restaurant and maybe five waiters/waitresses. They watched him standing there waiting to be seated. His reaction to it was that he wanted to leave. I understood why he would have reacted that way, because he felt that he was in no condition to be civil. He was ready to take the place apart and ... sometimes it's appropriate to behave that way. We hadn't gone the first step before going on to the next step. He didn't feel that he could comfortably and calmly take the first step, and I did. So I just asked him to please get back in the restaurant with me, and then you don't have to say a word, and let me handle it from there. It took some convincing, but I had to appeal to his sense of, this is not just you, this is not just for you. We are finally in a position as black people where there are some of us who can genuinely get their attention. And if they don't want to do this because it's right for them to do it, then they'd better do it because they're afraid to do otherwise. If it's fear, then fine, instill the fear.

This example provides insight into the character of modern discrimination. The discrimination was not the "No Negroes" exclusion of the recent past, but rejection in the form of poor service by restaurant personnel. The black response indicates the change in black-white interaction since the 1950s and 1960s, for discrimination is handled with vigorous confrontation rather than deference. The aggressive black response and the white backtracking underscore Brittan and Maynard's (1984, p. 7) point that black-white interaction today is being renegotiated. It is possible that the white personnel defined the couple as "poor blacks" because of their jeans, although the jeans were fashionable and white patrons wear jeans. In comments not quoted here the news director rejects such an explanation. She forcefully articulates a theory of rights—a response that signals the critical impact of civil rights laws on the thinking of middle-class blacks. The news director articulates the American dream: she has worked hard, earned the money and credit cards, developed the appropriate middle-class behavior, and thus has under the law a *right* to be served. There is defensiveness in her actions too, for she feels a need to legitimate her status by showing her purse and credit cards. One important factor that enabled her to take such assertive action was her power to bring a TV news team to the restaurant. This power marks a change from a few decades ago when very few black Americans had the social or economic resources to fight back successfully....

The confrontation response is generally so costly in terms of time and energy that acquiescence or withdrawal are common options. An example of the exit response was provided by a utility company executive in an east coast city:

> I can remember one time my husband had picked up our son... from camp; and he'd stopped at a little store in the neighborhood near the camp. It was hot, and he was going to buy him a snowball. And the proprietor of the store—this was a very old, white neighborhood, and it was just a little sundry store. But the proprietor said he had the little window where people could come up and order things. Well, my husband and son had gone into the store. And he told them, "Well, I can't give it to you here, but if you go outside to the window, I'll give it to you." And there were other [white] people in the store who'd been served [inside]. So, they just left and didn't buy anything.

... This site differed from the previous example in that the service was probably not of long-term importance to the black family passing through the area. In the previous site the possibility of returning to the restaurant for business or pleasure, may have contributed to the choice of a confrontational response. The importance of the service is a likely variable affecting black responses to discrimination in public accommodations....

The complex process of evaluation and response is described by a college dean, who commented generally on hotel and restaurant discrimination encountered as he travels across the United States:

> When you're in a restaurant and... you notice that blacks get seated near the kitchen. You notice that if it's a hotel, your room is near the elevator, or your room is always way down in a corner somewhere. You find that you are getting the undesirable rooms. And you come there early in the day and you don't see very many cars on the lot and they'll tell you that this is all we've got. Or you get the room that's got a bad television set. You know that you're being discriminated against. And of course you have to act accordingly. You have to tell them, "Okay, the room is fine, [but] this television set has got to go. Bring me another television set." So in my personal experience, I simply cannot sit and let them get away with it [discrimination] and not let them know that I know that that's what they are doing....
>
> When I face discrimination, first I take a long look at myself and try to determine whether or not I am seeing what I think I'm seeing in 1989, and if it's something that I have an option [about]. In other words, if I'm at a store making a purchase, I'll simply walk away from it. If it's at a restaurant where I'm not getting good service, I first of all let the people know that I'm not getting good service, then I [may] walk away from it. But the thing that I have to do is to let people know that I know that I'm being singled out for a separate treatment. And

then I might react in any number of ways—depending on where I am and how badly I want whatever it is that I'm there for.

This commentary adds another dimension to our understanding of public discrimination, its cumulative aspect. Blacks confront not just isolated incidents —such as a bad room in a luxury hotel once every few years—but a lifelong series of such incidents. Here again the omnipresence of careful assessments is underscored. The dean's interview highlights a major difficulty in being black —one must be constantly prepared to assess accurately and then decide on the appropriate response. This long-look approach may indicate that some middle-class blacks are so sensitive to white charges of hypersensitivity and paranoia that they err in the opposite direction and fail to see discrimination when it occurs. In addition, as one black graduate student at a leading white university in the Southeast put it: "I think that sometimes timely and appropriate responses to racially motivated acts and comments are lost due to the processing of the input." The "long look" can result in missed opportunities to respond to discrimination.

Using Middle-Class Resources for Protection

One advantage that middle-class blacks have over poorer blacks is the use of the resources of middle-class occupations. A professor at a major white university commented on the varying protection her middle-class status gives her at certain sites:

> If I'm in those areas that are fairly protected, within gatherings of my own group, other African Americans, or if I'm in the university where my status as a professor mediates against the way I might be perceived, mediates against the hostile perception, then it's fairly comfortable.... When I divide my life into encounters with the outside world, and of course that's ninety percent of my life, it's fairly consistently unpleasant at those sites where there's nothing that mediates between my race and what I have to do. For example, if I'm in a grocery store, if I'm in my car, which is a 1970 Chevrolet, a real old ugly car, all those things—being in a grocery store in casual clothes, or being in the car—sort of advertises something that doesn't have anything to do with my status as far as people I run into are concerned.
>
> Because I'm a large black woman, and I don't wear whatever class status I have, or whatever professional status [I have] in my appearance when I'm in the grocery store, I'm part of the mass of large black women shopping. For most whites, and even for some blacks, that translates into negative status. That means that they are free to treat me the way they treat most poor black people, because they can't tell by looking at me that I differ from that.

This professor notes the variation in discrimination in the sites through which she travels, from the most private to the most public. At home with friends she faces no problems, and at the university her professorial status gives her some protection from discrimination. The increase in unpleasant encounters as she moves into public accommodations sites such as grocery stores is attributed to the absence of mediating factors such as clear symbols of middle-class status —displaying the middle-class symbols may provide some protection against discrimination in public places. . . .

63

Joe R. Feagin

RESPONSES TO DISCRIMINATION: THE STREET

Reacting to White Strangers

As we move away from public accommodations settings to the usually less protected street sites, racial hostility can become more fleeting and severer, and thus black responses are often restricted. The most serious form of street discrimination is violence. Often the reasonable black response to street discrimination is withdrawal, resigned acceptance, or a quick verbal retort. The difficulty of responding to violence is seen in this report by a man working for a media surveying firm in a southern industrial city:

> I was parked in front of this guy's house. . . . This guy puts his hands on the window and says, "Get out of the car, nigger." . . . So, I got out, and I thought, "Oh, this is what's going to happen here." And I'm talking fast. And they're, "What are you doing here?" And I'm, "This is who I am. I work with these people. This is the man we want to put in the survey." And I pointed to the house. And the guy said, "Well you have an out-of-state license tag, right?" "Yea." And he said, "If something happened to you, your people at home wouldn't know for a long time, would they?" . . . I said, "Look, I deal with a company that deals with television. [If] something happens to me, it's going to be a national thing.". . . So, they grab me by the lapel of my coat, and put me in front of my car. They put the blade on my zipper. And now I'm thinking about this guy that's in the truck [behind me], because now I'm thinking that I'm going to have to run somewhere. Where am I going to run? Go to the police? [laughs] So, after a while they bash up my headlight. And I drove [away].

Stigmatized and physically attacked solely because of his color, this man faced verbal hostility and threats of death with courage. Cautiously drawing on his middle-class resources, he told the attackers his death would bring television crews to the town. This resource utilization is similar to that of the news director in the restaurant incident. Beyond this verbal threat his response had to be one of caution. For most whites threatened on the street, the police are a sought-after source of protection, this is often not the case. . . .

Responses to Discrimination by White Police Officers

Most middle-class blacks do not have such governmental authority as their personal protection. In fact, white police officers are a major problem. Encounters with the police can be life-threatening and thus limit the range of responses. A television commentator recounted two cases of police harassment when he was working for a survey firm in the mid-1980s. In one of the incidents, which took place in a southern metropolis, he was stopped by several white officers:

"What are you doing here?" I tell them what I'm doing here.... And so me spread on top of my car. [What had you done?] Because I was in the neighborhood, I left this note on these peoples' house: "Here's who I am. You weren't here, and I will come back in thirty minutes." [Why were they searching you?] They don't know. To me, they're searching, I remember at that particular moment when this all was going down, there was a lot of reports about police crime on civilians.... It took four cops to shake me down, two police cars, so they had me up there spread out. I had a friend of mine with me who was making the call with me, because we were going to have dinner together, and he was black, and they had me up, and they had him outside.... They said, "Well, let's check you out." ...And I'm talking to myself, and I'm not thinking about being at attention, with my arms spread on my Ford [a company car], and I'm sitting there talking to myself, "Man, this is crazy, this is crazy."

[How are you feeling inside?] Scared. I mean real scared. [What did you think was going go happen to you?] I was going to go to jail.... Just because they picked me. Why would they stop me? It's like, if they can stop me, why wouldn't I go to jail, and I could sit there for ten days before the judge sees me. I'm thinking all this crazy stuff.... Again, I'm talking to myself. And the guy takes his stick. And he doesn't whack me hard, but he does it with enough authority to let me know they mean business. "I told you stand still; now put your arms back out." And I've got this suit on, and the car's wet. And my friend's hysterical. He's outside the car. And they're checking him out. And he's like, "Man, just be cool, man." And he had tears in his eyes. And I'm like, oh, man, this is a nightmare. This is not supposed to happen to me. This is not my style! And so finally, this other cop comes up and says, "What have we got here Charlie?" "Oh, we've got a guy here. He's running through the neighborhood, and he doesn't want to do what we tell him. We might have to run him in." [You're "running through" the neighborhood?] Yeah, exactly, in a suit in the rain?! After they got through doing their thing and harassing me, I just said, "Man this has been a hell of a week."

And I had tears in my eyes, but it wasn't tears of upset. It was tears of anger; it was tears of wanting to lash back.... What I thought to myself was, man, blacks have it real hard down here. I don't care if they're a broadcaster; I don't care if they're a businessman or a banker.... They don't have it any easier than the persons on skid row who get harassed by the police on a Friday or Saturday night.

It seems likely that most black men—including middle-class black men—see white police officers as a major source of danger and death. (See "Mood of Ghetto America" 1980, June 2, pp. 32–34; Louis Harris and Associates 1989; Roddy 1990, August 26). Scattered evidence suggests that by the time they are in their twenties, most black males, regardless of socioeconomic status, have been stopped by the police because "blackness" is considered a sign of possible criminality by police officers (Moss 1990; Roddy 1990, August 26). This treatment probably marks a dramatic contrast with the experiences of young white middle-class males. In the incident above the respondent and a friend experienced severe police maltreatment—detention for a lengthy period, threat of arrest, and the reality of physical violence. The coping response of the respondent was resigned acceptance somewhat similar to the deference rituals highlighted by Goffman. The middle-class suits and obvious corporate credentials (for example, survey questionnaires and company car) did not protect the two black men. The final comment suggests a disappointment that middle-class status brought no reprieve from police stigmatization and harassment....

I have examined the sites of discrimination, the types of discriminatory acts, and the responses of the victims and have found the color stigma still to be very important in the public lives of affluent black Americans. The sites of racial discrimination range from relatively protected home sites, to less protected workplace and educational sites, to less protected workplace and educational sites, to the even less protected public places. The 1964 Civil Rights Act guarantees that black Americans are "entitled to the full and equal enjoyment of the goods, services, facilities, privileges, advantages, and accommodations" in public accommodations. Yet the interviews indicate that deprivation of full enjoyment of public facilities is not a relic of the past: deprivation and discrimination in public accommodations persist. Middle-class black Americans remain vulnerable targets in public places. Prejudice-generated aggression in public places is, of course, not limited to black men and women—gay men and white women are also targets of street harassment (Benokraitis and Feagin 1986). Nonetheless, black women and men face an unusually broad range of discrimination on the street and in public accommodations.

The interviews highlight two significant aspects of the additive discrimination faced by black Americans in public places and elsewhere: (1) the cumulative character of an *individual's* experiences with discrimination; and (2) the *group's* accumulated historical experiences as perceived by the individual. A retired psychology professor who has worked in the Midwest and Southwest commented on the pyramiding of incidents:

> I don't think white people, generally, understand the full meaning of racist discriminatory behaviors directed toward Americans of African descent. They seem to see each act of discrimination or any act of violence as an "isolated" event. As a result, most white Americans cannot understand the strong reaction manifested by blacks when such events occur. They feel that blacks tend to "over-react." They forget that in most cases, we live lives of quiet desperation generated by a litany of *daily* large and small events that whether or not by design, remind us of our "place" in American society.

Particular instances of discrimination may seem minor to outside white observers when considered in isolation. But when blatant acts of avoidance, verbal harassment, and physical attack combine with subtle and covert slights, and these accumulate over months, years, and lifetimes, the impact on a black person is far more than the sum of the individual instances.

The historical context of contemporary discrimination was described by the retired psychologist, who argued that average white Americans

> ... ignore the personal context of the stimulus. That is, they deny the historical impact that a negative act may have on an individual. "Nigger" to a white may simply be an epithet that should be ignored. To most blacks, the term brings into sharp and current focus all kinds of acts of racism—murder, rape, torture, denial of constitutional rights, insults, limited opportunity structure, economic problems, unequal justice under the law and a myriad of ... other racist and discriminatory acts that occur daily in the lives of *most* Americans of African descent—including professional blacks.

65

Particular acts, even antilocution that might seem minor to white observers, are freighted not only with one's past experience of discrimination but also with centuries of racial discrimination directed at the entire group, vicarious oppression that still includes racially translated violence and denial of access to the American dream. Anti-black discrimination is a matter of racial-power inequality institutionalized in a variety of economic and social institutions over a long period of time. The microlevel events of public accommodations and public streets are not just rare and isolated encounters by individuals; they are recurring events reflecting an invasion of the microworld by the macroworld of historical racial subordination.

REFERENCES

Allport, Gordon. 1958. The *Nature of Prejudice*. Abridged. New York: Doubleday Anchor Books.

Benokraitis, Nijole and Joe R. Feagin. 1986. *Modern Sexism: Blatant, Subtle and Covert Discrimination*. Englewood Cliffs: Prentice-Hall.

Blauner, Bob. 1989. *Black Lives, White Lives*. Berkeley: University of California Press.

Brittan, Arthur and Mary Maynard. 1984. *Sexism, Racism and Oppression*. Oxford: Basil Blackwell.

Doyle, Betram W. 1937. *The Etiquette of Race Relations in the South*. Port Washington, NY: Kennikat Press.

Feagin, Joe R. and Douglas Eckberg. 1980. "Prejudice and Discrimination." *Annual Review of Sociology* 6:1–20.

Feagin, Joe R. and Clairece Booher Feagin. 1986. *Discrimination American Style* (rev. ed). Melbourne, FL: Krieger Publishing Co.

Gardner, Carol Brooks. 1980. "Passing By: Street Remarks, Address Rights, and the Urban Female." *Sociological Inquiry* 50:328–56.

———. 1988. "Access Information: Public Lies and Private Peril." *Social Problems* 35:384–97.

Goffman, Erving. 1956. "The Nature of Deference and Demeanor." *American Anthropologist* 58:473–502.

Griffin, John Howard. 1961. *Black Like Me*. Boston: Houghton Mifflin.

"The Mood of Ghetto America." 1980. June 2. *Newsweek*, pp. 32–4.

Moss, E. Yvonne. 1990. "African Americans and the Administration of Justice." Pp. 79–86 in *Assessment of the Status of African-Americans*, edited by Wornie L. Reed. Boston: University of Massachusetts, William Monroe Trotter Institute.

Raper, Arthur F. 1933. *The Tragedy of Lynching*. Chapel Hill: University of North Carolina Press.

Roddy, Dennis B. 1990. August 26. "Perceptions Still Segregate Police, Black Community." *The Pittsburgh Press*, p. B1.

Rollins, Judith 1985. *Between Women*. Philadelphia: Temple University Press.

Wieseltier, Leon. 1989, June 5. "Scar Tissue." *New Republic*, pp. 19–20.

CHAPTER 3 Racism

3.1 LOUIS L. KNOWLES AND KENNETH PREWITT

Institutional and Ideological Roots of Racism

The mid-1960s witnessed an explosion of racial violence throughout the United States. Between 1964 and 1968 riots broke out in New York, Philadelphia, Rochester, Los Angeles, Chicago, Cleveland, Lansing, Omaha, Cincinnati, Buffalo, Detroit, and Newark. The federal government responded to the disorder by establishing social science commissions to investigate the social troubles—such as unemployment, inadequate education, and domestic violence—inundating the Black community. President Lyndon B. Johnson established the Commission on Civil Disorders, chaired by Otto Kerner, governor of Illinois, to investigate what had happened, why the riots had occurred, and what could be done to prevent further outbreaks.

In this selection, Louis L. Knowles and Kenneth Prewitt critically evaluate the findings of the Kerner Commission. They argue that the commission did not go far enough in its investigation to discover the root causes of racial violence in the United States. To these authors, the commission simply attributed the civil unrest to "black pathology"—a *blaming the victim* thesis. Knowles and Prewitt instead attribute racial disorder to America's "historical roots of institutional racism," which have prevented Blacks from attaining equality in society.

Key Concept: the historical roots of institutional racism

THE REPORT OF THE NATIONAL ADVISORY COMMISSION ON CIVIL DISORDERS: A COMMENT

The contemporary document perhaps most indicative of the ideology of official America is the influential "Kerner Commission Report." This is an important work. It is being widely read, and we cite from it frequently in the pages to follow. However, since our analysis operates from a premise fundamentally different from the Report, a few comments at this point will help introduce the substantive chapters to follow.

The Report asks: "Why Did It Happen?" A painful truth is then recorded: "White racism is essentially responsible for the explosive mixture which has been accumulating in our cities since the end of World War II." Unfortunately, the Report too quickly leaves this truth and emphasizes the familiar list of "conditions" of "Negro unrest." Paraded before the reader are observations about the frustrated hopes of Negroes, the "belief" among Negroes that there is police brutality, the high unemployment in the ghetto, the weak family structure and social disorganization in the Negro community, and so on.

It is the immediate conditions giving rise to civil disorders which the Report stresses, not the *causes behind the conditions*. Perhaps what is needed is a National Advisory Commission on White Racism. If a group of men sets out to investigate "civil disorders," their categories of analysis are fixed and, from our perspective, parochial. In spite of their admission that "white institutions created [the ghetto], white institutions maintain it, and white society condones it," the categories with which the commission operated screened out the responsibility of white institutions and pushed the commission back to the familiar account of "black pathology."

In the important section "What Can Be Done," this fault is even more clearly seen. Certainly it is true that much accumulated frustration would be relieved if the sweeping recommendations concerning administration of justice, police and community relations, housing, unemployment and underemployment, welfare thinking, and so forth were implemented. The Report merits the closest attention for its statement that issues of race and poverty must receive the highest national priority, and for its further argument that what is needed is a massive commitment by all segments of society. What disappoints the reader is that the section "What Can Be Done" only accentuates the shortsightedness of the section "Why Did It Happen." The recommendations are directed at ghetto conditions and *not* at the white structures and practices which are responsible for those conditions. Thus, while it is true that improved communication between the ghetto and city hall might defuse the pressures building up in the black community, the issue is not "better communication" but "full representation." Black people should not have to communicate with city hall; they should be represented at city hall.

The shallowness of the Report as social analysis is again reflected in its discussion of black protest movements. The Report does not uncover a critical social dynamic: militancy is first of all a response to white resistance and control, not its cause. The naiveté of the Report, and its ultimate paternalism, is nowhere better shown than in its attempt to draw parallels between the black power movement and the philosophy of Booker T. Washington. Accommodation stood at the center of Washington's thought; accommodation is explicitly and forcefully rejected by the ideology symbolized in the "black power" slogan. As Carmichael and Hamilton wrote, "Black people in the United States must raise hard questions which challenge the very nature of the society itself: its long-standing values, beliefs, and institutions."

Louis L. Knowles and Kenneth Prewitt

What we miss in the Kerner Commission Report is the capacity to ask "hard questions." The Commission members are to be saluted for their instinct that "white racism" is the culprit. They are to be faulted for their inability or unwillingness to pursue this theme. We do not have access to the professional resources available to the Kerner Commission, and therefore our study lacks the statistical detail of the national report. But we have tried to push the analysis of the race question into areas where the Report dared not tread: into the heart of institutional, which is to say white, America.

A new realization is dawning in white America. Under the insistent prodding of articulate blacks plus a few unusual whites, the so-called "Negro Problem" is being redefined. Just possibly the racial sickness in our society is not, as we have so long assumed, rooted in the black and presumably "pathological" subculture but in the white and presumably "healthy" dominant culture. If indeed it turns out that *the* problem" is finally and deeply a white problem, the solution will have to be found in a restructured white society.

Institutional racism is a term which describes practices in the United States nearly as old as the nation itself. The term, however, appears to be of recent coinage, possibly first used by Stokely Carmichael and Charles V. Hamilton in their widely read book, *Black Power*.[1] It is our goal to work with this term until we feel we have come to some full understanding of it, and to present an analysis of specific practices appropriately defined as "institutionally racist." Our strategy is to be self-consciously pragmatic. That is, we ask not what the motive of the individuals might be; rather we look at the consequences of the institutions they have created.

TOWARD A DEFINITION

The murder by KKK members and law enforcement officials of three civil rights workers in Mississippi was an act of individual racism. That the sovereign state of Mississippi refused to indict the killers was institutional racism. The individual act by racist bigots went unpunished in Mississippi because of policies, precedents, and practices that are an integral part of that state's legal institutions. A store clerk who suspects that black children in his store are there to steal candy but white children are there to purchase candy, and who treats the children differently, the blacks as probable delinquents and the whites as probable customers, also illustrates individual racism. Unlike the Mississippi murderers, the store clerk is not a bigot and may not even consider himself prejudiced, but his behavior is shaped by racial stereotypes which have been part of his un-conscious since childhood. A university admissions policy which provides for entrance only to students who score high on tests designed primarily for white suburban high schools necessarily excludes black ghetto-educated students. Unlike the legal policies of Mississippi, the university admission criteria are not intended to be racist, but the university is pursuing a course which perpetuates institutional racism. The difference, then, between individual and institutional racism is not a difference in intent or of visibility. Both the individual act of racism and the racist institutional policy may occur without the presence of conscious bigotry, and both may be masked intentionally or innocently.

In an attempt to understand "institutional racism" it is best to consider first what institutions are and what they do in a society. Institutions are fairly stable social arrangements and practices through which collective actions are taken. Medical institutions, for instance, marshal talents and resources of society so that health care can be provided. Medical institutions include hospitals, research labs, and clinics, as well as organizations of medical people such as doctors and nurses. The health of all of us is affected by general medical policies and by established practices and ethics. Business and labor, for example, determine what is to be produced, how it is to be produced, and by whom and on whose behalf products will be created. Public and private schools determine what is considered knowledge, how it is to be transmitted to new generations, and who will do the teaching. Legal and political institutions determine what laws regulate our lives, how and by whom they are enforced, and who will be prosecuted for which violations.

Institutions have great power to reward and penalize. They reward by providing career opportunities for some people and foreclosing them for others. They reward as well by the way social goods and services are distributed —by deciding who receives training and skills, medical care, formal education, political influence, moral support and self-respect, productive employment, fair treatment by the law, decent housing, self-confidence, and the promise of a secure future for self and children. No society will distribute social benefits in a perfectly equitable way. But no society need use race as a criterion to determine who will be rewarded and who punished. Any nation that permits race to affect the distribution of benefits from social policies is racist.

It is our thesis that institutional racism is deeply embedded in American society. Slavery was only the earliest and most blatant practice. Political, economic, educational, and religious policies cooperated with slaveholders to "keep the nigger in his place." Emancipation changed little. Jim Crow laws as well as residential and employment discrimination guaranteed that black citizens remained under the control of white citizens. Second-class citizenship quickly became a social fact as well as a legal status. Overt institutional racism was widely practiced throughout American society at least until World War II.

With desegregation in the armed forces and the passage of various civil rights bills, institutional racism no longer has the status of law. It is perpetuated nonetheless, sometimes by frightened and bigoted individuals, sometimes by good citizens merely carrying on "business as usual," and sometimes by well-intentioned but naive reformers. An attack on institutional racism is clearly the next task for Americans, white and black, who hope to obtain for their children a society less tense and more just than the one of the mid-1960's. It is no easy task. Individual, overt racist acts, such as the shotgun slaying of civil rights workers, are visible. Techniques of crime detection can be used to apprehend guilty parties, and, in theory, due process of law will punish them. To detect institutional racism, especially when it is unintentional or when it is disguised, is a very different task. And even when institutional racism is detected, it is seldom clear who is at fault. How can we say who is responsible for residential segregation, for poor education in ghetto schools, for extraordinarily high unemployment among black men, for racial stereotypes in history textbooks, for the concentration of political power in white society?

Louis L. Knowles and Kenneth Prewitt

Our analysis begins with attention to ideological patterns in American society which historically and presently sustain practices appropriately labeled "institutionally racist." We then turn attention to the procedures of dominant American institutions: educational, economic, political, legal, and medical. It is as a result of practices within these institutions that black citizens in America are consistently penalized for reasons of color.

Quite obviously the social arrangements which fix unequal opportunities for black and white citizens can be traced back through American history—farther back, as a matter of fact, than even the beginning of slavery. Our purpose is not to rewrite American history, although that needs to be done. Rather our purpose in this initial chapter is to point out the historical roots of institutional racism by examining the ideology used to justify it. In understanding how deeply racist practices are embedded in the American experience and values, we can come to a fuller understanding of how contemporary social institutions have adapted to their heritage.

HISTORY AND IDEOLOGY

Some form of white supremacy, both as ideology and institutional arrangement, existed from the first day English immigrants, seeking freedom from religious intolerance, arrived on the North American continent. From the beginning, the early colonizers apparently considered themselves culturally superior to the natives they encountered. This sense of superiority over the Indians, which was fostered by the religious ideology they carried to the new land, found its expression in the self-proclaimed mission to civilize and Christianize—a mission which was to find its ultimate expression in ideas of a "manifest destiny" and a "white man's burden."

The early colonists were a deeply religious people. The church was the dominant social institution of their time, and the religious doctrines brought from England strongly influenced their contacts with the native Indians. The goals of the colonists were stated clearly:

> *Principal and Maine Ends* [of the Virginia colony] ... ware first to preach and baptize into *Christian Religion* and by propogation of the *Gospell,* to recover out of the arms of the *Divell,* a number of poore and miserable soules, wrapt up unto death, in almost invincible ignorance ... and to add our myte to the Treasury of Heaven.[2]

Ignorance about the white man's God was sufficient proof in itself of the inferiority of the Indian and, consequently, of the superiority of the white civilization.

The mission impulse was doomed to failure. A shortage of missionaries and an unexpected resistance on the part of the Indian (who was less sure that the white man's ways were inherently superior) led to the dismantling of the few programs aimed at Christianization. It became clear that conquering was, on balance, less expensive and more efficient than "civilizing."

Thus began an extended process of genocide, giving rise to such aphorisms as "The only good Indian is a dead Indian." It was at this time that the ideology of white supremacy on the North American continent took hold. Since Indians were capable of reaching only the stage of "savage," they should not be allowed to impede the forward (westward, to be exact) progress of white civilization. The Church quickly acquiesced in this redefinition of the situation. The disappearance of the nonwhite race in the path of expansionist policies was widely interpreted as God's will. As one student of America's history has written, "It apparently never seriously occurred to [spokesmen for Christianity] that where they saw the mysterious law of God in the disappearance of the nonwhite races before the advancing Anglo-Saxon, a disappearance which apparently occurred without anyone's willing it or doing anything to bring it about, the actual process was a brutal one of oppression, dispossession, and even extermination."[3]

In short, what began as a movement to "civilize and Christianize" the indigenous native population was converted into a racist force, accompanied, as always, by a justificatory ideology. In retrospect, the result is hardly surprising. The English colonists operated from a premise which has continued to have a strong impact on American thought: the Anglo-Saxon race is culturally and religiously superior; neither the validity nor the integrity of alien cultures can be recognized. (The Indian culture, though native to the land, was considered the alien one.) When it became clear that Indians could not be "saved," the settlers concluded that the race itself was inferior. This belief was strengthened by such racist theories as the Teutonic Theory of Origins, which pointed out the superiority of the Anglo-Saxons. The institution of slavery and its accompanying justification would seem to have been products of the same mentality.

It has, of course, been the white man's relationship with the black man which has led to the most powerful expressions of institutional racism in the society. This is a history which hardly needs retelling, although it might be instructive to consider how closely related was the justification of Indian extermination to that of black slavery. It was the heathenism or savagery, so-called, of the African, just as of the Indian, which became the early rationale for enslavement. A particularly ingenious version of the rationale is best known under the popular label "Social Darwinism."

The Social Darwinian theory of evolution greatly influenced social thought, hence social institutions, in nineteenth-century America. Social Darwinists extended the concept of biological evolution in the development of man to a concept of evolution in development of societies and civilizations. The nature of a society or nation or race was presumed to be the product of natural evolutionary forces. The evolutionary process was characterized by struggle and conflict in which the "stronger, more advanced, and more civilized" would naturally triumph over the "inferior, weaker, backward, and uncivilized" peoples.

> The idea of natural selection was translated to a struggle between individual members of a society; between members of classes of society, between different nations, and between different races. This conflict, far from being an evil thing, was nature's indispensable method of producing superior men, superior nations, and superior races.[4]

Such phrases as "the struggle for existence" and "the survival of the fittest" became *lingua franca*, and white Americans had a full-blown ideology to explain their treatment of the "inferior race."

The contemporary expression of Social Darwinian thinking is less blatant but essentially the same as the arguments used in the nineteenth century. The poverty and degradation of the nonwhite races in the United States are thought to be the result of an innate lack of ability rather than anything white society has done. Thus a long line of argument reaches its most recent expression in the now famous "Moynihan Report": the focal point of the race problem is to be found in the pathology of black society.

Social Darwinism was buttressed with two other ideas widely accepted in nineteenth-century America: manifest destiny and white man's burden. Briefly stated, manifest destiny was simply the idea that white Americans were destined, either by natural forces or by Divine Right, to control at least the North American continent and, in many versions of the theory, a much greater share of the earth's surface. Many churchmen supported the idea that such expansion was the will of God. The impact of this belief with respect to the Indians has already been noted. Let it suffice to say that manifest destiny helped provide the moral and theological justification for genocide. The belief that American expansion was a natural process was rooted in Social Darwinism. Expansionism was simply the natural growth process of a superior nation. This deterministic argument enjoyed wide popularity. Even those who were not comfortable with the overt racism of the expansionist argument were able to cooperate in policies of "liberation" in Cuba and the Philippines by emphasizing the evils of Spanish control. Many, however, felt no need to camouflage their racism. Albert J. Beveridge, Senator from Indiana, stated his position clearly:

> The American Republic is a part of the movement of a race—the most masterful race of history—and race movements are not to be stayed by the hand of man. They are mighty answers to Divine commands. Their leaders are not only statesmen of peoples—they are prophets of God. The inherent tendencies of a race are its highest law. They precede and survive all statutes, all constitutions.... The sovereign tendencies of our race are organization and government.[5]

In any case, if racism was not invoked as a justification for imperialist expansion in the first place, it subsequently became a justification for continued American control of the newly "acquired" territories. This was particularly true in the Philippines. "The control of one country by another and the denial of rights or citizenship to the Filipinos were difficult ideas to reconcile with the Declaration of Independence and with American institutions. In order to make these opposing ideas of government compatible at all, the proponents of the acquisition of the Philippines were forced to rely heavily on race theories."[6]

An argument commonly expressed was that the Filipinos were simply incapable of self-government. " 'The Declaration of Independence,' stated Beveridge, 'applies only to peoples capable of self-government. Otherwise, how dared we administer the affairs of the Indians? How dare we continue to govern them today?' "[7] The decision, therefore, as to who was capable of self-government and who was not so capable was left to the United States Government. The criteria were usually explicitly racist, as it was simply assumed that whites, at least Anglo-Saxons, had the "gift" of being able to govern themselves while the inferior nonwhite peoples were not so endowed.

The ideology of imperialist expansion had an easily foreseeable impact on the domestic race situation. As Ronald Segal points out in *The Race War,*

> Both North and South saw and accepted the implications. What was sauce for the Philippines, for Hawaii and Cuba, was sauce for the Southern Negro. If the stronger and cleverer race is free to impose its will upon "new-caught sullen peoples" on the other side of the globe, why not in South Carolina and Mississippi? asked the *Atlantic Monthly.* "No Republican leader," proclaimed Senator Tillman of South Carolina, " . . . will now dare to wave the bloody shirt and preach a crusade against the South's treatment of the Negro. The North has a bloody shirt of its own. Many thousands of them have been made into shrouds for murdered Filipinos, done to death because they were fighting for liberty." Throughout the United States doctrines of racial superiority received the assent of influential politicians and noted academics. The very rationalizations that had eased the conscience of the slave trade now provided the sanction for imperial expansion.[8]

Another component of the ideology which has nurtured racist policies is that of "the white man's burden." This phrase comes from the title of a poem by Rudyard Kipling, which appeared in the United States in 1899. Whatever Kipling himself may have wished to convey, Americans soon popularized and adopted the concept as an encouragement for accepting the responsibility of looking after the affairs of the darker races. This notion of the "white man's burden" was that the white race, particularly Anglo-Saxons of Britain and America, should accept the (Christian) responsibility for helping the poor colored masses to find a better way of life.

It should be clear that this notion is no less racist than others previously mentioned. Behind the attitude lies the assumption of white supremacy. In exhorting Americans to follow British policy in this regard, the philosopher Josiah Royce stated the assumption clearly.

> . . . The Englishman, in his official and governmental dealings with backward peoples, has a great way of being superior without very often publicly saying that he is superior. You well know that in dealing, as an individual, with other individuals, trouble is seldom made by the fact that you are actually superior to another man in any respect. The trouble comes when you tell the other man, too stridently, that you are his superior. Be my superior, quietly, simply showing your superiority

in your deeds, and very likely I shall love you for the very fact of your superiority. For we all love our leaders. But tell me I am your inferior, and then perhaps I may grow boyish, and may throw stones. Well, it is so with the races. Grant then that yours is the superior race. Then you can say little about the subject in your public dealings with the backward race. Superiority is best shown by good deeds and by few boasts.[9]

Both manifest destiny and the idea of a white man's burden, in disguised forms, continue to shape white America's values and policies. Manifest destiny has done much to stimulate the modern day myth that colored peoples are generally incapable of self-government. There are whites who continue to believe that black Afro-Americans are not ready to govern themselves. At best, blacks must first be "properly trained." Of course, this belief influences our relations with nonwhites in other areas of the world as well.

The authors have found the concept of manifest destiny helpful in analyzing white response to "black power." Black power is based on the belief that black people in America are capable of governing and controlling their own communities. White rejection of black power reflects, in part, the widely accepted white myth that blacks are incapable of self-government and must be controlled and governed by whites. Many whites apparently still share with Albert Beveridge the belief that "organization and government" are among the "sovereign tendencies of our race."

The belief in a "white man's burden" also has its modern-day counterpart, particularly in the attitudes and practices of so-called "white liberals" busily trying to solve "the Negro problem." The liberal often bears a strong sense of responsibility for helping the Negro find a better life. He generally characterizes the Negro as "disadvantaged," "unfortunate," or "culturally deprived." The liberal generally feels superior to the black man, although he is less likely to publicly state his sense of superiority. He may not even recognize his own racist sentiments. In any case, much like Josiah Royce, he senses that "superiority is best shown by good deeds and by few boasts." Liberal paternalism is reflected not only in individual attitudes but in the procedures and policies of institutions such as the welfare system and most "war on poverty" efforts.

It is obvious that recent reports and action plans carry on a traditional, if diversionary, view that has long been acceptable to most white Americans: that it is not white institutions but a few bigots plus the deprived status of Negroes that cause racial tension. Such a view is mythical.... We are not content with "explanations" of white-black relations that are apolitical, that would reduce the causes of racial tension to the level of psychological and personal factors. Three hundred years of American history cannot be encapsulated so easily. To ignore the network of institutional controls through which social benefits are allocated may be reassuring, but it is also bad social history. America is and has long been a racist nation, because it has and has long had a racist policy. This policy is not to be understood by listening to the proclamations of intent by leading citizens and government officials; nor is it to be understood by reading off a list of compensatory programs in business, education, and welfare. The policy can be understood only when we are willing to take a hard look at the continuing and irrefutable racist consequences of the major institutions in American life. The policy will be changed when we are willing to start the difficult task of remaking our institutions.

NOTES

1. Stokely Carmichael and Charles Hamilton, *Black Power: The Politics of Liberation in America* (New York: Vintage Books, 1967).

2. Quoted in Thomas F. Gossett, *Race: The History of an Idea in America* (Dallas: SMU Press, 1963), p. 18.

3. *Ibid.*, p. 196.

4. *Ibid.*, p. 145.

5. *Ibid.*, p. 318.

6. *Ibid.*, p. 328.

7. *Ibid.*, p. 329.

8. Ronald Segal, *The Race War* (Baltimore: Penguin Books, 1967), p. 219.

9. Gossett, p. 334.

3.2 ELIZABETH MARTÍNEZ

Beyond Black/White: The Racisms of Our Time

A preponderance of the scholarship on racism in American society focuses on the African American experience. Consequently, the distinctive nature of racism in defining the sociohistorical experiences of Native Americans, Hispanic Americans, and Asian Americans in U.S. society remains obscure to most students of race and ethnic relations.

In the present article, Elizabeth Martínez explains why the Black-White framework remains pervasive in American thinking on racism. She then calls for a renewed understanding of racism beyond the Black-White model.

Key Concept: beyond the Black-White model of racism

BY WAY OF INTRODUCTION

Let me begin by admitting that I have an axe to grind. A bell to toll, a *grito* to shout, a banner to wave. The banner was fashioned during 10 years in the Black civil rights-human rights movement followed by 10 years in the Chicano *movimiento*. Those years taught that liberation has similar meanings in both histories: an end to racist oppression, the birth of collective self-respect, and a dream of social justice. Those years taught that alliances among progressive people of color can and must help realize the dream.

Such alliances require a knowledge and wisdom that we have yet to attain. For the present, it remains painful to see how divide-and-conquer strategies succeed among our peoples. It is painful to see how prejudice, resentment, petty competitiveness, and sheer ignorance fester. It is positively pitiful to see how often we echo Anglo stereotypes about one another.

All this suggests that we urgently need some fresh and fearless thinking about racism at this moment in history. Fresh thinking might begin with analyzing the strong tendency among Americans to frame racial issues in strictly Black-white terms. Do such terms make sense when changing demographics point to a U.S. population that will be 32% Latino, Asian/Pacific American, and Native American—that is, neither Black nor white—by the year 2050? Not to mention the increasing numbers of mixed people who incorporate two, three, or more "races" or nationalities? Don't we need to imagine multiple forms of racism rather than a single, Black-white model?

Practical questions related to the fight against racism also arise. Doesn't the exclusively Black-white framework discourage perception of common interests among people of color—primarily in the working class—and thus sustain White Supremacy? Doesn't the view of institutionalized racism as a problem experienced only by Black people isolate them from potential allies? Doesn't the Black-white definition encourage a tendency often found among people of color to spend too much energy understanding our lives in relation to Whiteness, obsessing about what the White will think? That tendency is inevitable in some ways: the locus of power over our lives has long been white (although big shifts have recently taken place in the color of capital)and the oppressed have always survived by becoming experts on the oppressor's ways. But that can become a prison of sorts, a trap of compulsive vigilance. Let us liberate ourselves, then, from the tunnel vision of Whiteness and behold the colors around us!

To criticize the Black-white framework is not simply a resentful demand from other people of color for equal sympathy, equal funding, equal clout, equal patronage. It is not simply us-too resentment at being ignored or minimized. It is not just another round of mindless competition in the victimhood tournament. Too often we make the categories of race, class, gender, sexuality, age, physical condition, etc., contend for the title of "most oppressed." Within "race," various population groups then compete for that top spot. Instead, we need to understand that various forms and histories of oppression exist. We need to recognize that they include differences in extent and intensity. Yet pursuing some hierarchy of competing oppressions leads us down dead-end streets where we will never find the linkage between oppressions or how to overcome them.

The goal in reexamining the Black-white definition is to find an effective strategy for vanquishing an evil that has expanded rather than diminished in recent years. Three recent developments come to mind. First is the worldwide economic recession in which the increasingly grim struggle for sheer survival encourages the scapegoating of working-class people—especially immigrants, especially those of color—by other working-class people. This has become so widespread in the West that a Klan cross-burning in London's Trafalgar Square or on Paris' Champs Élysée doesn't seem hard to imagine. The globalization of racism is mounting rapidly.

Second, and relatedly, the reorganization of the international division of labor continues, with changing demands for workers that are affecting demographics everywhere. History tells us of the close relationship between capital's need for labor and racism. If that relationship changes, so may the nature of racism.

Finally, in the U.S., we have passed through a dozen years of powerful reaction against the civil-rights agenda set in the 1960s. This has combined with the recession's effects and other socioeconomic developments to make people go into a defensive, hunkering-down mode, each community on its own, at a time when we need more rather than less solidarity. Acts of racist violence now occur in communities that never saw them before (although they always could have happened). An intensification of racism is upon us.

We see it in the anti-immigrant emotions being whipped up and new divisions based on racism and nativism. We see escalating white fears of becoming the minority population, the minority power, after centuries of domination. As U.S. demographics change rapidly, as the "Latinization" of major regions and cities escalates, a cross fire of fears begins to crackle. In that climate the mass media breed both cynical hopelessness and fear. Look only at the October 1992 *Atlantic* magazine cover proclaiming "BLACKS VS. BROWNS: Immigration and the New American Dilemma" for one chilling symptom of an assumed, inevitable hostility.

Today the task of building solidarity among people of color promises to be more necessary and difficult than ever. An exclusively Black-white definition of racism makes our task all the harder. That's the banner that will be raised here: an urgent need for 21st-century thinking, which can move us beyond the Black-white framework without negating its central, historical role in the construction of U.S. racism. We do need much more understanding of how racism and its effects developed, not only similarly, but also differently for different peoples according to whether they were victimized by genocide, enslavement, or colonization in various forms.

Greater solidarity among peoples of color must be hammered out, painstakingly. With solidarity a prize could be won even bigger than demolishing racism. The prize could be a U.S. society whose national identity not only ceases to be white, but also advances beyond "equality"—beyond a multiculturalism that gives people of color a respect equal to whites. Toni Morrison has written eloquently in *Playing in the Dark* of this goal from an Africanist perspective: "American means white, and Africanist people struggle to make the term applicable to themselves with ethnicity and hyphen after hyphen after hyphen.... In the scholarship on the formation of an American character [a]... major item to be added to the list must be an Africanist presence—decidedly not American, decidedly other" (Morrison, 1992: 47).

We need to dream of replacing the white national identity with an identity grounded in cultures oriented to respect for all forms of life and balance rather than domination as their guiding star. Such cultures, whose roots rest in indigenous, precolonial societies of the Americas and Africa, can help define a new U.S. identity unshackled from the capitalist worldview. Still alive today, they color my banner bright.

Let us begin that dialogue about the exclusively Black-white model of racism and its effects with the question: does that definition prevail and, if so, why?

Alas, it does prevail. Major studies of "minorities" up to 1970 rarely contain more than a paragraph on our second largest "minority," Mexican-Americans (Blauner, 1972: 165). In two dozen books of 1960s movement history, I found inadequate treatment of the Black Civil Rights Movement, but almost total silence about the Chicano, Native American, and Asian American movements of those years (Martínez, 1989). Today, not a week goes by without a major media discussion of race and race relations that totally ignores the presence in U.S. society of Native Americans, Latinos, Asian/Pacific Americans, and Arab-Americans.

East Coast-based media and publishers are the worst offenders. Even a progressive magazine like *The Nation* can somehow publish a special issue entitled "The Assault on Equality: Race, Rights, and the New Orthodoxy" (December 9, 1991) containing only two brief phrases relating to people of color other than African-Americans in 27 pages. Outbreaks of Latino unrest or social uprising, such as we saw in the Mt. Pleasant section of Washington, D.C. make little if any dent. New York, that center of ideological influence, somehow remains indifferent to the fact that in 1991, Latinos totaled 24.4% of its population while Asians formed 6.9%.

Even in California, this most multinational of the states, where Latinos have always been the most numerous population of color, it is not rare for major reports on contemporary racial issues to stay strictly inside the Black-white framework. Journalists in San Francisco, a city almost half Latino or Asian/Pacific-American, can see no need to acknowledge "This article will be about African-Americans, only"—which would be quite acceptable—in articles on racial issues. At best we may hear that after-thought construction, "Blacks and other minorities."

Again, momentous events that speak to Latino experience of racist oppression fail to shake the prevailing view. Millions of Americans saw massive Latino participation in the April 1992 Los Angeles uprising on their TV screens. Studies show that, taken as a whole, the most heavily damaged areas of L.A. were 49% Latino, and the majority of people arrested were Latino (Pastor, 1993). Yet the mass media and most people have continued to view that event as "a Black riot."

Predominantly Anglo left forces have not been much better than the mainstream and liberals. The most consistently myopic view could be heard from the Communist Party U.S.A., which has seen the African-American experience as the only model of racism. Left groups that adopted the Black Nation thesis rarely analyzed the validity of Chicano nationalism in the Southwest, or advocated giving lands back to the Native Americans, or questioned the "model minority" myth about Asian/Pacific Americans.

A semi-contemptuous indifference toward Latinos—to focus on this one group—has emanated from institutions in the dominant society for decades. Echoing this attitude are many individual Anglos. To cite a handful of personal experiences: Anglos will admit to having made a racist remark or gesture toward an African-American much more quickly than toward a Latino. Or if you bring up some Anglo's racist action toward a Latino, they will change the subject almost instantly to racism toward a Black person. Or they may respond to an account of police brutality toward Latinos with some remark of elusive relevance about Spanish crimes against indigenous people in the Americas.

A stunning ignorance also prevails. Race–relations scholar Robert (Bob) Blauner has rightly noted that:

> Even informed Anglos know almost nothing about La Raza, its historical experience, its present situation.... And the average citizen doesn't have the foggiest notion that Chicanos have been lynched in the Southwest and continue to be abused by the police, that an entire population has been exploited economically, dominated politically, and raped culturally (Blauner, 1972: 166).

Above all, there seems to be little comprehension of what it means to suffer total disenfranchisement in the most literal sense. Millions of Latinos, like many Asian/Pacific Americans, lack basic political rights. They are often extremely vulnerable to oppression and the most intense oppression occurs when people have problems of legal status. This means the borderlands, where vulnerability rests on having formal admission documents or not. Aside from South Africa's pass system, it is hard to imagine any mechanism in modern times so well designed to control, humiliate, and disempower vast numbers of workers than the border and its requirements.

WHY THE BLACK-WHITE FRAMEWORK?

Three of the reasons for the Black-white framework of racial issues seem obvious: numbers, geography, and history. African–Americans have long been the largest population of color in the U.S.; only recently has this begun to change. Also, African-Americans have long been found in sizable numbers in most of the United States, including major cities. On the other hand, Latinos—to focus on this group—are found primarily in the Southwest plus parts of the Northwest and Midwest and they have been (wrongly) perceived as a primarily rural people—therefore of less note.

Historically, it has been only 150 years since the U.S. seized half of Mexico and incorporated those lands and their peoples into this nation. The Black/white relationship, on the other hand, has long been entrenched in the nation's collective memory. White enslavement of Black people together with white genocide against Native Americans provided the original models for racism as it developed here. Slavery and the struggle against it form a central theme in this country's only civil war—a prolonged, momentous conflict —and continuing Black rebellion. Enslaved Africans in the U.S. and African-Americans have created an unmatched history of massive, pesistent, dramatic, and infinitely courageous resistance, with individual leaders of worldwide note. They cracked the structure of racism in this country during the first Reconstruction and again during the second, the 1960s Civil Rights Movement, as no other people of color have done.

Interwoven with these historical factors are possible psychological explanations of the Black-white definition. In the eyes of Jefferson and other leaders, Native Americans did not arouse white sexual anxieties or seem a threat to racial purity, as did Blacks. In any case, White Supremacy's fear of Indian resistance had greatly diminished by the late 1800s as a result of relentless genocide accompanied by colonization. Black rebelliousness, on the other hand, remains an inescapable nightmare to the dominant white society. There is also the fact that contemporary Black rebellion has been urban: right in the Man's face, scary.

A relative indifference toward Mexican people developed in Occupied America in the late 1800s. Like the massacre of Indians and enslavement of Africans, the successful colonization of Mexicans in what became the Southwest was key to U.S. economic growth. One would expect to see racist institutions and ideology emerge, and so they did in certain areas. Yet even in places like the

Texas borderlands, where whites have historically reviled and abused Latinos, the Mexican presence didn't arouse a high level of white sexual anxiety and other irrational fears. Today Latinos often say Anglo attitudes make them feel they are less hated than dismissed as inconsequential. "There's no Mau-Mau factor," observed a Black friend half-humorously about Latino invisibility.

Of course there may be an emergent Mau-Mau factor, called demographics. Anglo indifference to Latinos may be yielding to a new fear. The white response to anticipation of becoming a minority during one's own lifetime is often panic as well as hatred and those "hordes" at the gate are of colors other than Black. But the new frenzy has yet to show the same fear-stricken face toward Latinos—or Asian/Pacific Americans—as toward African-Americans.

Robert Blauner, an Anglo and one of the few authors on racism to have examined the Black-white framework, looks at these psychological factors as revealed in literature:

> ... We buy black writers, not only because they can write and have something to say, but because the white racial mind is obsessed with blackness.... Mexican-Americans, on the other hand, have been unseen as individuals and as a group.... James Baldwin has pointed to the deep mutual involvement of black and white in America. The profound ambivalence, the love-hate relationship, which Baldwin's own work expresses and dissects, does not exist in the racism that comes down on La Raza.... Even the racial stereotypes that plague Mexican-Americans tend to lack those positive attributes that mark antiblack fantasies—supersexuality, inborn athletic and musical power, natural rhythm. Mexicans are dirty, lazy, treacherous, thieving bandits—and revolutionaries (Blauner, 1972: 163–164).

(Not that I would want to choose between having Rhythm or Roaches.)

A final reason for the Black-white framework may be found in the general U.S. political culture, which is not only white-dominated, but also embraces an extremely stubborn form of national self-centeredness. This U.S.-centrism has meant that the political culture lacks any global vision other than relations of domination. In particular, the U.S. has consistently demonstrated contempt for Latin America, its people, their languages, and their issues. The U.S. refuses to see itself as one nation sitting on a continent with 20 others whose dominant languages are Spanish and Portuguese. That myopia has surely nurtured the Black-white framework for racism.

THE CULTURE OF COLOR

Color is crucial to understanding the Black-white framework of racial issues. Early in this nation's history, Benjamin Franklin perceived a tri-racial society based on skin color—"the lovely white," black, and "tawny," as Ron Takaki tells us in *Iron Cages*. Echoing this triad, we still have the saying "If you're white, you're all right; if you're Black, get back; if you're brown, stick around." As that old saying indicates, racism is experienced differently by Native Americans, African-Americans, Latinos, and Asian/Pacific Americans. In the case of

Latinos, we find them somewhat more likely to be invisibilized—rendered "un-seen"—than problematized (with thanks to writer/activist Linda Burnham for that concept). Color explains much of this.

The relatively light skin and "Caucasian" features of many Latinos mean they are less threatening in the eyes of white racism and can even can "pass" —unnoticed, invisible—much more often than African-Americans. Obviously this carries certain advantages in a racist society. Many Latinos would like to pass, work hard to assimilate, and succeed.

Until 1990 the U.S. Census categorized Latinos as "White," and even in that year it generated mass confusion on this issue: today the common term "Non-Hispanic Whites" certainly suggests a view of Latinos as white. At the same time, a 1992 poll of Latinos has shown an unexpectedly strong lack of self-identification as such. More than 90%, for example, said they did not be-long to any ethnic organizations and less than 13% participated in any political activities organized around their national groups.

The term Hispanic (Her Panic, His Panic), whose emergence accompa-nied the rise of a Latino middle-class in the late 1970s to 1980s, encourages the wannabe whites/don't wannabe Indians. Always the unspoken goal has been to sidestep racist treatment, and who can be criticized for that? But we must also recognize the difference between those whom racism's obsession with color al-lows to try, and those with no such choice. "Passing" is an option for very few African-Americans. If it is possible for some Latinos to assimilate, one cannot say that of most African-Americans; they can only accommodate.

Latinos themselves buy into the hierarchy of color. Too often we fail to recognize the way in which we sustain racism ideologically. We do it when we express prejudice against those among us who look *indio*, mulatto, or just Black. We do it when we favor being lighter. Such prejudice dehumanizes fel-low human beings, it divides our forces in the struggle for justice, and must be confronted....

THE COLOR OF CULTURE

If there is a culture of color in these racist United States, is it possible we also have a color of culture?

In trying to understand the Black/white construct, one might distinguish between racial oppression (derived from physical appearance, especially skin color), and national minority oppression (derived from cultural differences or nationality). According to these criteria Latinos—like Asian/Pacific Americans —would be victims of national minority rather than racial oppression. Racism itself, then, would indeed be strictly white on Black.

Does the distinction hold? Do Latinos suffer for reasons of culture and nationality, but not for their "race"?

On one hand, cultural difference (especially language) and nationality are indeed used in oppressing a colonized people like Mexicans or those of Mexican descent in the U.S. The right to speak Spanish on the job or in a school play-ground has been historically denied. A Spanish accent (though not a British or French accent) is a liability in many professional situations. Children are ridiculed at school for bringing Mexican lunches, their names are Anglicized by white teachers, humiliation is daily fare. Later in life, they will be treated as foreigners; citizens will be denied citizen rights and noncitizens will be denied human rights.

Culturally, Latinos are seen as exotica, outside the mainstream, alien. They speak a funny language, some say (the most beautiful in the world, others say), and nobody outside the barrio can understand their best jokes, their beloved play-on-words, or self-mocking style. This isolation largely results from tactics of self-defense: culture has provided a longstanding survival mechanism for many people of Latino origin in a hostile world. It is a mechanism whose strength has continued to flow, given the proximity of Mexico, Central America, and the Caribbean to the United States. Latino efforts to move from outside to inside have intensified in the last 25 years and will continue, but the sense of inhabiting a culturally distinct world remains, especially in newer generations.

Latinos are acknowledged—if at all—in a ghettoized cultural framework: as actors, film makers, musicians, and other kinds of artists; as a growing market with great promise if one caters to its cultural characteristics; perhaps as an "ethnic" electoral force—or, on the negative side, as immigrants who speak a "foreign" language and "swarm" across the border; as urban gangbangers with a culture of their own, *órale* Eddie Olmos! Even when these attitudes are not actively hostile, they are dehumanizing.

Does all this mean Latinos suffer for their culture and nationality, but not for their "race"? If we look at social conditions, at the actual experience of Latinos in the U.S., it makes more sense to conclude that the presence of national minority oppression doesn't signify the absence of racial oppression. It makes more sense to understand "racial" in terms of peoplehood and not only a supposed biology.

Social conditions affirm that combination of national, cultural, and racial oppression. The statistics for Latinos are grim: their national poverty rate (27%), high school drop-out rate (36%), and child poverty rate (42%) are even higher than for African-Americans, according to news reports on the 1990 Census. They are now reported to experience the most discrimination in housing markets of any U.S. population group (Lueck, 1991).

Life-endangering racism is not rare for Latinos in the Southwest, especially near the border, and especially for those who are poor and working class. For decades, Anglos in Texas, Arizona, and California have enslaved, tortured, and murdered Latinos because their victims were nonwhite "foreigners." Hundreds of Mexicans were lynched between 1847 and 1935, if not later.

On a recent visit, San Diego County in California felt to me for Mexicans and Central Americans like Mississippi felt for Blacks in the 1960s. Five years ago, in that county a pair of middle-class white youths spied two young, documented Latinos standing by the roadside; one shot them dead and later explained to the judge that he did it because he "didn't like Mexicans." Such attitudes are even more common in that county today. In urban areas Latinos number high among the victims of Los Angeles Police Department and Sheriff's Department brutality. It's far from chic to be a spic, as poet Gerardo Navarro rhymed it sardonically.

The borderlands remain the locus of the most intense oppression, for that is where Latinos are most vulnerable by virtue of nationality—with or without documents. Agents of the Border Patrol, the largest police force in the U.S., murder Latinos with impunity. Killing Latinos as they try to run back to Mexico, running them down with official vehicles, forcing them into the river to drown —all these seem to be favorite Border Patrol pastimes.

Women are among those most brutally abused at the border; their victimization has only recently attracted public attention. Officials rape and then sometimes murder Latinas trying to cross the border, at will. Latina women contracted in their home countries as housekeepers have been raped on the day of arrival here at a new job; worked 14 to 16 hours a day, seven days a week; never paid promised wages; and kept isolated from possible sources of assistance. What happens to young, "illegal" children has included separation from parents and being jailed.

Latino men, women, and children are victimized on the basis of nationality and culture, rendered vulnerable by their lack of documents and scant knowledge of English or of local institutions. More often than not, they are rendered additionally vulnerable by their skin color and other physical features. Nationality then combines with a nonwhite (though not Black) physical appearance to subject them to an oppression that is a form of racism. Even if a nonwhite appearance is lacking, however, nationality and culture create a separate peoplehood as the basis for oppression.

In a land where the national identity is white, nationality and race become interchangeable. We live today with a white definition of citizenship, which generates a racist dynamic. Think about our words, our codes, in the media and conversation. "Immigrants" today means only two things: Mexicans and Central Americans, or Asians. It doesn't mean French or Irish or Serbian people who have come to relocate (a nicer word than "immigrate").

A rigid line cannot be drawn between racial and national oppression when all victims are people of color. Both are racism, and in combination they generate new varieties of racism. All this suggests why we need to understand more than the Black-white model today.

RACISM EVOLVES

Racism evolves; as editor David Goldberg points out in his book *Anatomy of Racism*, it has no single, permanently fixed set of characteristics. New forms are being born today out of global events, in particular from the new international division of labor. He writes:

> ... all forms of racism may be linked in terms of their exclusionary or inclusionary undertakings. A major historical shift has been from past racist forms defining and fueling expansionist colonial aims and pursuits to contemporary expressions in nationalist terms. Insistence on racial inferiority in the past fed colonial appetites and imperialist self-definition. Racism is taken now to be expressed increasingly in terms of isolationist nationalist self-image, of cultural differentiation

tied to custom, tradition, and heritage, and of exclusionary immigration policies, anti-immigrant practices and criminality (Goldberg, 1990: xiv).

The increasing equation of racism with nationalism is spotlighted by the title of Paul Gilroy's provocative book, *There Ain't No Black in the Union Jack*. We need to look at that equation more closely here in the U.S. The challenge is to understand such new developments and to draw strength from our understanding. The challenge is to abandon a dead-end dualism that comprises two White Supremacist inventions: Blackness and Whiteness. The challenge is to extend a dialectical reach.

Black/white are real poles—but not the only poles. To organize against racism, as people in SNCC (the Student Nonviolent Coordinating Committee) used to say, Blackness is necessary but not sufficient. They were thinking of class, as I remember; today we can also think of other colors, other racisms. In doing so, we have to proceed with both boldness and infinite care. Talking race in these United States is an intellectual minefield; for every social observation, one can find three contradictions and four necessary qualifications. Crawling through the complexity, it helps to think: keep your eye on the prize, which is uniting against the monster.

REFERENCES

Blauner, Robert. 1972. Racial Oppression in America. New York: Harper and Row: 165.

Goldberg, David Theo (ed.). 1990. Anatomy of Racism. Minneapolis: University Of Minnesota Press.

Hayes-Bautista, David and Gregory Rodriguez. 1993. "Latinos Are Redefining Notions of Racial Identity." Los Angeles Times (January 15).

Lueck, T. J. 1991. "U.S. Study Finds Hispanic Minority Most Often Subject to Victimization." New York Times (November 3).

Martínez, Elizabeth. 1989. "A Certain Absence of Color." Social Justice 16,4.

Morrison, Toni. 1992. Playing in the Dark: Whiteness and the Literary Imagination. Cambridge: Harvard University Press.

Pastor, Manuel, Jr. 1993. Latinos and the L.A. Uprising. Tomas Rivera Center (TRC) Study, Occidental College, California.

3.3 NANCY STEIN

Affirmative Action and the Persistence of Racism

Affirmative action is one of America's most pressing social issues. The United States Commission on Civil Rights defines *affirmative action* as any measure that permits the consideration of race, national origin, sex, or disability in providing economic and educational opportunities to classes of individuals to whom U.S. society has historically denied those opportunities. Affirmative action has its origins in the post–Civil War Reconstruction period, when Congress enacted the Thirteenth, Fourteenth, and Fifteenth Amendments to the U.S. Constitution, thereby establishing the social and political rights of African American slaves. Ever since then U.S. society has used affirmative action in a variety of social and political contexts to dismantle the institutional barriers preventing non-White minorities and women from achieving economic and educational parity with the dominant White male majority. Whether or not affirmative action policies have been effective in admitting minority groups members into the mainstream of American society, however, is a hot topic of debate.

In the following reading from "Affirmative Action and the Persistence of Racism," *Social Justice* (Fall 1995), Nancy Stein explores the ideological assumptions underlying the social, political, and judicial assaults on affirmative action policies within the context of White racism in U.S. society. Stein denounces the rationale for attracking affirmative action as mythical, and she calls for a continued collective struggle to save affirmative action.

Stein, a social worker and activist, is on the editorial board of the journal *Social Justice.*

Key Concept: affirmative action policies

INTRODUCTION

The attack on affirmative action is only the latest in a series of efforts to roll back the rights of people of color, as seen in the passage of Proposition 187— California's anti-immigrant initiative—in the various three-strikes measures approved around the country, and in "welfare reform proposals," among others. Conservative ideologues seek to eliminate entitlement programs that benefit the poor by tapping into both the racism that has become increasingly legitimate since the Reagan administration and the fear engendered by the growing scarcity of jobs and economic opportunity.

Today's attack on affirmative action is represented most strongly in the politically motivated vote by the regents of the University of California in July 1995 to do away with affirmative action programs in admissions, hiring, and contracts. The regents are appointed by the governor and Governor Pete Wilson has received financial contributions from many of them. Wilson, who has made overturning affirmative action a centerpiece of his presidential election campaign, used this leverage to pressure the regents. In addition, conservative forces in California are proceeding with their efforts to place an initiative on the ballot in 1996 that would dismantle public affirmative action programs (CCRI, 1994; Dellios, 1994). Senator Dole and other Republican presidential candidates are also embracing the attack and conservative legislators are going after affirmative action at the national level.

There is a reservoir of resentment and bitterness in much of white America, particularly among white men, against any effort to eliminate discrimination by giving preferential treatment to people of color, who are seen as undeserving or as having already benefited enough from such programs. This article will examine the history of this contentious policy since its passage 30 years ago and the underlying values and ideological assumptions represented in the attack on affirmative action, particularly given the context of the persistence of racism in this society.

WHAT IS AFFIRMATIVE ACTION?

Affirmative action is a complex policy, designed to end discrimination in hiring, college admissions, and the awarding of contracts. The definition of affirmative action contained in the Uniform Guidelines on Employee Selection Procedures developed by the Equal Employment Opportunity Commission and other government agencies states that:

> ... affirmative action is one part of an effort to remedy past and present discrimination and is considered essential to assuring that jobs are "genuinely and equally accessible to qualified persons, without regard to their sex, racial, or ethnic characteristics" (Greene, 1989: 1).

Affirmative action was initially conceived as a temporary measure to compensate for the years of slavery and it was hoped that it would lead to equal opportunity for all (Edmonds, 1994: 22). Its purpose was to increase equity and opportunity, to permit race and, subsequently, gender to become a factor in hiring, contracting, admissions, and financial aid (Stimpson, 1993: 4). It justified using unequal means to achieve greater equality among diverse groups of people, which would contribute to the "public welfare because it reduces poverty and inequalities..." (Greene, 1989: 9).

Nancy Stein

The roots of affirmative action policy were contained in the provisions of the Civil Rights Act of 1964, specifically Title VII, which is the statutory basis of affirmative action in private employment. Title VII (as amended in 1972) bans all discrimination in employment based on race, color, religion, sex, or national origin. Although the language of Title VII refers to race in general, the impetus for this policy was to address the conditions of Black people in this country. For millions of African Americans, equal access to economic and educational opportunity was systematically denied for hundreds of years. The legacy of slavery resulted in separate and unequal institutions for the Black population and segregation in all aspects of life. African Americans have waged an ongoing struggle to challenge this inequality, using every arena from mass protests to the legal system. One of the most significant accomplishments of this struggle was the passage of the Civil Rights Act of 1964.

The initial focus of the legislation was to eliminate discrimination in hiring policies of the federal government and private corporations. Later, the provisions were extended to education and the awarding of federal contracts such that only firms that did not discriminate were eligible. Subsequent policies extended affirmative action protections to other people of color, women, and most recently, to disabled people.

However, the legislation went beyond declaring that discriminatory policies were no longer legal. The more comprehensive goal, revealed in congressional debates on Title VII in 1964 and 1972, was to eliminate economic disparities between the races (Greene, 1989: 55). Much of the debate on affirmative action concerns how the legislation has been interpreted and what its philosophical goals were.

If an analysis of an employer's work force indicates that certain groups are underrepresented due to gender, race, or ethnicity when compared with their proportion in the relevant job market, then the employer must establish "affirmative steps to remedy the situation." These steps can be race-conscious and include a variety of programs, including the establishment of goals, timetables, and focused recruitment drives, for example, to achieve a more balanced representation of workers. Comparable programs also exist to remedy the effects of discrimination in education.

Compensatory Versus Distributive Principles of Justice

The language of Title VII was vague enough that it could be interpreted differently, based on two underlying principles of justice: *compensatory* and *distributive* (Greene, 1989). The more narrow *compensatory* conception of justice construes affirmative action as a policy that allows *specific individuals* who have been discriminated against to seek compensation and sanctions for specific claims of discrimination. Conservative opponents of affirmative action want to limit its application solely to a compensatory role. In contrast, supporters of affirmative action go beyond that view to include all people of color, not only specific victims of discrimination; since "discrimination is systematic, so any remedy must also be systematic" (*Ibid.*: 3). In addition, supporters put forward a broader view of affirmative action as a *distributive* measure that seeks to distribute opportunities more fairly among the population in order to remedy the effects of discrimination. Under this broader principle, those who benefit from this policy may not have been discriminated against specifically, but suffer the historical *and* current effects of racist policies that have systematically excluded people of color from employment and educational opportunities. As Greene (*Ibid.*) summarizes this view,

> in the absence of discrimination (or the presence of equal opportunity) distributive inequities between whites and blacks [or all people of color] would not be as great as they presently are and affirmative action is justified as a means toward eliminating these inequities.

The Reagan and Bush administrations held to the narrow compensatory view of the Civil Rights Act, maintaining that affirmative action is "reverse discrimination" and, as such, is unconstitutional. Their appointments to the Supreme Court and the Equal Employment Opportunity Commission reflect this stand (e.g., Clarence Thomas was Reagan's appointee to head the Equal Employment Opportunity Commission, which dramatically changed the nature of that agency's focus such that it was limited almost exclusively to individual claims of discrimination, as opposed to claims of patterns or practices of discrimination affecting groups of people) (*Ibid.*: 4–5).

The legislative debate on the Civil Rights Act and subsequent judicial decisions have fluctuated between these two poles, often including elements of both. The current attack on affirmative action indicates that the conservative interpretation of Title VII is dominant. This does not bode well for policies that focus on redressing the effects of past and present discrimination, which are well documented and still pervasive. For example, white men hold 95% of senior management positions (Powell, 1995).

LEGISLATIVE HISTORY AND POLICY FORMATION

Brown v. Board of Education

Segregation was accepted as constitutional in the United States in the 1896 Supreme Court *Plessy* v. *Ferguson* decision. It remained in force until 1954, when the Supreme Court ruled in *Brown* v. *Board of Education* that the "separate but unequal" doctrine was unconstitutional. This landmark decision represented the culmination of a series of rulings that had been fought for by Black lawyers for the previous 20 years to open up historically white colleges and universities (Olivas, 1993: 18–19).

Attorneys Thurgood Marshall and Charles Houston successfully challenged the exclusion of Black students from the University of Maryland Law

School in 1936. In 1938, the Supreme Court overturned a Missouri plan that barred Black residents from attending the University of Missouri Law School, but paid their tuition at schools in other states. In 1948, the Court ordered Oklahoma to either enroll a Black law student or create a separate Black law school. In an effort to avoid integration, the state went so far as to create a separate school. When Oklahoma finally admitted its first Black student, he was given a separate room to eat in and attended classes by sitting in the hallway outside the classroom. The lawsuit protesting this treatment went all the way to the Supreme Court before it was successful.

Brown also signaled the beginning of the new Civil Rights Movement, which included sit-ins, the Montgomery bus boycott, and voter registration drives in the South. Dogs and fire hoses were used to attack peaceful protesters. In the course of the struggle, civil rights activists were murdered. In the 1963 March on Washington, hundreds of thousands of people demanded the passage of civil rights legislation. It is important to remember what it cost to win these rights and that conditions still exist that make it necessary to defend them.

Executive and Congressional Action

At the executive level, racial discrimination was not challenged directly until 1941, when President Franklin Roosevelt signed an order banning discrimination in employment by the federal government and defense contractors (Greene, 1989: 17). Congress did not successfully expand this policy until the passage of the 1964 Civil Rights Act.

President Kennedy proposed a relatively weak civil rights bill that was subsequently strengthened through congressional debate (*Ibid.*: 22–25). Kennedy included the redistributive principle of justice as part of the rationale for his bill by maintaining that the need to eliminate economic inequality between Blacks and whites was one of the main justifications for the legislation. While debate on Kennedy's bill was slowly developing in the House, the bombing of a Black church in Birmingham, Alabama, took place, killing four little girls. The effects of this violent act were to hasten the debate and strengthen the bill. When the debate moved to the Senate, thousands of civil rights activists came to Washington, holding vigils and rallies pressing for the final passage of the bill (*Ibid.*: 37).

Throughout the House and Senate debates on the Civil Rights Act, particularly on Title VII, speakers highlighted the disparity in income, employment, training, and educational opportunities between Blacks and whites. Improving the economic status of African Americans was a priority of Title VII. Conservatives, however, opposed this section of the act, preferring a narrower focus on compensation of victims of discrimination and expressing concern with an expansion of federal power (*Ibid.*: 31). Supporters of Title VII stated repeatedly that "nondiscrimination in employment alone was not enough to solve the economic problems of Blacks, but that any solution had to work toward a redistribution of Blacks throughout the job market" (*Ibid.*: 35).

After passage of the 1964 Civil Rights Act, one of the first express uses of the term was President Johnson's Executive Order No. 11246, which required federal contractors to "take affirmative action to ensure that applicants are employed and that employees are treated during employment without regard to their race, color, sex or national origin" (Edmonds, 1994: 22).

The Civil Rights Act was followed by the Voting Rights Act of 1965 and the Federal Housing Act of 1968. Interestingly enough, it was Nixon's Department of Labor, under George Shultz, that issued another order in 1970, mandating companies to create goals and timetables (later criticized for establishing quotas) for the increased hiring of minorities, and later women (Seligman, 1994).

A 1972 amendment to Title VII expanded its coverage to include companies of 15 or more employees, provided for minority set-asides for contracts for companies that received federal funds, an end to discrimination in education where federal funds were involved, and equal employment opportunity programs to provide for employment, training, and promotion in the business sector.

A report issued by the Senate Labor and Public Welfare Committee during the debate over the 1972 Amendment of Title VII (which created the Equal Employment Opportunity Commission) found that the Civil Rights Act was not effective enough in eliminating discrimination and that:

> ... while some progress has been made toward bettering the economic position of the Nation's black population, *the avowed goal of social and economic equality is not yet anywhere near a reality* (Greene, 1989: 52, emphasis added).

The Historical Context of the Passage of the Civil Rights Act

Many factors contributed to the passage of the Civil Rights Act. The attacks on peaceful protesters and the deaths of the children in Birmingham, as well as the growth of a broad-based Civil Rights Movement, created a moral imperative to pass a law guaranteeing the rights of Black Americans. Black people were finally able to register to vote and were developing political power as a voting bloc. This fact, in addition to the fear of social unrest if the demand for civil rights was not met, was not lost on the Democratic Party, which relied on the New Deal Coalition, including labor and people of color, to achieve power.

More important, the United States was in a period of economic expansion and needed a growing working class. It was possible to open up employment to previously excluded groups of people because it was thought that there would be an unlimited number of jobs for years to come. In fact, in the mid-1960s, an open-door immigration policy was developed, leading to an influx of poor and working-class people and their families. Furthermore, in the context of the Cold War, the United States did not wish to be vulnerable to Soviet accusations of racism. Therefore, the conjuncture of all of these factors made the 1960s an opportune time to press for and win policies to guarantee the rights of African Americans and other people of color.

An additional factor was the growing acceptance of the responsibility of government to redress discriminatory practices. While conservative economists argued that market forces alone would eventually open up the job market to people of color (Brimelow and Spencer, 1993; Green, 1981: Chapter 7), liberals maintained that government had to mandate employers and educational institutions to take affirmative acts to guarantee that discrimination would be eliminated (Greene, 1989). This was an extension of the activist role the government had played during the Depression.

The Civil Rights Movement supported affirmative action for several reasons. Without federally sanctioned policies to end discrimination against women and people of color, their access to America's prosperity would be even more difficult to obtain. As Audre Lorde stated, "institutionalized rejection of difference is an absolute necessity in a profit economy which needs outsiders as surplus people" (quoted in West, 1993: 63). In addition, if Black poverty was seen as being primarily due to an unequal distribution of wealth, power, and income, then it was important to promote redistributive measures, such as affirmative action, that would reduce that inequality and enhance the standard of living and quality of life of the Black community (*Ibid.*: Chapter 5).

However, according to West (1993), affirmative action was neither the solution to poverty nor a sufficient guarantee of equality. Because they do not challenge the roots of inequality, redistributive measures such as affirmative action are "a compromise with and concession from the caretakers of American prosperity—that is, big business and big government" (*Ibid.*: 63). This viewpoint is shared by Derrick Bell (1992:53), who also maintains that: "Whatever the civil rights law or constitutional provision, blacks gain little protection against one or another form of racial discrimination unless granting blacks a measure of relief will serve some interest of importance to whites."

THE ROLE OF THE COURT IN THE ATTACK ON AFFIRMATIVE ACTION

Title VII did not define what was meant by discrimination; this job fell to the courts. Early decisions by the U.S. Supreme Court developed three types of discrimination: disparate treatment (focusing on specific cases of discrimination), present effects of past discrimination, and adverse impact (Greene, 1989: 60). Adverse impact, which is based on racial imbalances in employment categories, opened the door to affirmative action remedies. Such remedies initially focused on individual victims of discrimination, but by the 1970s, "almost every circuit court had approved of race-conscious remedies" (*Ibid.*: 63).

The first volley in the legal attack on affirmative action occurred in 1976 when Allan Bakke sued the University of California Medical School at Davis for denying him admission in favor of Black candidates who he alleged were less qualified academically (Greene, 1989; Navarrette, Jr., 1993). Bakke maintained that since 16 out of 100 places in the medical school class were reserved for economically and educationally disadvantaged applicants, this violated his Fourteenth Amendment right to equal protection. Bakke was the first to argue that this was reverse racism—that is, that white men were being discriminated against and minorities were given preferential treatment.

The Supreme Court ruled in favor of Bakke, holding that the policy of reserving specified spots was a quota system and was illegal. However, the Court also said that race could be included as a factor in determining admission, as long as it was not the exclusive basis on which a decision was made. The Court ignored the fact that the "white race had in fact the power and advantages and that, notwithstanding the 14th Amendment, the black race has for decades been denied entry into California's medical schools" (Bell, 1992: 102). The holdings in the Bakke decision were to become the basis on which an entire ideological campaign was advanced to attack and weaken affirmative action policies in the years to come.

The *Croson* Decision

In 1989, another Supreme Court ruling further weakened affirmative action. In *The City of Richmond* v. *J. A. Croson,* the Court rejected minority set-asides in awarding municipal contracts. The City of Richmond maintained that "local, state, and national patterns of discrimination had resulted in all but complete lack of access for minority-owned businesses" (Williams, 1991: 104–105) and had required that 30% of the contracts be awarded to Black or minority contractors. Croson, a contractor, sued the city. The Court ruled that:

> the city has failed to demonstrate a *compelling* interest in apportioning public contracting opportunities on the basis of race. To accept Richmond's claim that past societal discrimination alone can serve as the basis for rigid racial preferences would be to open the door to competing claims for "remedial relief" for *every* disadvantaged group. The dream of a Nation of equal citizens in a society where race is irrelevant to personal opportunity and achievement would be lost in a mosaic of shifting preferences based on *inherently unmeasurable* claims of past wrongs (*Ibid.*: 105, emphasis added).

A few months after the *Croson* decision, the Court made additional rulings that threatened affirmative action policies. In *Martin* v. *Wilks,* the Court held that consent decrees setting goals for the hiring of Black firefighters in Birmingham, Alabama, were allowed to be challenged by those injured by the goals, that is, by white firefighters (*Ibid.*: 106).

The lawyer representing the City of Birmingham minced no words when he said: "I think whites have correctly perceived the new attitude of the U.S. Supreme Court, which seems to be giving encouragement to white citizens to challenge black gains in virtually every aspect of social and economic life" (*Ibid.*: 107).

ATTACKS ON RACE-BASED SCHOLARSHIPS

Scholarship programs designed to make higher education more accessible to students of color have also come under attack both in the courts and in government policy. Although most scholarship assistance is provided on the basis of need, many colleges and universities supplement this aid by other grants, some of which are awarded specifically to students of color. Although there are relatively few race-exclusive scholarships, accounting for only four percent of undergraduate scholarship funds and 14% of graduate funds (McClendon, 1994), they have become "a lightning rod for those opposed to affirmative action programs" (De Witt, 1991).

In 1990, organizers of the Fiesta Bowl, a college football championship game, offered a $100,000 scholarship fund for students of color from the two universities playing in the game (Marriott, 1990). This gesture was made because the game was being held in Arizona, a state that refused to recognize the holiday for Martin Luther King, Jr. Michael L. Williams, Assistant Secretary of Education for Civil Rights under President Bush, stated that such race-based scholarships were discriminatory and illegal, and institutions that offered such scholarships could lose their federal grants. Immediate protests forced the administration to back down while it reviewed existing policy. At the end of 1991, the administration proposed a ban on scholarships based exclusively on race except under specific circumstances. Race could be one factor among others in awarding scholarships and race-exclusive scholarships would be permitted only when used to remedy a proven history of past discrimination, when Congress specifically created them, or when the funds were from a private source (*Ibid.*).

A conservative public interest lawyer expressed his approval of the Bush ruling by asserting that, "the cycle of racial discrimination has got to be brought to an end if we are ever going to achieve the idea of a color-blind society" (De Witt, 1991). From this perspective, a color-blind society could only refer to the "good old days," when the dominance of white men was unchallenged.

In November 1994, a scholarship for African American students at the University of Maryland was struck down by a federal court as discriminatory (McClendon, 1994; Maxwell, 1994). The university, which is appealing this decision, provided detailed evidence of the history of past discrimination at the school, which justifies the continuation of a scholarship program to attract and support Black students. This case is also significant because it was brought by a Latino student, revealing the intense competition among ethnic groups for scholarships because of the scarcity of resources that would allow people of color to pursue higher education.

PUBLIC OPPOSITION TO AFFIRMATIVE ACTION

Business leaders have grown increasingly resentful of affirmative action policies. While conveniently ignoring factors such as international competition and a long-term recession, they blame affirmative action for a decline in U.S. productivity, undermining the economy, and adding to the cost of business due to being forced to hire "less competent" people (Brimelow and Spencer, 1993). They claim that qualified white male workers are being displaced by incompetent minorities and women and insist that "merit" and the pursuit of diversity are mutually exclusive concepts (McCoy, 1994). Corporations complain about the costs associated with complying with affirmative action policies to absorb Black workers and other previously excluded groups into the labor force (Brimelow and Spencer, 1993).

Affirmative action policies have been met with strong opposition by white people who are afraid they will not obtain jobs or their children will not be admitted into college. These fears intensified as the economy deteriorated, unemployment grew, and competition for jobs and affordable housing increased. As they worry more about their own economic futures, recent polls indicate that for the first time, slightly more than 50% of whites believe that efforts to improve the lives of people of color have "gone too far" (Fulwood, 1994). The fear tactic was used by Jesse Helms in 1990, when he came from behind to win an election against a Black opponent after airing a campaign ad showing a white person who lost his job to a Black man (Navarrette, Jr., 1993: 9).

Since the beginning of the economic downturn in the mid-1970s, opposition has grown to redistributive government policies that had been more acceptable when the economy was booming. Stagnant incomes, declining numbers of manufacturing jobs, and increases in marginal tax rates, combined with the perception of accelerating welfare dependency, illegitimacy, and crime and drug abuse, have made the struggle for public resources and benefits increasingly bitter and irreconcilable (Edsall and Edsall, 1991: 73).

Between 1964 and 1974, the economy pushed the earnings of both Blacks and whites steadily upward. Income differentials were reduced and there was a convergence of shared prosperity and growing racial equality (*Ibid.*: 81). Once the economy faltered, these trends were reversed. Now, "black gains are seen as a cost to whites, and white advantages are seen as a manifestation of racism" by Blacks. White people believe that Blacks are responsible for the problems they face; Black people believe their problems stem from a system based on racism and inequality (*Ibid.*: 84).

As mentioned above, an initiative is underway that would end affirmative action in California. Opportunistically entitled the "California Civil Rights Initiative," it holds that the state cannot discriminate against or grant preferential treatment to any group in public employment, education, or contracting. Claiming to "restore the meaning of civil rights," the initiative's creators emphasize individual liberty over group rights and entitlements. They talk about "overturning racial and sexual discrimination" without specifying that it is white men they wish to protect. Supporters such as Patrick Buchanan and William Buckley are overjoyed at the prospect of this initiative winning in California and being replicated throughout the country (Dellios, 1994; Greenberg, 1994; CCRI, 1994).

The Bell Curve

Coming in the midst of the attack on affirmative action, the publication of *The Bell Curve: Intelligence and Class Structure in American Life,* by Charles Murray and Richard Herrnstein, is dangerous because the authors try to use "scientific assertions of black inferiority to change public policy in America"

(Rowan, 1994). In an earlier work refuting similar assertions about the genetic inferiority of Black people by Arthur Jensen, Philip Green (1981: 18) stated:

> ... the alleged authority of "science" is placed squarely behind the notion that it is not just politically questionable but practically futile to propose collective social action to eliminate or attenuate the major inequalities that divide us, to redistribute social goods.

The covert purpose behind the questionable research of people like Jensen, Murray, and Herrnstein is that they offer irrefutable support for the status quo. By playing into the racist stereotypes and fears of the white majority, "they make whatever is appear natural and therefore right" (*Ibid.*: 17) in an effort to substitute social prejudice for social science (p. 26; see Green, 1981, for an in-depth expose of the fallacies in these arguments).

Conservative Black Views

Jumping into the fray against affirmative action has been a group of Black conservative scholars, including Shelby Steele, Glenn Loury, Stephen Carter, and Thomas Sowell. One of Steele's concerns is that affirmative action encourages feelings of inferiority in African Americans because of assumptions by white people that Black people were hired or admitted to a program due to a policy of racial preference, rather than ability (Steele, 1989). These blanket stereotypes plague people of color in every workplace and school, whether there is affirmative action or not, often leading to internalized racism that can undermine opportunities even when they do exist.

Steele emphasizes the personal responsibility of individuals to improve their lives and downplays both the role of racism in society and the structural barriers that hold people back. He blames affirmative action for the assumption that Black people are incompetent, but that assumption predates those policies. "Black Americans were not vilified and despised throughout most of this country's history because of affirmative action, but because of racism" (Payton, 1991).

Steele maintains that preference policies "rob the entire race of their power. I don't need help; I need fairness." He also believes that instead of affirmative action programs, you "ask the society to invest major resources in the development of deprived people" (Clayton, 1991: 14). His views are misguided in that white society has continually shown that it is not committed to fairness. Lacking such policies, people of color would continue to be excluded from employment and education. In addition, funding for social programs is under increasing attack because the dominant society is less inclined to provide assistance to those in need, particularly if they are not white.

Steele goes on to say that "you cannot have a group of preferred and another group who are unpreferred without stigmatizing the preferred," in this case people of color (*Ibid.*). Again, he overlooks the entire course of history in which whites have received preferential treatment, but have never been stigmatized for it. Implicit in this kind of critique is the assumption that while "it's never painful to be rewarded because you are in the majority ... it's always painful to be rewarded because you're in the minority or a marginal group" (Green, 1981: 186). Finally, Steele calls for "individual effort within the American mainstream—rather than collective action against the mainstream" to become "our means of advancement" (Williams, 1990).

Black conservatives assume that without affirmative action programs, white Americans will make choices on the basis of merit rather than race. However, Cornel West (1993: 52) believes that "affirmative action policies were political responses to the pervasive refusal of most white Americans to judge black Americans on that basis" and that "black conservative rhetoric about race-free hiring criteria (usually coupled with a call for dismantling affirmative action mechanisms) does no more than justify actual practices of racial discrimination."

Because analysts like Steele reinforce the opinions of white conservative policymakers, they are given a great deal of publicity and prominence in the mass media as the "true representatives" of the African American community.

MYTHS BEHIND THE ATTACKS
ON AFFIRMATIVE ACTION

Why have the attacks on affirmative action been successful in convincing the public that such policies are flawed and should be eliminated? To answer this, we must look behind the myths put forward to justify the attack on affirmative action.

The most important myth is that everyone in this country has an equal opportunity to succeed. In a recent poll, 60% of white people felt that people of color have the same opportunities as whites, while 70% of Black people disagreed (Fulwood, 1994). White people easily find this myth believable primarily because they refuse to view society in a historical context. Entertaining such a belief today—that everyone has an equal chance to enter college, get a job, be hired as a contractor, or live wherever they would like—ignores centuries of inequality in education, training, and preparation for work, as well as centuries of racist stereotypes depicting Black people, and other people of color, as inherently inferior. As Roger Wilkins (1995) put it, " ... blacks and whites remember America differently."

Affirmative action is mainly an attempt to level the playing field for disadvantaged people who are trying to compete under these conditions. The issue is deliberately confused by opponents who say that if discrimination by whites against Black people is unfair, then surely it is equally unfair to justify discrimination against whites by giving preferential treatment to people of color. Only by ignoring the context of history and the persistence of racism in this country, however, is it possible to equate the two situations (Fish, 1993).

Historically, the majority of white people have benefited from admissions and employment policies. Action to redress these inequalities is necessary because they will not change on their own. "To equate the efforts to remedy the plight with the actions that produced it is to twist history.... [T]he illness of racism is not equal to the therapy we use to redress it" (*Ibid.*). What is fair to each group—people of color and white people—must be considered in relation to the cultural and institutional histories of each group and how they have affected one another.

Directness is important when stating that affirmative action is based on unequal treatment based on race or gender, which can clearly lead individuals to consider themselves the "innocent victims" of such policies. Opponents of affirmative action emphasize that the infringement on *individual* rights "cannot be justified by the desire to advance the well-being of any ethnic group ... " (Green, 1981: 176). However, in an effort to build a society based on real and not merely formal equality, it is valid to protect the rights of groups of people to make up for a history and ongoing pattern of discrimination. How else are victims "ever to compete on truly equal terms with those who have victimized them for generations ... " (*Ibid.*: 187)? Those who oppose affirmative action are not interested in eliminating inequality. By longing for a time when the "individual" was what counted, they are conveniently ignoring the fact that it always mattered whether an individual was white or Black, male or female, rich or poor; and that opportunities in life are available based on those factors. They argue in favor of rolling back policies to the time when better-off white males did not have to contend with the intrusions of people of color or women.

Another underlying assumption of those who oppose affirmative action is that the opposite of a race-based policy is a race-neutral policy, that somehow the United States can operate on the color-blind assumption that race should not and cannot be a factor. Patricia Williams (1991: 48) explains that:

> Race-neutrality in law has become the presumed antidote for race bias in real life. With the entrenchment of the notion of race-neutrality came attacks on the concept of affirmative action and the rise of reverse discrimination suits. Blacks, for so many generations deprived of jobs based on the color of our skin, are now told that we ought to find it demeaning to be hired, based on the color of our skin.

Furthermore, employers hesitate to hire Black workers who are viewed as too confrontational because they raise racial issues, which the white majority does not wish to confront. A white employer often feels more comfortable hiring a white person, even if that person is less qualified than an applicant of color. Over the years, various studies have proved this to be the case. In one case, white and Black applicants were given equal credentials and sent out to look for jobs and rent apartments. In nearly every case, the white applicant was given preferential treatment (Fish, 1993).

Opponents of affirmative action also maintain that hiring policies based on "merit" are diametrically opposed to policies based on affirmative action, despite the fact that merit and standards of qualifications are often applied haphazardly. College admissions and employment are often based on personal connections or financial contributions to an institution, on geographical diversity, or on whether an applicant is a veteran. In fact, affirmative action plays the same role for people of color that patronage played for waves of immigrants from Ireland and Southern Europe (Edsall and Edsall, 1991). There have always been preferences, yet no one ever said they "lowered quality" until they began to be applied for the benefit of people of color. This attitude reflects the underlying persistence of racism and the belief that people of color are basically inferior, while white students and workers are assumed to be competent and superior.

In the ideological attack on affirmative action, merit and qualification standards are used as a smoke screen to justify a return to making decisions based on personal preference, which also reinforces racist stereotypes and patterns of institutional racism. Because so many unspoken factors go into determining "merit," Green (1981: 174–175) concludes that "there are no 'objective' criteria of merit such that it is wrong to 'discriminate' in favor of people who fulfill them, or right to 'discriminate' against those who do not." Merit is determined by those in positions of authority to justify their hiring policies.

Williams (1991: 103) goes on to say that:

> The whole historical object of equal opportunity, formal or informal, is to structure preferences for rather than against—to like rather than dislike—the participation of black people. Thus affirmative action is very different from numerical quotas that actively structure society so that certain classes of people remain unpreferred. "Quotas," "preference," "reverse discrimination," "experienced," and "qualified" are con words.... As a society, we have yet to look carefully beneath them to see where the seeds of prejudice are truly hidden.

Furthermore, opponents of affirmative action maintain that standardized qualifications should be based on test scores, grade point average, or other measurable standards. Despite evidence that many tests are culturally biased and inadequate, testing is still touted as providing an objective assessment of competence. The overreliance on test results also inhibits employers or admissions officers from considering other factors that indicate competence. There is a need to develop alternative methods for assessing ability that expand the range of qualifications to be considered. It has been found that there is only a modest relationship between test scores and college performance or professional achievement. Test scores also predict differently and less well for different populations, so that undue reliance on them is misplaced (Olivas, 1993: 20).

Finally, the fact is rarely acknowledged that "in a democratic, multiracial society, integrated institutions can provide higher levels of service than agencies run entirely by one race and sex" (Rockwell, 1989). For example, one study in Detroit found that after affirmative action policies resulted in an increased percentage of Black policemen on the police force, there was a significant improvement in relations between the police and the community. White officers who opposed implementing these policies did so not because they were guarding "high standards of service," but because they were protecting the "white buddy system" (*Ibid.*).

FIGHTING FOR AFFIRMATIVE ACTION IN THE FACE OF RACISM

The November 1994 elections emphasized that this country is divided along race and class lines. The polarization is so deep that not only are whites moving to the suburbs, they are also moving from states with a high percentage of people of color to those with less immigration and urban conflict (Tilove and Hallinan, 1993).

Three decades after the passage of the Civil Rights Act, racism is as integral a part of our society's institutional and private life as it ever was. It persists in the unquestioned assumptions that white people are competent and superior and people of color are incompetent and inferior; that white society must be protected from the demands of disadvantaged people for benefits they do not deserve; that undeserving people of color have already benefited too much at the expense of "innocent" white men. In the face of this reality, according to Green (1981: 198), "the demand of previously excluded groups to the suspension ... of the traditional rules in order to further their inclusion on equal terms into the polity is a demand that society undergo a moral revolution."

The right-wing attack on affirmative action is an attack on the fundamental concept of an egalitarian society and implies an acceptance of living in a racialized society where people are assigned their place according to race. Charles Murray's views and the Republican program for welfare "reform," along with other aspects of the Contract with America, exemplify a modified Darwinian notion that only the strong should survive and the weak (defined in various ways as the "other") neither deserve nor are "entitled" to any help in competing with the dominant society.

Progressive Black activists and scholars are critical of affirmative action because it has not gone far enough in addressing racial inequality, or because they see in these policies an overreliance on the legal system to address the endemic nature of racism in society. Derrick Bell (1992) and Patricia Williams (1991) recognize the importance of defending the principles of affirmative action while decrying the policy's overall limitations.

They also challenge the effectiveness of legal battles in attempting to protect the rights of people of color. In discussing the effort to achieve formal equal opportunity, Williams (*Ibid.*: 120) raises the fundamental contradiction:

> The rules may be color-blind, but people are not. The question remains, therefore, whether the law can truly exist apart from the color-conscious society in which it exists, as a skeleton devoid of flesh; or whether law is the embodiment of society, the reflection of a particular citizenry's arranged complexity of relations.

According to Bell (1992: 60), the goal of racial equality is illusory for Blacks who have worked for substantive reform, only to settle for less. He remains critical of laws (and fighting for laws) that "provide us the promise of protection without either the will or the resources to honor that promise." Bell calls for more self-reliance within the Black community and an increasing awareness of the limitations of struggling for social change within the legal system of this society.

However, despite the limitations of using the legal and legislative arenas as means to achieving equality, it is too dangerous to concede these methods or cease the fight to preserve the protections that currently exist. Cornel West (1993) maintains that progressives must cling to redistributive ideals and fight for policies that conform to those ideals, despite their weaknesses. Affirmative action is not the most effective mechanism to achieve Black progress in the United States, but it is part of a redistributive chain that must be strengthened if Black poverty is to be eliminated (*Ibid.*). Because of the persistence of discrimination and the lack of good will and commitment to redistribution within white America, the fight to save affirmative action policies from extinction is critical (*Ibid.*). However, this struggle must be waged in the context of a broader strategy for social change that unites people of color and all progressive people to work together to prevent the elimination of affirmative action. If this effort fails, the fight for equality and social justice in this country will be set back for years to come.

PART TWO

Theoretical Orientations to the Study of Race and Ethnicity in the United States

On the Internet . . .

Sites appropriate to Part Two

Founded in 1946, the American Immigration Lawyers Association (AILA) is a national bar association of over 5,200 attorneys who practice and teach immigration law. At this site, you can access general background about immigration, descriptions of the services that immigration lawyers provide, and updates on the latest changes to immigration-related laws and regulations.

    http://www.aila.org/

This is an experimental Black cultural studies site created to increase access to resources about ethnicity, race, and gender among populations of the African diaspora. The site lists bibliographical information on cultural workers in such areas as Black literary criticism, Black popular culture, critical race theory, and film theory.

    http://www.tiac.net/users/thaslett/

The bipartisan U.S. Commission on Immigration Reform was created to review and evaluate the implementation and impact of U.S. immigration policy and to transmit to Congress reports of its findings and recommendations. This is a useful site on which to begin research on immigration reform policies and legislation.

    http://www.utexas.edu./lbj/uscir/

This site offers the latest information on immigration law, employment verification, and naturalization. It also provides access to annual statistical reports and downloadable application forms.

    http://www.ins.usdoj.gov/index.html

4.1 MILTON M. GORDON

Assimilation in America: Theory and Reality

Assimilation refers to a process of accommodation by which members of minority groups are absorbed or integrated into a society's dominant or core culture. In this process, racially or ethnically diverse groups of people adapt and become indistinguishable from the dominant group.

This selection explores the dynamics of intergroup relations in American society from three conceptual models—Anglo-conformity, the melting pot thesis, and cultural pluralism. In his now classic work, Milton M. Gordon treats these conceptual models as ideologies of ethnic assimilation and suggests that they bear far-reaching consequences for ethnic diversity in American society.

Key Concept: assimilation theory

Three ideologies or conceptual models have competed for attention on the American scene as explanations of the way in which a nation, in the beginning largely white, Anglo-Saxon, and Protestant, has absorbed over 41 million immigrants and their descendants from variegated sources and welded them into the contemporary American people. These ideologies are Anglo-conformity, the melting pot, and cultural pluralism....

The story of America's immigration can be quickly told for our present purposes. The white American population at the time of the Revolution was largely English and Protestant in origin, but had already absorbed substantial groups of Germans and Scotch-Irish and smaller contingents of Frenchmen,

Dutchmen, Swedes, Swiss, South Irish, Poles, and a handful of migrants from other European nations. Catholics were represented in modest numbers, particularly in the middle colonies, and a small number of Jews were residents of the incipient nation. With the exception of the Quakers and a few missionaries, the colonists had generally treated the Indians and their cultures with contempt and hostility, driving them from the coastal plains and making the western frontier a bloody battleground where eternal vigilance was the price of survival.

Although the Negro at that time made up nearly one-fifth of the total population, his predominantly slave status, together with racial and cultural prejudice, barred him from serious consideration as an assimilable element of the society. And while many groups of European origin started out as determined ethnic enclaves, eventually, most historians believe, considerable ethnic intermixture within the white population took place. "People of different blood" [sic]—write two American historians about the colonial period, "English, Irish, German, Huguenot, Dutch Swedish-mingled and intermarried with little thought of any difference."[1] In such a society, its people predominantly English, its white immigrants of other ethnic origins either English-speaking or derived largely from countries of northern and western Europe whose cultural divergences from the English were not great, and its dominant white population excluding by fiat the claims and considerations of welfare of the non-Caucasian minorities, the problem of assimilation understandably did not loom unduly large or complex....

ANGLO-CONFORMITY

"Anglo-conformity"[2] is a broad term used to cover a variety of viewpoints about assimilation and immigration; they all assume the desirability of maintaining English institutions (as modified by the American Revolution), the English language, and English-oriented cultural patterns as dominant and standard in American life. However, bound up with this assumption are related attitudes. These may range from discredited notions about race and "Nordic"and "Aryan" racial superiority, together with the nativist political programs and exclusionist immigration policies which such notions entail, through an intermediate position of favoring immigration from northern and western Europe on amorphous, unreflective grounds ("They are more like us"), to a lack of opposition to any source of immigration, as long as these immigrants and their descendants duly adopt the standard Anglo-Saxon cultural patterns. There is by no means any necessary equation between Anglo-conformity and racist attitudes.

It is quite likely that "Anglo-conformity" in its more moderate aspects, however explicit its formulation, has been the most prevalent ideology of assimilation goals in America throughout the nation's history. As far back as colonial times, Benjamin Franklin recorded concern about the clannishness of the Germans in Pennsylvania, their slowness in learning English, and the establishment of their own native-language press.[3] ...

*Milton M.
Gordon*

The attitudes of Americans toward foreign immigration in the first three-quarters of the nineteenth century may correctly be described as ambiguous. On the one hand, immigrants were much desired, so as to swell the population and importance of states and territories, to man the farms of expanding prairie settlement, to work the mines, build the railroads and canals, and take their place in expanding industry. This was a period in which no federal legislation of any consequence prevented the entry of aliens, and such state legislation as existed attempted to bar on an individual basis only those who were likely to become a burden on the community, such as convicts and paupers. On the other hand, the arrival in an overwhelmingly Protestant society of large numbers of poverty-stricken Irish Catholics, who settled in groups in the slums of Eastern cities, roused dormant fears of "Popery" and Rome. Another source of anxiety was the substantial influx of Germans, who made their way to the cities and farms of the mid-West and whose different language, separate communal life, and freer ideas on temperance and sabbath observance brought them into conflict with the Anglo-Saxon bearers of the Puritan and Evangelical traditions. Fear of foreign "radicals" and suspicion of the economic demands of the occasionally aroused workingmen added fuel to the nativist fires. In their extreme form these fears resulted in the Native-American movement of the 1830s and 1840s and the "American" or "Know-Nothing" party of the 1850s, with their anti-Catholic campaigns and their demands for restrictive laws on naturalization procedures and for keeping the foreign-born out of political office. While these movements scored local political successes and their turbulences so rent the national social fabric that the patches are not yet entirely invisible, they failed to influence national legislative policy on immigration and immigrants; and their fulminations inevitably provoked the expected reactions from thoughtful observers.

The flood of newcomers to the westward expanding nation grew larger, reaching over one and two-thirds million between 1841 and 1850 and over two and one-half million in the decade before the Civil War. Throughout the entire period, quite apart from the excesses of the Know-Nothings, the predominant (though not exclusive) conception of what the ideal immigrant adjustment should be was probably summed up in a letter written in 1818 by John Quincy Adams, then Secretary of State, in answer to the inquiries of the Baron von Fürstenwaerther. If not the earliest, it is certainly the most elegant version of the sentiment, "If they don't like it here, they can go back where they came from." Adams declared:[4]

They [immigrants to America] come to life of independence, but to a life of labor —and, if they cannot accommodate themselves to the character, moral, political and physical, of this country with all its compensating balances of good and evil, the Atlantic is always open to them to return to the land of their nativity and their fathers. To one thing they must make up their minds, or they will be disappointed in every expectation of happiness as Americans. They must cast off the European skin, never to resume it. They must look forward to their posterity rather than backward to their ancestors; they must be sure that whatever their own feelings may be, those of their children will cling to the prejudices of this country....

Anglo-conformity received its fullest expression in the so-called Americanization which gripped the nation during World War I. While "Americanization" in its various stages had more than one emphasis, it was essentially a consciously articulated movement to strip the immigrant of his native culture and attachments and make him over into an American along Anglo-Saxon lines—all this to be accomplished with great rapidity. To use an image of a later day, it was an attempt at "pressure-cooking assimilation." It had prewar antecedents, but it was during the height of the world conflict that federal agencies, state governments, municipalities, and a host of private organizations joined in the effort to persuade the immigrant to learn English, take out naturalization papers, buy war bonds, forget his former origins and culture, and give himself over to patriotic hysteria.

After the war and the "Red scare" which followed, the excesses of the Americanization movement subsided. In its place, however, came the restriction of immigration through federal law. Foiled at first by presidential vetoes, and later by the failure of the 1917 literacy test to halt the immigrant tide, the proponents of restriction finally put through in the early 1920s a series of acts culminating in the well-known national-origins formula for immigrant quotas which went into effect in 1929. Whatever the merits of a quantitative limit on the number of immigrants to be admitted to the United States, the provisions of the formula, which discriminated sharply against the countries of southern and eastern Europe, in effect institutionalized the assumptions of the rightful dominance of Anglo-Saxon patterns in the land. Reaffirmed with only slight modifications in the McCarran-Walter Act of 1952, these laws, then, stand as a legal monument to the creed of Anglo-conformity and a telling reminder that this ideological system still has numerous and powerful adherents on the American scene.

THE MELTING POT

While Anglo-conformity in various guises has probably been the most prevalent ideology of assimilation in the American historical experience, a competing viewpoint with more generous and idealistic overtones has had its adherents and exponents from the eighteenth century onward. Conditions in the virgin continent, it was clear, were modifying the institutions which the English colonists brought with them from the mother country. Arrivals from non-English homelands such as Germany, Sweden, and France were similarly exposed to this fresh environment. Was it not possible, then, to think of the evolving American society not as a slightly modified England but rather as a totally new blend, culturally and biologically, in which the stocks and folkways of Europe, figuratively speaking, were indiscriminately mixed in the political pot of the emerging nation and fused by the fires of American influence and interaction into a distinctly new type?

Such, at any rate, was the conception of the new society which motivated that eighteenth-century French-born writer and agriculturalist, J. Hector St. John de Crèvecoeur, who, after many years of American residence, published his reflections and observations in *Letters from an American Farmer*.[5] Who, he asks, is the American?

> He is either an European, or the descendant of an European, hence that strange mixture of blood, which you will find in no other country. I could point out to you a family whose grandfather was an Englishman, whose wife was Dutch, whose son married a French woman, and whose present four sons have now four wives of different nations. He is an American, who leaving behind him all his ancient prejudices and manners, receives new ones from the new mode of life he has embraced, the new government he obeys, and the new rank he holds. He becomes an American by being received in the broad lap of our great Alma Mater. Here individuals of all nations are melted into a new race of men, whose labours and posterity will one day cause great changes in the world.

Some observers have interpreted the open-door policy on immigration of the first three-quarters of the nineteenth century as reflecting an underlying faith in the effectiveness of the American melting pot, in the belief "that all could be absorbed and that all could contribute to an emerging national character."[6] No doubt many who observed with dismay the nativist agitation of the times felt as did Ralph Waldo Emerson that such conformity-demanding and immigrant-hating forces represented a perversion of the best American ideals. In 1845, Emerson wrote in his Journal:[7]

> I hate the narrowness of the Native American Party. It is the dog in the manger. It is precisely opposite to all the dictates of love and magnanimity; and therefore, of course, opposite to true wisdom.... Man is the most composite of all creatures.... Well, as in the old burning of the Temple at Corinth, by the melting and inter-mixture of silver and gold and other metals a new compound more precious than any, called Corinthian brass, was formed: so in this continent,—asylum of all nations,—the energy of Irish, Germans, Swedes, Poles, and Cossacks, and all the European tribes,—of the Africans, and the Polynesians,—will construct a new race, a new religion, a new state, a new literature, which will be as vigorous as the new Europe which came out of the smelting-pot of the Dark Ages, or that which earlier emerged from the Pelasgic and Etruscan barbarism. *La Nature aime les croisements....*

It remained for an English-Jewish writer with strong social convictions, moved by his observation of the role of the United States as a haven for the poor and oppressed of Europe, to give utterance to the broader view of the American melting pot in a way which attracted public attention. In 1908, Israel Zangwill's drama, *The Melting Pot,* was produced in this country and became a popular success. It is a play dominated by the dream of its protagonist, a young Russian-Jewish immigrant to America, a composer, whose goal is the completion of a vast "American" symphony which will express his deeply felt conception of his adopted country as a divinely appointed crucible in which all the ethnic division of mankind will divest themselves of their ancient animosities and differences and become fused into one group, signifying the brotherhood of man. In the process he falls in love with a beautiful and cultured Gentile girl. The play ends with the performance of the symphony and, after numerous vicissitudes and traditional family opposition from both sides, with the approaching marriage of David Quixano and his beloved. During the course of these developments, David, in the rhetoric of the time, delivers himself of such sentiments as these:[8]

> America is God's crucible, the great Melting Pot where all the races of Europe are melting and reforming! Here you stand, good folk, think I, when I see them at Ellis Island, here you stand in your fifty groups, with your fifty languages and histories, and your fifty blood hatreds and rivalries. But you won't be long like that, brother, for these are the fires of God you've come to—these are the fires of God. A fig for your feuds and vendettas! Germans and Frenchman, Irishmen and Englishmen, Jews and Russians—into the Crucible with you all! God is making the American.

Here we have a conception of a melting pot which admits of no exceptions or qualifications with regard to the ethnic stocks which will fuse in the great crucible. Englishmen, Germans, Frenchmen, Slavs, Greeks, Syrians, Jews, Gentiles, even the black and yellow races, were specifically mentioned in Zangwill's rhapsodic enumeration. And this pot patently was to boil in the great cities of America.

Thus around the turn of the century the melting-pot idea became embedded in the ideals of the age as one response to the immigrant receiving experience of the nation. Soon to be challenged by a new philosophy of group adjustment (to be discussed below) and always competing with the more pervasive adherence to Anglo-conformity, the melting-pot image, however, continued to draw a portion of the attention consciously directed toward this aspect of the American scene in the first half of the twentieth century. In the mid-1940s a sociologist who had carried out an investigation of intermarriage trends in New Haven, Connecticut, described a revised conception of the melting process in that city and suggested a basic modification of the theory of that process. In New Haven, Ruby Jo Reeves Kennedy[9] reported from a study of intermarriages from 1870 to 1940 that there was a distinct tendency for the British-Americans, Germans, and Scandinavians to marry among themselves—that is, within a Protestant "pool"; for the Irish, Italians, and Poles to marry among themselves —a Catholic "pool"; and for the Jews to marry other Jews. In other words, intermarriage was taking place across lines of nationality background, but there was a strong tendency for it to stay confined within one or the other of the three major religious groups, Protestants, Catholics, and Jews. Thus, declared Mrs. Kennedy, the picture in New Haven resembled a "triple melting pot" based on religious division, rather than a "single melting pot." Her study indicated, she stated, that "while strict endogamy is loosening, religious endogamy is persisting and the future cleavages will be along religious lines rather than along nationality lines as in the past. If this is the case, then the traditional 'single-melting-pot' idea must be abandoned, and a new conception, which we term the 'triple-melting-pot' theory of American assimilation, will take its place as the true expression of what is happening to the various nationality groups in the United States."[10] The triple melting-pot thesis was later taken up by the theologian Will Herberg, and formed an important sociological frame of reference for his analysis of religious trends in American society, *Protestant-Catholic-Jew.*[11]

But the triple melting-pot hypothesis patently takes us into the realm of a society pluralistically conceived. We turn now to the rise of an ideology which attempts to justify such a conception.

CULTURAL PLURALISM

Probably all the non-English immigrants who came to American shores in any significant numbers from colonial times onward—settling either in the forbidding wilderness, the lonely prairie, or in some accessible urban slum—created ethnic enclaves and looked forward to the preservation of at least some of their native cultural patterns. Such a development, natural as breathing, was supported by the later accretion of friends, relatives, and countrymen seeking out oases of familiarity in a strange land, by the desire of the settlers to rebuild (necessarily in miniature) a society in which they could communicate in the familiar tongue and maintain familiar institutions, and, finally, by the necessity to band together for mutual aid and mutual protection against the uncertainties of a strange and frequently hostile environment. This was as true of the "old" immigrants as of the "new." In fact, some of the liberal intellectuals who fled to America from an inhospitable political climate in Germany in the 1830s, 1840s, and 1850s looked forward to the creation of an all-German state within the union, or, even more hopefully, to the eventual formation of a separate German nation, as soon as the expected dissolution of the union under the impact of the slavery controversy should have taken place.[12] Oscar Handlin, writing of the sons of Erin in mid-nineteenth-century Boston, recent refugees from famine and economic degradation in their homeland, points out: "Unable to participate in the normal associational affairs of the community, the Irish felt obliged to erect a society within a society, to act together in their own way. In every contact therefore the group, acting apart from other sections of the community, became intensely aware of its peculiar and exclusive identity."[13] Thus cultural pluralism was a fact in American society before it became a theory—a theory with explicit relevance for the nation as a whole, and articulated and discussed in the English-speaking circles of American intellectual life.

Eventually, the cultural enclaves of the Germans (and the later arriving Scandinavians) were to decline in scope and significance as succeeding generations of their native-born attended public schools, left the farms and villages to strike out as individuals for the Americanizing city, and generally became subject to the influences of a standardizing industrial civilization. The German-American community, too, was struck a powerful blow by the accumulated passions generated by World War I—a blow from which it never fully recovered. The Irish were to be the dominant and pervasive element in the gradual emergence of a pan-Catholic group in America, but these developments would reveal themselves only in the twentieth century. In the meantime, in the last two decades of the nineteenth, the influx of immigrants from southern and eastern Europe had begun. These groups were all the more sociologically visible because the closing of the frontier, the occupational demands of an expanding industrial economy, and their own poverty made it inevitable that they would remain in the urban areas of the nation. In the swirling fires of controversy and the steadier flame of experience created by these new events, the ideology of cultural pluralism as a philosophy for the nation was forged.

The first manifestations of an ideological counterattack against draconic Americanization came not from the beleaguered newcomers (who were, after all, more concerned with survival than with theories of adjustment), but from those idealistic members of the middle class who, in the decade or so before the turn of the century, had followed the example of their English predecessors and "settled" in the slums to "learn to sup sorrow with the poor."[14] Immediately, these workers in the "settlement houses" were forced to come to grips with the realities of immigrant life and adjustment. Not all reacted in the same way, but on the whole the settlements developed an approach to the immigrant which was sympathetic to his native cultural heritage and to his newly created ethnic institutions.[15] For one thing, their workers, necessarily in intimate contact with the lives of these often pathetic and bewildered newcomers and their daily problems, could see how unfortunate were the effects of those forces which impelled rapid Americanization in their impact on the immigrants' children, who not infrequently became alienated from their parents and the restraining influence of family authority. Were not their parents ignorant and uneducated "Hunkies," "Sheenies," or "Dagoes," as that limited portion of the American environment in which they moved defined the matter? Ethnic "self-hatred" with its debilitating psychological consequences, family disorganization, and juvenile delinquency, were not unusual results of this state of affairs. Furthermore, the immigrants themselves were adversely affected by the incessant attacks on their cultures, their language, their institutions, their very conception of themselves. How were they to maintain their self-respect when all that they knew, felt, and dreamed, beyond their sheer capacity for manual labor—in other words, all that they *were*—was despised or scoffed at in America? And—unkindest cut of all—their own children had begun to adopt the contemptuous attitude of the "Americans." Jane Addams relates in a moving chapter of her *Twenty Years at Hull House* how, after coming to have some conception of the extent and depth of these problems, she created at the settlement a "Labor Museum," in which the immigrant women of the various nationalities crowded together in the slums of Chicago could illustrate their native methods of spinning and weaving, and in which the relation of these earlier techniques to contemporary factory methods could be graphically shown. For the first time these peasant women were made to feel by some part of their American environment that they possessed valuable and interesting skills—that they too had something to offer—and for the first time, the daughters of these women who, after a long day's work at their dank "needletrade" sweat-shops, came to Hull House to observe, began to appreciate the fact that their mothers, too, had a "culture," that this culture possessed its own merit, and that it was related to their own contemporary lives. How aptly Jane Addams concludes her chapter with the hope that "our American citizenship might be built without disturbing these foundations which were laid of old time."[16]

This appreciative view of the immigrant's cultural heritage and of its distinctive usefulness both to himself and his adopted country received additional sustenance from another source: those intellectual currents of the day which, however overborne by their currently more powerful opposites, emphasized liberalism, internationalism, and tolerance. From time to time an occasional educator or publicist protested the demands of the "Americanizers," arguing that the immigrant too, had an ancient and honorable culture, and that this culture had much to offer an America whose character and destiny were still in the process of formation, an America which must serve as an example of the harmonious cooperation of various heritages to a world inflamed by nationalism and war. In 1916 John Dewey, Norman Hapgood, and the young literary critic Randolph Bourne published articles or addresses elaborating various aspects of this theme.

The classic statement of the cultural pluralist position, however, had been made over a year before. Early in 1915 there appeared in the pages of The Nation two articles under the title "Democracy versus the Melting-Pot." Their author was Horace Kallen, a Harvard-educated philosopher with a concern for the application of philosophy to societal affairs, and, as an American Jew, himself derivative of an ethnic background which was subject to the contemporary pressures for dissolution implicit in the "Americanization," or Anglo-conformity, and the melting-pot theories. In these articles Kallen vigorously rejected the usefulness of these theories as models of what was actually transpiring in American life or as ideals for the future. Rather he was impressed by the way in which the various ethnic groups in America were coincident with particular areas and regions, and with the tendency for each group to preserve its own language, religion, communal institutions, and ancestral culture. All the while, he pointed out, the immigrant has been learning to speak English as the language of general communication, and has participated in the over-all economic and political life of the nation. These developments in which "the United States are in the process of becoming a federal state not merely as a union of geographical and administrative unities, but also as a cooperation of cultural diversities, as a federation or commonwealth of national cultures,"[17] the author argued, far from constituting a violation of historic American political principles, as the "Americanizers" claimed, actually represented the inevitable consequences of democratic ideals, since individuals are implicated in groups, and since democracy for the individual must by extension also mean democracy for his group.

The processes just described, however, as Kallen develops his argument, are far from having been thoroughly realized. They are menaced by "Americanization" programs, assumptions of Anglo-Saxon superiority, and misguided attempts to promote "racial" amalgamation. Thus America stands at a kind of cultural crossroads. It can attempt to impose by force an artificial, Anglo-Saxon oriented uniformity on its peoples, or it can consciously allow and encourage its ethnic groups to develop democratically, each emphasizing its particular cultural heritage. If the latter course is followed, as Kallen puts it at the close of his essay, then,[18]

The outlines of a possible great and truly democratic commonwealth become discernible. Its form would be that of the federal republic: its substance a democracy of nationalities, cooperating voluntarily and autonomously through common institutions in the enterprise of self-realization through the perfection of men according to their kind. The common language of the commonwealth, the language of its great tradition, would be English, but each nationality would have for its emotional and involuntary life its own peculiar dialect or speech, its own individual and inevitable esthetic and intellectual forms. The political and economic life of the commonwealth is a single unit and serves as the foundation and background for the realization of the distinctive individuality of each *nation* that composes it and of the pooling of these in a harmony above them all. Thus "American civilization" may come to mean the perfection of the cooperative harmonies of "European civilization"—the waste, the squalor and the distress of Europe being eliminated—a multiplicity in a unity, an orchestration of mankind.

Within the next decade Kallen published more essays dealing with the theme of American multiple-group life, later collected in a volume.[19] In the introductory note to this book he used for the first time the term "cultural pluralism" to refer to his position. These essays reflect both his increasingly sharp rejection of the onslaughts on the immigrant and his culture which the coming of World War I and its attendant fears, the "Red scare," the projection of themes of racial superiority, the continued exploitation of the newcomers, and the rise of the Ku Klux Klan all served to increase in intensity, and also his emphasis on cultural pluralism as the democratic antidote to these ills. He has since published other essays elaborating or annotating the theme of cultural pluralism. Thus, for at least forty-five years, most of them spent teaching at the New School for Social Research, Kallen has been acknowledged as the originator and leading philosophical exponent of the idea of cultural pluralism.

In the late 1930s and early 1940s the late Louis Adamic, the Yugoslav immigrant who had become an American writer, took up the theme of America's multicultural heritage and the role of these groups in forging the country's national character. Borrowing Walt Whitman's phrase, he described America as "a nation of nations," and while his ultimate goal was closer to the melting-pot idea than to cultural pluralism, he saw the immediate task as that of making America conscious of what it owed to all its ethnic groups, not just to the Anglo-Saxons. The children and grandchildren of immigrants of non-English origins, he was convinced, must be taught to be proud of the cultural heritage of their ancestral ethnic group and of its role in building the American nation; otherwise, they would not lose their sense of ethnic inferiority and the feeling of rootlessness he claimed to find in them.

Thus in the twentieth century, particularly since World War II, "cultural pluralism" has become a concept which has worked its way into the vocabulary and imagery of specialists in intergroup relations and leaders of ethnic communal groups. In view of this new pluralistic emphasis, some writers now prefer to speak of the "integration" of immigrants rather than of their "assimilation."[20] However, with a few exceptions,[21] no close analytical attention has been given either by social scientists or practitioners of intergroup relations to the meaning of cultural pluralism, its nature and relevance for a modern industrialized society, and its implications for problems of prejudice and discrimination.

1. Allen Nevins and Henry Steele Commager, *America: The Story of a Free People* (Boston, Little, Brown, 1942), p. 58.

2. The phrase is the Coles'. See Stewart G. Cole and Mildred Wiese Cole, *Minorities and the American Promise* (New York, Harper & Brothers, 1954), ch. 6.

3. Maurice R. Davie, *World Immigration* (New York, Macmillan, 1936), p. 36, and (cited therein) "Letter of Benjamin Franklin to Peter Collinson, 9th May, 1753, on the condition and character of the Germans in Pennsylvania," in *The World of Benjamin Franklin, with Notes and Life of the Author,* by Jared Sparks (Boston. 1828), vol. 7, pp. 71–73.

4. *Niles Weekly Register,* vol. 18, 29 April 1820, pp. 157–158; see also Marcus L. Hansen, *The Atlantic Migration, 1607–1860,* pp. 96–97.

5. J. Hector St. John de Crèvecoeur, *Letters from an American Farmer* (New York, Albert and Charles Boni, 1925; reprinted from the 1st edn., London, 1782), pp. 54–55.

6. Oscar Handlin, ed., *Immigration as a Factor in American History* (Englewood, Prentice-Hall, 1959), p. 146.

7. Quoted by Stuart P. Sherman in his Introduction to *Essays and Poems of Emerson* (New York, Harcourt Brace, 1921), p. xxxiv.

8. Israel Zangwill, *The Melting Pot* (New York, Macmillan, 1909), p. 37.

9. Ruby Jo Reeves Kennedy. "Single or Triple Melting-Pot? Intermarriage Trends in New Haven, 1870–1940," *American Journal of Sociology,* 1944, 49:331–339. See also her "Single or Triple Melting-Pot? Intermarriage in New Haven, 1870–1950," *ibid.,* 1952, 58:56–59.

10. Kennedy, "Single or Triple Melting-Pot? . . . 1870–1940," p. 332 (author's italics omitted).

11. Will Herberg, *Protestant-Catholic-Jew* (Garden City, Doubleday, 1955).

12. Nathan Glazer, "Ethnic Groups in America: From National Culture to Ideology," in Morroe Berger, Theodore Abel, and Charles H. Page, eds., *Freedom and Control in Modern Society* (New York, D. Van Nostrand, 1954), p. 161; Marcus Lee Hansen, *The Immigrant in American History* (Cambridge, Harvard University Press, 1940), pp. 129–140; John A. Hawgood, *The Tragedy of German-America* (New York, Putnam's, 1940), *passim.*

13. Oscar Handlin, *Boston's Immigrants* (Cambridge, Harvard University Press, 1959, rev. edn.), p. 176.

14. From a letter (1883) by Sanuel A. Barnett; quoted in Arthur C. Holden, *The Settlement Idea* (New York, Macmillan, 1922), p. 12.

15. Jane Addams, *Twenty Years at Hull House* (New York, Macmillan, 1914), pp. 231–258; Arthur C. Holden, *op. cit.,* pp. 109–131, 182–189; John Higham, *Strangers in the Land* (New Brunswick, Rutgers University Press, 1955), p. 236.

16. Jane Addams, *op. cit.,* p. 258.

17. Horace M. Kallen, "Democracy *versus* the Melting-Pot," *The Nation,* 18 and 25 February 1915; reprinted in his *Culture and Democracy in the United States,* New York, Boni and Liveright, 1924; the quotation is on p. 116.

18. Kallen, *Culture and Democracy . . . ,* p. 124.

19. *Op. cit.*

20. See W. D. Borrie *et al., The Cultural Integration of Immigrants* (a survey based on the papers and proceedings of the UNESCO Conference in Havana, April 1956), Paris,

UNESCO, 1959; and William S. Bernard, "The Integration of Immigrants in the United States" (mimeographed), one of the papers for this conference.

21. See particularly Milton M. Gordon, "Social Structure and Goals in Group Relations"; and Nathan Glazer, "Ethnic Groups in America: From National Culture to Ideology," both articles in Berger, Abel, and Page, *op. cit.*; S. N. Eisenstadt, *The Absorption of Immigrants* (London, Routledge and Kegan Paul, 1954) and W. D. Borrie *et al., op. cit.*

4.2 RUTH W. GRANT AND MARION ORR

Language, Race and Politics: From "Black" to "African-American"

All-encompassing racial and ethnic labels such as *Asian American, Native American,* and *Hispanic* or *Latino American* are the result of populations' minority status in American society. While these labels provide convenient categorizations for social scientists, they systematically overlook or deny cultural variations within groups. For example, the label *Asian American* groups together dissimilar national elements—including Chinese, Japanese, Korean, Vietnamese, Thai, Khmer, and Asian Indian. Similarly, the terms *American Indian* and *Native American* obscure the multitude of tribal distinctions among these groups. These labels are also sensitive to change. For example, the traditional term assigned Asian Americans by Anglos is *Oriental.* Also, from the colonial era to the 1960s, Anglos identified people of African descent as *Negroes.* In response to the growing militancy of the civil rights era, however, people of African descent systematically rejected the White-imposed category of *Negro* and adopted *Black* instead. Most recently, Blacks have embraced the more inclusionary label *African American.*

In the following selection from "Language, Race and Politics: From 'Black' to 'African-American,'" *Politics and Society* (June 1996), Ruth W. Grant and Marion Orr explain the social and political implications of the label *African American* from a sociolinguistic approach. These authors contend that *African American* amounts to an ethnic term that will depreciate the historical struggle of persons of African descent for racial equality.

Grant is an associate professor of political science at Duke University who teaches political theory with particular interest in early modern philosophy and political ethics. The author of *John Locke's Liberalism* (University of Chicago Press, 1987), Grant earned her Ph.D. from the University of Chicago. Orr is an assistant professor of political science at Duke University who teaches urban politics and urban public policy and African American politics. She earned her Ph.D. from the University of Maryland.

Key Concept: racial and ethnic labels

My dear Roland:

Do not at the outset of your career make the all too common error of mistaking names for things. Names are only the conventional signs for identifying things. Things are the reality that counts. If a thing is despised, either because of ignorance or because it is despicable, you will not alter matters by changing its name. If men despise Negroes, they will not despise them less if Negroes are called "colored" or "Afro-Americans." ... Get this then, Roland, and get it straight even if it pierces your soul: a Negro by any other name would be just as black and just as white; just as ashamed of himself and just as shamed by others, as today. It is not the name—it's the Thing that counts. Come on, Kid, let's go get the Thing!

—W. E. B. DuBois[1]

One result of the civil rights struggle of the 1960s was the replacement of the term "Negro" by "black." Now, in the 1990s, there is some question whether "black" will itself be supplanted by "African-American" as the preferred term for America's largest racial minority. Is this change in terminology a politically significant event or a distinction without a difference? What's in a name?

Scholars in recent years have become increasingly sensitive to the ways in which language shapes political discourse and hence political options. Changes in terminology matter, it is argued, because terminology shapes conceptualization: some terms make certain conceptual associations seem obvious and others seem problematic; terms can constrain the way we perceive political alternatives; and so on. We have an intuitive sense that this is so. For example, "black separatism" makes conceptual sense in a way that "African-American separatism" does not. Or consider that the term "black" has an obvious opposite whereas the term "African-American" does not. The terms imply a different relation between members of the group and non-members. Terminological changes thus may influence the way we think about our political situation.

In what follows, we analyze the potential impact of the shift from "black" to "African-American." At the same time, we use this case to question, with DuBois, the extent to which language does indeed construct reality. The meaning of a term may be "given" to a certain extent by the circumstances of its use. We argue that, if "African-American" becomes the dominant term, it is likely to take on many of the same characteristics as earlier terms and that, consequently, it too will be challenged eventually, absent real political change in the condition of the races in America. However, this does not mean that the change from "black" to "African-American" is politically meaningless. We argue that it may matter a great deal, though not in the ways that people generally believe. Many proponents of this change believe that the new term will enhance the self-esteem of minority group members and the respect with which they are treated by the majority. The historical record as well as the psychological research do not confirm these expectations.

Politically, the importance of the shift from "black" to "African-American" lies in the fact that it implies a shift from race to ethnicity or culture as the defining characteristic of the group and consequently it evokes the notion of similarities between this group and other ethnic groups. Yet research in the social sciences has repeatedly demonstrated the uniqueness of the black experience in America. The analogy between blacks and immigrant groups is a weak analogy. We thus raise the possibility that the "African-American" label may mask the role of racism in our history and weaken, rather than strengthen, the political claims of this distinctive minority.[2]

*Ruth W. Grant
and Marion Orr*

LANGUAGE AND POLITICS

The tacit assumption behind the debate over the term "African-American" is that changes in language matter.[3] How and why language matters has been a central concern of scholarly investigation in recent years, particularly in philosophy, sociology, political theory, and linguistics. There has been a great deal of theoretical elaboration of the issue, and a variety of positions have emerged.[4] For our purposes, it suffices to articulate those few basic propositions which might provide essential theoretical support for the expectation that the change from "black" to "African-American" would be a significant change.

The importance of language is rooted in the broader notion that reality itself is socially constructed, rather than objectively or immutably given. Our very conception of ourselves, of our experience, and of the world is constituted by the society in which we live. This is what accounts for the relativity of reality: "what is 'real' to a Tibetan monk may not be 'real' to an American businessman."[5] Many identify language as the primary mechanism by which the social construction of reality takes place. The world is *as* it is only in and through language. "Learning to speak does not mean learning to use a preexistent tool for designating a world already somehow familiar to us; it means acquiring a familiarity and acquaintance with the world itself and how it confronts us."[6] A child learning a language does not merely learn which sounds express which ideas or stand for which objects. He learns a manner of thinking about the world around him. This observation is not new. Jean-Jacques Rousseau made a similar point over 200 years ago when he wrote that language is not

> only the study of words—that is to say, of figures or the sounds which express them ... in changing the signs, languages also modify the ideas which these signs represent. Minds are formed by languages; the thoughts take on the color of the idioms.[7]

Our understanding and experience are decisively shaped by the language within which they take place.

Moreover, our self-understanding is similarly constructed. It is for this reason that one might expect a name change to enhance self-esteem. In learning a language, the child learns about his own place in the world. "Language constitutes both the most important content and the most important instrument of socialization.[8] Language provides us with the conceptual classifications that differentiate things from each other, including those classifications that differentiate us from other people. For example, even our classification of ourselves and others as either feminine or masculine can be seen as the product of social and linguistic practices rather than as a reflection of an underlying biological reality. We identify ourselves with those who are called by the same name as we are, and each name carries expected characteristics that are important in the formation of identity. Clearly, naming, viewed in this way, is not a politically neutral process.

Indeed, language can be viewed as essentially political; language necessarily reflects, reinforces and reproduces the power relations within every society.[9] In advocating the adoption of the term "black," Stokely Carmichael and Charles Hamilton used Lewis Carroll to make precisely this point:

> "When I use a word," Humpty Dumpty said in a rather scornful tone, "it means just what I choose it to mean—neither more nor less."
> "The question is," said Alice, "whether you *can* make words mean so many different things."
> "The question is," said Humpty Dumpty. "which is to be master—that's all."[10]

If words have no fixed meanings, they become merely instruments of power. The process of definition, if not directly controlled by the powerful, at the very least could be said to serve the interests of the powerful. By implication, to attempt to be self defining is itself an important assertion of power. Where language is understood as the crucial medium for the construction of social reality and personal identity, both the control of the language and the terms we adopt take on enormous political significance.

Yet it is possible to make too much of this. Alice may also have a point (one rather like Dubois's) when she wonders "whether you *can* make words mean so many different things." Rousseau too indicates that the potential of language is not limitless. Language is intertwined with reason, mind, character, and so on so as to be both cause and effect. Immediately following the statement quoted above, Rousseau writes, "Only reason is common; in each language, the mind has its particular form. This is a difference that might very well be a part of the cause or of the effect of national characters."[11] Language is not simply an architectonic social force, but one that is itself limited by predetermined structures and realities. The advocates of terminological change may overestimate our ability to transform political reality through the collective manipulation of language.

The ambiguities in the relation of language and politics indicate the complexity of our initial question: "Does the change from 'black' to 'African-American' matter for politics, and if so, how?' In what follows, we suggest that this is a change that both does and does not matter. "African-American," like every term, exists in a linguistic web of relations with associated terms and conceptions. Its web differs from the one that encompasses the term "black." Consequently, the use of "African-American" can be expected to lead us to interpret the world differently than the use of "black." We will think about race relations differently as a result of the change, perhaps in a variety of subtle ways which we may only dimly perceive. But at the same time, the fact that the term "black" so recently replaced "Negro" and that this earlier change was justified in exactly the same terms as the more recent change to "African-American" leads us to question the limits of the linguistic construction of reality and the capacity of language to effect political change. As we will see, the history of racial nomenclature in the United States reinforces that doubt.

121

*Ruth W. Grant
and Marion Orr*

A HISTORY OF RACIAL
NOMENCLATURE IN AMERICA

The question as to what to call the descendants of African slaves is not new. In fact, the term used to designate America's largest racial minority has never been settled for long at any time since 1619, when the first African indentured servants landed at Jamestown. During most periods of our history, several terms have coexisted in common speech among different groups, and the precise history of the terminological transformations is far from clear. Nonetheless, what is striking about a brief survey of the history of racial nomenclature is that "African," "colored," "Negro" and "black" have each been adopted at one time by blacks themselves for political reasons, only to be rejected at a later time, also for political reasons.

During the colonial era, the most frequently used term by blacks, for free and slave blacks alike, was "African." When blacks organized their first churches they were called the African Episcopal Church or the First African Baptist Church. The first organized self-help organization was designated the Free African Society.[12] Indeed, the preamble of the Free African Society, which was founded in 1887, began: "We, the free Africans and their descendants of the City of Philadelphia or elsewhere..."[13] The African experience was still very immediate for most blacks. "The term *African* more often than not reflected a pride in blackness and racial inclusiveness."[14] The name had an "ideological function" and served as a "rallying point."[15]

"African" was widely used from the last quarter of the eighteenth century until the formation of the American Colonization Society in 1816.[16] Organized by wealthy whites, the Colonization Society led a movement to send free Africans "back" to Africa. Colonization was opposed by many blacks. In the North, black opposition reached fever pitch. It was in the reaction of blacks to the colonization movement of the 1820s and 1830s that the era of "colored" began and that of "African" declined.[17] With the establishment of the Colonization Society, growing numbers of blacks avoided use of the term *African*, opting for a safer appellation, *colored*, because to continue to refer to oneself as African might encourage colonizationists to believe one wanted to be shipped "back" to African A heated debate over what they should call themselves took place when they heard that colonizationists were promoting the view that America was not the African's home.[18]

The first switch in nomenclature, then, was initiated by blacks in response to the suggestion by whites that there was no place for Africans on American soil. Blacks responded loudly to this suggestion. Both the free and enslaved African populations were developing a new realization of their role in the development of America.[19] They had helped build this country. "The Africans reasoned that the European-dominated movements to resettle them in Africa would effectively disinherit them of their share of the American pie whose ingredients included not only their own blood, sweat, and tears, but that of many thousands gone."[20] Blacks' belief in the important role they played in the building of the American nation is reflected in a heightened mobilization in the nineteenth century, not to return to Africa, but toward emancipation as Americans.

The black community reacted to the colonization movement by abandoning the "African" designation and adopting instead the words "colored" and/or "free persons of color." Many prominent blacks in the North went so far as to advocate the removal of the word "African" from titles and from the marbles of churches and other institutions.[21] While it is true that terms were used interchangeably, Stuckey reports that "in any case, the term *colored* was by the late 1830's probably used more widely than any other in black leadership circles; it was used by integrationists and nationalists alike."[22] For example, David Walker's (1829) radical appeal calling for open rebellion against enslavement was addressed to the "Coloured Citizens of the World, but in Particular and very Expressly to Those of the United States of America."[23] Frederick Douglass, the leading public figure and abolitionist, used "colored" (as well as "Negro") in his speeches and writings. Even in the early twentieth century, "colored" was still an accepted racial designation. The oldest civil rights organization, founded in 1909, was (and still is) called the National Association for the Advancement of Colored People (NAACP).

"Colored" gradually began to lose its preferred status to "Negro" around the turn of the century, though the two terms coexisted in common usage for quite some time. Booker T. Washington favored the word "Negro" and urged its adoption by the U.S. Census Bureau.[24] Many viewed "Negro" as more accurate than "colored," as grammatically superior, and as the stronger term of the two.[25] Once again, one can see the development of linguistic change in the designation of the first "Negro" national organizations (the American Negro Academy, 1897; the National Negro Business League, 1901). By 1919, the *Negro Year Book* could report, "There is an increasing use of the word 'Negro' and a decreasing use of the words 'colored' and 'Afro-American'; to designate us as a people. The result is that the word 'Negro' is, more and more, acquiring a dignity that it did not have in the past."[26] Moreover, during this same period there was an aggressive campaign, led by the NAACP, for the capitalization of the word "Negro" on the grounds that the capital letter dignified the term by treating it as other group names were treated (e.g., Italian, Irish, etc.).[27] "Negro" continued to gain predominance, particularly during the period of the two world wars, "Although some Negroes continued to use 'colored,' and although some Negro leaders and intellectuals—DuBois among them—balanced 'Negro' with 'black,' 'Negro' became the label of choice, dominating discourse by and about Negroes for over forty years."[28]

By the 1950s "Negro" was accepted as the preferred term by both blacks and whites. But as the civil rights movement began making progress, the term "Negro" itself eventually fell under attack.[29] In its stead, "black" was promoted as a term that would not only designate a certain group of people, but would express at the same time racial pride, militancy, power, and rejection of the status quo.[30]

Perhaps the most famous proponent of the switch from Negro to black was Stokely Carmichael. In 1966 he helped to coin the phrase "black power," In *Black Power*, Carmichael and his coauthor, Charles Hamilton, urged the adoption of the term "black" as a means for black people to "redefine themselves."[31] Carmichael and Hamilton maintained that the designation "Negro" was the "invention" of whites, of the oppressors of black people, though the history we have just surveyed indicates the weakness of this claim.

For Carmichael and Hamilton, the term "Negro," because it was the "white" term, allowed whites to define black Americans, and their definition of "Negroes" carried definite negative connotations—"Negroes" were lazy, apathetic, dumb, shiftless, and so on. By using the term, blacks themselves were led to believe and to internalize the negative images that whites tended to associate with Negroes.

> There is a growing resentment of the word "Negro," for example, because this term is the invention of our oppressor; it is *his* image of us that he describes. Many blacks are now calling themselves African Americans, Afro-Americans or black people because that is *our* image of ourselves. When we begin to define our own image, the stereotypes—that is, lies—that our oppressor has developed will begin in the white community and end there. The black community will have a positive image of itself that *it* created.[32]

For a period of time, "black" continued to carry strong political messages. Slogans such as "black is beautiful" and "black pride" promoted solidarity within the black community.[33] Moreover, "black" was used to describe those who were "progressive," while "Negro" was used for those who were identified with the status quo.[34]

From the early 1970s to the late 1980s, "black" became the dominant designation. Smith presents public opinion data showing that "black" was preferred by a large majority (65 percent) of blacks by 1974.[35] Because of its association with radicals and extremists, whites were slower in adopting the new term.[36] By the mid-1970s, however, "black" had become the accepted term nationally in the press, in official documents, and for the vast majority of Americans in their common speech. But as the term gained acceptance, it also lost its political edge. "Black" was no longer coupled with its original associated term, "power," and it lost nearly all of its radical connotations.

In December 1988, a movement was launched to replace "black" with "African-American." At a meeting of black leaders in Chicago, Ramona H. Edelin, president of the National Urban Coalition, proposed the switch. Once again, the adoption of the new term was defended as a progressive step in the ongoing struggle for black dignity and liberation in contrast to the old term which was characterized as a symbol of oppression.[37] But in this case, the "old" term was one that had been introduced by radical black leaders only 25 years before as a symbol of black pride.

The evolution of racial labels from the early slavery period through the 1980s reveals a clear pattern. The established name is replaced for political reasons and in response to an initiative from within the black community. Each shift functions in part as an attempt to establish a positive black identity in a hostile environment.[38] Of course, the particular political mechanisms behind each name change vary considerably with the historical circumstances. For example, as we have seen, the change from "African" to "colored" was a response to a political movement among whites, whereas the change from "Negro" to "black" was part of an effort from within the Civil Rights movement involving a variety of factors, among them an attempt to change its political direction to address de facto segregation in the North, black self-determination, and so on. Nonetheless, in every case a new name is introduced by blacks themselves as an expression of some real dissatisfaction with their political situation. And as each new name gains acceptance and eventually comes to reflect the status quo, it too becomes subject to challenge by political forces within the black community. "African," "colored," "Negro," and "black" were each the preferred and progressive term at one time, and each lost that position in turn.

It is not the term itself, but its usage, acceptance and status, as well as the condition of that to which it refers, that determine its political significance and meaning. In our eagerness to investigate the impact of language on politics, we sometimes fail to notice the impact of politics on language. History leads us to expect that, should "African-American" become the established term, it too will succumb to a political challenge unless real conditions change. But in the meantime, what difference might the new term make for racial politics in America?

RACE AND ETHNICITY

Our earlier discussion of language and politics suggested that a terminological change might be expected to make a political difference in two quite different, though related, ways. Language can shape, consciously or unconsciously, our cognitive construction of political reality; how we understand our situation, how we perceive the available alternatives, and so on. Language can also function to shape feelings and attitudes, particularly in the process of the formation of identity. We are primarily concerned here with the first possibility, but it is the second that has dominated the discussion of the potential impact of "African-American" to date.

For example, when the new term was introduced at the December 1988 meeting in Chicago, Jesse Jackson, the groups' spokesperson, framed the rationale for the new term with the following statement.

> Just as we were called "colored," but were not that, and then "Negro," but were not that, to be called "black" is just as baseless. Just as you have Chinese Americans who have a sense of roots in China ... or Europeans, as it were, every ethnic group in this country has a reference to some historical cultural base ... There are Armenian Americans and Jewish Americans and Arab Americans and Italian Americans. And with a degree of accepted and reasonable pride, they connect their heritage to their mother country and where they are now.... To be called African American has cultural integrity.[39]

The central claim can be succinctly stated: because "African-American" refers individuals to their common cultural heritage, it can provide a basis for justifiable pride in membership in the group.

The expectation was that use of the new term would improve both individual self-esteem and attitudes among the public generally.[40] Interestingly, a similar claim was made on behalf of the term "black" when it was originally introduced, and psychological research was conducted in order to test the twin claims concerning the impact of the new term on blacks and on whites.[41] These studies do show some increases in self-esteem among blacks. However, among blacks who were strong advocates of the Black Power movement, several of these studies found "dramatic differences" in the level of self-esteem.[42] This raises the question of whether we can attribute the increase in black self-esteem to the switch from "Negro" to "black" or whether it is best described as an effect of the movement's emphasis on group pride. Significantly, this early research also suggests that a change in racial nomenclature should not be expected to have a significant impact on the general view of whites toward blacks. Whites' stereotypes of black Americans tend to remain relatively unchanged no matter what racial designation is in vogue.[43] Of course, in the case of the shift to "African-American," it is too early to assess lasting impact. It is certainly possible that the fact that the new name, unlike the old, refers to a cultural heritage will give it a more positive impact, as its proponents claim.

But it is precisely this emphasis on cultural heritage that raises significant questions about the political impact of the new term when we turn to consider its potential effect on our cognitive construction of political reality. In this area too it is difficult to predict: the term "African-American" resonates in a number of different ways in the language, at once suggesting affinities with "Afrocentrism" and with "Irish-American" or "Mexican-American." It is this latter possibility that concerns us here. The new term may subtly alter the way in which we understand the situation of the races in America by leading us to think of this group as part of the general category, "ethnic groups," or "hyphenated Americans." As Jackson's speech emphasizes, the major difference in the switch from "black" to "African-American" is that ethnicity or culture replaces race as the defining characteristic of the group. Jackson explicitly makes the connection between African culture and the cultures of other groups. But more importantly, an analogy between the *experience* of blacks in this country and the experience of immigrant groups is implicit in the term "African-American." How accurate is such an analogy? If such an analogy is false, might not the adoption of the new label tend to distort the general understanding of the black experience?

Some scholars have approached this issue by questioning the accuracy of the claim that there is an African culture that is analogous to the cultures of other groups, and, if there is, whether it has any relation to contemporary black American culture.[44] Controversies have arisen over such issues as whether the reference to a singular "African" culture obscures the diversity of cultures within Africa.[45] The concept of "Africa" itself has been described as an invention of European colonialism.[46] These controversies recall earlier exchanges among historians and other social scientists concerning the extent to which traditional and indigenous African cultural institutions have survived in the contemporary black American community. The writings of E. Franklin Frazier and Melville Herskovits provide the classic debate surrounding the "Negro" past.[47]

It is not our purpose to join in this debate. Instead, we question the accuracy of the analogy, not between African culture in America and immigrant cultures, but between the black experience in America and the experience of ethnic groups historically and politically.[48] Whether or not there is a common African culture that can serve to unite American blacks, there is clearly a common historical and political experience in America, and it is a unique experience,[49] one that differs from the experience of white ethnics even where one might expect to find the greatest similarity, that is, even among the black populations that migrated to the large Northern cities.[50]

Contrary to what several theorists argued in the early 1970s,[51] there seems to be a general agreement among scholars today that blacks and white ethnics had very different experiences historically in the North and that those differences go a long way toward explaining why white ethnics have become much more assimilated into American political and social life than have blacks.[52]

One of the preeminent works that seeks to explain why blacks have fared much worse than white immigrants over the last century is Stanley Lieberson's *A Piece of the Pie*.[53] Lieberson argues that the black experience differed from that of white immigrants in four significant ways. First, because blacks far outnumbered the members of any single, white ethnic group, blacks were unable to establish the job niches which were so crucial to the success of white immigrant groups. Secondly, because the standard of living of black migrants had been lower than that of Eastern European white immigrants, blacks had lower expectations and aspirations than did their white counterparts. Thirdly, though white immigration stopped after the immigration laws of the 1920s were passed, the numbers of blacks migrating to the North continued. Because these black migrants were unemployed and had low levels of skills and education, they served to undermine the ability of Northern blacks as a whole to gain social and political power. And fourthly, this continued influx of blacks to the North only exacerbated anti-black racism among whites as a whole.[54] For these reasons, blacks had a much tougher time establishing themselves in Northern cities than did white immigrants. Their difficulties stemmed from structural and economic conditions rather than from pre-migration (or pre-immigration) cultural characteristics,[55] the explanation that had been offered by Rosen and Glazer.[56]

Studies since Lieberson's work seem to support its basic thesis concerning the differences between blacks and white ethnics. Susan Olzak maintains that the structure of employment opportunities for white ethnics and blacks differed considerably as early as the 1870s.[57] Her research demonstrates that, in most big cities, the structure of opportunity for blacks deteriorated sharply just as occupational mobility for white immigrants improved. This was the case despite the fact that white ethnic groups had lower literacy rates than blacks in the same cities.[58] Thus Olzak questions human capital explanations of racial differences in occupational mobility. She maintains that "when African-Americans and white ethnics came to compete for the same jobs, skills mattered less than racial boundaries."[59] Similarly, Hirschman and Kraly argue that educational differences do not explain all of the discrepancies in black/white income levels in 1940 or in 1950.[60]

In terms of their political fortunes, blacks throughout the twentieth century have fared worse than white ethnics. As Roger Daniels argues, unlike white ethnics, blacks have faced a myriad of legal barriers in exercising their basic right to vote.[61] Dianne Pinderhughes makes similar claims in her study comparing the differences between blacks and white ethnics in Chicago politics. She argues that, contrary to pluralist models which assume few discriminatory structures against blacks, there have been many structures impeding black political success. In virtually all economic and political organizations, blacks have been discriminated against far more than any other ethnic minority.[62]

In a variety of ways, then, economically, legally, sociologically, and politically, blacks have been in a decidedly different and far less advantageous position than members of immigrant ethnic groups. To the extent that the term "African-American" suggests or implies an analogy between the black and the immigrant experience, it is bound to be misleading. The determining features of the black experience are unique and have had a great deal to do with race and racism as well as with historical contingencies. This is the reality that might be obscured, but cannot be altered, by the term "African-American."

CONCLUSIONS

It is not our goal to determine whether "black" or "African-American" is the more appropriate term. Instead, we are concerned both with understanding the significance of changes in racial nomenclature in general and with the possible political implications of the switch from "black" to "African-American" in particular.

With respect to the first concern, our findings would certainly challenge any unqualified claim that language shapes political reality. The historical survey of changes in racial nomenclature indicates instead that political realities often significantly limit linguistic meaning even as they spur linguistic change. The history suggests an ironic twofold conclusion; both that we are likely to see continued periodic terminological changes and that there is little reason to be optimistic about their results. With the recent emphasis on the power of language, perhaps we have paid insufficient attention to the ways in which language is politically constrained and directed. Analyses of language and politics need to be sensitive to both aspects of the relation between the two.

Our second observation turns to the particular implications of the switch from "black" to "African-American." What is distinctive about this most recent change is that it is a change that emphasizes ethnicity over race. In their quest to be accepted more fully and to be recognized as "other Americans" have been (i.e., Irish-Americans, Italian-Americans), black leaders have embraced a "hyphenated American" label. As Jesse Jackson put it, "to be called African-American has cultural integrity." We suggest that the new term is problematic precisely to the extent that it entails the reconceptualization of blacks as an ethnic group. The foundation of such a reconceptualization is a flawed analogy.

As our discussion above illustrated, opportunities for blacks and white ethnics were shaped differently by historical and sociological factors. Racial prejudice has exceeded ethnic intolerance. And moreover, the conduct of racial politics differs significantly from ordinary bargaining among competing interests.

> Because race is a highly evocative American social characeristic that provokes deep political and economic divisions, it is too broad and controversial a matter to be the subject of meaningful trading, or bargaining. It does not, in short, fit a pluralist analytical framework. When political institutions handle racial issues, conventional rules go awry, individuals react irrationally, and constitutional rules are violated.[63]

The danger in the switch from black to "African-American" is that, by emphasizing ethnicity over race, the new term runs the risk of distorting the unique history of American blacks, tacitly encouraging beliefs based on a false analogy, and confusing our understanding of contemporary racial politics.[64] The black experience in this country simply does not compare to the experience of any other group.

We appreciate that there is a real dilemma behind the choice of "African-American" as the new identifying term. Its strength lies in the fact that it is an attempt to refer to something positive, to a cultural inheritance generated from within the group and valued by its members. It is a step away from group identification based entirely on shared victimization, which is a healthy development. Yet, as we have tried to show, that very strength is, at the same time, the source of the problem. The problem lies in the tendency of the new term to distort our understanding of the black experience. A good part of what it means to be a black American is to be part of a group that has both suffered in unique ways and responded with unique strengths to that experience.

Finally, we raise the question DuBois asked Roland nearly seventy years ago: will a change in nomenclature change the "thing"; that is, the subordinate social, economic and political position of black Americans? Of course, it should be acknowledged that there has been substantial progress since then. We have seen over the last thirty years an intense and largely successful movement to end all government-sanctioned racial discrimination. Most socially significant, overt, racially discriminatory practices by private individuals and groups have also been eliminated, and there is now a substantial black middle class. Yet in spite of these developments, the gap between black and white well-being persists. It persists in every area of the country and for every category of educational attainment. Most analyses of socioeconomic data demonstrate conclusively that the gap between the well-being of blacks and whites remains a reality.[65] This is so even though the American economic system experienced unprecedented economic growth and expansion during the last quarter century. The frustrating search by blacks for a group designation reflects their continued subordination within the American political and economic system. Though its character has changed considerably, the "thing" is still very much with us.

Americans might do well to emulate Frederick Douglass who, in the midst of a similar "names controversy," "preferred to focus his energy and mind on changing the conditions that gave rise to the frustrating search for a group name rather than debate the names issue at great length."[66] DuBois was right: "It is not the name—it's the Thing that counts."

*Ruth W. Grant
and Marion Orr*

NOTES

1. W. E. B. DuBois, "The Name 'Negro'," *Crisis*, March 1928.

2. Ben Martin takes a contrasting view, though the contrast is not as sharp as it seems at first glance. He describes the introduction of "African-American" precisely as an attempt to strengthen black political claims by highlighting shared racial victimization as the basis of group identity. Those promoting the term certainly hope to strengthen black claims, though they do stress culture, national origin, and so on, along with racial victimization as the basis of group identity. We are concerned here with the long-range implications of the change for white attitudes, as well as black, should the campaign to establish "African-American" as the dominant term prove to be successful. See Ben L. Martin, "From Negro to Black to African American: The Power of Names and naming," *Political Science Quarterly* 106 (1991): 83–107.

3. Geneva Smitherman is one participant in the debate over racial terminology who grounds her arguments explicitly in linguistic theory. See, for example, Geneva Smitherman, "Black Language as Power," in *Language and Power,* edited by Chris Kramarae, Muriel Schulz, and William O'Barr (Beverly Hills, CA: Sage, 1984), 101–15; "A New Way of Talkin': Language, Social Change and Political Theory," *Race Relations Abstracts* (1989):5–23; and "What Is Africa to Me?" Language, Ideology, and African American," *American Speech* 66 (Summer): 115–32.

4. For some of the more important examples of the theoretical literature, see Michel Foucault, *The Archaeology of Knowledge,* translated by A. M. Sheridan (New York: Pantheon, 1972); *Language, Counter-Memory, Practice: Selected Essays and Interviews,* translated by Donald F. Bouchard and Sherry Simon, edited by Donald F. Bouchard (Ithaca: Cornell University Press, 1992); Hans-Georg Gadamer, *Philosophical Hermeneutics,* translated and edited by David E. Linge (Berkeley: University of California Press, 1975); *Truth and Method,* translated and edited by Garrett Barden and John Cumming (New York: Seabury, 1976); Jürgen Habermas, *The Theory of Communicative Action,* translated by Thomas McCarthy (Boston: Beacon, 1984); Maurice Merleau-Ponty, *Consciousness and Language Acquisition,* translated by Hugh J. Silverman (Evanston: Northwestern University Press, 1973); *Phenomenology, Language, and Sociology: Selected Essays of Maurice Merleau-Ponty,* edited by John O'Neill (London: Heinemann Educational, 1974).

5. Peter L. Berger and Thomas Luckmann, *The Social Construction of Reality: A Treatise in the Sociology of Knowledge* (Garden City, NY: Doubleday, 1967), 3.

6. Hans-George Gadamer, *Philosophical Hermeneutics,* translated and edited by David E. Linge (Berkeley: University of California Press, 1976), 63.

7. Jean-Jacques Rousseau, *Emile or on Education,* introduction and translation by Allan Bloom (New York: Basic Books, 1979), 109.

8. Berger and Luckmann, *The Social Construction of Reality,* 133.

9. As William E. Connolly observed, "The language of politics is not a neutral medium that conveys ideas independently formed; it is an institutionalized structure of meanings that channels political thought and action in certain directions... For to adopt without revision the concepts prevailing in a polity is to accept terms of discourse loaded in favor of established practices," *The Terms of Political Discourse,* 3rd ed.

(Princeton: Princeton University Press, 1993), 2–3. For analysis of the political uses of language, see also Murray Edelman, *Political Language: Words That Succeed and Policies That Fail* (New York: Academic Press, 1977); and his *The Symbolic Uses of Politics* (Urbana: University of Illinois Press, 1964).

10. Stokely Carmichael and Charles V. Hamilton, *Black Power: The Politics of Liberation in America* (New York: Vintage, 1967), 36.

11. Rousseau, *Emile or on Education*, 109.

12. John Hope Franklin and Alfred A. Moss, Jr., *From Slavery to Freedom: A History of Negro Americans* (New York: Knopf, 1988); Smitherman, "What Is Africa to Me?"

13. Quoted in Lerone Bennett, Jr., "What's In a Name?" *Ebony*, November 1967, 50.

14. Sterling Stuckey, *Slave Culture: Nationalist Theory and the Foundations of Black America* (New York: Oxford University Press, 1987), 199.

15. Smitherman, "What Is Africa to Me?" 118.

16. Franklin and Moss, *From Slavery to Freedom*, 155–57; Stuckey, *Slave Culture*; Bennett, "What's in a Name?"

17. Bennett, "What's in a Name?"; Smitherman, "What Is Africa to Me?"' John S. Butler, "Multiple Identities," *Society* 27 (May/June 1990): 8–13; Stuckey, *Slave Culture*.

18. Stuckey, *Slave Culture*, 202.

19. Franklin and Moss, *From Slavery to Freedom*.

20. Smitherman, "What Is Africa to Me?" 119–120.

21. Stuckey, *Slave Culture*, 204.

22. Idem., 208.

23. Quoted in Smitherman, "What is Africa to Me?" 120.

24. Kelly Miller, "Negroes or Colored People?" *Opportunity: Journal of Negro Life* 15 (May 1937): 144.

25. Idem; Tom Smith, "Changing Racial Labels: From 'Colored' to 'Negro' to 'Black' to 'African American'," *Public Opinion Quarterly* 58 (Winter 1992): 496–514.

26. Quoted in Bennett, "What's in a Name?" 51.

27. Irving Lewis Allen, "Sly Slurs: Mispronunciation and Decapitalization of Group Names," *Names* 36 (September-December 1988): 217–23; Stuckey, *Slave Culture*.

28. Smitherman, "What Is Africa to Me?" 121.

29. Smith, "Changing Racial Labels"; Smitherman, "What Is Africa to Me?"

30. "Black" received some competition in this period from "Afro-American" and "African-American."

31. Carmichael and Hamilton, *Black Power*, 37.

32. Idem.

33. Indeed, blacks often imposed sanctions on each other in the form of public ridicule and stereotyping to maintain their sense of community. For examples of literature of this type, see E. Franklin Frazier's *Black Bourgeoisie: The Rise of a New Middle Class* (New York: Free Press, 1957) and Nathan Hare's *Black Anglo Saxons* (New York: Marzani and Munsell, 1965). Both works are biting satires of black middle-class people and their imitations of white behavior. Each justifies hostility toward these blacks because they deny their black culture and cultural heritage.

34. Martin, "From Negro to Black to African American," 93; Smith, "Changing Racial Labels," 499.

35. Smith, "Changing Racial Labels," 502.

36. Ibid., 509.

37. Ibid., 508.

38. Relabeling strengthens group loyalty "by renewing a sense of differences from and grievances toward outsiders," Martin, "From Negro to Black to African American," 91.

39. Quoted in Smith, "Changing Racial Labels," 503–7.

40. Halford H. Fairchild, "Black, Negro, or Afro-American? The differences Are Crucial," *Journal of Black Studies* 16 (September 1985): 54. Martin, in "From Negro to Black to African American," undercuts the importance of this whole issue by arguing that "many studies have shown that blacks have self-esteem equal to or greater than whites," 101.

41. John E. Williams, Richard D. Tucker, and Frances Y. Dunham, "Changes in the Connotations of Color Names among Negroes and Caucasians," *Journal of Personality and Social Psychology* 19 (August 1971): 222–28; Douglas Longshore, "Color Connotations and Racial Attitudes," *Journal of Black Studies* 10 (1979): 183–97; Fairchild, "Black, Negro, or Afro-American?"

42. Williams et al., "Changes in the Connotations of Color Names," 228; Longshore, "Color Connotations and Racial Attitudes," 194–95.

43. Williams et al., "Changes in the Connotations of Color Names," 228; Longshore, "Color Connotations and Racial Attitudes."

44. Martin, "From Negro to Black to African American," 88–90.

45. See Anthony Appiah, "The Uncompleted Argument: DuBois and the Illusion of Race," *Critical Inquiry* 12 (Autumn 1985): 21–37; Molefi Kete Asante, *Kemet, Afrocentricity and Knowledge* (Trenton, NJ: Africa World Press, 1990).

46. V. Y. Mudimbe, *The Invention of Africa: Gnosis, Philosophy and the Order of Knowledge* (Bloomington: Indiana University Press, 1988).

47. Frazier, *Black Bourgeoisie*; Melville Herskovits, *The Myth of the Negro Past* (New York: Harper and Brothers, 1941).

48. We would like to thank Christopher Greenwald for his valuable assistance in helping to prepare this section of the article.

49. See Charles P. Henry, *Culture and African American Politics* (Bloomington: Indiana University Press, 1990); Matthew Holden Jr., *The Politics of the Black "Nation"* (New York: Chandler, 1973), 16–26; Robert C. Smith and Richard Seltzer, *Race, Class, and Culture* (Albany: State University of New York press, 1992); and Hanes Walton, Jr., *Invisible Politics: Black Political Behavior* (Albany: State University of New York Press, 1985), 21–42.

50. Even here, there is little reason to expect perfect similarity since there had been a long history of slavery and racial discrimination against blacks, who were, after all, not newcomers to America, though many were newcomers to the Northern cities.

51. Nathan Glazer, *Affirmative Discrimination* (New York: Basic Books, 1975); Andrew Greeley, *Why Can't They Be Like Us": America's White Ethnic Groups* (New York: E. P. Dutton, 1971); S. Makielski, Jr., *Beleaguered Minorities* (New York: W. H. Freeman, 1973); Daniel P. Moynihan and Nathan Glazer, *Ethnicity: Theory and Experience* (Cambridge: Harvard University Press, 1975).

52. There is a general consensus that blacks have not fared as well as white ethnics even when immigrants have faced significant political difficulties. See Eugene J. Cornacchia and Dale C. Nelson, "Historical Differences in the Political Experiences of American Blacks and White Ethnics: Revisiting an Unresolved Controversy," *Ethnic and Racial Studies* 15 (1992): 118–21; and Leonard Dinnerstein, Roger Nichols, and

David Reimers, *Natives and Strangers: Blacks, Indians, and Immigrants in America*, 2nd ed. (New York: Oxford University Press, 1990), esp. 328–32.

53. Stanley Liberson, *A Piece of the Pie: Blacks and White Immigrants Since 1880* (Berkeley: University of California Press, 1980).

54. Lieberson also notes that the continued influx of blacks after 1930 helps explain why anti-black racism was so much greater than anti-Asian racism. In addition, Lieberson notes the fact that slavery created negative stereotypes of blacks which have continued to persist throughout the twentieth century.

55. Ibid., 381.

56. B. Rosen, "Race, Ethnicity, and the Achievement Syndrome," *American Sociological Review* 24 (1959): 47–60; Glazer, *Affirmative Discrimination*.

57. Susan D. Olzak, *The Dynamics of Ethnic Competition and Conflict* (Stanford, CA: Stanford University Press, 1992).

58. Ibid., 143.

59. Idem.

60. See Charles Hirschman and Ellen Kraly, "Immigrants, Minorities, and Earnings in the United States in 1950," *Ethnic and Racial Studies* 11 (1988): 332–65. Joel Pearlmann, *Ethnic Differences: Schooling and Social Structure among the Irish, Jews, and Blacks in an American City, 1880–1935* (New York: Cambridge University Press, 1988), takes a similar position in his study of Providence, R.I., arguing that social stratification theories need to account for *racial* differences in order to explain discrepancies between blacks and white immigrants. Further support for Lieberson's general thesis can be found in John Bodnar, Roger Simon, and Michael Weber's *Lives of Their Own: Blacks, Italians, and Poles in Pittsburgh, 1900–1960* (Urbana: University of Illinois Press, 1982). They emphasize the important point that white ethnics were able to establish job niches, or what they call "kinship-occupational systems" primarily because they arrived before the great numbers of black migrants moved to the North after 1930. After 1930, however, the large, Northern, industrialized economy had already been established, thus leaving few occupational opportunities for blacks.

61. Roger Daniels, *The Politics of Prejudice* (New York: Anthenum, 1977), esp. chap. 4.

62. Diane Pinderhughes, *Race and Ethnicity in Chicago Politics* (Urbana: University of Illinois Press, 1987); see also Steven Erie, *Rainbow's End* (Berkeley: University of California Press, 1988).

63. Pinderhughes, *Race and Ethnicity in Chicago Politics*, 261.

64. For one example, see Allen, "Sly Slurs": "The new label [African-American] would please many social scientists, for it would denote ethnicity over color and connote equality in pluralism," 222. If Pinderhughes is correct, there is no "equality in pluralism" where racial groups are concerned.

65. Andrew Hacker, *Two Nations: Black and White, Separate, Hostile and Unequal* (New York: Ballentaine, 1992); Gerald David Jaynes and Robin M. Williams, Jr., eds., *A Common Destiny: Black and American Society* (Washington, DC: National Academy Press, 1989).

66. Stuckey, *Slave Culture*, 223.

4.3 LEWIS M. KILLIAN

Race Relations and the Nineties: Where Are the Dreams of the Sixties?

The 1991 beating of Black motorist Rodney King by four White Los Angeles police officers, which was captured on videotape, exemplified to many that the persecution historically suffered by African Americans is still a part of the social reality in American society. A year later, in response to the acquittal of the police officers, the worst civil unrest of this century occurred in Los Angeles. This turmoil signified to the nation that many Blacks are fiercely discontent with their position in American society. Ironically, the Los Angeles neighborhood where the 1992 disturbance occurred borders the area where 27 years earlier, in 1965, riots broke out in response to Black oppression. Despite the social and political discourse of the past 30 years, then, all is not racially and ethnically well in American society. Racial and ethnic minorities remain fully disenfranchised from equal participation in U.S. society. In sharp contrast to the "American dream" of equal opportunity for socioeconomic success, African Americans, Asian Americans, Hispanics, and Native Americans continue to suffer the realities of impoverishment, prejudice, and institutionalized discrimination.

What relative importance, then, can we place on the constructs of "assimilation" and "accommodation"? Lewis M. Killian, a faculty associate at the University of West Florida, addresses this question in the following article. Killian challenges the idea that U.S. society has moved effectively to fit minority populations into mainstream America. To Killian, race and ethnic assimilation and accommodation in the United States remains mythical. The civil rights and Black power movements, he argues, brought negligible social, political, and economic redress to the subjugation endured by racial and ethnic minorities.

Key Concept: race and ethnic disenfranchisement

One of the most inspiring events of the 1960s occurred on August 28, 1963, when Martin Luther King, Jr., stood on the steps of the Lincoln Memorial and declared, "I have a dream my four little children will one day live in a nation where they will not be judged by the color of their skin but by the content of their character. I have a dream today!" This was an era of brave, optimistic dreams. Those dreams began to take shape ten years before King's memorable speech, as the school desegregation decision of 1954 gave rise to brave hopes in the hearts of segregated, downtrodden blacks. The concept "a revolution of rising expectations" well described their situation. Victories over white southern resistance in Montgomery, Tallahassee, Little Rock, and New Orleans provided black Americans and their white allies with a sense of empowerment. The sit-ins of the early sixties, still nonviolent, still interracial, showed that the Movement could not be suppressed. As King said in his address, "Nineteen sixty-three is not an end, but a beginning. And those who hope that the Negro needed to blow off steam and will now be content will have a rude awakening if the nation returns to business as usual." Yet as we stand on the brink of the nineties the dreams have dimmed and the nation has indeed returned to business as usual. In his last presidential address to SCLC, ... King urged again, "Let us be dissatisfied until men and women, however black they may be, will be judged on the basis of the content of their character and not on the basis of the color of their skin." How sorely pained he would be were he to witness the state of ethnic relations today!

A SUCCESSION OF DREAMS

The Civil Rights vision formulated by King and his lieutenants was the first of a series of dreams. It was symbolized by its famous slogan, "black and white together."

Before the tragic end of his career King did place greater and greater emphasis on economic equality, particularly as he saw segregation diminishing while black unemployment and poverty persisted. He called for full employment, a guaranteed annual income, redistribution of wealth, and skepticism toward the capitalistic economy. "A true revolution of values," he declared, "will soon look uneasily on the glaring contrast of poverty and wealth."

During the height of the Civil Rights Movement the courage of the workers and the vicious violence of the white southern resistance engendered a national orgy of guilt and fear that provided the catalyst for the passage of the Civil Rights Act of 1964 and the Voting Rights Act the next year. The basic economic changes required if laws mandating desegregation and equal opportunity were to have more than a minimal effect had not come about, however. Moreover, the urban insurrections, brought to the forefront of the news by the Watts riot of 1965, awakened the nation to the fact that blacks were still far from content. King's dream of a revolution fueled by love and fought with nonviolence faded in the smoke of ghetto fires. The competing dream of Black Power dominated the last half of the decade.

The vision of black power as the way out of inequality and stigmatization had deep roots in black history in the United States. Even as King was emerging as a national black hero the nationalistic message preached so eloquently by Malcolm X resonated in the consciousness of hundreds of impatient, angry black people who saw no chance of entering white middle-class society. As far back as the middle of the nineteenth century Black Nationalism had been a strong ideological undercurrent in the United States, surfacing, as William J. Wilson has argued, when intense frustration and disillusionment follow a span of heightened expectations.

As limited as its human and financial resources may have been, the Black Power Movement was, with the aid of a titillated white press, able to drown out the voices of the leaders of the Civil Rights Movement. "Power," not "love"; "defensive violence" and "any means necessary," not nonviolence; and "soul" or "blood," not "black and white together," were the cries resounding in the ghettos and repeated on the nation's television screens.

Even more so than do most social movements, the Black Power Movement failed to achieve its stated objectives. Blacks did not win even veto power in the politics of the nation, the states, or the cities. The sort of power they gained in predominantly black cities and congressional districts resulted from demographic changes, not from concessions to the demands of the movement. Neither the extravagant dream of a black republic in the South nor the moderate one of viable all-black municipalities, such as Soul City, North Carolina, was realized. Real advances in self-chosen separatism, going beyond the historically black churches and fraternal organizations, primarily took the form of black studies departments, black cultural centers, and a few all-black dormitories in predominantly white universities.

Despite its near failure, the significance of the short-lived black power movement has been greatly underestimated. First of all, its very demise dramatized the lengths that the white power structure, at all levels, would go to suppress blacks who did not remain meek and mild. Of even greater importance was the change in the terms of the ongoing debate between whites and blacks and within each community about the future of blacks in U.S. society. King's shining grail of integration has lost its luster, at least for the time being. Assimilation had long been the dominant theme among both black Americans and white liberals, but now both its feasibility and desirability were being questioned. Various forms of pluralism gained legitimacy. At best, assimilation was a dream to be deferred until after a period of benign race consciousness.

The theme of black consciousness underscored the pervasive persistence of ethnic diversity in the society. It was accompanied by a novel concept, that of ethnic group rights. The idea of civil rights, individual rights based on citizenship, was now supplemented by the idea of rights based on membership in an ethnic group with a collective claim to being or having been an oppressed minority.

This seed fell on fertile soil, for other ethnic groups, not only Latinos and Native Americans, but also what Michael Novak called the "unmeltable white ethnics," began to advance their claims. A system of competitive pluralism coupled with what Barbara Lal has called "compulsory ethnicity" arose along with "the institutionalization of ethnic identification as a basis for the assertion of collective claims concerning the distribution of scarce resources." In this connection we should note that since 1980 citizens filling out the schedule of the decennial census have been called on to specify the ancestral group with which they identify—application of the rule of descent has received bureaucratic sanction at the federal level. Yet those are probably the most inaccurate data to be found in the census volumes. Careful research has shown about one-third of respondents are likely to change their ethnic responses from year to year. And, ironically, Stanley Lieberson suggests that a new ethnic group is now growing in the United States—unhyphenated whites. He identifies them for statistical purposes as that one sixth of the population who, in 1980, identified themselves simply as "American" or refused to report any ancestry.

One of the last demands addressed to United States society in the spirit of black power was the call for reparations. The Black Manifesto read by James Forman on the steps of New York's Riverside Church on May 4, 1969, was not an angry, quixotic whim of Forman and the few associates who accompanied him. It was a document drawn up by the National Black Economic Development Conference at a meeting set up by the Interreligious Foundation for Community Organization. The latter was created by most of the mainline protestant denominations in the nation.

In the Manifesto Forman and others charged that the white Christian churches and the Jewish synagogues were part and parcel of the capitalistic system which had exploited the resources, the minds, the bodies, and the labor of blacks for centuries. The NBEDC was demanding $500 million in reparations. The melodramatic rhetoric of the Manifesto proclaimed that this came to "$15 per nigger," but the demand was not for the distribution of such a pittance to 30 million black individuals. Instead it called for establishment of a southern land bank to enable displaced black farmers to establish farm cooperatives; black-controlled publishing houses and audio-visual networks; skills training centers; and other such collective enterprises. Whether such projects would have succeeded is beside the point. What is important is that the demand for reparations called for compensation to a group in the name of ethnic group rights; it was not a plea for the funding of "black capitalism."

THE DREAMS FADE

The principal outcome of the Manifesto was an outpouring of resolutions by churches. As Arnold Schucter observed, the "great orgy of American guilt" seemed to have subsided by the time, as had the urban insurrections. CointelPro was decimating the ranks of the Black Power Movement, and agents provocateurs were giving it a terrorist image. Even whites who had finally begun sympathizing with the goals of the Civil Rights Movement were asking, "Haven't we done enough for the blacks?"

Already the trend toward white acceptance of the principle of racial equality, particularly as applied to education and equal job opportunity, was discernible in public opinion polls. It was widely agreed that "white racism" was a terrible evil—but what did this mean?

The term "racism," usually meaning "white racism," became a catchword after the Kerner Commission declared in the summary of its Report to the President on the causes of civil disorders, "White racism is essentially responsible for the explosive mixture which has been accumulating in our cities since the end of World War II." But who are the white racists—particularly in the eyes of the majority of whites who now claim to accept the principle of racial equality? It is not they themselves but those Klansmen and American Nazis and Skinheads. They themselves are innocent, for they have accepted the victories of the Civil Rights Movement. They don't object to sharing public accommodations with blacks and they will let their children go to school with them as long as there aren't too many. They believe that blacks should have equal job opportunities and if a lot of them remain poor it must be because they don't take advantage of the changes open to them. Schucter was all too accurate when he wrote in 1970, "We are faced with a society in which racism has become institutionalized even though the majority of Americans vehemently protest their innocence."

THE FRUITS OF THE DREAMS

By the beginning of the 1970s both the Civil Rights Movement and the Black Power Movement were comparatively dormant. As pointed out earlier the Black Power Movement had consequences of greater significance than is generally recognized. These consequences are seen primarily in the world view of blacks in the U.S., symbolized by the fact that the vast majority now call themselves "Black," not "Negro," and some even prefer "African American." Concretely, black power is seen only in the political realm and then only dimly. There is an important but still very small black congressional caucus, but there has been no black senator since the defeat of Edward Brook in 1972. Numerous blacks have been elected to city, county, and state offices, but not until 25 years after the passage of the Voting Rights Act did a state elect a black governor. Black political power remains dependent upon a high degree of black residential concentration and the drawing of electoral boundaries to reflect that concentration.

The Civil Rights Movement, despite its apparent triumph with the passage of the Civil Rights Act and the Voting Rights Act, still won only intermediate objectives. *De jure* segregation was struck down. *De facto* segregation in public places was greatly reduced, but the illusion of equality created in the forum was not reflected at the hearth; American homes, neighborhoods, and private clubs remained highly segregated. King's dream of a society where people would not be judged on the basis of their color remained woefully unfulfilled. Even Latinos, a newer minority in many areas, find it easier to escape from the barrio than do blacks from the ghetto.

But what were the objectives unattained by either movement? Let us look again for a moment at the response of the white churches to the Black Manifesto. They placed new emphasis on preaching and teaching against "racism" and on welcoming blacks into the pews of white churches; they raised money—not a great deal—to put into the ghettos to aid the poor, the disenfranchised, and the uneducated. But the lesson of the failed dreams of the 1960s is that it is not sensitivity training, nor token integration, nor welfare that is needed to eradicate the destructive consequences of ethnic discrimination. It is drastic economic reform and that revolution of values that Martin Luther King said would "look uneasily on the glaring contrast of poverty and wealth." What the dreams did not produce was a society where black and white children would not only sit beside each other in school but also achieve equal gains in learning; a society where blacks would not only have equal rights to jobs but also have jobs; a society where poverty not only would ignore ethnic boundaries but also would actually diminish. How much closer are we to that sort of society than we were in 1970?

A GLASS HALF EMPTY

Many times after the publication of *The Impossible Revolution?* I heard myself characterized as a chronic pessimist who would always see a glass as half empty, never as half full. The analogy itself is flawed, of course—in life good or bad is never stable but is always rising or falling.

Today when I look about me, particularly in the South, and see whites and blacks eating, shopping, studying, working, and playing in each other's presence in places where once they were cruelly segregated, I think, "How great and wonderful the progress since 1954!" But when I look at the little clumps of black people sitting, talking, huddling together even in supposedly integrated settings, I wonder if we have not progressed only to that condition which Cayton and Drake called "the equality of anonymity." When I drive through a still segregated and often very poor black residential area, and when I look at the economic indicators, I am even more pessimistic. Indeed, I am convinced that the glass is surely half empty, for the level of black well-being is falling.

REPORTS AND REPORTS

Testifying before the Kerner Commission in 1968 Kenneth B. Clark said, "I read that report... of the 1919 riot in Chicago, and it is as if I were reading the report of the investigating committee on the Harlem riot of '35, the report of the investigating committee on the Harlem riot of '43, the report of the McCone Commission of the Watts riot. I must again in candor say to you members of this committee it is a kind of Alice in Wonderland—with the same moving picture shown over and over again, the same analysis, the same recommendations, and the same inaction."

Now we have the latest of the massive, comprehensive studies of how blacks are faring, *Blacks in American Society,* put together by a team of distinguished social scientists. It comes 70 years after the Chicago research, 45 years after *An American Dilemma,* and 20 years after the Kerner report. This volume starts out with refreshing honesty. While acknowledging many improvements, the authors declare, "We also describe the continuance of conditions of poverty, segregation, discrimination, and social fragmentation of the most serious proportions."

The analysis of trends since the great migration of blacks out of southern agriculture beginning in 1939 leads to the conclusion that the place of blacks in the American economy has been, and remains, that of a reserve army of labor. They have enjoyed some progress during periods of prosperity and high employment, usually war-induced. "But," says the study, "after initial reports of rising relative black economic status, black gains have stagnated on many measures of economic position since the early 1970s." Two examples of this stagnation are given. Poverty rates for blacks increased from 29.7% in 1974 to 31% in 1985. Blacks' real per capita income in 1984 was one-third higher than in 1968 but still stood in the same relationship to white income as in 1971—57%. Yet it is important to note that poverty had increased among whites also, from 7.3% in 1974 to 11% in 1985.

There is no need to repeat the much cited evidence of the accentuated differences in status among blacks, with some segments gaining drastically relative to whites and others losing ground. The major source of inequality within the black community, the authors note, is the increased fraction of black men with no earnings at all. The major reasons for black economic inequality are (1) the concentration of black workers, particularly men, in low-paying jobs and (2) the relatively high proportion of unemployed blacks, many of them not even in the labor force. In fact, while between 1973 and 1986 black men with jobs continued to approach whites in position on the occupational ladder and in hourly wage rates, the gains were offset by employment losses. The optimistic reports about employment rates released almost every month from Washington rarely note that black unemployment still continues at a rate twice that of whites and that the rates are based on persons in the labor force, not including the bitter, discouraged dropouts.

Jaynes and his coauthors reject the explanation that it is transfer payments —the much-maligned "welfare"—causing people to drop out of the labor force. They offer instead a structural explanation: "The shifting industrial base of the U.S. economy from blue-collar manufacturing to service industries, the slowdown in economic growth, and the consequent decline in real wages could be expected to produce a period of economic and social distress. For displaced and educationally or spatially misplaced workers, the rise in unemployment and increased competition for moderate-to-high-paying jobs might well lead to a rise in the number of discouraged workers."

The most ominous of the statistics drawn together by this committee pertain to poverty rates. We have seen a dramatic decline from the unbelievably high rates, in 1939, of 93% and 65% from black and white people, respectively. By 1974 the rates were 30% for blacks and 9% for whites, but by 1986 rates for both groups were higher, 31% and 11%. Even more alarming is the prevalence of poverty among black children—44% in 1985, compared with 16% among white children.

The pessimistic conclusion of the chapter "Blacks in the Economy" reads, "The economic fortunes of blacks are strongly tied (more so than those of whites) to a strong economy and vigorously enforced policies against discrimination. Without these conditions, the black middle class may persist, but it is doubtful it can grow or thrive. And the position of lower status blacks cannot be expected to improve."

To add my own pessimistic coda, a "strong economy" must achieve more than merely providing low-paying jobs in the service sector to replace those lost in the industrial sector through automation or export. Yet this seems to be what many secure people accept as a measure of solving the problem of unemployment. Moreover, with the insecurity felt by many whites it cannot be expected that they will willingly share with blacks the risk of falling into poverty.

Hence the crescendo of rhetoric decrying growing white racism and calling for more affirmative action programs is simplistic, avoiding the main problems facing both blacks and the society. In addition to focusing on the economic nature of these problems, we must also consider the changes in the nature of what is now called "racism."

HOW MUCH AND WHAT KIND OF "RACISM"?

Although there is no doubt that "racism" subsumes a multitude of sins, the term itself is very imprecise. Scholars defining it usually list a number of varieties. Since the 1960s it seems to have replaced the older concepts "prejudice" and "discrimination" to denote those negative attitudes and behaviors that result in the subordination and oppression of some groups which are socially defined as "races."

Focusing on the attitudinal components of racism, Schuman, Steeh, and Bobo found a paradox in the attitudes of white Americans in public opinion surveys from 1942 through 1983. On the one hand, they found strong positive trends toward acceptance of the principle of racial equality and the rejection of absolute segregation. On the other hand, questions concerning governmental implementation of these abstract principles got relatively low levels of support, and there are few signs showing that such support has increased over time. In 1989 the authors of *Blacks in American Society*, who found no reason to disagree with this observation, added their own finding that measures of black alienation from white society suggest an increase from the late 1960s to the 1980s.

Many theoretical explanations have been advanced for the paradox disclosed by Schuman and his associates. One theory focuses on the level of abstract principles, seeing agreement with them as evidence of a strong progressive trend. It underplays the contradictory aspect of the findings as well as the absence of proportional structural changes in society, such as the persistence of massive residential segregation.

A sharply contrasting explanation holds that underlying "racist" attitudes have not changed. Agreement with abstract principles of racial equality constitutes only lip service conforming to a new cultural norm rendering crude, overt expression of racial prejudice less than respectable. Racial prejudice is now expressed symbolically. Opposition to school busing, open housing laws, and affirmative action, as well as failure to vote for a black candidate for public office, is to be explained primarily in terms of symbolic, covert racism. The more complex explanation of competing values such as objections to governmental intrusion, individualism, and genuine concern about what happens to one's children is rejected out of hand.

In *Racial Formation in the United States* Michael Omi and Howard Winant similarly give little credence to attitudinal expressions of support for abstract principles unless they are paralleled by support for implementation. Unlike other sociologists they offer a theory of how the persistence of covert racism has affected racial politics in what they define as still being a "racial state."

They concede that a great transformation in ideas about race took place in the United States during the 1950s and 1960s. This had two major consequences. One was new, self-conscious racial identities which persisted even after the movements through which they were forged disintegrated. The second they call the "rearticulation of racial ideology" in reaction to the partial victories of the Civil Rights Movement and, I would add, of the Women's Liberation Movement. The conservative, right-wing trend in U.S. politics rests on racism, they suggest. "As the right sees it," they say, "racial problems today center on the new forms of racial injustice which originated in the great transformation. This new injustice confers group rights on racial minority groups, thus granting a new form of privilege—that of preferential treatment." Further developing this theme Omi and Winant assert, "In this scenario, the victims of racial discrimination have dramatically shifted from racial minorities to whites, particularly white males." They make a persuasive case that even though they were alluded to by code words racial issues were central to support for President Reagan in his two elections and for President George Bush. Who can question that the Republican Party's "southern strategy" has included a strong component of this rearticulated racial ideology, one appealing not only to voters such as those who elected David Duke to the Louisiana legislature, but also to numerous white voters outside the South?

This pessimistic view of the United States as basically a racial state in which racism changes its face but does not disappear is frightening to anyone who hopes for movement toward greater equality in the 1990s. An even more ominous view of a majority of the electorate is offered by Edna Bonacich, who attaches more importance to class as a factor than do Omi and Winant. She asserts, "The United States is an immensely unequal society in terms of distribution of material wealth, and consequently in the distribution of all the benefits and privileges that accrue to wealth.... This inequality is vast irrespective of race." Granting that people of color suffer disproportionately, she goes on to say, "I believe that racial inequality is inextricably tied to overall inequality and to an ideology that endorses vast inequality as justified and desirable." She concludes, "And even if some kind of racial parity at the level of averages could be achieved, the amount of suffering at the bottom would remain undiminished, hence unconscionable.

Bonacich cites dramatic statistics demonstrating the vastness of inequality and its frightening growth. In 1987, for example, 6.7 million American workers living on the minimum wage had incomes of $9,968 a year, while Lee Iacocca was paid over $20 million, or $9,615 an hour. In 1986 there were 26 billionaires in the country; in 1987, 49. "The Culture of Inequality" which Michael Lewis identified in 1978 is more entrenched than ever.

In the 1960s James Baldwin asked, "Who wants to be integrated into a burning house?" The house is still burning, being slowly consumed by the heat of greed and fear. Speculators gamble with the nation's wealth but pass the bill to the government when the dice roll against them. The CEO's of corporations have learned to live comfortably with affirmative action at the middle levels of the occupational scale but are equally comfortable with reductions in the total size of their work force. Often unnoted in optimistic studies of affirmative action is that increases in minority shares of employment are usually accompanied by contraction in the number of all persons employed. The size of the piece of the pie is not as critical in these times as is the shrinking of the fraction of the pie left for the have-nots in a class-polarized society.

The ideology of inequality Bonacich addresses is sustained also by the insecurities of people who have left the work force and are living on fixed incomes, either from interest and dividends or from those transfer payments now known as "entitlements." They do not see as their enemies the 0.5% of the families who in 1983 held 35% of the net wealth of the nation. Instead they fear the faceless people at the bottom of the heap. Have they not been told in campaign after campaign that it is the demands of the poor for welfare, social services, and higher wages that might cause higher taxes and increased prices? Polarization does not start near the top of the income distribution but near the bottom. One of Jonathan Rieder's subjects in *Canarsie* put it exactly, "We never join the have-a-littles with the have-nots to fight the haves. We make sure the have-a-littles fight the have-nots."

Now, ironically, as the crisis of capitalism in America intensifies the attention of American voters is distracted by the failures of socialist polities and economies abroad, as if that made their own plight less perilous and their own future more secure. The prospects for a radical rejection of the culture of inequality, with its concomitant acceptance of racial inequality, seem dim. To me, some pessimistic warnings from the past seem more appropriate today than do optimistic predictions for the 1990s.

VOICES FROM THE PAST

When I look at the retreat of the federal government from vigorous enforcement of civil rights laws, I am reminded of the warning of Frederick Douglass, issued as he witnessed a similar retreat. He wrote, "No man can be truly free whose liberty is dependent upon the thought, feeling, and actions of others, and who has himself no means in his own hands for guarding, protecting, defending, and maintaining that liberty."

During the Civil Rights and Black Power movements black Americans were catalysts in producing a national orgy of guilt, but they did not attain the sort of power Douglass described. After laws promising equal opportunity were passed, blacks lacked the political clout to get succeeding congresses to pass laws to implement these promises. They were forced to depend, instead, on sympathetic bureaucrats in the executive branch and a narrow majority in a relatively friendly Supreme Court to promote implementation in the absence of majority popular support. Now we see the administrative and judicial support fading because of the growing strength of a political party that does not depend on minority voters for victory and often appears downright hostile to their interests. As inadequate as were the responses of the liberal Kennedy, Johnson, and Carter administrations, they were magnificent when compared to those of elected officials who use "liberal" as a code word signifying softness on crime, welfare fraud, pauperism, reverse discrimination, and the spread of communism in the Third World.

Yet the black middle class still prospers relative to its past condition as the gap between the haves and have-nots grows in the black community, just as in the white. Here I am reminded of Stokely Carmichael's quip in the 1960s, "To most whites Black Power seems to mean that the Mau Mau are coming to the suburbs at night." Today we might say that, to most whites, actually accepting blacks as residents of their neighborhoods seems to mean that drug-ridden welfare recipients from the ghetto will be on their doorstep tomorrow. Julius Lester wrote at about the same time, "The black middle class is aware of its precarious position between the ghetto blacks and white society; and its members know that because they are black, they are dispensable." Even the qualified black person who seems to have achieved equality is regarded as the "exceptional" black and even then is often suspected of reaching that level because of affirmative action. Until the plight of the underclass is alleviated its shadow will continue to blight the lives and fortunes of those blacks who have partially escaped the bonds of past discrimination.

Lester said that the black middle class knew that it was dispensable. Sidney Willhelm asked, "Who needs the Negro?" Although asked in 1970, his question is still horrendously relevant today. Writing before the export of semiskilled jobs to Third World countries became another threat to workers in the United States, he warned about automation: "The Negro becomes a victim of neglect as he becomes useless to an emerging economy of automation. With the onset of automation the Negro moves out of his historical state of oppression into one of uselessness. Increasingly, he is not so much economically exploited as he is irrelevant."

Although he and Willhelm have been highly critical of each other's work, William J. Wilson pointed to the same problem in *The Declining Significance of Race*. He observed, "Representing the very center of the New American economy, corporate industries are characterized by vertically integrated production processes and technologically progressive systems of production and distribution. The growth of production depends more on technical progress and increases in physical capital per worker than on the growth of employment."

He added, "In short, an increasing number of corporate sector workers have become redundant because the demand for labor is decreased in the short run by the gap between productivity and the demand for goods. Perhaps we must ask today, "Who needs people, except as consumers?" Willhelm characterized our situation as one in which "the new standard of living entails both production and distribution of goods without, however, involving either a producer or distributor through large-scale employment." Hence this oft-disparaged but frighteningly accurate prophet among sociologists advanced a truly radical proposition: "It will be incumbent for a society relying upon automation and dedicated to the well being of human beings to accept a new economic gauge, namely: *services are to be rendered and goods produced, distributed and consumed in keeping with a designated standard of living.*" This is the sort of change in perspective of which Wilson said, in 1987, "It will require a radicalism that neither Democrat nor Republican parties have as yet been realistic enough to propose." Instead what we continue to see is platforms that imply that if profits are kept high and taxes low so that investment is encouraged, plenty of jobs will be created. Then, if blacks will get an education and develop the right attitudes toward work and family, they can enjoy that portion of the prosperity that trickles down to them. This, unfortunately, is the dream of many white voters today. It is not, however, an accurate vision of things to come but a rose-tinted stereotype of an industrial era which is gone forever and was never good for minority workers.

DREAMS OR NIGHTMARES FOR THE 1990s?

During those years after 1940 during which I studied, taught, and lived race relations in the South, I had my own dream. It was that my fellow white southerners, most of whom I knew as good, kind people, would have peeled from their eyes the veil which kept them from knowing what they were doing to black people. Someday they would see, I hoped, how segregation and discrimination, no matter how paternalistic, left cruel injuries which would handicap both current and future generations.

During the decade after 1954 I thought I was beginning to see that veil thinning under the assault of the Civil Rights Movement. I did witness heartening changes, but then I saw new complacency, with white America asking, "How much more are we supposed to do for them?" Now I see a new veil blinding people whom I still believe to be good-spirited. They are blind to institutional discrimination and to the poverty increasing in our nation even more rapidly than 20 years ago. Ironically, the behavior of most white people, particularly in the South, has changed more than have their attitudes. Now they mix with their black fellow citizens, yet blacks still remain largely invisible to them. They admit selected, acceptable blacks to their company as individuals but ignore the tragedy of the masses who yearly become more separated and alienated from what appears to those on top as an affluent society. Poverty, black and white, is concealed in a way different from when the rich and the poor lived closer to each other. It is known to many Americans only by flitting images in the mass media. In the meantime defense of what security and prosperity one does enjoy, rather than concern for the social problems threatening the nation, anchors successful political appeals with the dominant theme, "no new taxes."

In 1961 James E. Conant wrote in *Slums and Suburbs*, "We are allowing social dynamite to accumulate in our large cities." In the 1960s there were explosions of that dynamite, but its potential for destruction was far from exhausted. Now, in 1990, more dynamite is accumulating and in more cities.

Yet at this very time there appears to be a new basis for optimism. Many Americans are celebrating the end of the Cold War and looking forward to a "peace dividend." The case for deferring spending on domestic programs because of the demands for military defense loses its cogency. Journalists and novelists ask, "Who will be the enemy now that the Soviet Union is no longer the evil empire?"

There has been another cold war, however—a war of heartless neglect of the burgeoning needs of the truly disadvantaged in our own affluent society. A bright new dream would feature the end of this cold war and the beginning of a new war on poverty. We can expect increasingly urgent demands for a concerted attack on underemployment, undereducation, crime which preys on the poor, and the hopelessness that causes young people to drop out not only from school but also from the labor force. But these problems cannot be adequately addressed with the meager surplus left after the requirements for deficit reduction and new foreign aid are met. New taxes and a more equitable distribution of wealth will be required. But what if the response of the "haves" and the "have-littles" to this summons for self-sacrifice is a new wave of blaming the victim? If this is the case, the new enemy will be our own underclass.

5.1 WILLIAM RYAN

Blaming the Victim

American society is probably the most affluent of all developed nations. Yet America's poor constitutes about one-fifth of its population. The fact that literally millions of poor people live in a nation of exorbitant wealth raises considerable debate on poverty. One theory is the individualistic thesis, which holds that poor people themselves are to blame for their social plight. For example, professor emeritus of urban studies Edward Banfield, in *The Unheavenly City* (Little, Brown, 1970), asserts that perpetual impoverishment generates a distinctive lower-class subculture that deteriorates personal achievement and, in turn, leads the poor to perpetuate their own poverty. The opposing theory of poverty is discussed by William Ryan in the present article. Ryan maintains that poverty is the result of American society's unequal distribution of income, not individual inadequacies. He rejects individualistic explanations as instances of "blaming the victim."

Ryan is a professor in the Department of Psychology at Boston College in Chestnut Hill, Massachusetts, and a consultant in the fields of mental health, community planning, and social problems. His publications include *Distress in the City* (UPB, 1969).

Key Concept: blaming the victim

*T*wenty years ago, Zero Mostel used to do a sketch in which he impersonated a Dixiecrat Senator conducting an investigation of the origins of World War II. At the climax of the sketch, the Senator boomed out, in an excruciating mixture of triumph and suspicion, "What was Pearl Harbor *doing* in the Pacific?" This is an extreme example of Blaming the Victim.

Twenty years ago, we could laugh at Zero Mostel's caricature. In recent years, however, the same process has been going on every day in the arena of social problems, public health, anti-poverty programs, and social welfare. A philosopher might analyze this process and prove that, technically, it is comic. But it is hardly ever funny.

Consider some victims. One is the miseducated child in the slum school. He is blamed for his own miseducation. He is said to contain within himself the causes of his inability to read and write well. The shorthand phrase is "cultural deprivation," which, to those in the know, conveys what they allege to be inside information: that the poor child carries a scanty pack of cultural baggage as he enters school. He doesn't know about books and magazines and newspapers, they say. (No books in the home; the mother fails to subscribe to *Reader's Digest*.) They say that if he talks at all—an unlikely event since slum parents don't talk to their children—he certainly doesn't talk correctly. (Lower-class dialect spoken here, or even—God forbid!—Southern Negro. (*Ici on parle nigra.*) If you can manage to get him to sit in a chair, they say, he squirms and looks out the window. (Impulse-ridden, these kids, motoric rather than verbal.) In a word he is "disadvantaged" and "socially deprived," they say, and this, of course, accounts for his failure (*his* failure, they say) to learn much in school.

Note the similarity to the logic of Zero Mostel's Dixiecrat Senator. What is the culturally deprived child *doing* in the school? What is wrong with the victim? In pursuing this logic, no one remembers to ask questions about the collapsing buildings and torn textbooks, the frightened, insensitive teachers, the six additional desks in the room, the blustering, frightened principals, the relentless segregation, the callous administrator, the irrelevant curriculum, the bigoted or cowardly members of the school board, the insulting history book, the stingy taxpayers, the fairy-tale readers, or the self-serving faculty of the local teachers' college. We are encouraged to confine our attention to the child and to dwell on all his alleged defects. Cultural deprivation becomes an omnibus explanation for the educational disaster area known as the inner-city school. This is Blaming the Victim.

Pointing to the supposedly deviant Negro family as the "fundamental weakness of the Negro community" is another way to blame the victim. Like "cultural deprivation," "Negro family" has become a shorthand phrase with stereotyped connotations of matriarchy, fatherlessness, and pervasive illegitimacy. Growing up in the "crumbling" Negro family is supposed to account for most of the racial evils in America. Insiders have the word, of course, and know that this phrase is supposed to evoke images of growing up with a long-absent or never-present father (replaced from time to time perhaps by a series of transient lovers) and with bossy women ruling the roost, so that the children are irreparably damaged. This refers particularly to the poor, bewildered male children, whose psyches are fatally wounded and who are never, alas, to learn the trick of becoming upright, downright, forthright all-American boys. Is it any wonder the Negroes cannot achieve equality? From such families! And, again, by focusing our attention on the Negro family as the apparent *cause* of racial inequality, our eye is diverted. Racism, discrimination, segregation, and the powerlessness of the ghetto are subtly, but thoroughly, downgraded in importance.

The generic process of Blaming the Victim is applied to almost every American problem. The miserable health care of the poor is explained away on the grounds that the victim has poor motivation and lacks health information. The problems of slum housing are traced to the characteristics of tenants who are labeled as "Southern rural migrants" not yet "acculturated" to life in the big city. The "multiproblem" poor, it is claimed, suffer the psychological effects of impoverishment, the "culture of poverty," and the deviant value system of the lower classes; consequently, though unwittingly, they cause their own troubles. From such a viewpoint, the obvious fact that poverty is primarily an absence of money is easily overlooked or set aside.

The growing number of families receiving welfare are fallaciously linked together with the increased number of illegitimate children as twin results of promiscuity and sexual abandon among members of the lower orders. Every important social problem—crime, mental illness, civil disorder, unemployment —has been analyzed within the framework of the victim-blaming ideology....

I have been listening to the victim-blamers and pondering their thought processes for a number of years. That process is often very subtle. Victim-blaming is cloaked in kindness and concern, and bears all the trappings and statistical furbelows of scientism; it is obscured by a perfumed haze of humanitarianism. In observing the process of Blaming the Victim, one tends to be confused and disoriented because those who practice this art display a deep concern for the victims that is quite genuine. In this way, the new ideology is very different from the open prejudice and reactionary tactics of the old days. Its adherents include sympathetic social scientists with social consciences in good working order, and liberal politicians with a genuine commitment to reform. They are very careful to dissociate themselves from vulgar Calvinism or crude racism; they indignantly condemn any notions of innate wickedness or genetic defect. "The Negro is *not born* inferior," they shout apoplectically. "Force of circumstance," they explain in reasonable tones, "has *made* him inferior." And they dismiss with self-righteous contempt any claims that the poor man in America is plainly unworthy or shiftless or enamored of idleness. No, they say, he is "caught in the cycle of poverty." He is trained to be poor by his culture and his family life, endowed by his environment (perhaps by his ignorant mother's outdated style of toilet training) with those unfortunately unpleasant characteristics that make him ineligible for a passport into the affluent society.

Blaming the Victim is, of course, quite different from old-fashioned conservative ideologies. The latter simply dismissed victims as inferior, genetically defective, or morally unfit; the emphasis is on the intrinsic, even hereditary, defect. The former shifts its emphasis to the environmental causation. The old-fashioned conservative could hold firmly to the belief that the oppressed and the victimized were born that way—"that way" being defective or inadequate in character or ability. The new ideology attributes defect and inadequacy to the malignant nature of poverty, injustice, slum life, and racial difficulties. The stigma that marks the victim and accounts for his victimization is an acquired stigma, a stigma of social, rather than genetic, origin. But the stigma, the defect, the fatal difference—though derived in the past from environmental forces— is still located *within* the victim, inside his skin. With such an elegant formulation, the humanitarian can have it both ways. He can, all at the same time, concentrate his charitable interest on the defects of the victim, condemn the vague social and environmental stresses that produced the defect (some time ago), and ignore the continuing effect of victimizing social forces (right now). It is a brilliant ideology for justifying a perverse form of social action designed to change, not society, as one might expect, but rather society's victim.

As a result, there is a terrifying sameness in the programs that arise from this kind of analysis. In education, we have programs of "compensatory education" to build up the skills and attitudes of the ghetto child, rather than structural changes in the schools. In race relations, we have social engineers who think up ways of "strengthening" the Negro family, rather than methods of eradicating racism. In health care, we develop new programs to provide health information (to correct the supposed ignorance of the poor) and to reach out and discover cases of untreated illness and disability (to compensate for their supposed unwillingness to seek treatment). Meanwhile, the gross inequities of our medical care delivery systems are left completely unchanged. As we might expect, the logical outcome of analyzing social problems in terms of the deficiencies of the victim is the development of programs aimed at correcting those deficiencies. The formula for action becomes extraordinarily simple: change the victim.

All of this happens so smoothly that it seems downright rational. First, identify a social problem. Second, study those affected by the problem and discover in what ways they are different from the rest of us as a consequence of deprivation and injustice. Third, define the differences as the cause of the social problem itself. Finally, of course, assign a government bureaucrat to invent a humanitarian action program to correct the differences.

Now no one in his right mind would quarrel with the assertion that social problems are present in abundance and are readily identifiable. God knows it is true that when hundreds of thousands of poor children drop out of school —or even graduate from school—they are barely literate. After spending some ten thousand hours in the company of professional educators, these children appear to have learned very little. The fact of failure in their education is undisputed. And the racial situation in America is unusually acknowledged to be a number one item on the nation's agenda. Despite years of marches, commissions, judicial decisions, and endless legislative remedies, we are confronted with unchanging or even widening racial differences in achievement. In addition, despite our assertions that Americans get the best health care in the world, the poor stubbornly remain unhealthy. They lose more work because of illness, have more carious teeth, lose more babies as a result of both miscarriage and infant death, and die considerably younger than the well-to-do.

The problems are there, and there in great quantities. They make us uneasy. Added together, these disturbing signs reflect inequality and a puzzlingly high level of unalleviated distress in America totally inconsistent with our proclaimed ideals and our enormous wealth. This thread—this rope—of inconsistency stands out so visibly in the fabric of American life, that it is jarring to the eye. And this must be explained, to the satisfaction of our conscience as well as our patriotism. Blaming the Victim is an ideal, almost painless, evasion.

The second step in applying this explanation is to look sympathetically at those who "have" the problem in question, to separate them out and define them in some way as a special group, a group that is different from the population in general. This is a crucial and essential step in the process, for that difference is in itself hampering and maladaptive. The Different Ones are seen as less competent, less skilled, less knowing—in short, less human. The ancient Greeks deduced from a single characteristic, a difference in language, that the barbarians—that is, the "babblers" who spoke a strange tongue;—were wild, uncivilized, dangerous, rapacious, uneducated, lawless, and, indeed, scarcely more than animals. Automatically labeling strangers as savages, weird and inhuman creatures (thus explaining difference by exaggerating difference) not infrequently justifies mistreatment, enslavement, or even extermination of the *Different Ones.*

Blaming the Victim depends on a very similar process of identification (carried out, to be sure, in the most kindly, philanthropic, and intellectual manner) whereby the victim of social problems is identified as strange, different—in other words, as a barbarian, a savage. Discovering savages, then, is an essential component of, and prerequisite to, Blaming the Victim, and the art of Savage Discovery is a core skill that must be acquired by all aspiring Victim Blamers. They must learn how to demonstrate that the poor, the black, the ill, the jobless, the slum tenants, are different and strange. They must learn to conduct or interpret the research that shows how "these people" think in different forms, act in different patterns, cling to different values, seek different goals, and learn different truths. Which is to say that they are strangers, barbarians, savages. This is how the distressed and disinherited are redefined in order to make it possible for us to look at society's problems and to attribute their causation to the individuals affected....

Blaming the Victim can take its place in a long series of American ideologies that have rationalized cruelty and injustice.

Slavery, for example, was justified—even praised—on the basis of a complex ideology that showed quite conclusively how useful slavery was to society and how uplifting it was for the slaves.[1] Eminent physicians could be relied upon to provide the biological justification for slavery since after all, they said, the slaves were a separate species—as, for example, cattle are a separate species. No one in his right mind would dream of freeing the cows and fighting to abolish the ownership of cattle. In the view of the average American of 1825, it was important to preserve slavery, not simply because it was in accord with his own group interests (he was not fully aware of that), but because reason and logic showed clearly to the reasonable and intelligent man that slavery was good. In order to persuade a good and moral man to *do* evil, then, it is not necessary first to persuade him to *become* evil. It is only necessary to teach him that he is doing good. No one, in the words of a legendary newspaperman, thinks of himself as a son of a bitch.

In late-nineteenth-century America there flowered another ideology of injustice that seemed rational and just to the decent, progressive person. But Richard Hofstadter's analysis of the phenomenon of Social Darwinism[2] shows clearly its functional role in the preservation of the *status quo.* One can scarcely imagine a better fit than the one between this ideology and the purposes and actions of the robber barons, who descended like piranha fish on the America of this era and picked its bones clean. Their extraordinarily unethical operations netted them not only hundreds of millions of dollars but also, perversely, the adoration of the nation. Behavior that would be, in any more rational land (including today's America), more than enough to have landed them all in jail, was praised as the very model of a captain of modern industry. And the philosophy that justified their thievery was such that John D. Rockefeller could actually stand up and preach it in church. Listen as he speaks in, of all places, Sunday school: "The growth of a large business is merely a survival of the fittest.... The American Beauty rose can be produced in the splendor and fragrance which bring cheer to its beholder only by sacrificing the early buds which grow up around it. This is not an evil tendency in business. It is merely the working-out of a law of nature and a law of God."[3]

This was the core of the gospel, adapted analogically from Darwin's writings on evolution. Herbert Spencer and, later, William Graham Sumner and other beginners in the social sciences considered Darwin's work to be directly applicable to social processes: ultimately as a guarantee that life was progressing toward perfection but, in the short run, as a justification for an absolutely uncontrolled laissez-faire economic system. The central concepts of "survival of the fittest," "natural selection," and "gradualism" were exalted in Rockefeller's preaching to the status of laws of God and Nature. Not only did this ideology justify the criminal rapacity of those who rose to the top of the industrial heap, defining them automatically as naturally superior (this was bad enough), but at the same time it also required that those at the bottom of the heap be labeled as patently *unfit*—a label based solely on their position in society. According to the law of natural selection, they should be, in Spencer's judgment, eliminated. "The whole effort of nature is to get rid of such, to clear the world of them and make room for better."

For a generation, Social Darwinism was the orthodox doctrine in the social sciences, such as they were at that time. Opponents of this ideology were shut out of respectable intellectual life. The philosophy that enabled John D. Rockefeller to justify himself self-righteously in front of a class of Sunday school children was not the product of an academic quack or a marginal crackpot philosopher. It came directly from the lectures and books of leading intellectual figures of the time, occupants of professorial chairs at Harvard and Yale. Such is the power of an ideology that so neatly fits the needs of the dominant interests of society.

If one is to think about ideologies in America in 1970, one must be prepared to consider the possibility that a body of ideas that might seem almost self-evident is, in fact, highly distorted and highly selective; one must allow that the inclusion of a specific formulation in every freshman sociology text does not guarantee that the particular formulation represents abstract Truth rather than group interest. It is important not to delude ourselves into thinking that ideological monstrosities were constructed by monsters. They were not; they are not. They are developed through a process that shows every sign of being valid scholarship, complete with tables of numbers, copious footnotes, and scientific terminology. Ideologies are quite often academically and socially respectable and in many instances hold positions of exclusive validity, so that disagreement is considered unrespectable or radical and risks being labeled as irresponsible, unenlightened, or trashy.

Blaming the Victim holds such a position. It is central in the mainstream of contemporary American social thought, and its ideas pervade our most crucial assumptions so thoroughly that they are hardly noticed. Moreover, the fruits of this ideology appear to be fraught with altruism and humanitarianism, so it is hard to believe that it has principally functioned to block social change.

A major pharmaceutical manufacturer, as an act of humanitarian concern, has distributed copies of a large poster warning, "LEAD PAINT CAN KILL!" The poster, featuring a photograph of the face of a charming little girl, goes on to explain that if children *eat* lead paint, it can poison them, they can develop serious symptoms, suffer permanent brain damage, even die. The health department of a major American city has put out a coloring book that provides the same information. While the poster urges parents to prevent their children from eating paint, the coloring book is more vivid. It labels as neglectful and thoughtless the mother who does not keep her infant under constant surveillance to keep it from eating paint chips.

Now, no one would argue against the idea that it is important to spread knowledge about the danger of eating paint in order that parents might act to forestall their children from doing so. But to campaign against lead paint *only* in these terms is destructive and misleading and, in a sense, an effective way to support and agree with slum landlords—who define the problem of lead poisoning in precisely these terms.

This is an example of applying an exceptionalistic solution to a universalistic problem. It is not accurate to say that lead poisoning results from the actions of individual neglectful mothers. Rather, lead poisoning is a social phenomenon supported by a number of social mechanisms, one of the most tragic by-products of the systematic toleration of slum housing. In New Haven, which has the highest reported rate of lead poisoning in the country, several small children have died and many others have incurred irreparable brain damage as a result of eating peeling paint. In several cases, when the landlord failed to make repairs, poisonings have occurred time and again through a succession of tenancies. And the major reason for the landlord's neglect of this problem was that the city agency responsible for enforcing the housing code did nothing to make him correct this dangerous condition.

The cause of the poisoning is the lead in the paint on the walls of the apartment in which the children live. The presence of the lead is illegal. To use lead paint in a residence is illegal; to permit lead paint to be exposed in a residence is illegal. It is not only illegal, it is potentially criminal since the housing code does provide for criminal penalties. The general problem of lead poisoning, then, is more accurately analyzed as the result of a systematic program of lawbreaking by one interest group in the community, with the toleration and encouragement of the public authority charged with enforcing that law. To ignore these continued and repeated law violations, to ignore the fact that the supposed law enforcer actually cooperates in lawbreaking, and then to load a burden of guilt on the mother of a dead or dangerously ill child is an egregious distortion of reality. And to do so *under the guise* of public-spirited and humanitarian service to the community is intolerable.

But this is how Blaming the Victim works. The righteous humanitarian concern displayed by the drug company, with its poster, and the health department, with its coloring book, is a genuine concern, and this is a typical feature of Blaming the Victim. Also typical is the swerving away from the central target that requires systematic change and, instead, focusing in on the individual affected. The ultimate effect is always to distract attention from the basic causes and to leave the primary social injustice untouched. And, most telling, the proposed remedy for the problem is, of course, to work on the victim himself. Prescriptions for cure, as written by the Savage Discovery set, are invariably conceived to revamp and revise the victim, never to change the surrounding circumstances. They want to change his attitudes, alter his values, fill up his cultural deficits, energize his apathetic soul, cure his character defects, train him and polish him and woo him from his savage ways.

Isn't all of this more subtle and sophisticated than such old-fashioned ideologies as Social Darwinism? Doesn't the change from brutal ideas about survival of the fit (and the expiration of the unfit) to kindly concern about characterological defects (brought about by stigmas of social origin) seem like a substantial step forward? Hardly. It is only a substitution of terms. The old, reactionary exceptionalistic formulations are replaced by new progressive, humanitarian exceptionalistic formulations. In education, the outmoded and unacceptable concept of racial or class differences in basic inherited intellectual ability simply gives way to the new notion of cultural deprivation: there is very little functional difference between these two ideas. In taking a look at the phenomenon of poverty, the old concept of unfitness or idleness or laziness is replaced by the newfangled theory of the culture of poverty. In race relations, plain Negro inferiority—which was good enough for old-fashioned conservatives—is pushed aside by fancy conceits about the crumbling Negro family. With regard to illegitimacy, we are not so crass as to concern ourselves with immorality and vice, as in the old days; we settle benignly on the explanation of the "lower-class pattern of sexual behavior," which no one condemns as evil, but which is, in fact, simply a variation of the old explanatory idea. Mental illness is no longer defined as the result of hereditary taint or congenital character flaw; now we have new causal hypotheses regarding the ego-damaging emotional experiences that are supposed to be the inevitable consequence of the deplorable child-rearing practices of the poor.

In each case, of course, we are persuaded to ignore the obvious; the continued blatant discrimination against the Negro, the gross deprivation of contraceptive and adoption services to the poor, the heavy stresses endemic in the life of the poor. And almost all our make-believe liberal programs aimed at correcting our urban problems are off target; they are designed either to change the poor man or to cool him out.

We come finally to the question, Why? It is much easier to understand the process of Blaming the Victim as a way of thinking than it is to understand the motivation for it. Why do Victim Blamers, who are usually good people, blame the victim? The development and application of this ideology, and of all the mythologies associated with Savage Discovery, are readily exposed by careful analysis as hostile acts—one is almost tempted to say acts of war—directed against the disadvantaged, the distressed, the disinherited. It is class warfare in reverse. Yet those who are most fascinated and enchanted by this ideology tend to be progressive, humanitarian, and, in the best sense of the word, charitable persons. They would usually define themselves as moderates or liberals. Why do they pursue this dreadful war against the poor and the oppressed?

Put briefly, the answer can be formulated best in psychological terms—or, at least, I, as a psychologist, am more comfortable with such a formulation. The highly charged psychological problem confronting this hypothetical progressive, charitable person I am talking about is that of reconciling his own self-interest with the promptings of his humanitarian impulses. This psychological process of reconciliation is not worked out in a logical, rational, conscious way; it is a process that takes place far below the level of sharp consciousness, and the solution—Blaming the Victim—is arrived at subconsciously as a compromise that apparently satisfies both his self-interest and his charitable concerns. Let me elaborate.

First, the question of self-interest or, more accurately, class interest. The typical Victim Blamer is a middle-class person who is doing reasonably well in a material way; he has a good job, a good income, a good house, a good car. Basically, he likes the social system pretty much the way it is, at least in broad outline. He likes the two-party political system, though he may be highly skilled in finding a thousand minor flaws in its functioning. He heartily approves of the profit motive as the propelling engine of the economic system despite his awareness that there are abuses of that system, negative side effects, and substantial residual inequalities.

On the other hand, he is acutely aware of poverty, racial discrimination, exploitation, and deprivation, and, moreover, he wants to do something concrete to ameliorate the condition of the poor, the black, and the disadvantaged. This is not an extraneous concern; it is central to his value system to insist on the worth of the individual, the equality of men, and the importance of justice.

What is to be done, then? What intellectual position can he take, and what line of action can he follow that will satisfy both of these important motivations? He quickly and self-consciously rejects two obvious alternatives, which he defines as "extremes." He cannot side with an openly reactionary, repressive position that accepts continued oppression and exploitation as the price of a privileged position for his own class. This is incompatible with his own morality and his basic political principles. He finds the extreme conservative position repugnant.

He is, if anything, more allergic to radicals, however, than he is to reactionaries. He rejects the "extreme" solution of radical social change, and this makes sense since such radical social change threatens his own well-being. A more equitable distribution of income might mean that he would have less—a smaller or older house, with fewer yews or no rhododendrons in the yard, a less enjoyable job, or, at the least, a somewhat smaller salary. If black children and poor children were, in fact, reasonably educated and began to get high S.A.T.

scores, they would be competing with *his* children for the scarce places in the entering classes of Harvard, Columbia, Bennington, and Antioch.

So our potential Victim Blamers are in a dilemma. In the words of an old Yiddish proverb, they are trying to dance at two weddings. They are old friends of both brides and fond of both kinds of dancing, and they want to accept both invitations. They cannot bring themselves to attack the system that has been so good to them, but they want so badly to be helpful to the victims of racism and economic injustice.

Their solution is a brilliant compromise. They turn their attention to the victim in his post-victimized state. They want to bind up wounds, inject penicillin, administer morphine, and evacuate the wounded for rehabilitation. They explain what's wrong with the victim in terms of social experiences *in the past*, experiences that have left wounds, defects, paralysis, and disability. And they take the cure of these wounds and the reduction of these disabilities as the first order of business. They want to make the victims less vulnerable, send them back into battle with better weapons, thicker armor, a higher level of morale.

In order to do so effectively, of course, they must analyze the victims carefully, dispassionately, objectively, scientifically, empathetically, mathematically, and hardheadedly, to see what made them so vulnerable in the first place.

What weapons, now, might they have lacked when they went into battle? Job skills? Education?

What armor was lacking that might have warded off their wounds? Better values? Habits of thrift and foresight?

And what might have ravaged their morale? Apathy? Ignorance? Deviant lower-class cultural patterns?

This is the solution of the dilemma, the solution of Blaming the Victim. And those who buy this solution with a sigh of relief are inevitably blinding themselves to the basic causes of the problems being addressed. They are, most crucially, rejecting the possibility of blaming, not the victims, but themselves. They are all unconsciously passing judgments on themselves and bringing in a unanimous verdict of Not Guilty.

If one comes to believe that the culture of poverty produces persons *fated* to be poor, who can find any fault with our corporation-dominated economy? And if the Negro family produces young men *incapable* of achieving equality, lets' deal with that first before we go on to the task of changing the pervasive racism that informs and shapes and distorts our every social institution. And if unsatisfactory resolution of one's Oedipus complex accounts for all emotional distress and mental disorder, then by all means let us attend to that and postpone worrying about the pounding day-to-day stresses of life on the bottom rungs that drive so many to drink, dope, and madness.

That is the ideology of Blaming the Victim, the cunning Art of Savage Discovery. The tragic, frightening truth is that it is a mythology that is winning over the best people of our time, the very people who must resist this ideological temptation if we are to achieve nonviolent change in America.

1. For a good review of this general ideology, see I. A. Newby, *Jim Crow's Defense* (Baton Rouge: Louisiana State University Press, 1965).

2. Richard Hofstadter, *Social Darwinism in American Thought* (revised ed.; Boston: Beacon Press, 1955).

3. William J. Ghent, *Our Benevolent Feudalism* (New York: The Macmillan Co., 1902), p. 29.

5.2 EDNA BONACICH

Inequality in America: The Failure of the American System for People of Color

U.S. society is highly stratified: Persons in the upper echelon of the system control an inordinate amount of the nation's wealth. And the privilege of the upper class contrasts sharply with the poverty of the millions of poor people who struggle for survival on a daily basis.

In this selection, Professor Edna Bonacich argues that people of color are disproportionately relegated to the lower levels of the class structure to the extent that *social* inequality in the United States has become *racial* inequality. During her discussion, Bonacich poses and attempts to answer an interesting question: How unequal is the distribution of rewards in the United States?

Key Concept: class and racial inequality

INEQUALITY IN AMERICA

The United States is an immensely unequal society in terms of the distribution of material wealth, and consequently, in the distribution of all the benefits and privileges that accrue to wealth—including political power and influence. This inequality is vast irrespective of race. However, people of color tend to cluster at the bottom so that inequality in this society also becomes racial inequality. I believe that racial inequality is inextricably tied to overall inequality, and to an ideology that endorses vast inequality as justified and desirable. The special problems of racial inequality require direct attention in the process of attacking inequality in general, but I do not believe that the problem of racial inequality can be eliminated within a context of the tremendous disparities that our society currently tolerates. And even if some kind of racial parity, at the level of averages, could be achieved, the amount of suffering at the bottom would remain undiminished, hence unconscionable.

How unequal is the distribution of rewards in the United States? Typically this question is addressed in terms of occupation and income distribution rather than the distribution and control of property. By the income criterion, the United States is one of the more unequal of the Western industrial societies, and it is far more unequal than the countries of the Eastern European socialist bloc. The Soviet Union, for instance, has striven to decrease the discrepancy in earnings between the highest paid professionals and managers and the lowest paid workers, and as a consequence, has a much flatter income distribution than the United States (Szymanski 1979, pp. 63–9).

To take an extreme example from within the United States, in 1987 the minimum wage was $3.35 an hour, and 6.7 million American workers were paid at that level. That comes to $6,968 a year. In contrast, the highest paid executive, Lee Iacocca, received more than $20 million in 1986, or $9,615 per hour. In other words, the highest paid executive received more in an hour than a vast number of workers received in a year (Sheinkman 1987).

The excessive differences in income are given strong ideological justification—they serve, supposedly, as a source of incentive. Who will work hard if there is no pot of gold at the end, a pot that can be bigger than anyone else's? The striving for achievement leads to excellence, and we all are the beneficiaries of the continual improvements and advances that result.

Or are we? I believe a strong case can be made for the opposite. First of all, the presumed benefits of inequality do not trickle down far enough. The great advances of medical science, for example, are of little use to those people who cannot afford even the most basic health care. Second, instead of providing incentive, our steep inequalities may engender hopelessness and despair for those who have no chance of winning the big prize. When you have no realistic chance of winning the competition, and when there are no prizes for those who take anything less than fourth place, why should you run all out? Third, one can question how much inequality is necessary to raise incentives. Surely fairly modest inducements can serve as motivators. Does the person who makes $100,000 a year in any sense work that much harder than the person who makes the annual $7,000 wage? Altogether, it would seem that the justifications for inequality are more rationalizations to preserve privilege than they are a well-reasoned basis of social organization. The obvious wholesale waste of human capability (let alone life in and for itself) that piles up at the bottom of our system of inequality is testimony to the failure.

Even more fundamental than income inequality is inequality in the ownership of property. Here not only are the extremes much more severe, but the justification of incentives for achievement grow exceedingly thin. First, large amounts of property are simply inherited and the owner never did a stitch of work in his or her life to merit any of it. Second, and more important, wealth in property expands at the expense of workers. Its growth depends not on the achievements of the owner so much as on his or her ability to exploit other human beings. The owner of rental property, for example, gets richer simply because other people who have to work for a living cannot afford to buy their own housing and must sink a substantial proportion of their hard-earned wages into providing shelter. The ownership of property provides interest, rent or profit simply from the fact of ownership. The owner need only put out the capital itself to have the profits keep rolling in for the rest of his or her life.

The concentration of property in the United States is rarely studied—I assume because its exposure is politically embarrassing and even dangerous to those in power (who overlap substantially with, or are closely allied to those who own property). Only two such studies have been undertaken in the last 25 years, one in 1963 and one in 1983. The 1983 study was commissioned by the Democratic staff of the Congressional Joint Economic Committee (U.S. Congress 1986). It seems it may have been a political hot potato since shortly after its appearance, a brief 19-line article appeared in the *Los Angeles Times* stating that the committee withdrew some of its conclusions because of "an error in the figures" (*Los Angeles Times* 1986).

The 1983 study found that the top 0.5 percent of families in the United States owned over 35 percent of the net wealth of this nation. If equity in personal residences is excluded from consideration, the same 0.5 percent of households owned more than 45 percent of the privately held wealth. In other words, if this country consisted of 200 people, one individual would own almost half of the property held among all 200. The other 199 would have to divide up the remainder.

The remainder was not equally divided either. The top 10 percent of the country's households owned 72 percent of its wealth, leaving only 28 percent for the remaining 90 percent of families. If home equity is excluded, the bottom 90 percent only owned 17 percent of the wealth.

The super-rich top half of one percent consisted of 420,000 families. These families owned most of the business enterprises in the nation. They owned 58 percent of unincorporated businesses and 46.5 percent of all personally owned corporate stock. They also owned 77 percent of the value of trusts and 62 percent of state and local bonds. They owned an average of $8.9 million apiece, ranging from $2.5 million up to hundreds of times that amount.

Forbes publishes an annual list of the 400 richest Americans (*Los Angeles Times* 1986). In 1986, 25 individuals owned over a billion dollars in assets. The richest owned $4.5 billion. That is a 10-digit figure. The four-hundredth person on the list owned $180 million. So the concentration of wealth at the very top is even more extreme than the Congressional study reveals. In 1986, for the first time, a Black man made the *Forbes* list—he owned $185 million in assets. The super-rich property owners of this country are generally an all-white club.

By 1987, the number of billionaires in the country (as counted by Forbes) had grown from 26 in 1986 to 49 (Forbes 1987). The average worth of the top 400 had grown to $220 million apiece, a jump of 41 percent in one year. The top individual now owned $8.5 billion. Together, these 400 individuals commanded a net worth of $220 billion, comparable to the entire U.S. military budget in 1986, and more than the U.S. budget deficit, or total U.S. investment abroad.

RACIAL INEQUALITY

The gross inequalities that characterize American society are multiplied when race and ethnicity are entered into the equation. Racial minorities, especially

Blacks, Latinos and Native Americans, tend to be seriously overrepresented at the bottom of the scale in terms of any measure of material well-being.

In the distribution of occupations Whites are substantially overrepresented in the professional and managerial stratum. They are almost twice as likely as Blacks (1.71 times) and Latinos (1.97 times) to hold these kinds of jobs. On the other hand, Blacks and Latinos are much more concentrated in the lower paid service sector, and the unskilled and semiskilled of operators, fabricators and laborers. Whereas only 27 percent of White employees fall into these combined categories, 47 percent of Blacks and 43 percent of Latinos are so categorized. Finally, even though the numbers are relatively small, Blacks are more than three times and Latinos more than twice as likely as Whites to work as private household servants. This most demeaning of occupations remains mainly a minority preserve (U.S. Department of Labor 1987).

Occupational disadvantage translates into wage and salary disadvantage. The median weekly earning of White families in 1986 was $566, compared to $412 for Latino families and $391 for Black families. In other words, Black and Latino families made about 70 percent of what White families made. Female-headed households of all groups made substantially less money. Both Black and Latino female-headed families made less than half of what the average White family (including married couples) made (U.S. Department of Labor 1987).

Weekly earnings only reflect the take-home pay of employed people. In addition, people of color bear the brunt of unemployment in this society. In 1986, 14.8 percent of Black males, 14.2 percent of Black females, 10.5 percent of Latino males, and 10.8 percent of Latino females were unemployed officially. This compares to 6 percent of White males and 6.1 percent of White females (U.S. Department of Labor 1987).

The absence of good jobs or any jobs at all, and the absence of decent pay for those jobs that are held translates into poverty. Although the poverty line is a somewhat arbitrary figure, it nevertheless provides some commonly accepted standard for decent living in our society.

As of 1984, over one-third of Black households lived in poverty. If we include those people who live very close to the poverty line, the near poor, then 41 percent, or two out of five Blacks, are poor or near poor. For Latinos the figures are only slightly less grim, with over 28 percent living in poverty and 36 percent, or well over one-third, living in or near poverty. This compares to an official poverty rate of 11 percent for Whites.

Female-headed households, as is commonly known, are more likely to live in or near poverty. Over half of Black and Latino female-headed families are forced to live under the poverty line, and over 60 percent of each group live in or near poverty. The figures for White female-headed families are also high with over one-third living in or near poverty. But the levels for people of color are almost twice as bad (U.S. Bureau of the Census 1986).

The degree of racial inequality in property ownership is stark—more stark than the income and employment figures.... The average White family has a net worth of about $39,000, more than ten times the average net worth of about $3,000 for Black families. Latino families are only slightly better off, with an average net worth of about $5,000. The differences are even more marked among female-headed households. The average Black and Latino female-headed households have a net worth of only $671 and $478 respectively, less than 2 percent of the net worth of the average White household.

... The richest man in this country owned $8.5 billion in wealth in 1987 and there are a handful of others close behind him. Meanwhile, the average —not the poorest but the average—Black and Latino female-headed household only commands a few hundred dollars. How can one even begin to talk about equality of opportunity under such circumstances? What power and control must inevitably accompany the vast holdings of the billionaires, and what scrambling for sheer survival must accompany the dearth of resources at the bottom end?...

CAPITALISM AND RACISM

I want to consider the ways in which the American political-economic system is bound to racism. It is my contention that the racism of this society is linked to capitalism and that, so long as we retain a capitalist system, we will not be able to eliminate racial oppression. This is not to say that racism will automatically disappear if we change the system. If we were to transform to a socialist society, the elimination of racism would have to be given direct attention as a high priority. I am not suggesting that its elimination would be easily achieved within socialism, but it is impossible under capitalism.[1]

Stripped of all its fancy rationalizations and complexities, the capitalist system depends upon the exploitation of the poor by the rich. Property owners need an impoverished class of people so that others will be forced to work for them. We can see this ... on a world-wide scale, where, for example, poor Latin American countries sent to American investors and lenders (between 1982 and 1987) $145 billion more than they took in. And they still owe a principal of $410 billion in foreign debt, and all the billions of dollars of interest payments that will accrue to that (*Los Angeles Times* 1987).

Capitalism depends on inequality. The truth is, the idea of equality cannot even be whispered around here. It is too subversive, too completely undermining of the "American way." Liberals, conservatives, Democrats and Republicans are all committed to the idea of inequality and so, no matter how much they yell at each other in Congressional hearings, behind the scenes they shake hands and agree that things are basically fine and as they should be.

Perhaps not everyone agrees with my formulation, but I do not think anyone can disagree that there is a commitment to economic inequality in this system and that no attempt is made to hide it. It is part of the official ideology. However the same cannot be said for racial inequality today. At least at the official level it is stated that race should not be the basis of any social or economic distinction. Thus it should, in theory, be possible to eliminate racial inequality within the system, even if we do not touch overall inequality.

Even though an open commitment to racial inequality has been made illegitimate in recent years as a consequence of the Civil Rights and related social movements, I believe that it remains embedded in this system. Before getting into the present dynamics of the system, however, let me point out how deeply racism is embedded in the historical evolution of capitalism. First of all, one can make the case that, without racism, without the racial domination implicit in the early European "voyages of discovery," Europe would never have accumulated the initial wealth for its own capitalist "take off." In other words, capitalism itself is predicated on racism (Williams 1966).

But setting aside this somewhat controversial point, European capitalist development quickly acquired an expansionist mode and took over the world, spreading a suffocating blanket of White domination over almost all the other peoples of the globe. The motive was primarily economic, primarily the pursuit of markets, raw materials, cheap labor and investment opportunities. The business sector of Europe, linked to the state, wanted to increase its profits. They sought to enhance their wealth (see Cheng and Bonacich 1984).

The belief in the inferiority of peoples of color, the belief that Europeans were bringing a gift of civilization, salvation, and economic development, helped justify the conquest. They were not, they could think to themselves, hurting anyone. They were really benefactors, bringing light to the savages.

The world order that they created was tiered. On the one hand, they exploited the labor of their own peoples, creating from Europe's farmers and craftsmen an ownerless White working class. On the other hand, of the conquered nationalities they created a super-exploited work-force, producing the raw materials for the rising European industries, and doing the dirtiest and lowest paid support jobs in the world economy. Because they had been conquered and colonized, the peoples of color could be subjected to especially coercive labor systems, such as slavery, indentured servitude, forced migrant labor and the like.

Both groups of workers were exploited in the sense that surplus was taken from their labor by capitalist owners. But White "free labor" was in a relatively advantaged position, being employed in the technically more advanced and higher paid sectors. To a certain extent, White labor benefited from the super-exploitation of colonized workers. The capital that was drained from the colonies could be invested in industrial development in Europe or the centers of European settlement (such as the United States, Canada, Australia, New Zealand and South Africa). The White cotton mill workers in Manchester and New England depended on the super-exploitation of cotton workers in India and the slave South, producing the cheap raw material on which their industrial employment was built.

Although the basic structure of the world economy centered on European capital and the exploitation of colonized workers in their own homelands, the expansion of European capitalism led to movement of peoples all over the globe to suit the economic needs of the capitalist class. Internal colonies, the products of various forms of forced and semiforced migrations, replicated the world system within particular territories....

Still, we can ask: Is it not possible that within the United States, a redistribution could occur that would eliminate the racial character of inequality? Could we not, with the banning of racial discrimination and even positive policies like affirmative action, restructure our society such that color is no longer correlated with wealth and poverty? This is what is meant by racial equality within capitalism. The total amount of human misery would remain unaltered, but its complexion would change.

Assimilationism

It seems to me that, even if people of color are fully distributed along the capitalist hierarchy, resembling the distribution of White people, that does not necessarily spell the end of racism. The very idea of such absorption is assimilationist. It claims that people of color must abandon their own cultures and communities and become utilitarian individualists like the White men. They must compete on the white man's terms for the White man's values.

The notion that the American system can be "color blind," a common conservative position, is, of course, predicated on the idea that one is color blind within a system of rules, and those rules are the White man's. Even though he claims they are without cultural content, this is nonsense. They are his rules, deriving from his cultural heritage, and he can claim that they are universal and culturally neutral only because he has the power to make such a claim stick. There is an implicit arrogance that the White man's way is the most advanced, and that everyone else ought to learn how to get along in it as quickly as possible. All other cultures and value systems are impugned as backward, primitive or dictatorial. Only Western capitalism is seen as the pinnacle of human social organization, the height of perfection (see Bonacich 1987 and Bonacich in press for an elaboration of these points).

The absurdity of such a position need scarcely be mentioned. The White man's civilization has not only caused great suffering to oppressed nationalities around the globe, but also to many of its own peoples. It has not only murdered and pillaged other human beings but has also engaged in wanton destruction of our precious planet, so that we can now seriously question how long human life will be sustainable at all.

Let me give an example of the way in which the White man's seemingly universal rules have been imposed. In 1887 the U.S. government passed the Allotment Act, authored by Senator Henry Dawes. This law terminated communal land ownership among American Indians by allotting private parcels of land to individuals. Dawes articulated the philosophy behind this policy:

> The head chief [of the Cherokee] told us that there was not a family in that whole nation that had not a home of its own. There was not a pauper in that nation, and the nation did not owe a dollar.... Yet the defect in the system was apparent. They have got as far as they can go, because they own their land in common.... There is no enterprise to make your home any better than that of your neighbor's. There is no selfishness, which is at the bottom of civilization. Until this people consent to give up their lands and divide them among their citizens so that each can own the land he cultivates, they will not make much progress (Wexler 1982).

Needless to say, the plans to coerce American Indians into participation in the White man's system of private property did not work out according to official plan. Instead, White people came in and bought up Indian land and left the Indians destitute. People who had not been paupers were now pauperized. It is a remarkably familiar story. The workings of an apparently neutral marketplace have a way of leaving swaths of destruction in their wake.

The Role of the Middle Class

The growth of a Black, Latino and Native American middle class in the last few decades also does not negate the proposition that racial inequality persists in America. In order to understand this, we need to consider the role that the middle class, or professional-managerial stratum, plays in capitalist society, irrespective of race. In my view, middle class people (including myself) are essentially the sergeants of the system. We professionals and managers are paid by the wealthy and powerful, by the corporations and the state, to keep things in order. Our role is one of maintaining the system of inequality. Our role is essentially that of controlling the poor. We are a semi-elite. We are given higher salaries, social status, better jobs, and better life chances as payment for our service to the system. If we were not useful to the power elite, they would not reward us. Our rewards prove that we serve their interests. Look at who pays us. That will give you a sense of whom we are serving (see Ehrenreich and Ehrenreich 1979).

We middle class people would like to believe that our positions of privilege benefit the less advantaged. We would like to believe that our upward mobility helps others, that the benefits we receive somehow "trickle down." But this is sheer self-delusion. It is capitalist ideology, which claims that the people at the top of the social system are really the great benefactors of the people at the bottom. The poor should be grateful to the beneficent rich elites for all their generosity. The poor depend on the wealthy; without the rich elites, where would the poor be? But of course, this picture stands reality on its head. Dependency really works the other way. It is the rich that depend on the poor for their well-being. And benefit, wealth and privilege flow up, not down.

The same basic truths apply to the Black and Latino middle class with some added features. People of color are, too often, treated as tokens. Their presence in higher level positions is used to "prove" that the American system is open to anyone with talent and ambition. But the truth is, people of color are allowed to hold more privileged positions if and only if they conform to the "party line." They are not allowed real authority. They have to play the White man's game by the White man's rules or they lose their good jobs. They have to give up who they are, and disown their community and its pressing needs for change, in order to "make it" in this system. . . .

The rising Black and Latino middle class is, more often than not, used to control the poor and racially oppressed communities, to crush oppression and prevent needed social change. The same is the case, as I have said, with the White middle class. However, there was an implicit promise that the election of Black and Latino political officials, and the growth of a professional and business stratum, would trickle down to the benefit of their communities. This has worked as well as trickle down theory in general. Regardless of the intentions of the Black and Latino middle class, the institutional structures and practices of capitalism have prohibited the implementation of any of the needed reforms.

Black mayors, for example, coming in with plans of social progress, find themselves trapped in the logic of the private profit system and cannot implement their programs (see Lembeke in press).

This state of affairs is manifest on my campus. There has been a little progress in terms of affirmative action among the staff. However, if you look more closely, you discover that almost all of the Black and Chicano staff work under White administrators. Furthermore, those people with professional positions are highly concentrated in minority-oriented programs, like Student Affirmative Action, Immediate Outreach, Black and Chicano Student Programs and the like. Even here they are under the direction of White supervisors who ultimately determine the nature and limits of these programs.

What happens, more often than not, is that professional staff who are people of color become shock-absorbers in the system. They take responsibility for programs without having the authority to shape them. If recruitment or retention of students from racially oppressed communities does not produce results, it is the Black, Chicano and Native American professional staff who are held accountable, even though they could not shape a program that had any chance of succeeding. The staff people of color must accept the individualistic, meritocratic ethic of the institution and cannot push for programs that would enhance community development or community participation in the shaping of the university. They simply have to implement the bankrupt idea of plucking out the "best and brightest" and urging them to forsake their families and communities in the quest to "make it" in America.

Still, even if the ruling class can make use of people of color in middle class positions, I believe there are real limits to their willingness to allow enough redistribution to occur so that the averages across groups would become the same. The powerful and wealthy White capitalist class may be able to tolerate and even endorse "open competition" in the working and middle classes. However, they show no signs whatsoever of being willing to relinquish their own stranglehold on the world economy. They can play the game of supporting a recarving up of the tiny part of the pie left over after they have taken their share. Indeed, it is probably good business to encourage various groups to scramble for the crumbs. They will be so busy attacking each other that they will not think to join together to challenge the entire edifice.

The White establishment manipulates racial ideology. Even when it uses the language of colorblindness and equal opportunity, the words need to be stripped of their underlying manipulation. Right now it pays that establishment to act as though they are appalled by the use of race as a criterion for social allocation. But not too long ago, certainly within my memory, they were happy to use it openly. Have they suffered a real change of heart? Is a system that was openly built on racial oppression and that still uses it on a world scale, suddenly free from this cancer?

The truth is, a system driven by private profit, by the search for individual gain, can never solve its social problems. The conservatives promise that market forces will wipe out the negative effects of a history of racial discrimination. But this is a mirage. Wealth accrues to the already wealthy. Power and wealth enhance privilege.... The market system will not iron out this oppression. On the contrary, its operation sustains it. Only political opposition, only a demand for social justice, will turn this situation around.

NOTES

1. There is a major debate around the question of race versus class. See, for example, Alphonso Pinkney (1984) and Michael Omi and Harold Winant. The question is raised: Which is more important, race or class? Some argue that race cannot be "reduced" to class and that it has independent vitality. A similar argument is made by some feminists regarding gender. I do not contend that race can be reduced to class, but I do not think that race and class are independent systems that somehow intersect with one another. This imagery is too static.

REFERENCES

Bonacich, Edna. 1989. "Racism in the Deep Structure of U.S. Higher Education: When Affirmative Action Is Not Enough." In *Affirmative Action and Positive Policies in the Education of Ethnic Minorities,* edited by Sally Tomlinson and Abraham Yogev. Greenwich, CT: JAI Press.

——. 1987. "The Limited Social Philosophy of Affirmative Action." *Insurgent Sociologist* 14:99–116.

Cheng, Lucie and Edna Bonacich. 1984. *Labor Immigration Under Capitalism: Asian Workers in the United States Before World War II.* Berkeley: University of California Press.

Ehrenreich, Barbara and John. 1979. "The Professional-Managerial Class." Pp. 5–45 in *Between Labor and Capital,* edited by Pat Walker. Boston: South End Press.

Forbes. 1987. "The 400 Richest People in America." 140 (October):106–110.

Lembcke, Jerry. Forthcoming. *Race, Class, and Urban Change.* Greenwich, CT: JAI Press.

Los Angeles Times. "Hemisphere in Crisis." December 29, 1987.

——. " 'Super Rich' Control Misstated by Study." August 22, 1986.

——. "Walton Still Tops Forbes List of 400 Richest Americans." October 14, 1986.

Omi, Michael and Harold Winant. 1986. *Racial Formation in the United States: From the 1960s to the 1980s.* New York: Routledge and Kegan Paul.

Pinkney, Alphonso. 1984. *The Myth of Black Progress.* Cambridge: Cambridge University Press.

Sacks, Karen Brodkin and Dorothy Remy. 1984. *My Troubles are Going to Have Trouble With Me: Everyday Trials and Triumphs of Women Workers.* New Brunswick, New Jersey: Rutgers University Press.

Sheinkman, Jack. 1987. "Stop Exploiting Lowest-Paid Workers." *Los Angeles Times,* September 9.

Szymanski, Albert. 1979. *Is the Red Flag Flying? The Political Economy of the Soviet Union.* London: Zed Press.

U.S. Bureau of Census. 1986. Current Population Reports, Series P-60, No. 152. *Characteristics of the Population Below the Poverty Level: 1984.* Washington, D.C.: U.S. Government Printing Office.

U.S. Congress Joint Economic Committee. 1986. *The Concentration of Wealth in the United States: Trends in the Distribution of Wealth Among American Families.* Washington, D.C.: U.S. Government Printing Office.

U.S. Department of Labor, Bureau of Labor Statistics. 1987. *Employment and Earnings* 34:212. Washington D.C.: U.S. Government Printing Office.

Wexler, Rex. 1982. *Blood of the Land: The Government and Corporate War Against the American Indian Movement.* New York: Vintage.

Williams, Eric. 1966. *Capitalism and Slavery.* New York: Capricorn.

The Black "Underclass" Ideology in Race Relations Analysis

In the mid-1990s about 38 million people lived in poverty in the United States—about 15 percent of the total U.S. population. The rate of impoverishment has remined persistent over the last several decades, with non-White minorities and children disproportionately represented among the poor. Blacks and Latinos are more than three times as likely to be poor than Whites, and more than half of all Black and Latino children live in poverty. The poor live mostly in female-headed households where the head of the household has a very low level of educational attainment and skill development and is often functionally illiterate. When the poor can find work, it is usually in a dead-end job that pays at or below the minimum wage and has little intrinsic value. Poor people are heavily concentrated in segregated inner-city neighborhoods and in the rural South.

Social scientists are concerned with the persistence of poverty and the development of a permanent underclass. Researchers have developed ideological themes to explain the persistence of poverty, including *blaming the victim,* the *culture of poverty,* and the *black underclass.* Inherent within these explanatory frameworks is the notion that poor people are themselves accountable for poverty. The following critique of the *underclass* label is from "The Black 'Underclass' Ideology in Race Relations Analysis," *Social Justice* (Winter 1989). In it, Leslie Inniss and Joe R. Feagin contend that these explanations promote the idea of value deficiency and blameworthiness of poor people and essentially ignore discrimination as an exclusionary mechanism precluding poor peoples' accessibility to the opportunity structure of U.S. society.

Leslie Inniss is in the Department of Sociology at the University of Texas at Austin. Joe R. Feagin is a graduate research professor in sociology at the University of Florida. His publications include *The New Urban Paradigm: Critical Perspectives on the City* (Rowman & Littlefield, 1998) and *Racial and Ethnic Relations* (Prentice Hall, 1996), coauthored with Clairece Booher Feagin.

Key Concept: the "underclass"

Consider this city situation. A central city with 25% unemployment. One-third of the residents have moved out. There are many young men with no jobs collecting welfare checks and on the streets or playing pool with friends most of the day. There are many young women watching television all day. There are numerous unemployed adult children living with an unemployed parent. Many of these city residents have a problem with alcohol and drugs. Older men who once did heavy labor have been laid off; most have been out of work for years. Many young unmarried women, especially teenagers, in the public housing complexes are pregnant or have already had illegitimate children Most of the young do not expect to work in the near future. They seem resigned, angry, or fatalistic about their lives. They feel no one in government cares about them. These people certainly fit the definitions of the underclass used in recent literature in the United States.

Where is this "underclass"? What city are we describing? What are the likely racial characteristics of these urbanites? Many would guess the city is Chicago, New York, or Atlanta, but this city is actually Liverpool, England, once a prosperous city and the second great city of the British Empire. Interestingly, the people described are the *white* and British residents of a troubled city. Not one is Black. Many have educations and skills but no jobs in this northern England city, which has been neglected by the Conservative government ensconced in London in the affluent south of England ("Frontline," 1986).

Reflection on these Liverpool data suggest some of the serious problems with the current discussions of the "Black underclass" by scholars and journalists in the United States. Few U.S. scholars would seriously discuss these white, formerly middle-income families and individuals in Liverpool as some type of "underclass," as a new or distinctive class characterized by problematical values, a "subculture of poverty and deviance," teen pregnancies, crime-oriented males, and better-off families moving out.

To explain the tribulations of the white, formerly middle-income residents of Liverpool there is no need to use the interpretive language of individualized pathology and value aberration that is the focus of the Black underclass discussion in the United States. There is no need to consider these people as a self-reproducing subculture of pathological behavior that contrasts with the "healthy" behavior of their better-off counterparts elsewhere. Nor is there good reason to view the poor young women of Liverpool, with their illegitimate children and single-parent status, as major contributors to the larger underclass problem. The principal reason for the personal and family troubles in Liverpool is the flight of capital to more profitable locations outside the north of Britain; disinvestment is the cause of most unemployment and underemployment. Investors decide where the jobs go. Unemployment is reproduced from one generation to the next not by values, but rather through the working of capital investment markets.

The concept of the "underclass," as it has developed in the last decade in the United States, is not only ahistorical and noncomparative, but also highly ideological and political. It represents a casting about for a way of defining the problems of the poor, and particularly the Black poor, without substantial reference to the actions of U.S. investors and capital flight. A number of social scientists have testified before state legislatures and Congress on the problems of the underclass. The "underclass" problem thereby became politically defined and bureaucratized. An adequate interpretation of the underlying causes of the unemployment and poverty-related problems of Liverpool lies in the decisions of investors to invest or disinvest. And there is no reason not to interpret similar "underclass" phenomena in U.S. cities in the same fashion. There is no need for a new conceptual framework called the "Black underclass" theory which explains the Black situation as culturally distinctive. American scholars have largely failed to put the situation of Black Americans in proper international and comparative perspective.

In this article we will examine the origins of the underclass theory, assess why this wrongheaded viewpoint has taken such hold on the (mostly white) American mind, and provide a more accurate view of what is wrong in Black and white America.

THE CONCEPT OF THE UNDERCLASS

Early Conceptions of the Black Lower Class

The concept variously labelled the "rabble," the "dangerous class," the "lumpenproletariat," and the "underclass" has a long history in Western intellectual thought. Many European analysts have feared the cities because of the growth of sizeable, or organized, working populations. And this perspective migrated to North America. In the 1830s one of the founders of sociology, the French government official Alexis de Tocqueville, visited U.S. cities and wrote perhaps the first white assessment of the Black lower class; he noted that

> the lower ranks which inhabit these cities constitute a rabble even more formidable than the populace of European towns. They consist of freed blacks, in the first place, who are condemned by the laws and by public opinion to a hereditary state of misery and degradation.... [T]hey are ready to turn all the passions which agitate the community to their own advantage; thus, within the last few months, serious riots have broken out in Philadelphia and New York (de Tocqueville, 1945:299).

These words are from *Democracy in America, an* influential sociological analysis of the United States, and they reflect the fears of many educated whites about the "rabble" of Blacks and immigrants in the cities. This rabble is seen by white observers as disturbed, emotional, and dangerous. Note, too, that free Blacks in the cities are highlighted as a central part of the urban rabble. Thus, the idea of the Black underclass is not new with the debates of the 1960s or 1980s; the idea is at least a century and a half old. It is also interesting to note that while de Tocqueville saw free Blacks as dangerous and threatening, he also recognized the role of laws and public opinion in perpetuating the oppressive conditions of freed Blacks, a recognition of discrimination missing in much of the current discussion of the underclass.

Recent Discussions of the Black Underclass: The 1960s

According to *The Oxford English Dictionary,* the word "underclass" was first used in English in 1918 (Burchfield, 1986:1069). Its initial use was as a description of a process—for example, a "society moves forward as a consequence of an under-class overcoming the resistance of a class on top of them." It was not until 1963, in Gunnar Myrdal's *Challenge to Affluence,* that the term was used to describe in some detail a population—"an 'underclass' of unemployed and gradually unemployable persons and families at the bottom of society." The link between Blacks and the underclass was apparently first made in 1964. A January 1964 issue of the *Observer* noted that "the Negro's protest today is but the first rumbling of the underclass." Again in 1966 a connection between Blacks and the underclass was made in the August 19 *New Statesman:* "The national economic growth has been bought at the expense of industrial workers and the poor (largely Negro) underclass" (Burchfield, 1986: 1069).

Moreover, by the 1960s U.S. scholars were writing on the subject of the Black underclass, although the more common terms then were "the poor," "the lower class," and "the culture of poverty." The view of poor communities accenting pathological traits was particularly influenced by the culture-of-poverty generalizations of anthropologist Oscar Lewis. His culture-of-poverty perspective emphasizes the defective subculture of those residing in slum areas, at first in Latin America, and by the 1960s in the United States. Developing the "culture of poverty" concept for the U.S. poor in the book *La Vida,* Lewis (1965) argues that this culture is "a way of life which is passed down from generation to generation along family lines." The poor adapt in distinctive ways to their oppressive conditions, and these adaptations are transmitted through the socialization process.

During the 1960s the acceptance of this view by both scholars and policymakers was given greater legitimacy by its being featured in federal government publications. Published by the government, Catherine Chilman's scholarly publication entitled *Growing Up Poor* in effect gave governmental sanction to the culture-of-poverty portrait, with emphasis on personal disorganization, superstitious thinking, impulsive behavior, inadequate childrearing practices, and a lack of ability to defer gratification (Chilman, 1966). A second government publication, entitled *The Negro Family* (1965), focused on the alleged lack of social integration and pathology in *Black* communities. Here social scientist (later U.S. Senator) Daniel Patrick Moynihan argued that:

> at the heart of the deterioration of the fabric of Negro society is the deterioration of the Negro family. It is the fundamental source of the weakness of the Negro community at the present time (Moynihan, 1965:5).

The typical lower-class Black family was broken or disintegrated. Moynihan proceeded to argue that, in contrast, the typical white family "had maintained a high degree of stability." Black family disorganization was, in turn, tied to disintegration in other aspects of Black lower-class life. Moynihan accentuated the "tangle" of pathology and crumbling social relations—which in his view characterized Black communities—and argued further that "there is considerable evidence that the Negro community is, in fact, dividing between a stable middle class group that is steadily growing stronger and more successful and an increasingly disorganized and disadvantaged lower class group" (*Ibid.*, 1965: 5–6).

The policy impact of this lower-class-pathology emphasis in the social science literature can also be seen in the major government reports on Black/white conflict in the 1960s, including the *Report of the National Advisory Commission on Civil Disorders*. Writing about Black America under a heading of "Unemployment, Family Structure, and Social Disorganization," the authors of this report used a variety of disorganization codewords:

> The culture of poverty that results from unemployment and family breakup generates a system of ruthless, exploitative relationships within the ghetto. Prostitution, dope addiction, and crime create an environmental "jungle" characterized by personal insecurity and tension (National Advisory Commission on Civil Disorders, 1968: 7).

Critics of the Culture of Poverty View

There was much debate over the lower-class-pathology perspective during the 1960s and 1970s. Anyone returning to the discussion of the period will have a strong feeling of *déjà vu*. For example, in *Lower-Class Families* Hyman Rodinan argues that the lower-class view is a stereotyped view emphasizing negative aspects. Rodman contends that there are numerous responses made by lower-class persons in adapting to deprivation other than the lower-class-pathology adaptation. One response, the "lower-class value stretch," can be seen in the fact that many poor people share dominant middle-class values and aspirations and reflect these in actions, while at the same time reflecting lower-class values; their repertoire of values is usually greater than for middle-class individuals. Thus when conditions change, such as an availability of employment, most of the poor can rapidly adapt.

In the late 1960s and early 1970s, the junior author of this article also developed a critique. One point made then was that, although types of criminal behavior and drug use exist to a disproportionate degree in many Black communities, the extent of this behavior is exaggerated in many assessments of day-to-day life. It is too easy to move from characteristics of a minority of the Black residents of a given urban community, however unconventional or criminal, to ungrounded generalizations about Black areas overall. In addition, there is much unheralded white-collar crime and drug use in white suburban communities, but scholars have not developed a deviant subculture perspective for these communities. Moreover, the quick typification of Black areas in pathological organization terminology, with its overtones of character flaws and individual blame, tends to play down the intimate relationship between these areas and the larger racial system surrounding them (Feagin, 1974: 123–146).

THE LOWER CLASS BECOMES THE UNDERCLASS

The Underclass Debate

In the 1970s and 1980s, the debates between the neoconservatives and liberals over the character and constitution of the underclass have mirrored the debates of the 1960s. Numerous analysts have underscored the significant growth in the problems confronting central city Blacks since the 1970s. The emphasis on Black problems has coincided with a major economic crisis (for example, disinvestment in many cities) and, thus, a legitimacy crisis for U.S. capitalism. This crisis of legitimacy has involved ordinary Americans questioning the actions and legitimacy of U.S. elites. Commentators and social scientists such as Charles Murray, Glenn Loury, Ken Auletta, Nicholas Lemann, Nathan Glazer, and Daniel P. Moynihan have played an important role in refurbishing the legitimacy of the existing system of inequality by moving the public discussion away from such issues as decent-paying jobs, capital flight, racism, and militarism and back onto the old 1960s' issues of crime, welfare, illegitimacy, ghetto pathologies, and the underclass. For example, in his 1975 book entitled *Affirmative Discrimination,* Nathan Glazer described a "tangle of pathology in the ghetto" which cannot be explained by "anything as simple as lack of jobs or discrimination in available jobs." Although Glazer does not use the term underclass, he does conjure up its image with comments that suggest that many Black youth prefer illicit activities because they do not want to work at regular jobs. From his perspective, neither rapid economic growth nor affirmative action will benefit unskilled and culturally impoverished Black males reluctant to do low-wage work (Glazer, 1975:71–72).

A Cover Story in *Time*

One of the first national discussions of the underclass appeared in the cover story of *Time* magazine in August 1977, not long after the burning and looting of a store by unemployed Blacks during the New York City electrical blackout in July 1977. The *Time* portrait anticipates that which appears later in both scholarly and journalistic sources: "The underclass has been... left behind.... Its members are victims and victimizers in the culture of the street hustle, the quick fix, the rip-off, and, not least, violent crime" (*Time*, 1977: 14). Although the article tends to focus on the culture, welfare involvement, illegitimacy, street values, and feelings of hopelessness among the members of the underclass, it does also discuss the impact of long-term unemployment on the Black underclass' self-esteem and identification. However, the increasing conservatism of the late 1970s can be seen in the emphasis on individual and private sector initiatives. Asserting that there is no political consensus for governmental job creation or War-on-Poverty programs—which the journalists argue would increase inflation—the article retreats to the mostly conservative strategies of education, tougher law enforcement, a lower minimum wage, work requirements for welfare recipients, and giving private business control of job training programs. The conservative tone of much subsequent discussion of the underclass was foreshadowed in this mass media article.

In the late 1970s prominent intellectual magazines began to carry articles defining the situation of the Black poor in terms of the "underclass." For example, Ken Auletta produced an influential series of articles for the *New Yorker*, which he later developed into a book called *The Underclass*. For Auletta the underclass only includes the nine million people who are permanently poor. Auletta discusses the Black, white, and Hispanic underclasses, but the emphasis is on impoverished Blacks. The central issue is class culture. The underclass is grouped by Auletta into four distinct categories: the passive poor, hostile street criminals, hustlers, and the drunks, homeless, and released mental patients who roam city streets (Auletta, 1982: 198–304). (He leaves out the underemployed and unemployed Poor.) For Auletta, racism plays no significant part in the formation of the underclass. Auletta uses "Black underclass" to describe those with a lifestyle characterized by poverty and antisocial behavior: "The underclass suffers from behavioral as well as income deficiencies" *(Ibid.,* 1982: 28). These behavioral deficiencies include immorality, broken families, and a poorly developed work ethic. Auletta's accent on the old "culture of poverty" characteristics is linked to his argument that the plight of the Black underclass has little to do with racial discrimination but instead is the product of cultural deprivation. While he makes occasional concessions to environmental factors, the general tone of this analysis indicates that he prefers the culture-of-poverty perspective.

Similarly, in a 1980 *New York Times Magazine* article, Carl Gershman argued that it is the worsening condition of the underclass, not racial discrimination, which requires the greatest policy attention (Gershman, 1980: 24–30). Critical to his argument is the old idea that the conditions of poorer Black Americans are due to the "tangle of pathology" in which they find themselves. He, too, argues that poor Black Americans are locked into a lower-class sub-culture, a culture of poverty, with its allegedly deviant value system of immorality, broken families, juvenile delinquency, and lack of emphasis on the work ethic.

Moreover, in a widely read 1986 article in the *Atlantic Monthly*, Nicholas Lemann wrote that:

> every aspect of the underclass culture in the ghettos is directly traceable to roots in the South—and not the South of slavery but... in the nascent underclass of the sharecropper South.... In the ghettos, it appears that the distinctive culture is now the greatest barrier to progress by the black underclass rather than either unemployment or welfare (Lemann, 1986: 35).

The culture of the underclass is seen as the greatest barrier to Black advancement. The poor Black communities lack positive values. In the 1970s, the ghettos went from being diversified to being "exclusively Black lower-class" and this resulted in complete social breakdown. "Until then the strong leaders and institutions of the ghetto had promoted an ethic of assimilation," but with the movement away of institutions and leaders there was a "free fall" into "social disorganization." Echoes of the 1960s arguments can again be heard in these views; the criminalized underclass flourished because there was no middle class to reign it in.

Moreover, a 1988 article in the *Chronicle of Higher Education* reviewed the research on the underclass and concluded:

> Although the underclass constitutes a minuscule portion of the total U.S. population and a very small proportion of all those living in poverty, the lives of the ghetto poor are marked by a dense fabric of what experts call "social pathologies" —teenage pregnancies, out-of-wedlock births, single-parent families, poor educational achievement, chronic unemployment, welfare dependency, drug abuse, and crime—that, taken separately or together, seem impervious to change (Coughlin, 1988: A5).

The language of pathology was given legitimacy in this important journal of higher education.

The Mass Media Picks Up the Underclass

Not only the intellectual magazines but also the mass media proclaimed the culturally oriented underclass theory in the mid-1980s. Using social science scholarship, the journalistic accounts had their own special twist. For example, a 1987 *Fortune* magazine author commented as follows:

> Who are the underclass? They are poor, but numbering around five million, they are a relatively small minority of the 33 million Americans with incomes below the official poverty line. Disproportionately Black and Hispanic, they are still a minority within these minorities. What primarily defines them is not so much their poverty or race as their behavior—their chronic lawlessness, drug use, out-of-wedlock births, welfare dependency, and school failure. "Underclass" describes a state of mind and a way of life. It is at least as much a cultural as an economic condition (Magnet, 1987:130).

An *Esquire* article excerpted in a 1988 *Reader's Digest* put it this way:

> The heart of the matter is what has come to be called the underclass—those nine million impoverished black Americans (of a total of 29 million blacks), so many of whom are trapped in welfare dependency, drugs, alcohol, crime, illiteracy, and disease, living in isolation in some of the richest cities of the earth (Hamill, 1988:105).

A Leading Scholar: William J. Wilson

In the late 1970s and 1980s, the University of Chicago sociologist William J. Wilson, a leading Black scholar, became an effectual exponent of the Black underclass perspective. Wilson's 1980 work, *The Declining Significance of Race*, had a major influence on the misconceptions surrounding the "Black underclass." Wilson contended that affirmative action programs had actually widened the gap between the Black middle class and the rest of Black America and had produced a Black underclass that has fallen behind the larger society in every aspect. Wilson's book opened the door for assumptions that racial discrimination had little significance for those who were moving up into the Black middle class and, by extension, that class (status) discrimination was more important than racial discrimination. The Black middle class had become a central part of the underclass argument. Racial discrimination, in employment at least, was not considered to be significant for middle-class Black Americans.

More recently, Wilson has argued that the underclass is composed of individuals who lack training and skills and who either experience long-term unemployment or are not a part of the labor force; individuals who engage in street criminal activity and other aberrant behavior; and families who experience long-term spells of poverty or welfare dependency. He developed these ideas most extensively in a widely discussed 1987 book, *The Truly Disadvantaged*. There Wilson targets the underclass and demonstrates numerous fallacies in the recent neoconservative analysis of the Black poor. Wilson shows, for example, that there is no consistent evidence that welfare programs decrease work effort or increase dependency and that the growing percentage of out-of-wedlock Black births is not the result of immorality or welfare, but instead results from the declining birth rate among married women as well as young women's difficulty in finding marriageable Black men—young men who are not chronically unemployed. In reply to the neoconservative emphasis on the subculture of poverty, Wilson develops the concepts of *social isolation* and *concentration effects*. A central Black underclass dilemma is the departure of stable middle-class families from traditional ghetto areas into better residential neighborhoods farther away. The poor thus face social isolation unlike that of the past. Not only are there fewer role models, but there are also fewer supportive institutions, including family stores, churches, and other voluntary associations. This deterioration brings a decline in sense of community, neighborhood identification, and norms against criminal behavior. Coupled with isolation are the concentration effects of having single-parent families, criminals, and the unemployed crowded into one area. Wilson rejects the neoconservative notion that the causes of current Black problems lie in self-perpetuating cultural traits.

Other Black Scholars

By the 1980s the term "underclass" was being used by white and Black social scientists. A number of Black scholars have made use of, and thereby helped to legitimate, the terminology of the Black underclass. However, although they accept the language of pathology, they have tended to accent the structural causes of the underclass dilemma. For example, in a 1984 book Pinkney has argued that

> Perhaps two of the major defining characteristics of the black underclass are their poverty and the social decay in which they are forced to survive.... Often they are forced to engage in criminal activities, a rational response to the circumstances in which they find themselves. And it must be noted that since these people are treated as animals, they frequently respond in kind (Pinkney, 1984:117).

He goes on to place emphasis on the structural conditions faced by Black Americans. Moreover, in a 1987 analysis of the Black family, Billingsly notes in passing the growth of the underclass:

The black underclass continues to grow, due in part to extensive poverty, unemployment, and family instability.... Composed of those families and individuals at the bottom of the economic and social scales—perhaps a third of all black families—this sector of the population experiences an enormous portion of suffering (Billingsly, 1987:101).

Douglas G. Glasgow published *The Black Underclass* in 1981; his book has been unnecessarily neglected. Although Glasgow uses the underclass terminology by defining the underclass as a "permanently entrapped population of poor persons, unused and unwanted," his analytical focus is on structural factors. He addresses institutional racism as it operates in the educational system and the job market. Programs like affirmative action have failed to improve life for the inner-city poor because these programs have been "aimed at correcting superficial inequities without addressing the ingrained societal factors that maintain such inequities." Moreover, in a recent article Glasgow notes that the concept of the Black underclass has become widespread and generally has negative connotations. The portrait is one of ne'er-do-well welfare recipients an irresponsible fathers of illegitimate children on the dole. Glasgow takes issue with three of the major assumptions in underclass theory: the implication that there is a value deficiency in the Black community which created the underclass; the notion that the underclass problem is mainly a female/feminization problem rather than a racial one; and the notion that it was antipoverty programs that created the underclass. Nonetheless, he does accept the concept of the underclass as useful and suggests that the underclass concept adds another dimension to the traditional class structure of upper, middle, working, and lower class (Glasgow, 1987:129–145).

A Report by Local Government

Just as in the 1960s, governmental reports in the 1980s have picked up on the underclass theory in analyzing urban problems. A report of the New York City Commission on the Year 2000, established by Mayor Ed Koch, reviews the health of that city and finds it to be "ascendant," with a strong economy and the "exuberance of a re-energized city." While this Koch report does recommend some job creation and development control actions, one section provides an underclass interpretation of poverty in the city. Contrasting conditions of earlier immigrants with the contemporary poor, it portrays the latter as not having the churches and other institutions that aided the mobility of earlier immigrants:

A city that was accustomed to viewing poverty as a phase in assimilation to the larger society now sees a seemingly rigid cycle of poverty and a permanent underclass divorced from the rest of society.

The report takes a limited "the city can only do so much" attitude to the solution of the poverty problem; the first two solutions proposed are for the "city to do what it can to discourage teenagers from becoming pregnant" and to provide troubled families at an early point with a caseworker. Some attention is given to the need to find job training programs for the welfare mothers, and a brief paragraph outlines how the city needs to develop programs to employ in its own division young unemployed males. As in many previous governmental reports, education is accented as the long-term solution to poverty in the city. There is no attention to the role of racial discrimination in Black poverty, nor is there any analysis of urban capital investment and disinvestment. From the beginning the orientation is "to make more sections of the city attractive to business" (Commission on the Year 2000, 1988: 33).

A CRITIQUE OF THE UNDERCLASS THEORY

A Politicized Theory

The concept of the underclass, as it has developed in the last decade, is highly political and represents a defining of the problems of the Black or in ways that do not involve an indictment of the existing structure of U.S. society. Neoconservatives use a reconstituted culture-of-poverty explanation, while liberals like Wilson mix some of the culture-of-poverty language with an emphasis on the social isolation and concentration of the Black poor. All theories, including the underclass theory, reflect the bias and societal situations of the theorists. Much of the underclass theorizing of the neoconservative theorists—and the white policymakers propagating it—is replete with white fears, assumptions, and biases. Liberal analysts, moreover, have generally fallen into the trap of accepting the language of the underclass theory even though they may place emphasis on demographic or structural factors.

The Problem of Definition

A major indicator of the problems in underclass theory is the ambiguity in various definitions. Auletta, for example, excludes the underemployed and includes street criminals, welfare mothers, hustlers, and the homeless. Wilson includes those who are among the long-term unemployed or who lack skills. For some, the underclass includes both rich criminals and the very poor. Most, but not all, see the underclass as made up primarily of minorities.

Behavior seems to be a common theme. Gephart and Pearson (1988: 3) claim that "most current definitions center around the concepts of concentrated and persistent poverty and/or a profile of 'underclass behaviors' that are judged dysfunctional by their observers." Neoconservatives and liberals alike use the language of illegitimacy, disorganization, and pathology. Many use income to count the underclass, but use behavior as the focus of the discussion. This means that the working poor and the elderly are sometimes included in the total count of those in the underclass, but are not part of the behavioral discussion. Even putting numbers on the size of the underclass has been problematical. Some estimates of the underclass include only a small share of the poor, while others expand the notion to include a much larger population. In a 1988 policy journal article, Ricketts and Sawhill have tried to make the definition of the underclass more concrete and specific, and thus to make it more useful for policymakers. They noted that "estimates of the underclass vary widely—from 3% to 38% of the poor. Persistence-based measures generally lead to higher estimates than location-based measures" (Ricketts and Sawhill, 1988: 318). They develop a definition using census data for geographical areas of cities:

> an underclass area [is] a census tract with a high proportion of (1) high school dropouts... ; (2) prime-age males not regularly attached to the labor force... ; (3) welfare recipients... ; and (4) female heads (Ricketts and Sawhill, 1988: 321).

They found that 2.5 million Americans live in these census tracts, although they admit that many nonpoor also live in there. Their final estimate is 'that there are about 1.3 million non-elderly adults living in underclass areas.

There is also a problem with the use of "class" in the term "underclass." The underclass distinction is not really a class distinction, because it does not focus on the hierarchy of classes or the relationship of classes, as does the tradition of class analysis since Karl Marx and Max Weber. While some argue that the underclass is outside the production (work) system, this is not actually the case, as we will see below. Moreover, if there is a Black underclass, presumably there is an "overclass." Yet the mainstream discussion does not discuss this "overclass."

Capitalism and Capital Flight

The underclass theory has arisen during an era when American capitalism is undergoing great change. There has been much capital flight out of central cities into suburban areas, cities in the Sunbelt, and foreign countries. Capital and corporate flight is at the heart of Black joblessness and poverty. Workers, Black or white, do not have the same ability to flee the community as do large corporations (Feagin and Parker, 1990: 37–50). Indeed, the threat of corporate flight has become a type of coercion, in that it forces workers to agree to wage reductions and other concessions—or in some cases to accept low-wage jobs. In addition, social scientists have functioned to legitimate a view of the U.S. capitalist system which suggests that Black workers should accept low-wage jobs.

Perhaps the strongest feature of Wilson's book, *The Truly Disadvantaged*, is the emphasis on joblessness as an important causal factor in the isolation of the Black underclass. Wilson argues that the scarcity of young Black males with regular jobs substantially accounts for the growing numbers of female-headed households and the increase in out-of-wedlock births. If young men and women cannot afford to get married, rent an apartment, and live together in a stable economic situation, young women set up their own households, raise their children, and often depend on welfare benefits. Wilson concludes his analysis with a call for a traditional job training and full employment policy, coupled with macroeconomic policy to generate a tight labor market and growth.

Among leading industrial nations the U.S. government has provided the weakest job training and creation programs. One important reason for this is that the U.S. state is substantially under the control of corporate capital, whose leadership seeks the freedom to invest or disinvest wherever profit margin and market control dictate and, thus, to weaken labor, cut taxes, and reduce employment programs. Wilson and other liberal analysts generally do not deal critically with the structure and operation of the contemporary capitalist system. The movement of jobs from northern cities to the Sunbelt cities and overseas, which Wilson does note, is not just part of a routine fluctuation in U.S. capitalism, but rather signals that investors are moving much capital, on a long-term basis, to areas with cheap labor and weak state regulation. Without a radical new policy restructuring the undemocratic investment policy of U.S. capitalism, it is not possible to deal fundamentally with job problems of central city dwellers. In *Black in a White America*, Sidney Wilhelm has pointed to the major problem facing large nonwhite groups concentrated in racially stratified low-wage jobs—the abandonment of whole populations as capitalism restructures to meet the chronic need for renewed profits. The U.S. economy no longer needs the majority of Black workers for full-time jobs (Willhelm, 1983).

Neoconservative and liberal analysts suggest that either the private sector or the government can provide enough jobs to solve the Black underclass problem. Yet, to quote from Adolph Reed (1988:170),

> what if there is no upward mobility queue—or at least not one either fat enough to accommodate the large populations of marginalized blacks and Hispanics or sturdy enough to withstand the dynamics of racial and class subordination?

Contemporary Discrimination: The Matter of Race

For most underclass analysts the concept of the Black underclass accents class culture or social isolation and downplays racial discrimination. A major weakness in Wilson's book is the rejection of current race discrimination as a significant reason for Black problems. Underclass analysts fail to consider the ways in which current discrimination perpetuates the effects of past discrimination. This results in, among other misconceptions, an ahistorical analysis, a too positive evaluation of the situation of middle-income Black Americans, and insufficient attention to the effect of discrimination on the Black underclass.

The discrimination of the past is much more substantial and thorough going for Black Americans. There is a view among some neoconservative scholars that "blacks today are like white immigrants yesterday," and that there is no need for governmental intervention on behalf of Blacks. In an article in the *New York Times Magazine* in 1966, social scientist Irving Kristol argued that "The Negro Today is Like the Immigrant of Yesterday" (Kristol, 1966: 50–51, 124–142). In his view the Black experience is not greatly different from that of white immigrant groups, and Black Americans can and will move up, just as the white immigrants of yesterday did. Similarly, Glazer argues that there are some important differences between the experiences of Blacks and those of white immigrants, but that there are more similarities than differences. He emphasizes that the difference is one of degree: "the gap between the experience of the worst off of the [white] ethnic groups and the Negroes is one of degree rather than kind. Indeed, in some respects the Negro is better off than some other groups" (Glazer, 1971: 45–59). Glazer further avers that, for the most part, the employment conditions faced by Black migrants to northern cities were no worse than those encountered by white immigrant groups.

Yet historical research by Hershberg, Yancey, and their associates has demonstrated that economic conditions at the time of entry into cities and the level of anti-Black racism at that time made the experiences of Blacks far more oppressive and difficult than those of white immigrant groups in northern cities. In the case of white immigrant groups, and of their children and grandchildren, group mobility was possible because:

1. Most arrived at a point in time when jobs were available,when capitalism was expanding and opportunities were more abundant;
2. Most faced far less severe employment and housing discrimination than Blacks did; and
3. Most found housing, however inadequate, reasonably near the workplaces (Hershberg, 1981: 462–464).

From an historical perspective there is no new underclass of the Black poor. For more than half a century there have been many Blacks in and outside cities without jobs; from the beginning of urban residence many Blacks have been locked into the segregated housing in cities.

Moreover, much "past" discrimination that reduced Black resources and mobility is not something of the distant past, but rather is recent. *Blatant* discrimination against Blacks occurred in massive doses until 25 years ago, particularly in the South. All Blacks (and whites) over the age of 30 years were born when the U.S. still had massive color bars both North and South. Most Blacks over 40 years of age were educated in *legally* segregated schools of lower quality than those of whites, and many felt the weight of massive *blatant* racial discrimination in, at least, the early part of their employment careers. And the majority of those Black Americans under the age of 30 have parents who have suffered from blatant racial discrimination. Moreover, most white Americans have benefited, if only indirectly, from past racial discrimination in several institutional areas.

A second misconception can be seen in the conceptualization of the Black middle class. By focussing on the middle class, scholars and other writers can argue that the problem of "race" is solved, that the only problem is that of the underclass, which is not racially determined. For example, it is often assumed that Black women hold favored positions in the labor market because affirmative action programs and equal opportunity programs have been most beneficial to middle-class Black women. This in turn leads to the assumption that Black professional women have experiences, interests, and concerns which are very substantially at variance with Black women who belong to the underclass (i.e., welfare mothers). However, whatever their class position, there are certain fundamental commonalties of experiences and perceptions shared by Black women as a racial-gender group.

Research on upper-middle-income Blacks in corporate America shows them to be suffering from widespread discrimination. Jones' research on Black managers has found that the predominantly white corporate environment, with its intense pressures for conformity, creates regular problems. Jones describes one Black manager working his way up the executive ranks. One day he met with other Black managers who wanted his advice on coping with discrimination:

> Charlie concluded that this should be shared with senior management and agreed to arrange a meeting with the appropriate officers. Two days before the scheduled meeting, while chatting with the President at a cocktail affair, Charlie was sobered by the President's disturbed look as he said, "Charlie I am disappointed that you met with those black managers. I thought we could trust you" (Jones, 1986:89).

Jones has also reported racial climate data from his nationwide survey of a large number of Black managers with graduate-level business degrees. Nearly all (98%) felt that Black managers had not achieved equal opportunity with white managers, and more than 90% felt there was much anti-Black hostility in corporations. The leaders in white (male) oriented organizations are willing, often grudgingly, to bring Blacks and women into important positions but in token numbers and under the existing rules (Jones, 1985).

In addition, members of the Black middle class do not have the same long-term financial security of comparable whites. Thus, a 1984 Census Bureau study of wealth found that the median Black household had a net worth of about $3,400, less than one-tenth of the median white household's net worth. This means that a crisis could easily wipe out most Black middle-class families (U.S. Bureau of the Census, 1987: 440–41).

Moreover, in the 1980s many Black workers at all status levels have faced layoffs and sharp reductions in income, including auto and steel workers. A Federal Service Task Force study found that in the early 1980s minority workers were laid off at 50% higher rate than whites. As Robert Ethridge of the American Association for Affirmative Action put it in 1988: "There are a lot [of Blacks] in peripheral areas like affirmative action and community relations, but as companies downsize, restructure, and merge, they want to cut off those fluff areas" (Ellis, 1988:68). The eight years of attacks on affirmative action under the Reagan administration took their toll. There is today less commitment to affirmative action in the business community.

The Reality of Discrimination

White Americans tend not to see the actual racial discrimination that exists in U.S. society, while Black Americans are acutely aware of it. In reply to an early 1980s Gallup poll question ("Looking back over the last ten years, do you think the quality of life of Blacks in the U.S. has gotten better, stayed the same, or gotten worse?"), over half of the nonwhites in the sample (mostly Blacks) said "gotten worse" or "stayed the same" (Gallup Opinion Index, 1980:10). Yet only a fifth of the *white* respondents answered in a negative way. Three-quarters of the whites said "gotten better." The survey also asked this question: "In your opinion, how well do you think Blacks are treated in this community: the same as whites are, not very well, or badly?" Sixty-eight percent of the whites in this nationwide sample said Blacks were treated the same as whites; only 20% felt they were not well treated or were badly treated.

In the spring of 1988, a *Business Week* article reported on a national survey showing that about half of the Blacks interviewed felt that they had to work harder than whites; just 7% of whites agreed. Over half the Blacks interviewed felt that most Blacks are paid less than whites "doing the same job." The comparable percentage for whites was 18%; 70% of the whites interviewed felt there was pay equality. Eighty percent of the Black respondents, and just 32% of the whites, felt that if an equally well qualified Black and white were competing for the same job, that the Black applicant would be less likely to be hired. Furthermore, 62% of Black respondents said that the chances for Blacks to be promoted to supervisory jobs were not as good as those for whites; even 41% of whites agreed (Ellis, 1988: 65).

Residential Dispersion and Desegregation

Current theories of the Black underclass emphasize the importance of Black middle-class flight from previously all-Black areas and into all-white areas. Underclass theorists argue that middle-class Blacks can and do abandon the ghetto to "move on up" to integrated suburban neighborhoods. The implication is that there is widespread housing integration, at least at the middle-class level. However, theories that focus on middle-class abandonment cannot explain the overwhelming statistical evidence of continuing residential segregation at all class levels (Newman, 1978; Peterson, 1981; Johnston, 1984). To take one example, in the city of New Orleans most Blacks at all income levels remain in traditionally Black areas; the four census tracts with the largest concentrations of Blacks are three public housing projects and one large Black suburban subdivision adjacent to poor Black areas (Inniss, 1988).

Black suburbanization has been low. Only one-tenth of Black Americans live in the suburbs today. Housing segregation data suggest that many stable-income, middle-income Black families have not moved far from ghetto areas, but rather live in nearby suburbs on the ghetto fringe. Thus, one study conducted in the 1980s of New Jersey found that most of the increase in Black suburban population in that state occurred in or near existing Black neighborhoods (Lake, 1981). A 1988 study by Denton and Massey also questioned the middle-class abandonment thesis. Using data from the 1980 census, Denton and Massey found that within the 20 metropolitan areas with the largest Black populations, Blacks continue to be highly segregated residentially, at all socioeconomic levels. Even for the best-educated Blacks, those with one year or more of postgraduate work, the index of segregation was very high. They conclude that if the Black middle class is abandoning the Black poor, "they are not moving to integrated Anglo-Black neighborhoods" (Denton and Massey, 1988: 814).

Moreover, in a recent national survey the majority of the whites interviewed said that the percentage Black in their neighborhood had stayed the same or gone down in the past five years; only 29% said the percentage Black had increased—even a little. Among the Black respondents only 10% reported that the percent Black in their neighborhood had gone down in the last five years. Thirty-five percent reported that the percentage had gone up (Ellis, 1988:65). The surveys suggest no great changes in the mid-1980s.

CONCLUSION

The solution to the problem of Blacks in America is neither obscure nor novel. The vestiges and badges of slavery are still very much in evidence in the terrible statistics that the underclass theorists repeat. But these statistics are not the result, at base, of some underclass subculture or isolation from the Black middle class. They reflect past and present discrimination. One problem is that most commentators have gotten so used to Black poverty that their language of pathology and ghettos seems relatively accurate and harmless. Yet like other forms of discrimination and segregation Black "ghettos" go back to, and are a residue of, slavery; we should not speak of them cavalierly as though they were just areas of cities somehow comparable to other areas such as "suburbs." Ghettos are terrible places reflecting the *result* of white racism, no less.

To get rid of these badges and vestiges of slavery, we not only need some broad restructuring of modern capitalism to meet the needs of ordinary workers, Black and white, but in our view we also require race-specific solutions such as expanded—and aggressive—affirmative action. In theory at least, the concept of affirmative action is radical; affirmative action recognizes that past wrongs are structured-in and must be specially addressed with race-specific structural programs. Some previous affirmative action plans have been successful in opening up institutions for Black Americans.

The opponents of equal opportunity and affirmative action have scored a brilliant coup by getting the mass media to discuss affirmative action in terms of the simplistic phrase "reverse discrimination." Yet the term is grossly inaccurate. Traditional discrimination has meant, and still means, the widespread practice of blatant and subtle discrimination by whites against Blacks in most organizations in all major institutional areas of society—in housing, employment, education, health services, the legal system, and so on. For three centuries now, tens of millions of whites have participated directly in discrimination against millions of Blacks, including routinized discrimination in the large-scale bureaucracies that now dominate this society. The reverse of traditional discrimination by whites against Blacks would mean reversing the power and resource inequalities for a long time: for several hundred years, massive institutionalized discrimination would be directed by dominant Blacks against most whites. That societal condition would be "reverse discrimination." It has never existed.

Moreover, Kenneth Smallwood (1985) has argued that white America has historically benefited from huge federal "affirmative action" plans for whites only, programs which laid the foundation for much of white prosperity in the United States. To take one major example, from the 1860s to the early 1900s, the Homestead Act provided free land in the West for whites, but because most Blacks were still in the semislavery peonage of Southern agriculture, most could not participate in this government affirmative action program giving land to U.S. citizens. That billion-dollar land giveaway became the basis of economic prosperity for many white Americans and their descendants. Recent affirmative action plans for Black Americans pale in comparison with that single program. Moreover, most New Deal programs in the 1930s primarily subsidized white Americans and white-controlled corporations. Thus, Federal Housing Administration (FHA) actions helped millions of white American families secure housing while that agency also encouraged the segregation of Black Americans in ghetto communities. Massive New Deal agricultural programs and the Reconstruction Finance Corporation kept many white American bankers, farmers, and corporate executives in business, again providing the basis for much postwar prosperity in white America.

Yet similar, massive multibillion dollar aid programs have never been made available to most Black Americans. Preferential treatment for white Americans has always been legitimate, and was for more than three centuries an essential part of government development in U.S. society. If so, one might add, why not provide three centuries of equivalent, legitimate, large-scale affirmative action to build up the wealth of the Black American victims of white discrimination?

Leslie Inniss and Joe R. Feagin

PART THREE

Race and Ethnicity in American Institutions

On the Internet . . .

Sites appropriate to Part Three

This site, sponsored by the American Fidelity Educational Services, offers over 50,000 pages that can be referenced. Search under the topics "race" and "ethnicity" for education resources related to these categories.

    http://www.education-world.com/

This Web site, sponsored by the U.S. Department of Education, leads to numerous documents related to elementary and early childhood education, as well as other curriculum topics and issues.

    http://www.ed.gov/pubs/pubdb.html

Studies by the National Center for Education Statistics (NCES) cover the entire educational spectrum, providing the facts and figures needed to help policymakers understand the condition of education in the United States today, to give researchers a foundation of data to build upon, and to help teachers and administrators to identify the best practices for their schools. This site provides information about reports and data products that NCES has released and the results of a variety of educational surveys.

    http://nces.ed.gov/

This site is a major source of social, demographic, and economic information, such as income/employment data and income distribution and poverty data. Search the terms "race, ethnic" to find the results of the 1996 Race and Ethnic Targeted Test (RAETT) and U.S. population projections by race, as well as other race-related information.

    http://www.census.gov/

CHAPTER 6 The Educational Institution

6.1 NOEL JACOB KENT

The New Campus Racism: What's Going On?

The politics of racial hate, fear, and anger is significantly increasing on U.S. college and university campuses. Hate literature, graffiti in public places, name-calling, denigrating epithets, and violence continue to disrupt the lives of racial minorities attempting to get a college education. The National Institute Against Prejudice and Violence claims that hundreds of incidents of racial violence and assaults have taken place on college campuses within the last several years. Recently, Asian American students at the University of California, Irvine, were threatened via e-mail with being "hunted down and killed."

In the following selection from "The New Campus Racism: What's Going On?" *Thought and Action* (1997), Noel Jacob Kent contends that the racial and ethnic intolerance on U.S. campuses reflects a growing racial polarization in the greater society that, in turn, is the product of a "profound moral crisis." Kent proposes that to end the escalating campus racism, colleges and universities must adopt "transformative" strategies that include meaningful curriculum reform comprising more realistic explications of racism in U.S. society, faculty awareness of their own personal microcultures, and the adoption of conflict mediation programs.

Kent is a professor of ethnic studies at the University of Hawaii at Manoa. His research interests focus on ethnic and race relations and U.S.

history and political economy. His most recent endeavor of study is on how colleges and universities handle the issues of ethnic and racial diversity and conflict.

Key Concept: campus racism

"Racism and bigotry are back on the campus with a vengeance."
—Professor William Damon, Clark University

Colleges and universities could once pretend to offer a refuge from the swirling antagonisms of a highly racialized society. But no longer.

The incidence of verbal and physical harassments and abuses directed against Latino, Asian and Jewish-Americans, foreign students, and, above all, African-Americans has been surging on our campuses since at least the late 1980s.

Why so much bigotry and intolerance at institutions long seen as dedicated to reason and the search for truth?

Part of the answer is that life on campus closely mirrors the dominant patterns and attitudes of the larger society. In both, racial structures and meanings are in flux and hotly contested, and racism, driven by a profound "moral crisis," has proven an entrenched and virulent social force.

Another part of the answer: Our economy in the late 20th Century is going through its most profound restructuring since the dawn of the Industrial Age. The consequences of that restructuring—diminished opportunity, stagnating wages, a decline in the quality of life for many families—directly conflict with the mythic American dream. The result: depression, confusion, and wide-ranging anger throughout the society, a reaction that the campus is not immune from.

Here we will attempt to demonstrate how these interrelated phenomena fuel the rise of intolerance on our campuses. We also hope to suggest how campuses might respond to the current crisis with transformative solutions, rather than the current response, which has usually been reactive, after-the-fact, and too little-too late.

THE CONTEXT OF THE "NEW RACISM"

The great triumph of the civil rights movement of the 1960s was to end legal segregation in the United States. A consequence of that movement was that white attitudes toward African-American inclusion shifted demonstrably. The idea of Black participation in formerly white-monopolized spheres of national life became widely accepted throughout the society. A wholly new set of opportunities and possibilities seemed to open up.

The transformation, however, remained both uneven and incomplete—an odd "mixture of striking movement and surface change." The belief in equal opportunity did not lead to widespread acceptance of equal opportunity in practice. Rather than the steady decline of discrimination and maturing of the "colorblind society" envisioned by integrationists, "racial meanings" remained bitterly contested. The battle for full participation continued as "trench warfare" in bureaucracies and courts.

Given the nation's history and the psychological and material advantages that skin pigmentation confers upon whites, the emergence of a "New Racism" is hardly surprising. Anti-Black prejudice continues as a cultural norm central to the white American worldview and identity. Indeed, as a "fluid, variable and open ended process," racism simply plays too many essential roles to be easily abandoned.

If the United States in 1996 no longer perfectly fits the "two societies, one Black, one white—separate and unequal," described by the National Advisory Commission on Civil Disorders in 1969, it is not so very different either. Older theories of biological inferiority and white supremacy have given way to a new view that combines negative Black stereotypes with the glorification of individualism and meritocracy.

The accepted "wisdom" of the "new racism" is that "a racially balanced society" now provides equal opportunity for all to pursue the American Good Life. Individuals can rise above their environment. There is opportunity for all. Failure results from personal inadequacies, splintered families, and a culture of failure.

Minority poverty, labor market ghettoization, segregated neighborhoods, and disproportionate rates of incarceration are attributed to the moral failure of the people involved. Groups "lagging behind are in essence faulted for their own circumstances."

Crudely overt displays of racism represent a second level of the "New Racism." Its proponents are the fairly large number of whites who remain unable "to perceive Black members as legitimate full members of the polity."

These undisguised acts of bigotry take the form of everyday harassment, violence, and intimidation, ranging from street epithets and the primitive stereotypes bandied about during radio talk shows to the vicious assaults orchestrated by vanguard neo-Nazis, Klan, and other white supremacists. What marks the latter groups, notes Robert Cahill, who monitored white supremacist movements in the Northwest, are their "proudly explicit" racial beliefs, "radical alienation from racial amalgamation," and violence.

The "New Racism" also has its political front. The New Right, the champion of white protectionism and identity, has been a key player in an unlikely coalition of Southern whites, Northern blue collars, religious fundamentalists, and the affluent that practically monopolized the White House from 1968 through 1992. The GOP has been especially effective in turning *crime, busing, welfare,* and *quotas* into highly charged codewords.

All these approaches feed into each other. In Professor Mari Matsuda's succinct phrase: "Gutter racism, parlor racism, corporate racism and government racism work in coordination, reinforcing existing conditions of domination."

The timing is certainly opportune: For the first time since the civil rights era, a majority of whites believe equal rights have been "pushed too far in this country." Much of the Republican Party's 1994 electoral success stemmed from playing to white voter anger at federal social programs and "enforced diversity." The leading 1996 Republican presidential candidates uniformly bashed affirmative action programs, and one, Pat Buchanan, made their abolition a central plank of his platform.

In retrospect, the right-wing success in shifting the national debate from the historic foundations of minority poverty and disadvantage toward the twin myths of total individual responsibility and "color-blindness" has been nothing short of phenomenal.

That our colleges and universities are not immune to the racial polarization of society at large should come as no surprise. Well before entering college, young people have gotten the message—subtle and not-so-subtle—from family, peers, and the media about the appropriate racial hierarchy.

Many white college students, those from highly segregated suburbs and smaller cities, carry the larger society's stereotypes of Blacks as violent criminals/willing welfare dependents. Given their narrow cultural framework, it is difficult for these students to accept non-white presence and cultural expressions on campus. For them, African-American students may appear to be intruders. At least some whites associate difference in skin color with disadvantage and, often, deviance.

But there are also many white students who genuinely support the idea of a color-blind society. For them, the intense skepticism of Blacks to this idea is troubling if not bewildering. They have come face to face with a basic obstacle to real communication: the radically differing views Black and white students have about the meaning of racism. That even the most well intentioned whites and Blacks have entirely different reference points becomes startlingly evident not only over campus issues, but in national and international events like the Gulf War, the O.J. Simpson trial verdict, the Million Man March.

Professor Robert Blauner of the University of California at Berkeley argues that there "care two languages of race in America" and that young whites and Blacks are talking past each other when they discuss "racism." What whites see as peripheral and mainly an historic artifact, Blacks view as absolutely "central" to U.S. history and contemporary society. "Whites," he says, "locate racism in color consciousness and its absence in color-blindness," whereas Blacks expand the meaning to include power, position, and equality in the structuring of American society.

Blauner points out that when Black students act in conventionally American *ethnic* ways—by forming Black Student Unions, for instance—whites interpret this as racial exclusion. White students don't understand why "students of color insistently underscore their sense of difference, their affirmation of racial and ethnic membership." In contrast, minorities of color "sense a kind of racism in the whites' assumption that minorities must assimilate to mainstream values and styles."

This is an increasing point of conflict as campus Blacks mirror the "defensive ethnicity" many whites have adopted. Integration has always taken a psychic toll. Now across the spectrum of African-American society—and especially on campuses—cynicism about the entire undertaking is increasing. Black separatism, once a tactic in the integration struggle, has emerged as an end in itself.

African-American students have always had difficulty in "recognizing" themselves and their heritage on white majority campuses. "I know that whites are never going to respect me on face value," says an Atlanta student. "It feels like I don't exist here," commented one Black student in the midst of a 1995 dispute at the College of the Holy Cross over the barring of whites from a Black campus organization.

Since most campuses don't provide a supportive infrastructure, and have a generally unfavorable racial climate, African-Americans increasingly form their own campus enclaves. "It's a Black thing. You wouldn't understand" read the t-shirts worn by college students, who increasingly choose to segregate themselves from whites in dormitories.

To comprehend the larger forces driving campus racism, we should look at recent structural changes in the United States and the flourishing of old and new fears.

THE MORAL CRISIS

The escalating racial polarization of American society is intertwined with what Professor Charles Maier calls a national "moral crisis." Americans are no longer able to make sense of, much less respond to, the massive changes now confronting them.

Moreover, many certainties and rituals that once provided meaning and stability are now threatened. A public—adrift and dislocated—no longer knows what social progress means. That same public has grown disenchanted with traditional political processes incapable of providing protection.

Americans recite a litany of fears, ranging from loss of jobs and medical coverage to rising taxes. The sense of every-citizen-as-victim is mirrored on prime-time television sitcoms and is the food and drink of immensely popular, immensely spiteful talk-show hosts.

Public discussion is saturated with mean-spirited rhetoric catering to knee-jerk instinct and irrationality. Working people rant at being victimized, yet direct their rage at those even more powerless. The inevitable search for different "others" to blame helps to repress both conflicts within the white majority itself and the need to address society's most deep rooted problems.

At the heart of this contemporary crisis is the collision between the American Dream's myth of individual upward mobility and the reality of the radical restructuring of the U.S. political-economy.

The American Dream tells us that if you work hard, you succeed. The nation's vast resources, technical ingenuity, and fluid social system will reward the conscientious, thrifty individual—and, if not her or him, then surely, that person's children. "Americans," remarks Paul Wachtel, "have viewed the future as rightfully providing them with more.

Today, however, pessimism reigns. Forty-three percent of those surveyed shortly before the 1994 election expected life to be worse by the end of the century. A 1995 survey found 55 percent convinced the nation was in long-term decline.

Such pessimism flows from a quarter-century of stagnant and declining family and individual incomes and wages. Personal savings have fallen dramatically, along with discretionary incomes. The buying power of most families remains approximately at late 1970s levels.

The more than 10 million new jobs generated during the Clinton era, significant increases in the rate of women working, and multiple job holding have not reversed income stagnation and decline. A large majority of the population has lost ground absolutely or relatively. People in the lowest income groups have lost the most.

Big Business has jettisoned the post-war social contract and consciously conducted anti-union campaigns with a vengeance and outsourced millions of high-paying jobs to cheaper labor areas. "Downsizing" has become this decade's *leitmotif* [dominant, recurring theme]. Internal corporate labor markets now feature a core of stable, relatively privileged employees surrounded by low-paid, casual, contingent workers lacking rights or benefits. Solid primary sector jobs, with middle class incomes, career ladders, and job security, are driven out by what Chris Tilly calls "firms that have adopted a low-wage, low skill, high turnover employment policy."

College educated workers—middle managers, engineers, professionals, and other white collar workers—have been displaced at a previously unimaginable rate, as corporations flatten hierarchies and hire fewer permanent, well-paid staff.

Youth are at the epicenter of this social earthquake. Today's young adult man is less likely than his father was at the same age to own his own home or have a secure career and opportunities for future mobility. American society now mocks young people's needs for a long-term, secure place in society. The decline of homeownership opportunities has led to a sharp increase in the "unexpected homecomings" of married and unmarried 20- to 30-year olds.

Young adults share the prevailing pessimism about the future. Meanwhile, they continue to desperately cling to the disintegrating American Dream. Throughout the '90s, about three-quarters of college freshmen surveyed agreed they are in school "to be able to get a better job" and "to be able to make more money." Large majorities believe that "the chief benefit of college is that it increases one's earning power."

The latter belief does contain some truth. Higher education credentials have become more crucial than ever before for those aspiring to middle class lives. Yet the hopes of collegians for professional jobs and pay are simply out of line with new labor market realities. Higher education no longer offers a guaranteed payoff.

The collapsed job market for college graduates of the 1970s reappeared in the early 1990s. Job prospects for the 1993 graduating class were "dismal," as fewer recruiters arrived on campuses offering fewer jobs. The mid-'90s "prosperity" has improved things only marginally. More college graduates are working at jobs not requiring college level training.

Even students at the most prestigious institutions are digesting the unpalatable truth that they will wind up poorer than their parents. "There's a general sense of helplessness that students have that they're not going to be able to find a job that will pay them enough to live on," notes one college counselor.

This perception drives the often frantic pressures to link college and professional career. Job hunting becomes a preoccupation almost from the freshman year. The college years become more a financial investment in the future and less a *rite de passage*.

Contemporary young people, perhaps more than any other American generation before them, are trapped between the prevailing "psychology of entitlement" and an economic environment that demands austerity and sacrifice.

We have already seen how the "question of color" arrives on the campus laden with extensive ideological baggage. Now the struggle toward the always elusive goal of racial justice takes on the added dimension of scarcity: The possibility of a livable future has become scarce—for whites as well as Blacks.

Given their increasing financial worries and their deteriorating job prospects, white college students readily perceive of themselves as victims. From a zero sum game perspective, affirmative action programs seem to further stack a deck already loaded against them. The feelings of self-doubt, inadequacy, and difficulties in identity formation now epidemic among youth have been identified with the propensity to scapegoat minorities.

In a culture where very often expressions of rage and frustration are directed at race, terms like "reverse racism" and "terminally Caucasian" take on real power. A white student leader organizing against the white student union at the University of Florida has summarized the mood: "There is a growing realization by white males that they no longer have their privileged advantages, who feel they may not do as well as their fathers, and they are looking for scapegoats."

At UC Berkeley, one embittered student complains that "being white means that you're less likely to get financial aid. It means that there are all sorts of tutoring groups and special programs that you can't get into, because you're not a minority."

Underscoring these intense feelings is the fiscal crisis of higher education in the United States, which *is* victimizing white students (among others). Cutbacks in federal, state, and local funding over the last decade have meant that, at a time of growing enrollments, institutions have left faculty and support positions unfilled, pared back classes, eliminated departments, and shortened library hours.

Meanwhile, as tuition and fee increases soar well beyond inflation rates, financial aid awards have diminished. Financial pressures compel many white students to spend more time working and less in school. Ironically, even as students are being whipsawed between the demands of school, work, and family life, counseling services are being cut back, too. Some would-be full-timers are now part-timers with a long trajectory to graduation. A "ratcheting down" process forces many students to attend a lower prestige school than they might have attended only recently.

White students, reacting out of helplessness and free-floating anger, scapegoat minority students. This demonization leads to the overtly racist acts that occur on our campuses.

Colleges and universities have, of course, never been "ivory towers." The racial divisions and economic dislocation that plague society as a whole play themselves out on our campuses. And never more than today.

A COMMITMENT TO TRANSFORMATIVE EDUCATION

How to break this vicious cycle of escalating campus racism and polarization? Senator Bill Bradley maintains that racism will thrive as long as "white Americans resist relinquishing the sense of entitlement skin color has given them throughout our history." Seldom, however, does the college experience cause students to question whether such entitlements exist. Neither do they find their own, nor their society's, racial biases seriously challenged by the curriculum they study or the associations they make.

Few institutions mandate study of cultural identities and values. Only infrequently do white undergraduates investigate the framework in which African-Americans (among others) are marginalized by both university and larger society. For the vast majority of white students, then, *college does not change their sense of race and race relations in the United States.*

College and university administrators trying to address the race issue have tended to be *reactive.* They draw up guidelines for conduct, promulgate hate speech codes, and mete out punishments for campus offenders. This has raised a storm of protest and a slew of court actions.

Given the campus racial climate, firm rules to define acceptable behavior are certainly needed. Every student has a basic right to a safe and secure campus learning and living environment free from harassment. No college or university should tolerate violations of those rights. But such policies should be part of a *transformative* strategy that takes as its point of departure white and minority student attitudes, fears, and self-conceptions. This strategy should help students learn "the different languages of race" cited by Blauner. Make these languages mutually intelligible and students will begin to "get it." Mutual empathy is an indispensable step toward mutual respect and cooperation.

Curriculum reform—as when Stanford broadens the canon to include non-western literature and Wisconsin-Madison requires undergraduates to take courses with an ethnic studies component—is probably the most widely used transformative vehicle. Conflict mediation programs, such as the one at UCLA which emphasizes resolving diversity related conflicts, are also critical. But developing empathy across subcultures demands more. Majority white colleges and universities must take some risky initiatives along uncharted ground. Black sensibilities and experiences must be given wide-spread voice. White students, too, must have a safe and dignified way to express and work out their greivances and fears and find answers to their own questions of identity. *We must not underestimate the mutual hunger for honest talk across racial bunkers.* Interracial campus activities and dialogues should be encouraged, so students can appreciate each other as (different) equals and members of a community sharing similar goals. White students should have the opportunity to experience the daily realities of being "otherness" by living in a majority African-American dorm, volunteering in a minority neighborhood, or studying abroad.

Faculty are critical agents in the process. As Gay Reed suggests, learning about other cultures and "celebrating diversity" is only a minor part of understanding "the cultural and historical roots of diversity which have made it so problematic in American society." Reed sagely argues that faculty "need to become aware of their own personal microcultures and understand how this microculture affects and is affected by the larger macroculture."

Programs must move beyond the campus to creatively challenge racism in the community. White children and teenagers at the K–12 level need to be educated about the harsh historical realities of who were not allowed to be "We the People of the United States." Researchers at the University of Massachusetts-Amherst are conducting racial and ethnic diversity and tolerance programs in those Boston elementary schools from which the university has drawn some of its more aggressively racist students. Public and private colleges might, as an institutional mission, adopt local schools for race relations education.

Higher education has a vital role to play in reversing the tide of bigotry and hate in the country, but, right now, the best contribution we can make is to begin getting our own academic houses in order.

American Indians in Higher Education: A History of Cultural Conflict

Unique to the Native American educational experience is the legal relationship that was established with the federal government through hundreds of treaties providing specific governmental services to Indian nations in exchange for access to tribal lands. Education was one such service. The history of Native American access to formal education in the United States, however, is one of racial isolation. In the late 1800s, the federal government viewed educational programs for Native American children as a means to assimilate these children into the Anglo-dominated culture of the United States. This was the underlying philosophy of boarding schools for Native American children, which were often located great distances from the children's family and tribal ties. The boarding school essentially isolated the children and thereby eased their indoctrination into mainstream American culture. Native American culture, including language, values, traditions, and customs, was viewed as negative and a hindrance to the educational process.

Bobby Wright, of the Chippewa-Cree tribe, is an assistant professor and a research associate in the Center for the Study of Higher Education at Pennsylvania State University. His colleague William G. Tierney is an associate professor and a senior research associate at the center. In the present selection, Wright and Tierney suggest that the cultural conflict associated with Native Americans' educational processes continues today.

Key Concept: Native Americans in higher education

*C*aleb Cheeshateaumuck, an Algonquian Indian from Martha's Vineyard, graduated from Harvard College, class of 1665. An outstanding scholar, Caleb could read, write, and speak Latin and Greek as well as English—not to mention his own native language. Although fully able to meet Harvard's rigorous academic demands, the young native scholar did not escape the dangers associated with life in an alien environment.

Caleb was among the first in a long line of American Indians who have attended colleges and universities during the past three centuries. He represents, too, the challenge and the triumph, as well as the failure and tragedy, that characterize the history of American Indian higher education. These conflicting outcomes reflect the clash of cultures, the confrontation of lifestyles, that has ensued on college campuses since colonial days. Euro-Americans have persistently sought to remold Native Americans in the image of the white man—to "civilize" and assimilate the "savages"—but native peoples have steadfastly struggled to preserve their cultural integrity. The college campus has historically provided a stage for this cross-cultural drama.

Within a decade of the first European settlement in America, plans for an Indian college were already underway. The earliest colonial efforts to provide Indians with higher education were designed to Christianize and "civilize" the Indians, thus saving them from the folly of their "heathenish" and "savage" ways. The hope was that educated Indians, as schoolmasters and preachers, would become missionary agents among their own brethren.

In 1617, King James I launched the initial design, when he enjoined the Anglican clergymen to collect charitable funds for "the erecting of some churches and schools for ye education of ye children of these [Virginia] Barbarians." The following year, the English set aside 1,000 acres at Henrico, Virginia for construction of a "college for Children of the Infidels." However, the Virginia natives resisted such cultural intrusions. Their rebellion in 1622, an attempt to rid their lands of the English forever, was only partially and temporarily successful, but it abruptly ended the scheme for an Indian college in Virginia.

In New England, the 1650 charter of Harvard College heralded the next educational design. It provided for the "education of the English and Indian youth of this country in knowledge." Charitable contributions from England supported the construction of the Indian College building on Harvard's campus, completed in 1656. During the four decades of its existence, although it had a capacity for 20 students, the structure housed no more than six Indian scholars—Caleb Cheeshateaumuck among them. Most of that time, the "Indian college" housed English students and the college printing press.

In Virginia, the native rebellion of 1622 had ended the initial plans for an Indian college. Seven decades later, the 1693 charter of the College of William and Mary reaffirmed the English desire to educate and "civilize" the Indians. It established William and Mary, in part, so "that the Christian faith may be propagated amongst the Western Indians." Robert Boyle, an English scientist and philanthropist, inspired this divine mission when he willed a bequest for unspecified charitable and pious uses. The president of William and Mary obtained the lion's share of this charity, which he used to build the Brafferton building in 1723, purportedly to house resident native scholars. No Indian students were in residence for two decades following its completion, however, and only five or six attended during the life of the Brafferton school. Following feeble efforts and insignificant results, the American Revolution stopped the flow of missionary funds from England, and William and Mary has since ignored the pious mission on which it was founded.

In the mid-18th century, Eleazar Wheelock, a Congregational minister, passionately engaged in the academic training of Indian youth. Wheelock founded Dartmouth College, chartered in 1769, for "the education & instruction of Youth of the Indian tribes in this Land in reading, wrighting [sic] and all parts of Learning which shall appear necessary and expedient for civilizing and Christianizing children of pagans... and also of English Youth." He built the College with charity collected by Samson Occum, Wheelock's most successful convert and a noted Indian scholar, who solicited a substantial endowment for native education. Nonetheless, by the time he established Dartmouth, Wheelock's interest in Indian schooling waned in favor of the education of "English youth." As a result, the College became increasingly inaccessible to potential Native American converts. While a total of 58 Indians attended from 1769 to 1893, Dartmouth produced only three Indian graduates in the 18th century and eight in the 19th.

The College of New Jersey (now Princeton University), although not specifically professing an Indian mission, admitted at least three Indian students. The first, a Delaware youth, attended the College in 1751 under the sponsorship of the Society in Scotland for the Propagation of Christian Knowledge, benefactors also of Dartmouth's Indian program. Although reportedly proficient in his learning and "much beloved by his classmates and the other scholars," the unfortunate young Delaware died of consumption a year later. Jacob Woolley, one of Wheelock's first students, enrolled in 1759, though he was expelled before completing his degree. Finally, Shawuskukhkung—also known by his English name, Bartholomew Scott Calvin—attended the College in 1773. During his second year of residence, however, the charitable funds from Great Britain that supported his attendance ceased, as a consequence of the Revolutionary War, forcing Calvin to abandon his studies.

TRIBAL RESISTANCE

The colonial experiments in Indian higher education proved, for the most part, unsuccessful. Targeted tribal groups resisted missionary efforts and tenaciously clung to their traditional life ways. Among those who succumbed to education, their physical inability to survive the alien environment compounded the failure. Hugh Jones, an 18th-century historian of Virginia, admitted that, at the College of William and Mary

> hitherto but little good has been done, though abundance of money has been laid out.... [An] abundance of them used to die... Those of them that have escaped well, and been taught to read and write, have for the most part returned to their home, some with and some without baptism, where they follow their own savage customs and heathenish rites.

The general Indian sentiment is illustrated by the Six Nations' response to the treaty commissioners from Maryland and Virginia, who in 1744 invited the Indians to send their sons to the College of William and Mary. "We must let you know," the Iroquois leaders responded,

> We love our Children too well to send them so great a Way, and the Indians are not inclined to give their Children learning. We allow it to be good, and we thank you for your Invitation; but our customs differing from yours, you will be so good as to excuse us.

The colonial era ended and, with the birth of the new nation, Indian education increasingly became a matter of federal policy. Influenced by the limited results of the colonial educational missions, George Washington voiced a shift in policy from an emphasis on higher learning to vocational training for American Indians. "I am fully of the opinion," he concluded,

> that this mode of education which has hitherto been pursued with respect to these young Indians who have been sent to our colleges is not such as can be productive of any good to their nations. It is perhaps productive of evil. Humanity and good policy must make it the wish of every good citizen of the United States that husbandry, and consequently, civilization, should be introduced among the Indians.

This educational philosophy unfolded in the 19th century and dominated until the 20th, even in the midst of tribal efforts to gain a foothold in higher education.

TRIBAL SUPPORT

While some tribes violently resisted attempts to "civilize" them through education, other Indian groups eagerly embraced higher learning. At the same time that Dartmouth was educating 12 members of the Five Civilized Tribes, the Cherokees and the Choctaws organized a system of higher education that had more than 200 schools, and sent numerous graduates to eastern colleges. The 1830 Treaty of Dancing Rabbit Creek set aside $10,000 for the education of Choctaw youth. The first official use of the funds provided under this treaty occurred in 1841, when the tribe authorized the education of Indian boys at Ohio University, Jefferson College, and Indiana University. The 1843 Report of the Commissioner of Indian Affairs mentioned the education of 20 Choctaw boys, 10 at Asbury University, and 10 at Lafayette College.

Choctaw graduates from tribally operated boarding schools were selected on the basis of their promise and allowed to continue their education until they had completed graduate and professional study at colleges in the states. Several members of the Five Civilized Tribes entered Dartmouth in 1838, and, in 1854, Joseph Folsom, a Choctaw, received a degree. In all, 12 Choctaw and Cherokee students received support to attend Dartmouth from the "Scottish Fund"—the legacy of their predecessor, Samson Occum. Ironically, the Choctaw academic system, responsible for a literacy rate exceeding that of their white neighbors, collapsed when the federal government became involved in the late 1800s.

The first university in which Indians were to play a significant role was proposed in 1862. As was the case at Harvard, however, the Ottawa Indian University was more a dream than a reality. The Ottawas never received the promised university, as they were removed by the federal government to Oklahoma in 1873.

Bacon College, founded by the Baptists in 1880, also received Indian support, which came in the form of a land grant from the Creek tribe. Dedicated to training of Indian clergy, the college opened to three students. By the end of its fifth year, 56 students had enrolled. Bacon College still operates today with a strong (but not exclusive) commitment to educate American Indians.

EDUCATION AS ASSIMILATION

Indians who attended universities and colleges during the 17th, 18th, and 19th centuries, for the most part, studied the same subjects as did the white students. However, as the federal government began to dominate Indian education in the late 19th century, significantly reducing the role of missionary groups, private individuals, and the states, the result was a continual de-emphasis on higher learning. Instead, the role of higher education changed to vocational training.

In 1870 Congress appropriated $100,000 for the operation of federal industrial schools. The first off-reservation boarding school was established at Carlisle, Pennsylvania in 1879. The boarding school, exemplified at Carlisle, dominated the federal approach to Indian education for half a century. Its methods included the removal of the students from their homes and tribal influences, strict military discipline, infusion of the Protestant work ethic, as well as an emphasis on the agricultural, industrial, and domestic arts—*not* higher academic study.

Most importantly, these institutions were designed to make their Indian charges in the image of the white man. Luther Standing Bear, a Sioux, attended Carlisle in 1879. He recalled the psychological assaults he and others encountered during the educational process.

> I remember when we children were on our way to Carlisle School, thinking that we were on our way to meet death at the hands of the white people, the older boys sang brave songs, so that we would meet death according to the code of the Lakota. Our first resentment was in having our hair cut. It has ever been the custom of Lakota men to wear long hair, and old tribal members still wear the hair in this manner. On first hearing the rule, some of the older boys talked of resisting, but realizing the uselessness of doing so, submitted. But for days after being shorn we felt strange and uncomfortable.... The fact is that we were to be transformed.

Fueled by a large congressional appropriation in 1882, 25 boarding schools opened by the turn of the century—among them, Santa Fe Indian School, which became the Institute of American Indian Arts, a two-year postsecondary school, and Haskell Institute (now Haskell Indian Junior College) in Lawrence, Kansas. These institutes, like the normal schools of the 19th century, were not true colleges. Their standards of training, at best, approximated only those of a good manual-training high school. The range of occupational futures envisioned for Indian students was limited to farmer, mechanic, and housewife.

By the turn of the century, only a few talented Indian youth went on for further training at American colleges and universities. Ohiyesa, a Sioux, was among them. Adopting the notion that "the Sioux should accept civilization before it was too late," Charles A. Eastman (his English name) graduated from Dartmouth College in 1887, and three years later received a degree in medicine at Boston University. Eastman was keenly aware that his academic success depended on his acceptance of American civilization and the rejection of his own traditional culture. "I renounced finally my bow and arrow for the spade and the pen," he wrote in his memoirs. "I took off my soft moccasins and put on the heavy and clumsy but durable shoes. Every day of my life I put into use every English word that I knew, and for the first time permitted myself to think and act as a white man."

Ohiyesa's accomplishments were rare in the 19th and early 20th centuries. The education of Native Americans—although still preserving the centuries-old purpose of civilizing the "savages"—seldom exceeded the high school level. The impact of this neglect on Indian educational attainment is reflected in enrollment figures. As late as 1932, only 385 Indians were enrolled in college and only 52 college graduates could be identified. At that time, too, American Indian scholarships were being offered at only five colleges and universities.

FEDERAL EFFORTS

Not until the New Deal era of the 1930s, a period of reform in federal Indian policy, did Indian higher education receive government support. The Indian Reorganization Act of 1934, among other sweeping reforms, authorized $250,000 in loans for college expenses. By 1935, the Commissioner of Indian Affairs reported 515 Indians in college. Although the loan program was discontinued in 1952, the Bureau of Indian Affairs had established the higher education scholarship grant program in 1948, allocating $9,390 among 50 students. Indian veterans returning from World War II and eligible for GI Bill educational benefits added to the growing number of college students. According to estimates, some 2,000 Native Americans were enrolled in some form of postsecondary education during the last half of the 1950s. The enrollment grew to about 7,000 by 1965. Sixty-six Indians graduated from four-year institutions in 1961, and by 1968 this figure had almost tripled. Still, in 1966, only one percent of the Indian population was enrolled in college.

During the 1970s, a series of federal task force and U.S. General Accounting Office reports called attention to the academic, financial, social, and cultural problems that Indian students encountered in pursuing a college education. These reports fell on attentive Congressional ears. By 1979 the Bureau of Indian

Affairs Higher Education Program was financing approximately 14,600 under-graduates and 700 graduate students. Of these, 1,639 received college degrees and 434 earned graduate degrees. In addition, federal legislation, including the Indian Self-Determination and Education Assistance Act of 1975 and the Tribally Controlled Community College Assistance Act of 1978, spawned striking new developments in Indian higher education.

Perhaps the most dramatic policy change reflected in the new legislation was the shift to Indian control of education. For the first time, Indian people —who had thus far been subjected to paternalistic and assimilationist policies —began to take control of their own affairs. Higher education was among the targets of the new Self-Determination programs, best illustrated by the development of tribally controlled community colleges.

TRIBAL COLLEGES

Tribal colleges evolved for the most part during the 1970s in response to the unsuccessful experience of Indian students on mainstream campuses. Today, there are 24 tribally controlled colleges in 11 western and midwestern states —from California to Michigan, and from Arizona to the Dakotas. These institutions serve about 10,000 American Indians and have a full-time equivalent enrollment of about 4,500 students.

Because Indian students most often live in economically poor communities, tuition is low and local tax dollars do not offer much assistance. Congress has authorized up to $6,000 per student, but, in reality, the amount released to the colleges decreased throughout the Reagan era so that by 1989 the amount generated for each student was only $1,900. Tribal leaders point out how odd it is that those students who are most at-risk receive the least assistance. One would think that if the government was serious about increasing opportunities for Indian youth, then colleges would be provided the funds necessary to aid those youth. Such has not been the case.

CURRENT DEMOGRAPHICS

By all accounts the Native American population of the United States is growing at a fast pace and becoming increasingly youthful. Current estimates place the total population of American Indians in the United States at slightly less than two million. Between 1970 and 1980, Indians between the ages of 18 and 24 increased from 96,000 to 234,000. The average age of this population is 16.

Although Native Americans live throughout the United States, over half live in the southwest. California, Oklahoma, Arizona, and New Mexico account for slightly less than 50 percent of the total Indian population. Native Americans are equally split between those who live in rural and urban areas. Los Angeles, Tulsa, Oklahoma City, Phoenix, and Albuquerque have the largest numbers of urban Indians. The largest reservations in the United States are the Navajo Reservation in what is now New Mexico and Arizona and the Pine Ridge Reservation in the present state of South Dakota.

American Indians are among the most economically disadvantaged groups in the United States. The unemployment rate for American Indians who live on reservations often approaches 80 percent, with the median family income hovering around $15,000. The percentage of Native Americans who live below the poverty line is three times the national average. About 50 percent of the Native American population over 30 years old has not completed high school.

Given the propensity for Native American students to leave one institution prior to an academic year's completion, valid estimates of how many high school graduates actually participate in a freshman year at a postsecondary institution are difficult to determine. A student, for example, may graduate from high school and decide to attend a particular college and he or she may leave relatively soon thereafter; a few months later the student may re-enroll at another institution. Meanwhile, the previous college may not even be aware the student has left. Consequently, a valid national percentage of Native American high school graduates who are college freshmen is unknown.

We do know that in 1980 there were 141,000 high school graduates, and 85,798 students were enrolled in postsecondary education. The general lesson to be learned here is that less than 60 percent of Native American high school students complete the 12th grade, and that less than 40 percent of those students go on to college. More simply, if 100 Indian students enter the 9th grade, only 60 will graduate from high school. Of these graduates, a mere 20 will enter academe, and only about three of these will receive a four-year degree.

Not surprisingly, more than half of those students who go on to college will enter a two-year institution, and over 70,000 of the students will attend public institutions. The proportion of American Indian students who enroll full-time is around 50 percent, and Native American women outnumber their male counterparts on college campuses by about 20 percent.

THE TASK AHEAD

What does this information tell us about American Indian participation in postsecondary education? The composite population of Native Americans is economically poorer, experiences more unemployment, and is less formally educated than the rest of the nation. A greater percentage of the population lives in rural areas, where access to postsecondary institutions is more limited. Although a majority of the population lives in the southwest, they attend postsecondary institutions throughout the country.

They have a population that is increasingly youthful, yet only three out of 100 9th-graders will eventually receive a baccalaureate. Those four-year institutions that have the largest percentage of Indian students are either in economically depressed states of the country such as Montana and South Dakota, and those colleges that have the highest proportion of Indian students—tribal colleges—receive only a fraction of what they should receive from the federal government to carry out their tasks.

This overview highlights the problems and challenges that American Indians have faced regarding higher education. One certainly is that the federal government must renew its support for at-risk college students. Society can no longer afford excluding populations simply because they are different from the mainstream or prefer to remain within their own cultural contexts. All evidence suggests that Indian students and their families want equal educational opportunities. They seek better guidance in high school, more culturally relevant academic programming and counseling, and more role models on campus. Indian students do not want to be excluded from a university's doors because they cannot afford the education, and they do not want to be lost on a campus that doesn't value and accommodate their differences.

Many of the same challenges that confronted Caleb Cheeshateaumuck at Harvard face Indian college students today. A Native American senior recently reflected on her four years at school and the dysfunction between the world of higher education and the world from which she had come. "When I was a child I was taught certain things," she recalled, "don't stand up to your elders, don't question authority, life is precious, the earth is precious, take it slowly, enjoy it. And then you go to college and you learn all these other things, and it never fits."

Now, more than three centuries after Caleb Cheeshateaumuck confronted the alien environment of Harvard, the time is long overdue for cultural conflict and assimilationist efforts to end. American Indians must have opportunities to enter the higher education arena on their own terms—to encounter challenge without tragedy and triumph without co-optation. Only then can higher education begin a celebration of diversity in earnest.

6.3 JONATHAN KOZOL

Savage Inequalities

The educational process for most Americans is a vehicle for personal achievement and socioeconomic advancement. A fundamental premise of the so-called American dream, for example, is that the postponement of personal gratificaiton, especially in the pursuit of educational goals, will result in social rewards attached to a prestigious occupational position. Yet for many people of color the American dream amounts to little more than a dream. Sociologists have argued that since its inception, the American educational system has functioned systematically to exclude minorities from full and equal educational opportunity. The educational system so dramatically limits opportunity through discriminatory practices that many minorities never reach their full potential nor do they acquire access to social opportunity. Throughout its history in the United States, public education has legitimized the unequal treatment of non-White students by schooling them differently than White students. A hidden curriculum, intelligence testing, and the categorical assignment of students to different types of educaitonal programs all act to perpetuate privilege and ideas supporting the status quo.

In *Savage Inequalities: Children in America's Schools* (Harper Perennial, 1992), from which this selection has been excerpted, social critic Jonathan Kozol contrasts two public schools—one poor and one rich. Kozol's examination of these two schools reveals that the gross disparity in school funding has ensured White students teachers, facilities, and educational programs that are superior to those found in predominantly non-White schools.

Key Concept: inequalities in U.S. education

*E*ast of anywhere," writes a reporter for the *St. Louis Post-Dispatch*, "often evokes the other side of the tracks. But, for a first-time visitor suddenly deposited on its eerily empty streets, East St. Louis might suggest another world." The city, which is 98 percent black, has no obstetric services, no regular trash collection, and few jobs. Nearly a third of its families live on less than $7,500 a year; 75 percent of its population lives on welfare of some form. The U.S. Department of Housing and Urban Development describes it as "the most distressed small city in America."

Only three of the 13 buildings on Missouri Avenue, one of the city's major thoroughfares, are occupied. A 13-story office building, tallest in the city, has been boarded up. Outside, on the sidewalk, a pile of garbage fills a ten-foot crater.

The city, which by night and day is clouded by the fumes that pour from vents and smokestacks at the Pfizer and Monsanto chemical plants, has one of the highest rates of child asthma in America.

It is, according to a teacher at Southern Illinois University, "a repository for a nonwhite population that is now regarded as expendable." The *Post-Dispatch* describes it as "America's Soweto."

Fiscal shortages have forced the layoff of 1,170 of the city's 1,400 employees in the past 12 years. The city, which is often unable to buy heating fuel or toilet paper for the city hall, recently announced that it might have to cashier all but 10 percent of the remaining work force of 230. In 1989 the mayor announced that he might need to sell the city hall and all six fire stations to raise needed cash. Last year the plan had to be scrapped after the city lost its city hall in a court judgment to a creditor. East St. Louis is mortgaged into the next century but has the highest property-tax rate in the state....

The dangers of exposure to raw sewage, which backs up repeatedly into the homes of residents in East St. Louis, were first noticed, in the spring of 1989, at a public housing project, Villa Griffin. Raw sewage, says the *Post-Dispatch*, overflowed into a playground just behind the housing project, which is home to 187 children, "forming an oozing lake of ... tainted water." ... A St. Louis health official voices her dismay that children live with waste in their backyards. "The development of working sewage systems made cities livable a hundred years ago," she notes. "Sewage systems separate us from the Third World." ...

The sewage, which is flowing from collapsed pipes and dysfunctional pumping stations, has also flooded basements all over the city. The city's vacuum truck, which uses water and suction to unclog the city's sewers, cannot be used because it needs $5,000 in repairs. Even when it works, it sometimes can't be used because there isn't money to hire drivers. A single engineer now does the work that 14 others did before they were laid off. By April the pool of overflow behind the Villa Griffin project has expanded into a lagoon of sewage. Two million gallons of raw sewage lie outside the children's homes....

... Sister Julia Huiskamp meets me on King Boulevard and drives me to the Griffin homes.

As we ride past blocks and blocks of skeletal structures, some of which are still inhabited, she slows the car repeatedly at railroad crossings. A seemingly endless railroad train rolls past us to the right. On the left: a blackened lot where garbage has been burning. Next to the burning garbage is a row of 12 white cabins, charred by fire. Next: a lot that holds a heap of auto tires and a mountain of tin cans. More burnt houses. More trash fires. The train moves almost imperceptibly across the flatness of the land.

Fifty years old, and wearing a blue suit, white blouse, and blue headcover, Sister Julia points to the nicest house in sight. The sign on the front reads MOTEL. "It's a whorehouse," Sister Julia says.

When she slows the car beside a group of teen-age boys, one of them steps out toward the car, then backs away as she is recognized.

The 99 units of the Villa Griffin homes—two-story structures, brick on the first floor, yellow wood above—form one border of a recessed park and playground that were filled with fecal matter last year when the sewage mains exploded. The sewage is gone now and the grass is very green and looks inviting. When nine-year-old Serena and her seven-year-old brother take me for a walk, however, I discover that our shoes sink into what is still a sewage marsh. An inch-deep residue of fouled water still remains.

Serena's brother is a handsome, joyous little boy, but troublingly thin. Three other children join us as we walk along the marsh: Smokey, who is nine years old but cannot yet tell time; Mickey, who is seven; and a tiny child with a ponytail and big brown eyes who talks a constant stream of words that I can't always understand.

"Hush, Little Sister," says Serena. I ask for her name, but "Little Sister" is the only name the children seem to know.

"There go my cousins," Smokey says, pointing to two teen-age girls above us on the hill.

The day is warm, although we're only in the second week of March; several dogs and cats are playing by the edges of the marsh. "It's a lot of squirrels here," says Smokey. "There go one!"

"This here squirrel is a friend of mine," says Little Sister.

None of the children can tell me the approximate time that school begins. One says five o'clock. One says six. Another says that school begins at noon.

When I ask what song they sing after the flag pledge, one says, "Jingle Bells."

Smokey cannot decide if he is in the second or third grade.

Seven-year-old Mickey sucks his thumb during the walk.

The children regale me with a chilling story as we stand beside the marsh. Smokey says his sister was raped and murdered and then dumped behind his school. Other children add more details: Smokey's sister was 11 years old. She was beaten with a brick until she died. The murder was committed by a man who knew her mother.

The narrative begins when, without warning, Smokey says, "My sister has got killed."

"She was my best friend," Serena says.

"They had beat her in the head and raped her," Smokey says.

"She was hollering out loud," says Little Sister.

I ask them when it happened. Smokey says, "Last year." Serena then corrects him and she says, "Last week."

"It scared me because I had to cry," says Little Sister.

"The police arrested one man but they didn't catch the other," Smokey says.

Serena says, "He was some kin to her."

But Smokey objects, "He weren't no kin to me. He was my momma's friend."

"Her face was busted," Little Sister says.

Serena describes this sequence of events: "They told her go behind the school. They'll give her a quarter if she do. Then they knock her down and told her not to tell what they had did."

I ask, "Why did they kill her?"

"They was scared that she would tell," Serena says.

"One is in jail," says Smokey. "They cain't find the other."

"Instead of raping little bitty children, they should find themselves a wife," says Little Sister.

"I hope," Serena says, "her spirit will come back and get that man."

"And *kill* that man," says Little Sister.

"Give her another chance to live," Serena says.

"My teacher came to the funeral," says Smokey.

"When a little child dies, my momma say a star go straight to Heaven," says Serena.

"My grandma was murdered," Mickey says out of the blue. "Somebody shot two bullets in her head."

I ask him, "Is she really dead?"

"She dead all right," says Mickey. "She was layin' there, just dead."

"I love my friends," Serena says. "I don't care if they no kin to me. I *care* for them. I hope his mother have another baby. Name her for my friend that's dead."

"I have a cat with three legs," Smokey says.

"Snakes hate rabbits," Mickey says, again for no apparent reason.

"Cats hate fishes," Little Sister says.

"It's a lot of hate," says Smokey.

Later, at the mission, Sister Julia tells me this: "The Jefferson School, which they attend, is a decrepit hulk. Next to it is a modern school, erected two years ago, which was to have replaced the one that they attend. But the construction was not done correctly. The roof is too heavy for the walls, and the entire structure has begun to sink. It can't be occupied. Smokey's sister was raped and murdered and dumped between the old school and the new one." ...

The problems of the streets in urban areas, as teachers often note, frequently spill over into public schools. In the public schools of East St. Louis this is literally the case.

"Martin Luther King Junior High School," notes the *Post-Dispatch* in a story published in the early spring of 1989, "was evacuated Friday afternoon after sewage flowed into the kitchen.... The kitchen was closed and students were sent home." On Monday, the paper continues, "East St. Louis Senior High School was awash in sewage for the second time this year." The school had to be shut because of "fumes and backed-up toilets." Sewage flowed into the basement, through the floor, then up into the kitchen and the students' bathrooms. The backup, we read, "occurred in the food preparation areas."

School is resumed the following morning at the high school, but a few days later the overflow recurs. This time the entire system is affected, since the meals distributed to every student in the city are prepared in the two schools that have been flooded. School is called off for all 16,500 students in the district. The sewage backup, caused by the failure of two pumping stations, forces officials at the high school to shut down the furnaces.

At Martin Luther King, the parking lot and gym are also flooded. "It's a disaster," says a legislator. "The streets are under water; gaseous fumes are being emitted from the pipes under the schools," she says, "making people ill."

In the same week, the schools announce the layoff of 280 teachers, 166 cooks and cafeteria workers, 25 teacher aides, 16 custodians and 18 painters, electricians, engineers and plumbers. The president of the teachers' union says the cuts, which will bring the size of kindergarten and primary classes up to 30 students, and the size of fourth to twelfth grade classes up to 35, will have "an unimaginable impact" on the students. "If you have a high school teacher with five classes each day and between 150 and 175 students . . . , it's going to have a devastating effect." The school system, it is also noted, has been using more than 70 "permanent substitute teachers," who are paid only $10,000 yearly, as a way of saving money. . . .

East St. Louis, says the chairman of the state board, "is simply the worst possible place I can imagine to have a child brought up. . . . The community is in desperate circumstances." Sports and music, he observes, are, for many children here, "the only avenues of success." Sadly enough, no matter how it ratifies the stereotype, this is the truth; and there is a poignant aspect to the fact that, even with class size soaring and one quarter of the system's teachers being given their dismissal, the state board of education demonstrates its genuine but skewed compassion by attempting to leave sports and music untouched by the overall austerity.

Even sports facilities, however, are degrading by comparison with those found and expected at most high schools in America. The football field at East St. Louis High is missing almost everything—including goalposts. There are a couple of metal pipes—no crossbar, just the pipes. Bob Shannon, the football coach, who has to use his personal funds to purchase footballs and has had to cut and rake the football field himself, has dreams of having goalposts someday. He'd also like to let his students have new uniforms. The ones they wear are nine years old and held together somehow by a patchwork of repairs. Keeping them clean is a problem, too. The school cannot afford a washing machine. The uniforms are carted to a corner laundromat with fifteen dollars' worth of quarters. . . .

In the wing of the school that holds vocational classes, a damp, unpleasant odor fills the halls. The school has a machine shop, which cannot be used for lack of staff, and a woodworking shop. The only shop that's occupied this morning is the auto-body class. A man with long blond hair and wearing a white sweat suit swings a paddle to get children in their chairs. "What we need the most is new equipment," he reports. "I have equipment for alignment, for example, but we don't have money to install it. We also need a better form of egress. We bring the cars in through two other classes." Computerized equipment used in most repair shops, he reports, is far beyond the high school's budget. It looks like a very old gas station in an isolated rural town. . . .

The science labs at East St. Louis High are 30 to 50 years outdated. John McMillan, a soft-spoken man, teaches physics at the school. He shows me his lab. The six lab stations in the room have empty holes where pipes were once attached. "It would be great if we had water," says McMillan. . . .

Leaving the chemistry labs, I pass a double-sized classroom in which roughly 60 kids are sitting fairly still but doing nothing. "This is supervised study hall," a teacher tells me in the corridor. But when we step inside, he finds there is no teacher. "The teacher must be out today," he says.

Irl Solomon's history classes, which I visit next, have been described by journalists who cover East St. Louis as the highlight of the school. Solomon, a man of 54 whose reddish hair is turning white, has taught in urban schools for almost 30 years. A graduate of Brandeis University, he entered law school but was drawn away by a concern with civil rights. "After one semester, I decided that the law was not for me. I said, 'Go and find the toughest place there is to teach. See if you like it.' I'm still here....

"I have four girls right now in my senior home room who are pregnant or have just had babies. When I ask them why this happens, I am told, 'Well, there's no reason not to have a baby. There's not much for me in public school.' The truth is, that's a pretty honest answer. A diploma from a ghetto high school doesn't count for much in the United States today. So, if this is really the last education that a person's going to get, she's probably perceptive in that statement. Ah, there's so much bitterness—unfairness—there, you know. Most of these pregnant girls are not the ones who have much self-esteem....

"Very little education in the school would be considered academic in the suburbs. Maybe 10 to 15 percent of students are in truly academic programs. Of the 55 percent who graduate, 20 percent may go to four-year colleges: something like 10 percent of any entering class. Another 10 to 20 percent may get some other kind of higher education. An equal number join the military....

"I don't go to physics class, because my lab has no equipment," says one student. "The typewriters in my typing class don't work. The women's toilets..." She makes a sour face. "I'll be honest," she says. "I just don't use the toilets. If I do, I come back into class and I feel dirty."

"I wanted to study Latin," says another student. "But we don't have Latin in this school."

"We lost our only Latin teacher," Solomon says.

A girl in a white jersey with the message DO THE RIGHT THING on the front raises her hand. "You visit other schools," she says. "Do you think the children in this school are getting what we'd get in a nice section of St. Louis?"

I note that we are in a different state and city.

"Are we citizens of East St. Louis or America?" she asks....

In a seventh grade social studies class, the only book that bears some relevance to black concerns—its title is *The American Negro*—bears a publication date of 1967. The teacher invites me to ask the class some questions. Uncertain where to start, I ask the students what they've learned about the civil rights campaigns of recent decades.

A 14-year-old girl with short black curly hair says this: "Every year in February we are told to read the same old speech of Martin Luther King. We read it every year. 'I have a dream....' It does begin to seem—what is the word?" She hesitates and then she finds the word: "perfunctory."

I ask her what she means.

"We have a school in East St. Louis named for Dr. King," she says. "The school is full of sewer water and the doors are locked with chains. Every student in that school is black. It's like a terrible joke on history."

It startles me to hear her words, but I am startled even more to think how seldom any press reporter has observed the irony of naming segregated schools for Martin Luther King. Children reach the heart of these hypocrisies much quicker than the grown-ups and the experts do....

The train ride from Grand Central Station to suburban Rye, New York, takes 35 to 40 minutes. The high school is a short ride from the station. Built of handsome gray stone and set in a landscaped campus, it resembles a New England prep school. On a day in early June of 1990, I enter the school and am directed by a student to the office.

The principal, a relaxed, unhurried man who, unlike many urban principals, seems gratified to have me visit in his school, takes me in to see the auditorium, which, he says, was recently restored with private charitable funds ($400,000) raised by parents. The crenellated ceiling, which is white and spotless, and the polished dark-wood paneling contrast with the collapsing structure of the auditorium at [another school I visited]. The principal strikes his fist against the balcony: "They made this place extremely solid." Through a window, one can see the spreading branches of a beech tree in the central courtyard of the school.

In a student lounge, a dozen seniors are relaxing on a carpeted floor that is constructed with a number of tiers so that, as the principal explains, "they can stretch out and be comfortable while reading."

The library is wood-paneled, like the auditorium. Students, all of whom are white, are seated at private carrels, of which there are approximately 40. Some are doing homework; others are looking through the *New York Times*. Every student that I see during my visit to the school is white or Asian, though I later learn there are a number of Hispanic students and that 1 or 2 percent of students in the school are black.

According to the principal, the school has 96 computers for 546 children. The typical student, he says, studies a foreign language for four or five years, beginning in the junior high school, and a second foreign language (Latin is available) for two years. Of 140 seniors, 92 are now enrolled in AP [advanced placement] classes. Maximum teacher salary will soon reach $70,000. Per-pupil funding is above $12,000 at the time I visit.

The students I meet include eleventh and twelfth graders. The teacher tells me that the class is reading Robert Coles, Studs Terkel, Alice Walker. He tells me I will find them more than willing to engage me in debate, and this turns out to be correct. Primed for my visit, it appears, they arrow in directly on the dual questions of equality and race.

Three general positions soon emerge and seem to be accepted widely. The first is that the fiscal inequalities "do matter very much" in shaping what a school can offer ("That is obvious," one student says) and that any loss of funds in Rye, as a potential consequence of future equalizing, would be damaging to many things the town regards as quite essential.

The second position is that racial integration—for example, by the busing of black children from the city or a nonwhite suburb to this school—would meet with strong resistance, and the reason would not simply be the fear that certain standards might decline. The reason, several students say straightforwardly, is "racial" or, as others say it, "out-and-out racism" on the part of adults.

The third position voiced by many students, but not all, is that equity is basically a goal to be desired and should be pursued for moral reasons, but "will probably make no major difference" since poor children "still would lack the motivation" and "would probably fail in any case because of other problems."

At this point, I ask if they can truly say "it wouldn't make a difference" since it's never been attempted. Several students then seem to rethink their views and say that "it might work, but it would have to start with preschool and the elementary grades" and "it might be 20 years before we'd see a difference."

At this stage in the discussion, several students speak with some real feeling of the present inequalities, which, they say, are "obviously unfair," and one student goes a little further and proposes that "we need to change a lot more than the schools." Another says she'd favor racial integration "by whatever means—including busing—even if the parents disapprove." But a contradictory opinion also is expressed with a good deal of fervor and is stated by one student in a rather biting voice: "I don't see why we should do it. How could it be of benefit to us?"

Throughout the discussion, whatever the views the children voice, there is a degree of unreality about the whole exchange. The children are lucid and their language is well chosen and their arguments well made, but there is a sense that they are dealing with an issue that does not feel very vivid, and that nothing that we say about it to each other really matters since it's "just a theoretical discussion." To a certain degree, the skillfulness and cleverness that they display seem to derive precisely from this sense of unreality. Questions of unfairness feel more like a geometric problem than a matter of humanity or conscience. A few of the students do break through the note of unreality, but, when they do, they cease to be so agile in their use of words and speak more awkwardly. Ethical challenges seem to threaten their effectiveness. There is the sense that they were skating over ice and that the issues we addressed were safely frozen underneath. When they stop to look beneath the ice they start to stumble. The verbal competence they have acquired here may have been gained by building walls around some regions of the heart.

"I don't think that busing students from their ghetto to a different school would do much good," one student says. "You can take them out of the environment, but you can't take the environment out of *them*. If someone grows up in the South Bronx, he's not going to be prone to learn." His name is Max and he has short black hair and speaks with confidence. "Busing didn't work when it was tried," he says. I ask him how he knows this and he says he saw a television movie about Boston.

"I agree that it's unfair the way it is," another student says. "We have AP courses and they don't. Our classes are much smaller." But, she says, "putting them in schools like ours is not the answer. Why not put some AP classes into *their* school? Fix the roof and paint the halls so it will not be so depressing."

The students know the term "separate but equal," but seem unaware of its historical associations. "Keep them where they are but make it equal," says a girl in the front row.

A student named Jennifer, whose manner of speech is somewhat less refined and polished than that of the others, tells me that her parents came here from New York. "My family is originally from the Bronx. Schools are hell there. That's one reason that we moved. I don't think it's our responsibility to pay our taxes to provide for *them*. I mean, my parents used to live there and they wanted to get out. There's no point in coming to a place like this, where schools are good, and then your taxes go back to the place where you began."

I bait her a bit: "Do you mean that, now that you are not in hell, you have no feeling for the people that you left behind?"

"It has to be the people in the area who want an education. If your parents just don't care, it won't do any good to spend a lot of money. Someone else can't want a good life for you. You have got to want it for yourself." Then she adds, however, "I agree that everyone should have a chance at taking the same courses...."

I ask her if she'd think it fair to pay more taxes so that this was possible.

"I don't see how that benefits me," she says.

CHAPTER 7 The Political Institution

7.1 LEOBARDO F. ESTRADA ET AL.

Chicanos in the United States: A History of Exploitation and Resistance

Chicanos as an ethnic group emerged from the conquest of Mexico by the United States in the mid-1800s. Chicanos today constitute about 90 percent of the Hispanic population living in the American Southwest. Chicanos have a common ethnic heritage rooted in collectively experienced oppression, exploitation, and social conflict. The capitalist economic system of the United States has been identified as a major factor in the oppression of Chicanos.

In the present selection, Leobardo F. Estrada and his colleagues state that Chicanos are a colonized people in the United States. According to Estrada et al., the sociohistorical factors that have shaped the presence of Chicanos in the United States continue to relegate the population to the lower echelons of U.S. society. The institutionalization of Anglo dominance in the Southwest occurred during the second half of the nineteenth century, and it included the establishment of a racial division of labor. Overwhelmingly concentrated in the working class, Chicanos became integrated into the economy on a restricted basis, with most located in unskilled manual labor positions and in a reserve army of labor. The pervasive practice of

White capitalists of hiring Mexican labor at low wages has further restricted the socioeconomic mobility of Chicanos already living in the United States. The authors conclude that the historical treatment of Chicanos in the U.S. economic society has put them in a position of severe disadvantage today.

Key Concept: the exploitation of Chicanos

This essay seeks to provide material that will contribute to an understanding of Chicanos[1] in the United States today. The task calls for a historical perspective on the Mexican people within the context of the U.S. political economy.

It is essential to examine first the early and continued influence of Mexicans in the development of what is today the southwestern United States. Unlike those who believe that social, political, and economic influences in the region were largely the result of Anglo penetration, we argue that practices and institutions indigenous to Mexicans were largely taken over by colonizing Anglos.[2] The military conquest of the Southwest by the United States was a watershed that brought about the large-scale dispossession of the real holdings of Mexicans and their displacement and relegation to the lower reaches of the class structure. Anglo control of social institutions and of major economic sectors made possible the subsequent exploitation of Mexican labor to satisfy the needs of various developing economic interests. . . .

THE MILITARY CONQUEST

Mexicans were incorporated into the United States largely through military conquest. The period that brought the northern reaches of Mexico under the U.S. flag begins approximately in 1836 with the Battle of San Jacinto, and ends in 1853 with the Gadsden Purchase. The military conquest was preceded by a period of Anglo immigration.

In 1810 Mexico began its struggle to gain independence from Spain, an objective finally achieved in 1821. Mexico, recognizing the advantage of increasing the size of the population loyal to its cause, granted permission to foreigners in 1819 to settle in its northern area, what is now Texas. Two years later Stephen Austin founded San Felipe de Austin: by 1830, one year after Mexico had abolished slavery, it is estimated that Texas had about twenty thousand Anglo settlers, primarily Southerners, with approximately two thousand "freed" slaves who had been forced to sign lifelong contracts with former owners. This trickle of immigrants soon became an invading horde.

Immigrants into the territories of Mexico were required to meet certain conditions: pledge their allegiance to the Mexican government and adopt Catholicism. The settlers' initial acceptance of these conditions, however, soon turned to circumvention. The distance of the settlements from Mexico's capital city, together with the internal strife common in the period, made enforcement of these settlement agreements difficult, almost impossible. The foreigners' attitudes toward their hosts only aggravated the situation. Eugene C. Barker, a historian, wrote that by 1835 "the Texans saw themselves in danger of becoming the alien subjects of a people to whom they deliberately believed themselves morally, intellectually, and politically superior. Such racial feelings underlay Texan-American relations from the establishment of the very first Anglo-American colony in 1821."

A constellation of factors—attitudes of racial superiority, anger over Mexico's abolition of slavery, defiance of initially agreed-upon conditions for settlement, and an increasing number of immigrants who pressed for independence from Mexico—strained an already difficult political situation. Direct and indirect diplomatic efforts at negotiation failed. The result was the Texas Revolt of 1835–36, which created for Anglo-Texans and dissident Mexicans the so-called independent Texas Republic, which was to exist until 1845. This republic, while never recognized by the Mexican government, provided the pretext for further U.S. territorial expansion and set the stage for the war between Mexico and the United States (1846–48).

Despite significant and conflicting regional interests in the war, imperialist interests allied with proponents for the expansion of slavery carried the day. When the United States granted statehood to Texas in 1845, almost a decade after recognizing it as a republic, war was inevitable; it was officially declared on May 13, 1846. It has been argued that U.S. politicians and business interests actively sought this war, believing Mexico to be weak, a nation torn by divisive internal disputes that had not been resolved since independence.

When hostilities ended in 1848, Mexico lost over half its national territory. The United States, by adding over a million square miles, increased its territory by a third. Arizona, California, Colorado, New Mexico, Texas, Nevada, and Utah, as well as portions of Kansas, Oklahoma, and Wyoming, were carved out of the territory acquired....

A final portion of Mexican land was acquired by the United States through purchase. James Gadsden was sent to Mexico City in 1853 to negotiate a territorial dispute arising from the use of faulty maps in assigning borders under the Treaty of Guadalupe Hidalgo. Mexico's dire need for funds to rebuild its war-ravaged economy influenced its agreement to sell more land. Gadsden purchased over 45,000 square miles in what is now Arizona and New Mexico, land the United States wanted for a rail line to California. The Gadsden Purchase territories were in time seen to contain some of the world's richest copper mines.

The importance for the United States of this imperialist war and the later Gadsden Purchase cannot be overstated. Vast tracts of land, rich in natural resources, together with their Mexican and Indian inhabitants, provided conditions very favorable to U.S. development and expansion. The United States had done very well in its "little war" with Mexico.

DISPOSSESSION AND DISPLACEMENT

To make matters worse, the social and economic displacement of Mexicans and their reduction to the status of a colonized group proceeded rapidly, in clear violation of the civil and property rights guaranteed both by treaty and protocol. In Texas, a wholesale transfer of land from Mexican to Anglo ownership took place. That process has started at the time of the Texas Revolt and gained momentum after the U.S.-Mexico War. Mexican landowners, often robbed by force, intimidation, or fraud, could defend their holdings through litigation, but this generally led to heavy indebtedness, with many forced to sell their holdings to meet necessary legal expenses. With depressing regularity, Anglos generally ended up with Mexican holdings, acquired at prices far below their real value.

The military conquest, the presence of U.S. troops, racial violence, governmental and judicial chicanery—all served to establish Anglos in positions of power in economic structures originally developed by Mexicans. Anglos adopted wholesale techniques developed by Mexicans in mining, ranching, and agriculture. Because this major transfer of economic power from Mexicans to Anglos varied by region, it is important to say something about each.

Texas, responding to a significant expansion in the earlier Mexican-based cattle and sheep industries, was quick to cater to increased world demands. Acreage given over to cotton also expanded, helped greatly by improvements in transport facilities. These industries helped create and develop the mercantile towns that soon became conspicuous features on the Texas landscape. Mexicans, instead of reaping the economic rewards of ownership, found themselves only contributing their labor. Mexicans were increasingly relegated to the lower ranks of society. By the end of the century, ethnicity, merged with social class, made Mexicans a mobile, colonized labor force.

The social structure of *New Mexico* in the beginning was quite different from that of Texas. The state, sparsely populated, was more densely settled in the north, in and about Santa Fé, than in the south; communal villages with lands granted to each community were common in the north. Communal water and grazing rights were assigned by community councils; only homestead and farming land were privately owned. Southern New Mexico, by contrast, boasted *haciendas* that had been established by grantees. This system consisted of *patrónes,* with settlers recruited to perform the necessary chores. It was a social structure organized on a debt-peonage system.

Anglo penetration into New Mexico after the war was more limited and did not occur on a large scale until the mid-1870s. Indian and Mexican defense of the territory served to keep out many settlers. Only an established U.S. military presence in the area made it at all accessible to Anglo cattlemen and farmers. Encountering a diversified class structure among the resident Mexicans, the Anglos generally chose to associate with the U.S. armed forces, creating a quasi-military society in the process. By the early 1880s, however, the railroads had helped to stimulate a new economic expansion. There was a further swelling of the Anglo population, and as pressure for land increased, the process of Mexican dispossession also dramatically accelerated....

Arizona offers the example of the development of a colonial labor force in yet another mode. Arizona, not a separate entity at the time of conquest, was originally part of New Mexico, administered from Santa Fé. The small Mexican population was concentrated in the south, largely in Tucson and Tubac. One of the reasons for the sparseness of the settlements was the failure of the Spanish missionaries to impose Christianity on the nomadic Indian inhabitants; another was the aridity of the soil, which made agricultural pursuits difficult. The presence of the U.S. Army in the 1880s began to have its effects on the region. The Army fought the Indians, allowing the mining of copper and silver to resume; it was soon to become a large-scale economic enterprise. As with other industries, Anglo ownership was the norm; Mexicans contributed their labor, employing the familiar techniques they had developed long before. Railroads accelerated the migration of Anglos and the establishment of new towns. The growth of all these major industries called for a cheap wage labor pool. Mexicans who migrated north, mostly to work in these industries, discovered that the wages they received for tasks identical to their Anglo counterparts were considerably lower. Restricted to menial and dangerous work, and forced to live in segregated areas in the mining and railroad communities that had created their jobs, they felt the indignity of their situation.

California differed from the other regions: New England clipper ships had established very early ties with California; Franciscans, founding missions in the area in the 1830s, forced Christianized Indians into agriculture and manufacturing, to work alongside mulatto and *mestizo* Mexicans. This labor force helped to make California—economically, politically, and socially distant—independent of Mexico City. Excellent climate and abundant natural resources contributed to make this the most prosperous province in Mexico. Strong ties bound the missions to the *ranchos*. Missions, given large parcels of land to carry out their Christianizing enterprise, were neighbors of private individuals who owned vast tracts of land. Eventually, however, the privately owned *ranchos* established their supremacy throughout the province....

A few Anglos had come to Alta California before the U.S.-Mexico War; some were recipients of land grants, and many of them apparently assimilated into Mexican society. After the Texas revolt, however, Anglo foreigners coming to California were more reluctant to mingle or assimilate, and openly showed their antagonism towards Mexicans. The U.S. government was at the same time stepping up its efforts to secure California. In 1842, in fact, the U.S. flag was prematurely raised in Monterey, when Commodore Thomas Jones imagined that the war with Mexico had already begun.

The transfer of land titles from Mexicans to Anglos in California differed significantly from the transfer of title in other areas conquered by the U.S. forces. To begin with, the vast majority of Mexicans did not own land in California. The original *Californios* began to lose title to their lands to better-financed Anglo newcomers very early; there was no possibility of competing with wealth established through banking, shipping, railroads, and other such enterprises. The holdings of these new elites ran into the hundreds of thousands of acres early in the nineteenth century.

Congress established the Land Commission in 1851 to judge the validity of grant claims made by *Californios* whose titles came down through the Spanish and Mexican periods. The commission served mainly to hasten the process of dispossession. Litigation costs often involved a contingent lawyer's fee of one quarter of the land in question. Some Mexican landowners borrowed money at high interest rates to carry on their legal fights, and frequently found themselves in the end selling their lands to meet their debts. Anglo squatters only added to the burden; they formed associations to apply political pressure favorable to their own interests, and were generally successful in retaining land forcefully taken from Mexicans. Violence and murder in California, as in other parts of the conquered territories, was the order of the day....

By the turn of the century, Mexicans had been largely dispossessed of their property. Relegated to a lower-class status, they were overwhelmingly dispossessed landless laborers, politically and economically impotent. Lynchings and murder of both Mexicans and Indians were so common that they often went unreported. Long-term residents of the region were reduced to being aliens in their native lands. The common theme that united all Mexicans was their conflict with Anglo society. The dominant society, profoundly racist, found it entirely reasonable to relegate Mexicans to a colonial status within the United States....

THE U.S. SOUTHWEST AND BEYOND, 1900–1930

... The conditions that greeted new immigrants from Mexico were essentially like those Mexicans already in the United States knew only too well. There was powerful racial hostility; Mexicans were thought to be inferior beings and inherently unassimilable and foreign. Their economic niche was insecure; their work was often seasonal in nature. In agricultural and related pursuits they were forced into a dual-wage system where they received low wages, frequently below those received by Anglos for the same type and amount of work. Many found themselves barred from supervisory positions. The situation in mining and related industries was not much different.

The railroad companies offered only slightly better conditions. By 1908 the Southern Pacific and the Atchison, Topeka, and Santa Fe were each recruiting more than a thousand Mexicans every month. The vast majority worked as section crews, laying track and ensuring its maintenance. The major difference between this industry and others in which Mexicans found work was that it seemed somewhat more stable and less seasonal; wages, however, were uniformly low.

The Southwest was growing; its urban centers—in most instances, expanded versions of earlier Mexican towns—were often inhabited by Mexicans overwhelmingly concentrated in the lower range of the urban occupational structure. The wage differentials common to the rural sector were not as obvious in the urban areas. Access to particular occupations and industries, however, was limited and channeled. There was no mobility out of the unskilled and semiskilled positions in which Mexicans found themselves. They formed a reserve labor pool that could be called up as the situation dictated. When the economy expanded and jobs were created, these might be filled by Mexicans in specific sectors. Contractions of the economy relegated Mexicans quickly to the ranks of the unemployed; it was then they were reminded that they could be technically subject to another "sovereign," Mexico.

Mexicans served the industrial economy in other ways, also. As a reserve labor pool, employers used them as a sort of "strike insurance," much as female and child labor were used to undercut unionizing efforts in other parts of the country. Such policies tended to generate ethnic antagonism between working-class Mexicans and working-class Anglos. Trade union practices, which excluded Mexicans and contributed to their exploitation, also helped to maintain them as a reserve labor pool, forcing them in the end to organize their own unions and associations....

The Mexican government regularly lodged formal complaints with the State Department, protesting the abusive treatment its citizens received from industrial, mining, and agricultural enterprises. Those protests went largely unheeded; the U.S. government generally chose not even to verify the assertions, let alone make efforts to correct abuses....

MIGRATION 1900–1930

... The passage of the 1924 Immigration Act made Mexicans conspicuous by their continued free access to the United States. Debate on the issue continued to agitate Congress.... The powerful economic arguments for the continued importation of Mexican laborers had been articulated two years earlier before a congressional committee by John Nance Garner, who was to become Franklin Roosevelt's vice president: "In order to allow land owners now to make a profit of their farms, they want to get the cheapest labor they can find, and if they can get the Mexican labor it enables them to make a profit."

At the same time, control of the "immigrant" population came to include measures that could be applied to the domestic Mexican population. The Americanization activities of the early twentieth century spread throughout the country and were used to bleach all vestiges in the national flock. These activities included intensive English instruction—with retribution for those who chose to speak other tongues—and success defined as a capacity to speak as did the English-speaking middle class; and intensive "civic" classes to socialist the "foreign" population. The norm for success became the Anglo middle class, and standardized IQ and achievement tests measured this success. The widespread institution of high schools that traced the population into occupational or college preparatory curricula, with immigrants and racial minorities tracked into the former—when they entered high schools at all—became common. English oral proficiency became a requirement for immigration, as did English literacy for voting.... Segregated Mexican schools were maintained. In the early 1930s, through federal court litigation, segregation based on race was challenged, and segregation based on grouping for language instruction was initiated and legitimized....

THE GREAT DEPRESSION AND REPATRIATION

The decade of the Great Depression was another watershed for Mexicans. Social forces during this period significantly shaped the lives of Mexicans and are in many ways still responsible for their status half a century later. The decade began with a massive economic collapse that started late in the 1920s and continued until World War II. There was a major decline in economic activities, with wage rates in both industry and agriculture suffering, and rampant unemployment. With this came a major acceleration of government intervention in social welfare, with bureaucracies developing and expanding to meet the urgent needs of a dislocated populace. There was also a large-scale westward migration out of the Dust Bowl. In the Southwest, this was a time of accelerated rates of concentration into larger and larger units in both agriculture and mining, where increased mechanization led to a further displacement of labor. The industrial sector in the Southwest lagged behind the rest of the nation and could contribute little to absorb either the locally displaced labor or the dust-bowl migrants. These major economic dislocations fell on Mexicans with even greater force than on other groups. Already relegated to a marginal status, Mexicans were particularly vulnerable. The situation worked to eliminate for all practical purposes further northward migration from Mexico.

The Great Depression had another sobering effect: it engendered a collective social atmosphere of insecurity and fear that set the tone in allocating blame for the major social and economic traumas. Mexicans were singled out as scapegoats and made to bear the guilt for some of the ills of the period. It was not long before great numbers of unemployed Mexicans, like other citizens in the country, found themselves on the rolls of the welfare agencies.

One response to the strain placed on limited economic resources throughout the country was the demand for large-scale repatriations. To reduce the public relief rolls and agitation to organize labor, the Mexican became both the scapegoat and the safety valve in the Southwest. It is estimated that in the early years of the Depression (1929–34) more than 400,000 Mexicans were forced to leave the country under "voluntary repatriation." Those who applied for relief were referred to "Mexican Bureaus," whose sole purpose was to reduce the welfare rolls by deporting the applicants. Indigence, not citizenship, was the criterion used in identifying Mexicans for repatriation. . . .

Repatriations took place both in the Southwest and Midwest, where Mexicans, recruited to the area by employers with promises of work, had lived since the early twenties. Approximately half of the "returnees" actually were born in the United States. Shipment to Mexico was a clear violation of both their civil and human rights. The Immigration and Naturalization Service, in concert with the Anglo press, identified the Mexican labor migrant as the source of (Anglo) citizen unemployment, for the increase of public welfare costs (and taxes), and as having entered the country "illegally" and in large numbers. The scapegoating tactics of an earlier nativist generation, with its xenophobic memories and myths, were used against the Mexicans. There was a good deal of sentiment also against Mexico's expropriation and nationalization of its oil industry, which U.S. oil companies had once controlled. Repatriation caused widespread dissolution of family and community, and contributed to an even more acute distrust among Mexicans of all government—local, state, or federal....

WORLD WAR II TO 1960

... After a regulated labor pool was firmly reestablished for agribusiness, in 1954 the Immigration and Naturalization Service vigorously launched "Operation Wetback." Undocumented workers, unstable and intractable as a labor source, were now to be removed. An astonishing 3.8 million Mexican aliens (and citizens) were apprehended and expelled in the next five years. Of the total number deported during that time, fewer than 2 percent left as a result of formal proceedings. The vast majority were removed simply by the *threat* of deportation. "Looking Mexican" was often sufficient reason for official scrutiny. The search focused initially on California and then Texas; it soon extended as far as Spokane, Chicago, St. Louis, and Kansas City....

World War II posed a major dilemma for the United States. In its official pronouncements and acts, the country strongly condemned the racism explicit in Nazism. Yet at the same time, the United States had a segregated military force. This was also a time when President Roosevelt issued Executive Order No. 9066, which authorized the internment of Japanese who were U.S. citizens and whose sole "crime" was living and working on the West Coast.

This contradiction also manifested itself in ugly confrontations between Mexicans and Anglos. The press, for its part, helped to raise feelings against Mexicans. The violent confrontations between servicemen and local police against Mexican residents began late in 1942 and continued until mid-1943....

The Mexican community, in responding to the situation of World War II, acted as it had done in previous times of hostility and exploitation—with organizational efforts and litigation, and occasionally with armed resistance. Unity Leagues, created in the early 1940s, had as their principal purpose the election of Mexicans to city councils in Southern California communities; they also conducted voter registration drives, attempted fund-raising, and worked to get voters to the polls. The basic theme uniting these leagues was the fight against racial discrimination, particularly in the schools. The League of United Latin American Citizens (LULAC), founded in South Texas in 1928, expanded into a national organization in the post-World War II period, and was soon heavily involved in anti-discrimination activity, again particularly in the educational arena.

A landmark court decision in 1945 (*Méndez v. Westminster School District*) barred *de jure* segregation of Chicano students. A similar legal action in Texas in 1948 was also successfully pressed. The results of both court actions, as well as others during the 1950s, helped set the stage for the Supreme Court's *Brown v. Board of Education* decision in 1954, and clearly established the illegality of the deliberate segregation of Chicano and Mexican school children on the basis of race, and of bilingual education as a partial remedy for segregation. The success of these efforts served to encourage civil rights suits in other areas, notably against job discrimination in New Mexico....

GROWTH AND NATIONAL VISIBILITY

... The century-old relationship between the United States and Mexico continues to affect both nations. Immigrants, natural resources, and profits continue to flow north. Legal immigration from Mexico to the United States at present allows between forty and fifty thousand visas each year for permanent residence. Those looking for "commuter status," which allows them to work in the United States while living in Mexico, have to endure, barring political connections, a three-year waiting period.

Mexican workers caught in Mexico's economic sluggishness are aware that wages in the United States for identical work are sometimes seven times higher than at home, and many are thus led to risk illegal entry. Such illegal entry is only increased by the active recruitment by "coyotes," who transport Mexicans across the border for a fee. Undocumented workers are a significant part of the U.S. labor force, particularly for work that most American citizens regard as demeaning, low paying, dirty, and unstable. Undocumented workers have always come to the United States in circumstances of multiple jeopardy, as minorities unprotected from employer exploitation and abuse. Such conditions continue unabated today. ...

CURRENT STATUS

Chicanos lag behind the rest of the U.S. population by every measure of socioeconomic well-being—level of education, occupational attainment, employment status, family income, and the like. Some say that Chicanos are no different from other immigrants who arrived in the United States impoverished, and who managed by hard work to gain advantages for their children, taking the first important step toward assimilation. The substantial achievements of the American-born first generation over that of the immigrant generation are thought to be conclusive. Such an optimistic view overlooks major changes in the society and the historical relationship of over a century and a half of racial discrimination and economic exploitation. Although economic expansion and dramatic social change characterized the postwar years, economic contraction and dislocation, possibly exaggerated by the new conservative retrenchment, are the hallmarks of more recent times. ... Although second-generation and later Chicanos made large gains relative to those of the first generation, such gains did not allow for their thorough absorption into the economic and social structure of U.S. society. The data of the late 1970s suggest how different generations of Chicanos have fared. The median education for second-generation Chicanos was 11.1 years, only two years more than for U.S.-born first-generation, but decidedly more than for the immigrant generation (5.8 years).

All generations of Chicano males are underrepresented in white-collar jobs; Mexican-born males are least likely to be found in such positions. Farm labor is the one area where there is a significant difference between the U.S.-born and immigrant Chicano populations. Over 15 percent of Mexican-born men are employed as farm laborers, twice the number for sons of Mexican immigrants, five times the number of third-generation Chicanos. Labor force participation figures, however, also show that second-generation Chicanos had the highest unemployment rate, while the immigrant generation had the lowest. The data on incomes indicate first-generation Chicano families as having the highest median income, with the second-generation following, and the Mexican-born as having the lowest incomes. The range, however, was not great—about $1,500.

That Mexicans who have resided for the longest time in the United States —second generation—have the highest unemployment rates and only very modest representation in white-collar, professional, and managerial categories suggests the limited structure of opportunity for Chicanos. They are entering the industrial sector at a time when its socioeconomic structure is increasingly tertiary, demanding highly trained personnel in high-technology industries such as aerospace, communications, and the like. Although Chicanos may be making "progress" relative to their immigrant parents, they are actually falling farther behind when looked at in the context of the opportunity structure in an increasingly post-industrial social order and compared to the dominant population. Also, there is evidence that Chicano technical and occupational skills will increasingly limit them to the secondary labor market, with its unfavorable wage rates, limited fringe benefits, and general instability. These conditions to not promise either full equity or full participation for Chicanos in the decades immediately ahead. Still, that the Anglo population growth is at or near a steady state, with its income-generating population increasingly aging, suggests that the younger and expanding Chicano work force will be shouldering a growing and disproportionate burden in the future. Social Security, Medicare, Medicaid, and the myriad of other social programs funded from taxes on the work force will be more and more borne by youthful employed Chicanos.

Historically, Chicanos' economic rewards have been disproportionate to their contribution to U.S. industrial development. Now that the society is increasingly post-industrial, Chicanos find themselves still carrying the burden. The federal government, which played a prominent role throughout the history of Mexicans in the United States, has been repressive, supporting industries and employers, and generally frustrating Chicanos' efforts to advance.

NOTES

1. The terms "Chicano" and "Mexican" are used interchangeably in this essay, because the U.S. Southwest and northern Mexico were initially a cultural and geographic unit, the border being only an invisible line between the two nations.
2. The term "Anglo" will be used to refer to U.S. residents of European origin. It is used, for convenience, as a generic term for all European immigrants to the United States.

7.2 SU SUN BAI

Affirmative Pursuit of Political Equality for Asian Pacific Americans: Reclaiming the Voting Rights Act

As with other minority groups, Asian Americans have been systematically excluded from equal participation in the American political arena. In 1990 the U.S. Commission on Civil Rights identified several social impediments to Asian American political participation. Among these obstacles are policies that weaken the voting strength of Asian Americans; the unavailability of Asian-language ballots and other election materials; problems with reapportionment; anti-Asian sentiments among non-Asian voters and the media; and the absence of Asian American political candidates.

In the present selection, Su Sun Bai challenges contemporary explanations for Asian American exclusion from American politics. The author outlines the problem of low Asian American political awareness and points out that available legal remedies fail to safeguard Asian Americans from exclusion. Additionally, Su suggests that the 1965 Voting Rights Act be amended to ensure more realistic protections for Asian American political participation.

Key Concept: Asian Americans and political equality

227

THE PROBLEM OF LOW ASIAN PACIFIC AMERICAN POLITICAL PARTICIPATION

Complete Integration Hypothesis Refuted

A common assertion that the lack of political participation by a cohesive Asian Pacific American group is due to their complete integration into the American political process and assimilation into American society is disproved by empirical evidence. Disproportionately low levels of Asian Pacific American participation in both electoral and nonelectoral politics, as compared to that of the general population, suggests that Asian Pacific Americans actually are not assimilated into the American political mainstream. This Comment focuses on three areas with significant Asian Pacific American populations—Los Angeles, San Francisco, and New York City—to investigate the present problem of low political participation by Asian Pacific Americans.

Lack of Electoral Political Participation.

LOW VOTER REGISTRATION FIGURES   The *UCLA Asian Pacific American Voter Registration Study (UCLA Study)* found that Asian Pacific Americans accounted for 6.0% of the total Los Angeles County population and comprised between 2.9%–4.3% of the total electorate of that county in 1980. In all of the communities studied, Asian Pacific Americans demonstrated a lower voter registration rate than other residents, and the "proportion of Asian Pacific American voters in relation to local electorates [wa]s usually far less than the proportion of Asian Pacific Americans in the total population of these communities." The Asian Pacific American voter registration rate was well below the overall county average of 60% for all individuals 18 or older. Specifically, the highest Asian Pacific American registration rate of 43.0% was that of Japanese Americans, followed by a rate of 35.5% for Chinese Americans, 27.0% for Filipino Americans, 13.0% for Korean Americans, 16.7% for Asian Indians, 28.5% for Samoans, and the extremely low 4.1% for Vietnamese Americans.

A similar study done in San Francisco compared Chinese and Japanese American voter registration rates to those of the general population in three electoral districts with high concentrations of Asian Pacific American populations and found Asian Pacific American rates to be extremely low. For instance, only 30.9% of the Chinese Americans in the San Francisco area were registered to vote in contrast to the 69.1% voter registration rate for non-Chinese (and non-Asian Pacific American) citizens. The estimated number of Chinese American voters in the San Francisco area was about 5.5% of the total number of voters when the Chinese American population in 1980 was 12.1% of the city's total population. Japanese Americans in these districts also demonstrated overall low registration figures with only about 39% registered to vote. Even if the low Chinese American voter registration rate can be explained partly by the high percentage of those who are foreign born, the possibility of noncitizenship status still fails to explain adequately the low registration rate of Japanese Americans who are predominantly American born.

In sum, Asian Pacific Americans are "grossly underrepresented in terms of their voting power in relation to their numbers in the population." As a consequence, the study of San Francisco accurately predicted that Asian Pacific Americans will have "a lack of say in decisions that affect them the most, such as bilingual ballots, Chinatown development... and less of a likelihood to elect Asian/Pacific candidates than their numbers would indicate."

Although no formal study has been done for the New York City area, the problem of low voter registration among the Asian Pacific American community in New York has been documented. For instance, a 1984 informal survey by a community organizer found that

> the percentage of voting-age adults who registered to vote in [New York's] Chinatown that year was only 25 per cent compared with 47.2 per cent for Manhattan as a whole: in addition, in districts where Chinese represented more than 90 per cent of the total population, only 30 per cent of the voters in the 1984 Democratic primary were Chinese.

This survey indicates that the lower registration rate of Chinese Americans in New York City cannot be attributed simply to the possibility of their noncitizen status.

Consequently, as the New York State Advisory Committee to the United States Commission on Civil Rights reports, because of a perceived lack of political power, Asian Pacific Americans are not consulted in formulating policies that affect them, are deprived of benefits, are subject to subtle discrimination, and have "no place... in the regular Democratic or Republican party machinery."

THE LOW NUMBER OF ELECTED OFFICIALS RELATIVE TO THE NUMBER OF ASIAN PACIFIC AMERICAN VOTERS   The three urban areas with high concentrations of Asian Pacific American populations also exhibited disproportionately low numbers of elected officials of Asian Pacific American descent relative to their population numbers—a further sign of political exclusion.

California, for example, has the largest concentration of Asian Pacific Americans in the nation, and many estimate that Los Angeles County's Asian Pacific American population will have doubled in size by 1990 with current rates of overseas immigration and domestic, secondary migration.

Nevertheless, as of 1986, no Asian Pacific American had ever been elected to a county-level position in Los Angeles, there had been only one Asian Pacific American member of the state legislature from Los Angeles, and there had been only two Asian Pacific American congressmen from California (moreover, both Robert Matsui and Norman Mineta were elected from Northern California). The *UCLA Study*, however, does recognize some improvement, stressing that the existence of elected Asian Pacific American public officials "nonetheless represents a significant degree of progress, especially when it is measured against the long history of *total* non-representation of Asian Pacific Americans in local politics." Similar underrepresentation by elected officials is evident in San Francisco, New York City, and across the nation in general.

WEAK PARTY AFFILIATION   Another possible sign of the political exclusion of an identifiable group is the lack of strong political party identification within the group. Although the Democratic party has been the overwhelming choice of minority groups, this does not necessarily seem the case with Asian Pacific Americans. In Los Angeles County, for instance, most political subdivisions show a plurality or majority of Democrats among Asian Pacific Americans. This figure, however, is usually less than that of the electorate as a whole. The San Francisco study also points out weak party affiliations of Chinese Americans in San Francisco, and in particular, the significant percentage that declined to state any party affiliation.

In addition, exit polls conducted by the Asian American Legal Defense and Education Fund (AALDEF) after the recent presidential and mayoral elections at New York City voting sites revealed a "willingness among Asians to cross party boundaries." In the mayoral race, for instance, 53% of the Asian Pacific Americans surveyed in the Flushing area voted for Republican Rudolph Giuliani and 40% voted for Democrat David Dinkins even though only 30% claimed to be registered Republicans.

This lack of party identification, however, does not mean that Asian Pacific Americans do not form a politically cohesive group. Rather, it only indicates that Asian Pacific Americans are not fully integrated into the political mainstream and thus are not bound by traditional party ties.

In sum, the low Asian Pacific American voter registration rates, along with weak party affiliations and the low number of elected officials of Asian descent, all attest to the political exclusion of Asian Pacific Americans....

Incomplete Socio-Cultural Explanations

Commentators on the problem of Asian Pacific American political inactivity have focused primarily on personality and cultural traits of Asian Pacific Americans to explain their "disinterest" and lack of activity in American politics. Scholars in Asian Pacific American studies have also called for greater education and mobilization of the Asian Pacific American population to combat the problem of political inactivity. A common theory asserts that this problem stems mostly from within the Asian Pacific American communities because of the innate socio-psychological characteristics of Asian Pacific Americans which hinder the formation of an effective political power base. This Section argues, however, that socio-cultural explanations rely on incomplete analysis and false assumptions and do not adequately address the problem of Asian Pacific American political exclusion.

Elements of Validity in Theories.   Socio-cultural explanations do assert some valid points and observations. A degree of divisiveness within the generic Asian Pacific American group stems from generational, national, and historical differences among the various subgroups. This "internal diversity—of ethnic origins, generations, social classes, political perspectives, and organizational aims—has ofttimes prevented [Asian Pacific Americans] from being perceived as a unified actor in articulating their stands on public policy."

Another often cited factor with some validity is the Asian Pacific American community's unfamiliarity with American political processes due to the fact that a majority of the community consists of recent immigrants with neither the time nor resources to engage in politics. This unfamiliarity in turn has led to a certain level of disaffection with the political system, which furthers skepticism among Asian Pacific Americans about their political efficacy. In addition, a historical lack of political responsiveness to Asian Pacific American interests has forced many Asian Pacific Americans into segregated ethnic enclaves such as the Chinatowns, little Tokyos, Manila towns, and Koreatowns of the United States, with very few resources to integrate into mainstream society. A prediction of the future of Asian Pacific Americans' political participation thus cannot ignore the possibility that they may become even further alienated from the system.

Problems With Theories. The basic thrust and erroneous assumption of the socio-cultural hypothesis is that the lack of political participation by Asian Pacific Americans is their own fault, and not that of the system. A 1966 article for the *New York Times*, entitled *Success Story, Japanese American Style*, can be credited with first imposing the egregious honor of the "model minority" on the Asian Pacific American community. This first positive assessment of Japanese Americans was transferred to a similar discussion about Chinese Americans in a 1966 *U.S. News & World Report* article entitled *Success Story of One Minority Group in U.S.* Thus the image of Asian Pacific Americans changed from the "yellow peril" of the World War II era to the "model minority" of the 1960s at a time when the country was facing a racial crisis. Similar media accounts of Asian American "success" have continued to the present....

This "model minority" myth, however, amounts to just an ethnic stereotype; it characterizes all Asian Pacific Americans as quiet, obedient, and non-adversarial yet economically successful minorities. One of the myth's most dangerous fallacies is that it portrays Asian Pacific Americans as either choosing not to participate in politics or of not needing political empowerment. It is interesting to note that most "proponents" of the success model are either non-Asian scholars or reporters of the mass media, while critics of the model are scholars of Asian ancestry or representatives of government agencies, such as the U.S. Commission on Civil Rights. As one study observes, "[i]mplicit in the success theme are three crucial political messages": the "benefit denying function," the "system preserving function," and the "minority blaming function." The "model minority" theory, then, is largely a myth to preserve existing inequalities and is unsubstantiated by the facts....

Historical evidence... does not support the claim that Asian Pacific Americans are culturally averse to politics. Asian Pacific American history is replete with instances of collective efforts to combat common experiences of discrimination and exclusion. This tradition of political unification and protest is presently evident in the Asian Pacific Americans' fight against increasing anti-Asian violence, against quotas in university admissions, for inclusion in affirmative action programs, for Japanese American reparations, for immigration reforms, and for access to the ballot.

Finally, socio-cultural theories also dismiss the history of institutional discrimination faced by Asian Pacific Americans, denying responsibility for their present situation and serving a "minority blaming function." These theories do not recognize subtle exclusionary barriers faced by Asian Pacific Americans attempting to enter the political process, and ignore the history of arbitrary exclusion and racial attacks against the entire group if any individual or subgroup "made trouble."

On the other hand, AALDEF's analyses of its exit polls offer a more realistic assessment of the factors that forge the political habits of Asian Pacific Americans. The AALDEF polls revealed "that most Asian Americans who vote are long-time citizens, American-born, or very familiar with American customs and the language." The exit polls also suggested that immigrants who have only recently become citizens and those who "feel that their needs will not be represented by non-Asian candidates" often do not vote. Furthermore, 20% stated that they were "'not very fluent' in English," and 74% said they were only "moderately fluent." Most significantly, 71% said they would vote more often *"if more Asian candidates ran for office."*...

CURRENT BARRIERS TO EFFECTIVE POLITICAL PARTICIPATION

Although a closer examination of the socio-cultural explanations for Asian Pacific American political inactivity reveals many fallacies in the theories and indicates that Asian Pacific Americans have not been, and are not being, incorporated into the political process, case law concerning Asian Pacific American vote dilution or other barriers to the franchise is almost nonexistent. That neither the Asian Pacific American community nor the Justice Department has been able or willing to initiate legal challenges to the systematic exclusion of Asian Pacific Americans from the political process is itself a powerful indicator of the lack of Asian Pacific American political participation. Reasons for the absence of litigation in this area can be gleaned from an examination of the available vote dilution case law concerning both racial and language minorities.

Modern Vote Dilution

In addition to legislative action such as the Voting Rights Act of 1965 and its subsequent amendments, the Supreme Court has, at least recently, constitutionally guaranteed minority access to the ballot. Voting and registration restrictions based on race have been judicially and legislatively invalidated and other more ingenious ways to keep "nonwhites" from the voting booth have also been declared void. Some scholars still argue that the right to vote equals the right to cast a ballot, and that the right was achieved when direct barriers to casting ballots were eliminated.

The Voting Rights Act, as amended in 1982, however, implies a broader view of the right to vote. As the Senate Report discussing the 1982 amendments noted, "the political effectiveness of minority groups" has been hampered by new and more sophisticated methods of impeding minority "access to the ballot box"; these methods fall under the umbrella term of "minority vote dilution." Vote dilution, as recognized and specifically prohibited by section 2 of the Voting Rights Act, is the submergence of a minority group's voting strength and the denial of an equal opportunity to participate in the political process caused by discriminatory mechanisms or practices.

The Supreme Court first construed and applied the amended section 2 of the Voting Rights Act in *Thornburg v. Gingles.* The plaintiffs, a group of black registered voters in North Carolina, claimed that the 1982 redistricting scheme by the North Carolina General Assembly "impaired black citizens' ability to elect representatives of their choice in violation of the... Constitution and of § 2 of the Voting Rights Act." In affirming the lower court's holding for the plaintiffs, the Court emphasized that "[m]inority voters who contend that the multimember form of districting violates § 2 must prove that the use of a multimember electoral structure operates to minimize or cancel out their ability to elect their preferred candidates." The plaintiffs must thus demonstrate a causal relationship between the challenged electoral scheme and the submergence of their voting power in a white majority.

According to the Court, the most relevant of the Senate Report factors in assessing a section 2 claim were those that helped to evaluate the situation from a "functional" view of the political process. From this evolved a three-prong test as a section 2 liability threshold. The plaintiff must demonstrate that: (1) the minority group is *geographically compact* with sufficiently large numbers "to constitute a majority in a single-member district," (2) that there is *political cohesion* within the group as demonstrated by *distinctive interests and bloc voting,* and (3) that there is sufficient racial *bloc voting* by the majority that operates "usually to defeat the minority's preferred candidate."...

From the perspective of Asian Pacific Americans, the main difficulty with the *Gingles* approach lies in the first prong of the liability threshold, which requires geographic compactness of the minority group. This first prong assumes the virtues of residential concentration because most section 2 vote dilution claims challenge multimember districts or at-large elections. However, when the minority group is not concentrated enough to form a single-member district, the obsessive focus on geography becomes misplaced and fails to protect Asian Pacific Americans, most of whom are geographically dispersed. This dispersal is often not voluntary. Thus the geographic insularity requirement does not address the problem of discrimination despite nonsegregation.

Additionally, even in those areas of high Asian Pacific American concentration, Asian Pacific Americans do not comprise a majority so as to form aesthetically simple and judicially manageable single-member districts. Therefore, the remedy of redistricting would not cure Asian Pacific Americans' lack of an equal opportunity to participate.

The bloc voting components of the second and third prongs present further difficulties for Asian Pacific Americans in establishing the liability threshold under the *Gingles* approach to vote dilution claims. Specifically, a group's political cohesion, which is necessary to satisfy the second prong of *Gingles,* is most easily demonstrated by group bloc voting. In the absence of a clear choice such as an Asian Pacific American candidate, however, the Asian Pacific American community's political cohesion cannot be measured in this manner.

Nevertheless, there is ample evidence to demonstrate that, in other respects, Asian Pacific Americans are politically cohesive and therefore can meet the second prong requirement of *Gingles*. Not only do they more readily identify with Asian Pacific American candidates, but they share an ever-increasing number of common interests and needs distinctive to the group. Furthermore, to counter the indiscriminate anti-Asian directives, from both the populace and the legislature, Asian Pacific Americans have learned to build and utilize an Asian Pacific American collective.

Similarly, there is evidence (other than bloc voting) suggesting that the majority population "usually" votes to defeat Asian Pacific American candidates; this would satisfy the third prong of *Gingles*.

Disfranchisement by Unremedied Language Barriers

In addition to the indirect dilution of Asian Pacific Americans' voting power, a persistent *direct* barrier for Asian Pacific Americans is their status as language minorities. Although the 1975 amendments to the Voting Rights Act "broadened the 1965 law to include the issue of discrimination against 'citizens of language minorities' and banned practices denying the right of any citizen of the United States to vote" because of her language minority status, empirical evidence demonstrates that non-English speaking Asian Pacific Americans have remained effectively disfranchised. For example, the UCLA study of Asian Pacific American voter registration in the Los Angeles county area reveals that

> 26.7% of all Asian Pacific Americans eighteen years and older, and therefore of voting age, in Los Angeles county in 1980 indicated that they did not speak English well or not at all; and in every city or Asian Corridor area which was surveyed, Asian Pacific Americans had a higher proportion of such individuals than their local communities.... [But] [n]o city or area in Los Angeles county has ever had Asian language electoral materials, be they for election purposes or encouraging individuals to register to vote.

The analysis of San Francisco's voter registration data also shows that low registration rates among Chinese Americans are partly caused by being born in a foreign country, but more importantly, are caused by their lack of English skills. In New York, the AALDEF's exit poll showed that 83% of those who said they were not fluent in English would vote more often if bilingual ballots were available. This data demonstrates the existence of "de facto discrimination that is in part a product of their [Asian immigrants'] unfamiliarity with the language and ways of their new country."

The coverage formula that triggers protection for members of a single language minority provides only minimal protection for non-English speaking Asian Pacific Americans. This problem, however, is not evidenced by litigation involving Asian Pacific Americans. Instead, cases involving non-English speaking Hispanic Americans reveal the inadequacies of the multilingual provision of the Voting Rights Act. These inadequacies are exacerbated in the case of Asian Pacific Americans because of the diverse languages spoken by the "generic" Asian Pacific American group. Thus, although Asian Pacific Americans as a group may form more than five percent of the voting age population in a jurisdiction, it is extremely difficult for one language minority (i.e., Chinese, Japanese, or Korean) to constitute five percent of the relevant population....

In addition to the difficulties previously mentioned, the inability to acquire English language skills stems from the stress of immigration, psychological and emotional conflicts, and the resultant identity change with a loss in self-esteem. Difficulty in learning to read and write English is thus not an indication of Asian Pacific Americans' unwillingness to learn the language. The dangers of a lack of bilingual assistance for such a significant activity as voting include exclusion and isolation from the surrounding society.

SUGGESTED MODIFICATIONS OF PRINCIPLES/POLICY AND ALTERNATIVE REMEDIES

Dismantling the subtle and effective discriminatory barriers against Asian Pacific Americans' voting rights demands an affirmative commitment to the political equality of Asian Pacific Americans. Without such a commitment, "true equality [for Asian Pacific Americans]... remains elusive so long as the law is merely passive in conferring equality. Discrimination will persist in a system that is indifferent to the social realities confronting Asian immigrants." The federal government and the judiciary must utilize the Voting Rights Act to pursue its intended goals affirmatively.

Affirmative Judicial Intervention and Fashioning of Innovative Remedies

When faced with vote dilution cases, courts should not hesitate to intervene to invalidate the electoral structure being challenged and to fashion innovative remedies. Political equality for Asian Pacific Americans consists of equality in opportunity to participate, to have an effective voice, and to have an Asian Pacific American presence in the voting booth and in public offices. A determination of political cohesion of Asian Pacific Americans should not depend exclusively on geographic insularity and polarized voting, but should also consider their distinctive interests and demonstrated collective action. Thus where the electoral system being challenged is not an at-large system, or the minority group is not geographically compact, alternative theories of inclusion and alternative remedies to single member districts must be utilized.

Alternative remedies that "lower the threshold of exclusion" and promote "greater diversity on governing bodies by increasing the number of groups large enough to elect the representatives of their choice" have already been tested. For instance, limited voting and cumulative voting are credited with lowering the threshold of exclusion, and with allowing the election of greater numbers of minority candidates.

Furthermore, the *Gingles'* interpretation of section 2 (or at least the lower courts' construction of the *Gingles'* interpretation) is not necessarily the only approach to section 2 cases. As Judge Myron Thompson proposed in *Dillard v. Crenshaw County*, and as Karlan encourages, courts should "take *Gingles* at its word: dilution occurs when 'minority voters [would] possess the *potential* to elect representatives in the absence of the challenged structure or of practice....'"

In sum, the courts should take a "functional view"—that of a very local appraisal in light of present realities—to define the *Gingles'* prongs....

Legislative Changes

To protect Asian Pacific Americans' voting rights, modifications to the multilingual provisions of the Voting Rights Act also need to be made when the Act is considered for renewal in 1992. The most significant modification is altering the trigger factor for determining coverage under the Voting Rights Act. The five percent trigger for coverage should be replaced with a fixed number of language minority voters. A lower trigger figure for bilingual assistance will help to ensure that non-English speaking Asian Pacific Americans who comprise less than five percent of the voting age population are protected. In turn, when greater numbers of Asian Pacific Americans are provided with bilingual voting assistance, greater numbers will register to vote, and the Asian Pacific American electorate will grow in strength.

CONCLUSION

Currently, Asian Pacific Americans' impact on electoral politics is significant in terms of its *potential* rather than present impact. In order to realize that potential, any situation in which it is shown that Asian Pacific Americans "have less opportunity than other members of the electorate to participate in the political process and to elect representatives of their choice" must be effectively remedied. To include Asian Pacific Americans in the electoral process, "specific local communities and ethnic groups which deserve greater attention" must be pinpointed and served. The final goal of political equality for Asian Pacific Americans, then, is a guarantee of an equal opportunity for Asian Pacific Americans to participate in politics and to have an effective voice which will encourage greater and more active participation.

7.3 FRANK HAROLD WILSON

Housing and Black Americans: The Persistent Significance of Race

Despite legal safeguards, such as the federal Fair Housing Act, many Black and other non-White minorities experience housing discrimination. Approximately three out of four Blacks in American cities currently live in segregated neighborhoods. Racial minorities are excluded from many neighborhoods by the illicit practices of real estate agents who manipulate White fears and attitudes toward minorities.

In the present selection, sociology professor Frank Harold Wilson, of the University of Wisconsin–Milwaukee, examines the changes that have occurred in Black housing during the post–World War II years and since the 1970s. He discusses some of the financial and real estate practices, such as *redlining* and *racial steering,* that contribute to the maintenance of segregated neighborhoods. Wilson suggests that the contemporary housing status of Blacks is characterized by persistent racial differentials.

Key Concept: race and housing segregation

INTRODUCTION

This paper describes changes in the housing status of blacks during the post-World War II period as a context for examining black housing conditions since 1970. While these overall trends illustrate actual improvements and "upgrading" in black housing through the late 1980s, there are persistent trends of racial differentials in homeownership, housing quality, and housing costs. Underlying these differences are macro-sociological changes in the economy and social policy. This paper is organized around the following questions:

1. To what extent has the absolute and relative status of housing among blacks changed during the post-World War II period in general and since 1970 in particular?

2. What complex combination of macro- and micro-sociological factors account for change and persistence in black housing patterns?
3. To what extent have federal governmental policies provided possibilities and limitations for changing the status of black housing?

A related concern in this paper centers on assessing how these changing housing conditions of blacks fit different models of changing racial and class stratification.

HOUSING AND RACE IN THE BLACK COMMUNITY: CLASSICAL PERSPECTIVES

Social scientists who have studied the social and economic status of Black Americans have long been concerned with questions of race and housing. In W. E. B. DuBois's pioneering study, *The Philadelphia Negro* (1899), housing and race questions at the turn-of-the-century were addressed in a chapter entitled "The Environment of the Negro" (DuBois, 1899; Chapter XV). DuBois showed how the growth of the black population during the nineteenth century was segregated and concentrated by housing discrimination resulting in high rents, crowding, and slums. DuBois was clear in indicating that the housing conditions of blacks were primarily conditioned by racial discrimination and economics.

Investigators who examined relationships between housing and race between the turn-of-the-century and the "Great Migration" further articulated urban patterns of racial segregation and racial differentials in homeownership, rentership, physical housing conditions, and quality of life. Social scientists influenced by the University of Chicago tradition such as Ernest Burgess, Charles S. Johnson, and E. Franklin Frazier examined the housing of blacks within the "growing city" model characterized by rapid population growth, in-migration, high density, and succession (Burgess, 1928; Johnson, 1943; Drake and Cayton, 1944; Frazier, 1949). In a classic essay, "Residential Segregation in American Cities," Ernest Burgess hypothesized that the distribution of black residences in urban space and their movement from central to peripheral locations was part of a more universal process of city growth and radical expansion (Burgess, 1928). Charles S. Johnson, in *Patterns of Negro Segregation*, described the variability in spatial and institutional forms of racial residential segregation in the North and South and within urban and rural communities. While Johnson identified a pattern of large concentrations of black neighborhoods across cities, historic and economic factors conditioned these differently by region. In northern cities, black neighborhoods and housing were intensely concentrated into "Black Belts" or black ghettos which more nearly approached complete segregation. In southern cities, black neighborhoods and housing approximated more "islands" configurations with at least one large black cluster of neighborhoods and a scattering of smaller black clusters (Johnson, 1943; 8–11). E. Franklin Frazier noted an internal differentiation of the urban black community by concentric zones varying by social and economic status. Amid racial segregation, homeownership, structural quality, and social organization increased directly with status and radial movement (Frazier, 1949). Outside of the University of Chicago, Robert Weaver's studies of black neighborhoods in the *Negro Ghetto* constitutes one of the most comprehensive and early statements of housing and race (Weaver, 1948).

During the post-World War II period, questions of race and housing retained traditional concerns with discrimination and segregation that were increasingly influenced by social policy concerns associated with civil rights reforms (McEntire, 1960; Taeuber and Taeuber, 1965; National Advisory Commission on Civil Disorders; 1968). By the late 1960s, the National Advisory Commission on Civil Disorders (Kerner Commission) identified deteriorating conditions of ghetto housing for blacks among the causes of urban riots and rebellions. The Kerner Commission Report identified three areas of differential housing conditions by race. First, blacks were disproportionately represented in older, substandard, and overcrowded housing structures. Second, blacks in large cities were forced to pay the same rents as whites and receive less in return for their money or pay higher rents for similar housing. Third, a high proportion of housing in ghetto neighborhoods at the time contained building and housing code violations which were not corrected (National Advisory Commission on Civil Disorders, 1968; 468–472).

RACE AND HOUSING IN CONTEMPORARY AMERICA: HAS THE SIGNIFICANCE OF RACE DECLINED?

The civil rights movement during the early 1940s and post-World War II period was salient in institutionalizing federal-level reforms in policies of social and economic equality that changed the structure of race relations in the United States. Through the cumulative effects of executive orders, legislation, and supreme court decisions that undermined the historic bases of racial exclusion and segregation, the status of blacks with respect to education, employment, and income changed dramatically. During the height of the civil rights movement, the beginnings of fair housing policy were initiated. In 1962, President Kennedy signed Executive Order 11063 barring discrimination in federal housing programs. With the enactment of Title VI of the Civil Rights Act of 1964, Congress barred discrimination in federally funded activities including housing. In 1968 after the assassination of Martin Luther King, Congress passed with more specificity Title VIII of the Civil Rights Act or the "Fair Housing Act" which broadly prohibited discrimination in private and public housing. In the same year, the Supreme Court in *Jones vs. Mayer* reexamined the reach of the Reconstruction Civil Rights Act and concluded that it was broad enough to provide blacks with redress against private as well as government discrimination in housing activities (See: Schwemm, 1988; Citizens Commission on Civil Rights, 1983).

How Black Americans have fared with respect to housing since the late 1960s is subject to different interpretations. These competing interpretations are based on different models of the changing nature of racial stratification in the United States and the level and type of social indicator(s) used as evidence. These models may be defined as: 1) "the declining significance of race" model; 2) the "inclining significance of class" model; 3) the "persistence of institutional discrimination" model.

The "declining significance of race" model advances that civil rights policies including the Fair Housing Act have either diminished or ended the effects of racial discrimination and segregation in housing and blacks have been primary beneficiaries. According to this view, the social segregation of blacks and whites is analogous to general land economics where similar land uses tend to cluster together. Although racial segregation may exist, it is associated with lower rental and homeowner costs for black households and does not necessitate racial discrimination (Muth, 1985; Muth, 1969). Consequently, racial differential costs are theorized as increasingly and disproportionately borne by whites more than blacks. The evidence for the "declining significance of race" model may include the following: (1) Trends in public opinion polls that show increasing favorability if not acceptance among whites of the principle of fair housing (Schuman, Steeh, and Bobo, 1985); (2) Recent trends in metropolitan- and central city-level segregation which show decreasing black scores (Clark, 1986); (3) The increasing rate and scale of black suburbanization during the 1970s (Nelson; 1985); (4) The "gentrification" of central area neighborhoods that has resulted in whites coming "back to the city" with increased neighborhood-level integration with blacks (Lee, Spain, and Umberson, 1985).

The "inclining significance of class model" advances that while civil rights policies have decreased the significance of historic discrimination, the persistence of racial concentration and segregation are a consequence of economic factors in general and recent patterns of social dislocation and poverty among blacks specifically. According to this perspective, decreasing discrimination does not necessarily result in decreasing segregation. Socio-economic characteristics of blacks are primary factors explaining housing differentials and segregation. First, the generally lower and depressed incomes of black households "naturally select" them to rental and owner markets in central cities. For those upper- and middle-income black households who have the necessary income to purchase housing in suburban markets, their lower wealth limits them to older suburbs (U.S. Census, 1990). Second, the growth of the urban black underclass and the "mismatch" in education and skills between central city black jobless and suburban employers may indirectly through unemployment result in marginal housing status and concentration in inner city ghetto areas.

On a more micro-sociological level, black preferences may be hypothesized as factors in persistent racial segregation. Since blacks are assumed to prefer to live in neighborhoods that are at least half black, and whites prefer to live in neighborhoods that are largely white, a self-fulfilling prophecy results in racially mixed areas being perceived as inherently unstable and favorable for racial "tipping." The most typical modes of locating housing such as asking friends and co-workers or searches along familiar transportation routes may reinforce ghettoization.

The "persistence of institutional discrimination" model advances an interactive relationship between class and race rather than the "zero-sum" and "independence" assumptions contained in the other models. This perspective assumes that despite civil rights policies including the Fair Housing Act there is a continuation of discrimination and segregation in the rental and sale of housing which largely restricts blacks to central city and racially changing suburban markets. Accordingly, the persistence of high levels of segregation and "hyper-segregation" (Massey, 1990) are explained by racially exclusionary historic and current practices of an institutional nature....

Although de jure discrimination in principle is illegal according to the Fair Housing Act, there are a complex of institutional and interpersonal factors that maintain racial discrimination and segregation in housing. First, institutional "redlining" with respect to developmental and home mortgage loans may still be practiced by private financial and insurance institutions resulting in the disinvestment of inner city areas and lessened opportunities for black homeownership and equity (Squires and Velez, 1987). Second, "racial steering," a real estate practice where prospective buyers or renters of properties are directed to racially changing or segregated markets, exists independent of income, social class and life style (Turner, Struyk, and Yinger, 1991; Wienk, 1979; Pearce, 1979). In a recent Housing Discrimination Study (HDS), black and Hispanic homeseekers were less likely than comparable whites to be told about available units and when available units were shown or recommended, these were likely to be in neighborhoods with a higher percent minority, lower incomes, and lower property values (Turner, Struyk, and Yinger, 1991). Third, exclusionary zoning in building and land use may prohibit privately built low- and moderate-income housing and public housing resulting in its segregation in central cities. Within central cities, decisions to build low-income housing in dense, single-site rather than in low-density and scattered-site patterns can involve actions that are racist in consequence if not intention. Despite its range, the "institutional discrimination" model does not advance that "race explains all."

These three models of the contemporary context of housing and race advance different and sometimes contradictory explanations of the social structures and social relationships underlying racial segregation and discrimination. While each of these offer different explanations, when used separately and independently each may have distinct limitations. Why do separatist uses of each model have limitations in understanding housing and race? The complexity of housing and race requires accounts that link different levels of sociological analysis such as micro-level patterns of individuals and households, middle-range levels of neighborhood and community, and macro-level patterns of metropolitan and national land and housing market organization. Where the "declining significance of race" and "inclining significance of class" models are strongest in accounting for micro- and middle range linkages, the "persistence of institutional discrimination" more directly accounts for macro- and middle range linkages....

POST-WORLD WAR II CHANGES
IN BLACK HOUSING TENURE

The empirical assessment of selected housing changes among blacks in this paper will be limited to the following: homeownership, housing quality, and costs. The statistics and summaries presented provide an insight of long-term and contemporary patterns. Since only aggregate patterns are summarized, caution is advised in generalizing from these.

... Before the United States entry in World War II (1940), black households were disproportionately represented as tenants in renter occupied units in both urban and rural communities. In 1940, 76 percent of black households as compared to 54 percent of white households were renters. This racial differential reflected not only the relatively greater poverty and depressed incomes of blacks coming out of the New Deal recovery of the 1930s but the historic effects of racial exclusion in land and homeownership.

The most significant change since 1940 has been the growth in homeownership. Black homeownership between 1940 and 1980 grew steadily nearly doubling in percentages. In absolute terms, the number of black homeowners during these four decades increased more than fivefold—from 778,000 to 5,124,000 (1940 and 1980 figures, respectively). As might be expected, black homeownership increased most dramatically during those periods when white homeownership grew rapidly. Black ownership increased more than 12 percent between 1940 and 1960 going from 23.6 to 38.4 percent. At the same time, white homeownership increased from 45.6 to 64.4—a 19 point increase. Since 1960, black homeownership grew more slowly increasing only 6 percent through 1980. White homeownership during the same twenty year period was even smaller increasing only 3 percent. Although the momentum of homeownership growth across race slowed down during the 1960s and 1970s, it should be noted that the actual increases in homeowners were larger than at any time in history.

This primary trend in post-World War II black homeownership growth can be largely explained by three factors. First, the urbanization of blacks during these years was generally characterized by increasing educational and occupational opportunities which translated into greater incomes and purchasing power. Second, new housing opportunities in previously crowded central city housing markets opened up as a direct consequence of the vacancies created by white out-movement and suburbanization. Third, black social and residential mobility were primarily accommodated in moderately-priced racially changing and established black urban housing markets. Improved black homeownership was part of a larger and unprecedented expansion of the U.S. housing inventory during the post-World War II period which was accompanied by unparalleled gains in renter-occupied units (Taeuber and Taeuber, 1965; Sternlieb and Hughes, 1983)....

A secondary and emergent trend of housing deprivation has accompanied the post-World War II trends in housing upgrading which has increased in significance during the 1970s and 1980s. While macroeconomic forces are primary in this development, the intersection of social class and race is evident in the persistence of housing deprivation and racial differentials. The most significant change since 1980 is the recent reversal in black homeownership. Although

Frank Harold
Wilson

homeownership among blacks increased during the post-World War II period, these figures underscore the importance of viewing and tempering contemporary black housing within the larger context of changing tenureship patterns. First, while actual black homeownership increased, the level of homeownership has lagged far behind white households. Between 1940 and 1987, the racial differential increased from 22 to 24 percent. Second, the level of black homeownership growth since 1980 has slowed down and reversed. By 1987, the level of black homeownership (43 percent) was smaller than the beginning of the decade. Third, a majority (57 percent) of black households remain as renters not homeowners. This representation of black households as renters in 1987 is higher than the white renter figure in 1940 (54 percent)....

CONTEMPORARY TRENDS IN HOUSING QUALITY

How have the larger trends in housing upgrading been reflected in the physical conditions of Black Americans housing and to what extent have differences by race decreased? At the beginning of the post-World War II period, a number of studies documented the absolute and relative deprivation experienced by blacks in general and blacks within ghetto housing specifically. One of the more frequently cited sources, The Kerner Commission Report (1968) noted: (1) blacks living in central cities occupied substandard housing at more than three times the rate of whites (16 vs. 5 percent; 1960); (2) black occupied units were three times more likely to be overcrowded (25 vs. 8 percent; 1960); (3) blacks in most metropolitan areas were at least twice as likely to be housed in older structures built before 1939 (National Advisory Commission on Civil Disorders, 1968; 468–470). The physical quality of housing and neighborhood has implications for other "quality of life" dimensions such as health, safety, and access to services.

Table 1 shows that since the publication of the Kerner Report, the absolute levels of physical deprivation in the traditional criteria of housing structural quality have improved steadily since 1970 for blacks. Between 1970 and 1983, levels of crowding decreased more than half for renters and nearly two-thirds for homeowners. These recent levels of crowding for renters (9 percent) and owners (9 percent) are faint reminders of the depressed and substandard conditions cited in the Kerner Report. Black households living in housing units lacking some or all plumbing decreased more than two-thirds for both tenure classes. Blacks who shared or had no bathroom facilities still characterized at least 15 percent of black households in 1970....

The persistent racial differentials in housing quality are significantly smaller than earlier. Still, compared to all renters blacks experience significantly greater structural inadequacies in contemporary housing. Compared to all renters, black renters lived in housing with 38 percent greater sharing of bath or no bath, 40 percent greater crowding, and 75 percent plumbing deficiencies. Black homeowners lived in housing where they experienced 60 percent greater

TABLE 1

Summary of Physical Housing Conditions by Race, 1970–1983

	1970	1975	1979	1983
CROWDED (1.01 or more persons per room)				
RENTERS				
Blacks and other races	22.2	13.2	10.2	9.0
All Races	10.6	6.7	5.8	5.6
OWNERS				
Blacks and other races	15.5	10.9	8.5	5.8
All Races	6.4	4.0	3.1	2.3
LACKING SOME OR ALL PLUMBING				
RENTERS				
Blacks and other races	17.6	10.0	7.3	5.3
All Races	7.9	4.8	3.6	2.9
OWNERS				
Blacks and other races	14.4	7.0	4.9	4.4
All Races	4.2	1.8	1.4	1.4
SHARED OR NO BATH				
RENTERS				
Blacks and other races	19.2	10.8	7.9	5.8
All Races	9.2	6.7	4.3	3.6
OWNERS				
Blacks and other races	15.3	7.2	5.2	4.7
All Races	4.8	2.0	1.7	1.7

Source: U.S. Statistical Abstract and Annual Housing Survey.

crowding, 63 percent greater sharing of bath or no bath, and 68 percent greater plumbing deficiencies.

The trends of housing upgrading have been slower to reach the poor. The report, "A Place to Call Home," notes that 11 percent of poor black households as compared to 6 percent of all black households in 1985 lived in crowded conditions. Relatedly, the percentage of black poor households in substandard housing was roughly 33 percent. These levels were markedly higher than those reported for white poor households living in overcrowded units (4 percent) and substandard conditions (14 percent) (Leonard, Dolbeare, and Lazere, 1989; 55–56). By 1987, 33 percent of black poor households remained in substandard housing with the white poor percentage rising to 17 percent (Joint Center for Housing Studies, 1990; 34).[1]

CONTEMPORARY TRENDS IN HOUSING COSTS

How have the larger trends of housing upgrading translated into lower housing costs for Black Americans and to what extent have racial and class differentials persisted? There is a classic and contemporary body of research documenting the restrictive effects of racial discrimination on black housing supply and the consequences of these in terms of differential costs. Traditionally, racial discrimination has channeled black demand for homeownership and high quality housing to parts of metropolitan areas and central cities where the supply of high quality housing available for owner occupation is low. This discrimination has generally been found to result in a mark-up for housing in black areas and lower levels of housing consumption for black households. When controlling for socio-economic and tenure characteristics, the costs at both the "supply-side" and "demand-side" have been found higher for blacks. Black households consume on the average less dwelling quality, neighborhood quality, and exterior space than white households of identical size, composition, and labor force (Leigh, 1982; Wilson, 1979; Kain and Quigley, 1974; King and Mieszkowski, 1973). During the 1960s, the Kerner Commission noted that within the context of racial discrimination and segregation, there existed an interaction of high rents and low incomes resulting in cost deprivation for blacks. In the most expensive metropolitan areas, blacks paid nearly 40 percent of their incomes for housing (National Advisory Commission on Civil Disorders, 1968; 469–470).

... [T]he median percent of income paid by black households increased to 32 percent in 1987. The effects of rising housing costs and lower incomes are most evident in nearly two-fifths (39 percent) of black renters who paid at least 40 percent or more of their incomes for housing. Among black homeowners, the median costs paid for housing was significantly lower at 21 percent but 18 percent of black homeowners paid 40 percent or more of their earnings on housing. This housing deprivation becomes clearer when racial differentials are examined. Within the lower costs categories, black renters and homeowners are less represented; within the highest category (40 percent or more) blacks are more frequent....

CONCLUSION

The post-World War II years have been characterized by actual improvements in the housing status of blacks in the United States. These trends indicate that: 1) black homeownership has increased significantly; 2) the structural quality of housing and crowded living conditions improved; 3) historic differentials in housing costs have decreased. These trends occurred at a time when the urbanization of blacks was generally characterized by increasing educational and occupational opportunities which translated into greater incomes and purchasing power and new housing opportunities via the turnover process. Housing opportunities opened up largely as a consequence of the vacancies created by white central city out-movement and suburbanization. This housing upgrading among blacks was part of the larger expansion of the post-World War II housing inventory which was accompanied by unparalleled gains in owner- and renter-occupied units and "fair housing" policies. The role of the federal government in this post-war housing expansion and upgrading was broad including financing, construction, ownership, management, and urban renewal activities.

Although blacks experienced actual improvements in housing during the post-World War II years, the momentum of upgrading slowed during the late 1970s and 1980s. The contemporary housing status of blacks is characterized by persistent racial differentials and emergent trends of reversals. While actual and percentage levels of homeownership show overall increases since the 1940s, the gap between black and white homeownership widened during the 1980s as new black homeownership has fallen. In contrast to whites, a majority of black households in 1987 (57 percent) remain as renters not homeowners and this representation of black renters is higher than white renter levels in 1940 (54 percent). Despite housing quality structural improvements, both black homeowners and renters experienced significantly greater crowding, sharing of bath or no bath, and plumbing deficiencies. Contemporary housing costs have nearly two-fifths of black renters paying at least 40 percent of their incomes for housing and 60 percent of poor black households paying at least half.

Recent trends are occurring in a context where the urbanization of blacks is characterized by increasing decentralization, suburbanization, slowed central city growth, and inner city "emptying out." At the same time, increasing costs of land, materials, labor, financing, and tax changes are creating a "vicious cycle" which is conducive for builders, speculators, realtors, and landlords to produce a larger supply of higher-priced housing and decrease the supply of moderate- and lower-income housing. During the 1980s, the federal government has reduced public intervention in housing and in turn has relied more on the private sector.

There are two categories of federal policies in housing relevant to accounting for the current housing deprivation experienced among blacks and potentially ameliorating these housing conditions in the future: universalistic housing policies, targeted housing policies.

Universalistic housing policies include those federal programs that have focused on general housing problems such as low-rent public assistance, mortgage assistance, and rental assistance. The earliest of these, the 1937 Housing Act, established a federal governmental role in the construction of low-rent public housing projects. Currently, the federal government through the Department of Housing and Urban Development (HUD) funds the construction of public housing while locally operated housing authorities (LHAs) and public housing authorities (PHAs) manage these. The Federal Housing Authority, an entity within HUD, provides mortgage insurance guaranteeing private lenders repayment of their mortgage loans in cases of default. Rental assistance includes programs such as the Section 8 voucher program where HUD pays landlords the difference between 30 percent of income and a payment standard for low-income renters (Leigh, 1990; 78–81).

Targeted housing policies include those federal and local programs that have specifically focused on the implementation of fair housing and nondiscrimination. According to Noel and Wertheim, four elements essential to this "interracial" strategy include enforcement of existing laws, education, economic equity, and affirmative integration (Noel and Wertheim, 1990; 136). More effective enforcement includes elements of empowerment through greater re-sources to expose discrimination, obtain compliance with other laws, adopt affirmative action plans, cooperative coordination with other agencies and prosecuting discrimination. Although HUD and other agencies recognize the illegality of discrimination in principle, measures to correct discrimination and segregation have not been systematically enforced resulting in the maintenance of "colorblind" public pronouncements in a context of "colorconcious" private and public practices (Noel and Werthem, 1990).

Continuing housing deprivation by race is not a zero-sum condition to be addressed by mutually exclusive approaches that emphasize either universal or race-specific targeted programs. The post-World War II and contemporary record shows that while long-term trends of economic growth and housing con-struction resulted in black social and residential mobility, these macro-economic developments have not been sufficient to impact high levels of racial segrega-tion or costs. In the absence of increased federally articulated housing programs to proactively and affirmatively address inequities of access and costs, the emer-gent patterns of contemporary housing deprivation experienced by the poor across races will increase in significance.

247

*Frank Harold
Wilson*

NOTES

1. The figures for "substandard" or inadequate housing contained in the Joint Center for Housing Studies of Harvard University and Center on Budget and Policy Priori-ties reports include the presence or absence of plumbing fixtures, heating equipment, and other mechanical subsystems, and other information on the repair and upkeep of properties. See: Joint Center for Housing Studies of Harvard, The State of the Nation's Housing, 1990; Center on Budget and Policy Priorities and Low Income Housing Information Service, A Place to Call Home.

CHAPTER 8 The Economic Institution

8.1 REYNOLDS FARLEY

Blacks, Hispanics, and White Ethnic Groups: Are Blacks Uniquely Disadvantaged?

The economy is an institutionalized system for the production, distribution, and consumption of goods and services. Labor is the mechanism by which people involve themselves in the economy. Approximately 116.9 million persons participated in the American labor force in 1991. But in the United States, not all racial and ethnic groups participate fully and equally in the nation's economy.

In the present selection, research scientist Reynolds Farley suggests that some racial and ethnic groups enjoy more affluence and wider participation in the economy than other groups. In terms of educational attainment, occupational status, and income, Farley explains that while Blacks are not uniquely disadvantaged in comparison to other racial and ethnic groups, non-Hispanic White ethnic groups are uniquely advantaged.

Key Concept: race and ethnicity in the economy

*T*he National Academy's *A Common Destiny* described black Americans, and observed that while substantial progress was made, blacks remained far behind whites on social, health, and economic indicators.

Are blacks unique? If we consider Hispanics, other racial minorities, and white ethnic groups, will we find that some groups are even less prosperous than African-Americans? Is the black-white comparison too simple? This paper, part of my larger investigation of racial-ethnic differences (1989), addresses these issues.

I. DEFINING RACIAL AND ETHNIC GROUPS

The 1980 Census asked persons to identify their race by checking one of 15 circles. All respondents also answered a question about their Hispanic origin. A 19.3 percent sample answered a question about their ancestry. This query, used for the first time in 1980, replaced questions about birthplace of parents. Respondents could write any terms they wished, and typically the first two were coded. There was no allocation for nonresponse to the ancestry question, and about 11 percent left the question unanswered. Another 6 percent wrote the single term, American.

An exhaustive and mutually exclusive array of racial/ethnic groups was created using these questions (see also Stanley Lieberson and Mary Waters, 1988, ch. 2). First, 4 Hispanic groups were defined from the Spanish-origin question. Next, non-Hispanics were classified by their race. Aleuts and Eskimos were grouped with American Indians (by race) to form an American Natives category, and then 7 nonwhite racial groups were identified. A residual category of "other races" included Hawaiians, Guamanians, and other infrequently reported races.

Those who identified themselves as white by race and were not Hispanics were classified by their first reported ancestry. I identified 37 white ethnic groups, each having 60,000 persons between the ages 25–54; a number that allowed the fitting of models of earnings using the one-percent sample. The list of white ethnic groups includes American Indians. There were numerous individuals (approximately 2 million) who selected white as their race and then wrote American Indian for their ancestry. This group should be distinguished from the smaller Native American group (C. Matthew Snipp, 1980, ch. 2). The list includes a category of whites who write American for their ancestry, those who left the ancestry question blank, and whites not elsewhere classified (NEC): people whose first ancestry was not among the 36 used in this analysis. English and Germaneach made up about 15 percent of the population. The third

TABLE 1

Size and Characteristics of 50 Mutually Exclusive
Racial/Ethnic Groups in 1980

	Percent			Men 25–54	
	Below Poverty Line	Affluent[a]	Per Capita Income[b]	Mean Yrs. College	Percent Prof./ Mgr.[c]
U.S. Total	11	12	$11.2	1.7	28
Hispanic Groups					
Cuban	12	9	10.6	1.7	25
Mexican	22	3	6.8	.7	11
Puerto Rican	34	2	6.1	.6	13
Other Spanish	16	7	8.9	1.5	21
Racial Minorities					
Amer. Natives	25	5	6.9	1.0	19
Asian Indians	8	12	13.2	5.3	60
Black	27	4	7.1	1.0	14
Chinese	13	16	11.9	3.6	42
Filipino	6	9	10.9	2.8	27
Japanese	5	23	14.6	2.9	42
Korean	8	11	10.2	3.4	36
Vietnamese	34	3	5.8	1.4	17
Other Races	21	7	8.8	2.2	26
Other Ethnic Groups					
American	10	9	10.0	1.0	18
Amer. Indian	13	6	9.0	.8	15
Armenian	9	19	13.6	2.6	38
Austrian	5	25	15.5	3.3	49
Belgian	7	14	12.3	2.0	36
Canadian	6	7	13.4	2.2	40
Croatian	4	16	13.2	2.1	38
Czech	6	16	13.3	2.2	35

(Table 1 continued on next page)

[a]This reports the percent of individuals in households whose pre-tax cash income equalled at least six times the poverty line.
[b]Shown in thousands: 1987$.
[c]This shows the percent of employed men holding professional or managerial jobs in April 1980.

Source: U.S. Bureau of the Census, *Census of Population: 1980*; Public Use Microdata Sample.

largest group, blacks, was the only other one comprising 10 percent or more. The 4 smallest groups (Croatian, Rumanian, Lebanese, and Armenian) each comprised less than .1 percent.

II. ECONOMIC CHARACTERISTICS

Table 1 shows the percent in households whose pre-tax cash incomes either fell below the poverty line or exceeded six times the poverty line (a group I label

| | Percent | | | Men 25–54 | |
	Below Poverty Line	Affluent[a]	Per Capita Income[b]	Mean Yrs. College	Percent Prof./ Mgr.[c]
Danish	5	16	$13.2	2.3	34
Dutch	8	12	11.7	1.7	29
English	8	15	12.5	2.0	32
Finnish	7	13	11.5	2.1	31
French	8	10	11.6	1.5	27
French- Canadian	6	11	11.7	1.5	25
German	6	14	12.3	1.8	30
Greek	7	16	12.2	2.0	35
Hungarian	6	18	13.5	2.3	36
Irish	8	13	11.8	1.8	29
Italian	6	14	12.1	1.8	31
Lebanese	7	17	13.1	2.8	40
Lithuanian	5	20	14.6	2.6	42
Norwegian	6	15	12.7	2.2	33
Polish	5	11	12.8	2.0	32
Portugese	7	10	10.9	1.1	19
Rumanian	6	27	15.3	3.3	49
Russian	6	32	17.9	4.0	59
Scandinavian	5	16	12.3	2.7	41
Scots-Irish	5	18	14.1	2.4	37
Scottish	5	20	14.4	2.7	40
Slovak	4	13	13.4	1.8	27
Swedish	5	17	13.7	2.4	37
Swiss	6	18	13.6	2.5	36
Ukranian	5	17	13.6	2.5	36
Welsh	5	18	13.0	2.6	39
Yugoslavian	7	18	13.7	2.1	33
NEC	6	14	12.4	2.4	36
Not Rpt.	5	11	11.7	2.3	23

affluent). To be impoverished, a household of four had to have an income of less than $11,600 in 1987 dollars; to be affluent, in excess of $69,600.

The white ethnic groups (except Americans and American Indians) had poverty rates between 4 and 8 percent, or well below the national average of 11 percent. Among Filipinos, Japanese, Koreans, and Asian Indians, poverty rates were equivalent to those of white ethnic groups, but 6 groups were distinguished by elevated poverty. The most impoverished, Puerto Ricans and Vietnamese, had rates triple the national average, while among blacks, American Natives, Mexicans, and Other Races, poverty was double the national rate. Only two groups, Vietnamese and Puerto Ricans, were more frequently impoverished than blacks.

Several white groups and one Asian race were overrepresented among the affluent. Nationally, about one person in eight lived in such a household, but one-third of Russians did so. More than one-fifth of Rumanians, Austrians, Lithuanians, and Japanese were in prosperous circumstances.

Per capita incomes are shown in Table 1 in 1987 dollars. Two groups stood out for their meager incomes: Vietnamese (92 percent born outside the United States) had a per capita income just one-half the national average, while Puerto Ricans (about one-half island born) had incomes only $300 above that of the Vietnamese. American Natives, Mexicans, and blacks had small incomes, about 60 percent of the national average. The least prosperous European group (the Portuguese) had incomes exceeding those of blacks by 54 percent.

Russians, whose incomes were $2,500 greater than those of their closest rivals, Austrians and Rumanians, were exceptionally prosperous. Three others (Japanese, Lithuanians, and the Scottish) had incomes $3,000 or more in excess of the overall average.

Information about the educational attainment and occupational achievements of men aged 25–54 is also presented in Table 1. The summary assessment of attainment is per capita years of college education. The national average was 1.7 years, but Asian Indians were exceptional in that they averaged in excess of 5 years of college, or 1.3 years more than the second ranking group, the Russians. Austrians, Chinese, Koreans, and Rumanians had averages exceeding 3 years. At the other extreme were Americans, American Natives, and blacks who averaged just 1 year of college, and 2 groups, Mexicans and Puerto Ricans, whose average was below 1 year.

The final column reports the percent of employed men holding professional or managerial jobs. Overall, 28 percent worked at these positions, but 2 groups stood out for their unusually high proportions: Asian Indians and Russians. In 8 groups, fewer than 20 percent were so employed. Mexicans were least likely to be working as professionals or managers followed by Puerto Ricans, blacks, American Indians, Vietnamese, Americans, American Natives, and one European-origin group, the Portuguese.

III. THE EARNINGS OF MEN

Does race or ethnicity make a difference? Why are there such substantial discrepancies in economic status? Do some groups invest in education and live in high wage areas, while others quit school and remain in the rural South? Or, are there systematic differences in the rates of financial return groups receive for their human capital investments? A complete disaggregation of differences is beyond the scope of this paper, but groups differ greatly in the characteristics associated with earnings and racial minorities, and Hispanics receive smaller returns for human capital investments than white ethnic groups.

Table 2 describes men aged 25–54 who reported any positive earnings in 1979. To facilitate a comparison, I eliminated men who were foreign born and considered only those 40 groups in which there were 300 or more in the 1980 one-percent sample. In the table, Puerto Rican refers to men born in the United States.

The first column shows mean earnings in 1987 dollars, while the second reports earnings as a percent of the national average of $23,400. There is additional evidence of the prosperity of Eastern European ancestries since Russian,

TABLE 2

*Annual Earnings of Men 25–54 and Differences from the National
Average for 40 Mutually Exclusive Racial/Ethnic Groups in 1980*

| | 1979 Annual Earnings[a] | As Percent of Total | Differences Attributable to | |
			Own Characteristics[b]	Own Rates of Return[c]
U.S. Total	$23.4	100		
Hispanic Groups				
Mexican	19.3	83	−11	−6
Puerto Rican	19.6	83	−8	−3
Other Spanish	21.3	91	−2	−7
Racial Minorities				
Amer. Natives	19.1	82	−12	−12
Black	18.6	80	−12	−8
Chinese	26.8	115	+18	−13
Japanese	26.4	113	+14	−6
Other Races	20.3	87	−1	−16
White Ethnic Groups				
American	21.3	91	−9	0
Amer. Indian	20.8	89	−10	−4
Austrian	29.4	126	+17	+6
Belgian	27.2	116	+7	+8
Canadian	23.7	101	+7	0
Czech	25.5	109	+7	+3

(Table 2 continued on next page)

[a]Shown in thousands: 1987$. Estimates of earnings assume a person worked 2000 hours. Analysis is restricted to all persons reporting positive earnings in 1979.
[b]This is the percent difference between the overall average earnings and the hypothetical earnings of a group assuming their own characteristics and the rates of return of the entire sample.
[c]This is the percent difference between the overall average earnings and the hypothetical earnings of a group assuming their own rates of return but the characteristics of the entire sample.
Source: See Table 1.

Austrian, and Yugoslavian men had earnings 20 percent or more above average. Other white ethnic groups (with the exception of Americans and American Indians) had earnings 95 to 119 percent of the mean. At the low end were Puerto Ricans, Mexicans, and American Natives, but blacks were at the bottom with earnings 80 percent of the national average. The procedure used here underestimates actual racial-ethnic differences by assuming full employment. In fact, only 83 percent of black men ages 25–54 reported any earnings in 1979, compared to 96 percent of the Russians.

To investigate causes of these differences, I used an earnings model and a regression standardization procedure. The log of hourly earnings was regressed upon years of precollege education, years of college, marital status (to distinguish married men who earn more), age, and a series of variables that identified

	1979 Annual Earnings[a]	As Percent of Total	Differences Attributable to	
			Own Characteristics[b]	Own Rates of Return[c]
Danish	$25.4	109	+9	+2
Dutch	23.5	101	+2	−1
English	24.1	103	+1	+1
Finnish	27.3	117	+5	+5
French	23.2	99	−1	+1
French-Canadian	23.8	102	+2	+2
German	24.4	104	+3	+1
Greek	25.7	110	+10	+1
Hungarian	27.8	119	+10	+8
Irish	24.5	105	+2	+3
Italian	25.5	109	+5	+6
Lithuanian	27.3	117	+11	+3
Norwegian	24.7	106	+6	+3
Polish	25.6	110	+6	+3
Portuguese	25.4	119	+3	−3
Russian	32.4	139	+22	+8
Scandinavian	25.7	110	+8	+2
Scots-Irish	25.4	109	+7	+1
Scottish	25.7	110	+9	+1
Slovak	26.5	114	+9	+3
Swedish	25.6	110	+9	+2
Swiss	24.2	104	+8	−4
Ukranian	25.5	109	+8	+3
Welsh	25.7	110	+10	+2
Yugoslavian	28.0	120	+9	+15
NEC	24.6	105	+4	+1
Not Rpt.	22.1	95	−7	0

the regions and men who lived outside metropolises. Equations were fit for the entire sample and for every group.

For each race-ethnicity, I took the earnings equation for the entire sample and inserted the characteristics of the group to estimate what their earnings would have been if they had the rates of return of the entire sample but their own characteristics. These hypothetical earnings were compared to the national average to assess the net effects of a group's characteristics. They are shown in Table 2 as a percent of the overall mean. Mexicans, for example, had characteristics that cost them an amount equal to 11 percent of the national average.

Next, I used the earnings equations for each group and inserted the characteristics of the total sample. This produced a second hypothetical earnings estimate for every group which was compared to the national average to assess the effects of a group's rate of return. This disaggregation does not unambiguously account for a group's overall difference from the national average.

We expect that groups differ in their earnings because of differences in their geographic locations, education, age, and marital status. Figures in the column Own Characteristics confirm this. The earnings of Russian, Chinese, Austrian, Japanese, and Lithuanian men were raised by 10 percent or more above the average because of their favorable characteristics, while those of Mexicans, American Natives, and blacks were limited because of their characteristics.

Title VII of the 1964 Civil Rights Act outlawed discrimination in the labor market. If this earnings model is appropriate, and if employers comply with the law, we would expect that the numbers showing differences attributable to a group's rates of return would be close to zero. This is the situation for most white ethnic groups. Four white ethnic groups (Belgians, Hungarians, Russians, and Yugoslavians) had earnings that were augmented, but the racial minorities and Hispanics had their earnings limited by lower than average rates of return. The net cost of being an American Native, black, Chinese, or Other Races exceeded 8 percent of the overall mean earnings. It is impossible to demonstrate discrimination using census samples, but these numbers imply that if a specific set of characteristics were possessed by Hispanics or racial minorities, they were less rewarded than if they were possessed by white ethnic groups.

Several additional conclusions may be drawn. First, the high earnings of Eastern European men came about primarily because of their characteristics. Second, Chinese and Japanese reported large earnings but the net effect of membership in these groups was a reduction in earnings. To earn a great deal, Chinese and Japanese must have greater educational attainments than whites (see Ronald Takaki, 1989). Third, the least prosperous of the white groups were those who wrote American or American Indian for their ancestry or left the question blank. Their low earnings were due to their characteristics: their meager educations and concentrations in rural areas. Finally, Mexicans, American Natives, and blacks were at a double disadvantage. Their characteristics limited their earnings, and their rates of return were also below average.

IV. CONCLUSION

Would the National Academy's Committee have drawn different conclusions if they had considered an array of racial, Hispanic, and ethnic minorities? Is the black-white comparison too simple? The answer to both questions is no. After examining the characteristics of 50 racial-ethnic groups, I found that the Vietnamese and Puerto Ricans were more impoverished than blacks and, in terms of per capita income, Mexicans and American Natives were similar to blacks. There was considerable variation in the status of the 37 white ethnic groups and Eastern European groups had exceptionally high incomes. However, all of the white ethnic groups were more prosperous than blacks. The only white group whose educational attainment or occupational status approximated that of blacks were people who identified themselves as white by race but American Indian by ancestry.

When the analysis focused on earnings of native born men, blacks were the most disadvantaged with earnings below those of Native Americans, Mexicans, and Puerto Ricans. Blacks and men from these three groups had characteristics associated with low earnings. In addition, blacks, other racial minorities (including Asians), and Hispanic groups had rates of return that were lower than those of white ethnic groups.

REFERENCES

Chapter 8
The Economic
Institution

Farley, Reynolds, "Race and Ethnicity in the U.S. Census: An Evaluation of the 1980 Ancestry Question," unpublished manuscript, Population Studies Center, University of Michigan, 1989.

Jaynes, Gerald and Williams, Robin, *A Common Destiny: Blacks and American Society*, Washington: National Academy Press, 1989.

Lieberson, Stanley and Waters, Mary C., *From Many Strands*, New York: Russell Sage, 1988.

Snipp, C. Matthew, *American Indians: The First of This Land*, New York: Russell Sage, 1988.

Takaki, Ronald, *Strangers from a Different Shore*, Boston: Little Brown, 1989.

U.S. Bureau of the Census, *U.S. Census of Population: 1980*, PC80–S1–10, Special Report, *Ancestry of the Population by State: 1980*, Washington, 1983.

8.2 GEORGE E. TINKER AND LORING BUSH

Native American Unemployment: Statistical Games and Coverups

During the recession of the early 1990s nearly 9.1 million persons were listed as unemployed in the United States. This statistic, however, is misleading because it does not account for discouraged workers who gave up looking for jobs and those who were working part-time because they could not find full-time work. Inclusion of discouraged and underemployed workers could double the unemployment rate. Similarly, not all racial and ethnic groups are equally represented in the official unemployment statistics.

In the present selection, George E. Tinker and Loring Bush explain that sometimes the Native American unemployment rate is nearly 20 times higher than what is officially reported. They point out that institutional racism in the national economy, exemplified by this misrepresentation of unemployment rates, prevents Native Americans from securing economic well-being.

Key Concept: Native American unemployment

*U*nemployment is a tragedy for any American citizen old enough to work, but this tragedy is compounded for Native Americans by (1) a dramatic difference between Indian and non-Indian unemployment figures reported for any particular locale in the United States, and (2) what appears to be a severe undercount of Native American unemployment rates reported by federal and state government agencies. In part, this chapter tries to find some explanation of the discrepancy between these government statistics and the figures reported unofficially by many tribes themselves. These undercounts mask the reality of Native American unemployment rates that are apparently, in some cases, almost twenty times higher than what is reported by government agencies. Furthermore, such undercounts result in less funding for government programs that attempt to alleviate these high rates of unemployment. Most important, the undercounts point to the continuation of the corporate and institutional racism

257

entrenched in a system that prevents Native Americans from improving their situation and procuring the resources necessary to ensure their well-being, both as individuals and as culturally discrete communities of people.

The chronic nature of Native American unemployment is well known in Indian circles. Although the reports referred to here were published in various years, it is precisely the chronic problem of Native American unemployment that allows us to validly compare these figures. Despite chronological gaps in the reporting of rates, it seems a virtual certainty that the high rate of unemployment has remained relatively constant. While overall unemployment statistics in the United Stats are relatively volatile, depending on general and/or local economic factors, Native American unemployment statistics have been relatively static and at an extraordinarily high level for an extended period of time. In this chapter, both published and unpublished reports are compared and used for a survey of three states with high populations of Native Americans and high rates of Native American unemployment.

NATIVE AMERICAN
UNEMPLOYMENT STATISTICS

Definitions

Before beginning our analysis, the issue of the definitions used for determining members of the labor force and calculating unemployment rates must be addressed. Indeed, the fact that different government agencies use different definitions for unemployment has particular implications for unemployed Native Americans. These implications are addressed after surveying the data. But even before terms such as labor force and unemployment are defined, it must be noted that there is confusion over the definition of *Indian* or *Native American* on the part of government agencies. The Bureau of Indian Affairs (BIA), for instance, bases its Native American statistics on persons

> who are members of Indian tribes, or who are one-fourth degree or more blood quantum descendants of a member of any Indian tribe, band, nation, rancheria, colony, pueblo, or community, including Alaska Native Villages or regional village corporations defined in or established pursuant to the Alaska Native Claims Settlement Act.

On the other hand, the U.S. Department of Labor (DOL) defines Native Americans as those who classified themselves as such on 1980 census forms.

The DOL uses what is called the Local Area Unemployment Statistics (LAUS) methodology to measure unemployment. The data for this methodology are derived from a Current Population Survey (CPS), which is performed by the Bureau of the Census under a contract with the DOL. The CPS combines monthly surveys of approximately 60,000 households nationwide with unemployment claims activity to provide a statistical reflection of what is actually happening in the labor market.

Characteristic data, such as race and age, are collected with the CPS. However, the data by race are collected only for white, black, and Hispanic populations and exclude Native Americans. Thus, DOL does not track unemployment statistics for Native Americans. Some state labor divisions, particularly in areas with high Native American populations, do calculate Native American unemployment. These states use a census methodology of "sharing out" CPS figures by making future labor force projections for racial/ethnic groups based on proportions from the most recent national census data. It must be noted that individuals are not actually counted in this census methodology of sharing out data among racial/ethnic groups. Rather, a cumulative figure derived from the CPS is proportionally divided among racial/ethnic groups, including Native Americans, based on the racial/ethnic proportions from 1980 census information. It seems that assignment of numbers to categories that are over a decade old would result in arbitrary conclusions about the reality of Native American unemployment.

The DOL defines the *civilian labor force* as "All persons, 16 years of age and over, who are not in institutions nor in the Armed Forces and are either 'employed' or 'unemployed.'"

DOL defines *those not in the labor force* as "Persons, 16 years old and over, who are not employed and not seeking employment or are unable or unavailable to work regardless of the reason, such as homemakers, students, retirees, disabled persons, or institutionalized persons."

The *unemployed*, according to DOL, are

> Individuals, 16 years of age and older, who are not working, but are looking for work and are available to work. Looking for work requires specific efforts such as sending resumes or canvassing employers. Discouraged workers (those who have given up looking for work because they feel there are no jobs available) are not counted as unemployed.

Clearly implied, but never baldly stated in state labor reports, is that in addition to not counting as unemployed, *discouraged workers* are not included as part of the labor force in DOL unemployment statistics. According to Richard Pottinger, one reason for this exclusion of discouraged workers from the state labor force counts is that the LAUS methodology is structured with a "logical contradiction" between being trained and unemployed. In the LAUS methodology, it is assumed that those who have training and are unemployed will secure work again within the time limit set by DOL (four weeks). Pottinger explains DOL actions toward those who do not fall within the parameters established by the Department:

> If these unemployed stop actively looking for jobs, through disillusionment or despair in confrontation with a lack of opportunity, they are actually dropped from the statistical tabulation of the "labor force"! Irrespective of the actual availability of jobs, they are no longer considered part of the labor force and are therefore no longer statistically "unemployed."

This exclusion of discouraged workers from the parameters of DOL's official labor force definition has particular implications for Native Americans. The experience of the Native American work force consists primarily of isolation from job opportunities. Hence, a great many unemployed Native Americans do not have access to employers whom they can canvass for employment. As a result, we would argue that most unemployed Native Americans fall under DOL's definition of discouraged workers and are consequently dropped from calculations of Native American unemployment.

In addition to its methodological oversight of discouraged workers, DOL masks Native Americans unemployment statistics by calculating overall unemployment rates with figures for all races. When very low unemployment rates for whites are figured in with very high unemployment rates for racial/ethnic groups, and especially the high rates for Native Americans, the overall figure becomes diluted to the point where Native American rates are calculated out of the picture.

It would be expected that the Bureau of Indian Affairs (BIA) would account for this oversight. In its biannual *Indian Service Population and Labor Force Estimates,* the BIA gives an indication that Native American unemployment statistics are consistently higher than figures for the rest of the population. A breakdown of BIA methodology does reveal the percentage of the labor force who are discouraged workers, and the BIA publishes statistics that account for Native American discouraged workers. In order to understand more fully the distinction of the BIA and DOL reports, it is necessary to look at the entire BIA unemployment statistic methodology.

According to its *Population and Labor Force Estimates,* local BIA agencies gather data from the tribes themselves—actual house-to-house surveys conducted by tribal programs and contracts, school and employment records, tribal election statistics, tribal membership rolls maintained by the tribes, and BIA program services records.

... The BIA differs from the DOL in that the BIA only counts Native Americans, so its official unemployment rate comes somewhat closer to the reality of Native American unemployment than does the DOL. But this provides only minimally greater accuracy that does not yet reflect the true magnitude of Indian unemployment.

Data Comparisons

The 1985 "First Friday Report," *American Indian Unemployment: Confronting a Distressing Reality,* contrasts BIA unemployment figures for Native Americans and overall DOL unemployment figures. The "First Friday Report" uses BIA figures but not those officially reported as Indian unemployment. It uses statistics tucked away in the BIA report that do indeed include discouraged workers. By contrasting these figures with the figures derived from DOL methodology, the "First Friday Report" publicly articulates for the first time the severity of Native American unemployment and the nature of the undercounts in official government reporting.

The problem is best illustrated with actual data. According to the 1980 census, Arizona had the third highest population of Native Americans in the

ployment rates for Arizona with DOL figures for that state. While DOL reported
overall unemployment in the state to be 11.2 percent in 1985, BIA reported Indian unemployment in the state at 41 percent. Using BIA estimates, the "First
Friday Report" puts Navajo unemployment as high as 75 percent.

The Navajo Nation is the most populated reservation in the United States,
with a population of 94,451 in its Arizona sector in 1989 (the tribe also has
some land holdings in Utah and extensive holdings in New Mexico). Of these
residents, 88,739 (93.8 percent) are Native Americans, which is certainly to be
expected on tribal lands. Further, Native Americans comprise 88 percent of the
labor force on Navajo lands in Arizona. The overall 1989 Navajo reservation
unemployment rate, which includes all races, is reported by the Arizona Labor Market Information (ALMI) report as 17.8 percent. A 1985 study of Navajo
unemployment, however, estimates a reservation ratio of about 1 job for every
100 people.... [M]any of the scarce jobs on reservations are being filled by non-
Indians. Given this information, the ALMI 1989 report records a surprisingly
low Native American unemployment rate of 19.8 percent on the Navajo reservation. This is in stark contrast to the 75 percent estimate of the "First Friday
Report." Because Native American unemployment has been a chronic problem,
it is appropriate to assume that their community's unemployment rate has not
fluctuated by 55 percent over a 4-year period. This discrepancy demands some
explanation.

The ALMI report does break down statistics with reference to racial/
ethnic heritage, and the statistics reported are consistent with the already noted
general tendency of a much higher unemployment figure for Native Americans
than for the general population and other racial/ethnic groups. In 1985, there
were between 6,000 and 7,000 jobs held by non-Navajos on the reservation.
Of the 188 Hispanics who were in the reservation work force, none were unemployed. Of the 2,396 whites in that particular labor force, 2.2 percent were
unemployed.

The discrepancy between Indian and non-Indian unemployment on the
Navajo reservation and indeed on every reservation has its explanation in differences in Indian and non-Indian inculturation and in psychological factors
related to the self-image of the people as aggressive, independent, and "in control" or as conquered and dependent. Non-Indians on a reservation typically
are agriculturalists who lease Indian lands, small business traders who have
the capital or access to the capital to run successful businesses targeting Indian
people as their primary market, and management-level specialists brought in
by the federal government or corporate business structures to provide administrative or technical expertise that the Indians are assumed unable to provide.
Hence non-Indian unemployment figures are always characteristically low in
any reservation context....

The complexities at the heart of conflicting statistics and government undercounts of Native American unemployment are issues of the psychology of
Indian versus white, historical factors, and structures of power in this country. The complexities involve decisions that were made by the federal government, such as the 1887 Dawes Severalty Act, the 1934 Indian Reorganization
Act, the disastrous relocation policy initiated by the Eisenhower administra-

tion, and a multiplicity of other federal government attempts to "solve" the Indian "problem."

One important factor that has not been considered among these complexities is the perspective of the Indian people themselves. What do Native Americans see as the root of these problems, particularly concerning issues of unemployment?

Karen Thorne, Job Training and Partnership Administration (JTPA) director of the Phoenix Indian Center, and Charlee Hoyt, of the Pascua Yaqui Tribal Job Training and Placement Program, point to some of the major reasons that Native Americans not only have high rates of unemployment but also why they are discouraged workers and thus uncounted in the DOL methodology. Thorne states that the high level of migration between the reservation and the urban area of Phoenix is a major factor in analyzing Native American unemployment. According to Thorne, Native Americans come to Phoenix because the job opportunities seem relatively better, yet most do not find jobs. As a result, many return to the reservation, to what is at least a marginally better support system, in part because of the continuing role of kinship systems and extended family and the comfort provided by cultural placement in some continuing traditional structure. This forces families to make difficult choices because the urban areas afford more employment opportunities. Families become separated so that one member can work in the city while the others stay on the reservation. Hoyt concurs on this point. She states that apart from the unavailability of jobs on the reservation, transportation problems invariably pose another major obstacle to Native American unemployment.

Both Thorne and Hoyt refer to cultural differences as another important barrier to full Indian employment. Thorne states that on the reservation, the pace of life is not as fast as in the urban centers. Punctuality and new technology are difficult for more traditional people. Furthermore, tribal cultures tend to teach cooperation rather than individual competition. By rising above the rest, an individual violates the culture.

Again, Hoyt offers a similar view. She gives the example of job interview techniques to illustrate the divergent cultural values of Native Americans and the dominant white culture. According to Hoyt, the Pascua Yaqui people are not as aggressive as those in the white culture, and thus they do not extol their virtues or talk about their talents during employment interviews. They do not maintain direct eye contact when they are speaking. These actions are often taken by majority culture employers as signs of passivity or lack of accomplishment on the part of Native Americans. Therefore, people such as Thorne and Hoyt, from job training programs, educate potential Native American employees in interview techniques and "front-run" through contact with personnel officers to answer cultural questions that they may have. Because of the realities in training Native Americans to function in a labor market driven by the majority culture, Thorne says that Native Americans must wear multiple hats. She notes that this causes difficulties in adjusting.

The issues raised by these two women are, for the most part, common concerns among members of the Native American community as they address their unemployment crisis. These issues must be kept in mind as we turn to a sample of unemployment statistics for Minnesota.

The Native American community of Minnesota resides largely on reservations that are much more distant from major metropolitan centers than in the case of reservations in Arizona. The Minnesota urban centers are found in Minneapolis and St. Paul, where the "First Friday Report" indicates a 1985 unemployment rate of 49 percent. Because of the chronic nature of Native American unemployment rates, it is assumed that this statistic remains roughly the same today.

As was the case in Arizona, the unemployment figures derived from DOL methodology that pertain directly to the Native American community are misleading because they show, with few exceptions, single-digit unemployment rates in areas where much higher unemployment rates can be expected due to the higher numbers of Native Americans in those particular populations. For the counties that intersect the Minneapolis/St. Paul area, however, the December 1989 state unemployment figures do not reflect the large numbers of unemployed Native Americans in the area....

[I]t is appropriate to question the validity of the Department of Labor LAUS methodology of counting the unemployed as it applies to Native Americans. In October of 1988, this challenge was taken up jointly by Job Service North Dakota, the South Dakota Department of Labor, and the Standing Rock Sioux Tribe, whose reservation straddles both North and South Dakota. In response to "longstanding and substantial controversy" over the unemployment rates for counties containing Indian reservations, these three parties collaborated to contract with the Bureau of the Census for a special census of the Standing Rock reservation.... Standing Rock has a very high unemployment rate as reported by the "First Friday Report." According to the Standing Rock study, the collaboration among these three entities to conduct a special census amounts to a governmental recognition of flaws in counting unemployed Native Americans. The study states, "There is concern that the official unemployment rates are not adequately reflecting the worsening economic situation nor the human capital available on Indian reservations, and are in turn impeding job development."

In conducting the special census, the Standing Rock study located what was believed to be the major factor, overlooked in standard LAUS methodology, which could account for the consistent undercount and might provide a corrective to reflect more accurately Native American unemployment.

> Employment opportunities are closely related to the availability of federal and tribal funds and to the starting and ending of programs administered by the federal and tribal governments. People enter the labor market as employment opportunities expand. For many workers on reservations, however, it is not possible to work long enough or earn enough wage credits to qualify for unemployment insurance and be counted in the claims data.
>
> The results of the special census indicate that the major difference between the estimates derived from the LAUS methodology and those shown by the special census occur in the area of labor force entrants and reentrants.... [T]his makes perfect sense for a geographic area where the timing of work search is determined by news of job openings for short-term tribal or federal government programs or other short-term, seasonal work.

TABLE 1

Standing Rock Special Census Highlights

Population

| | Stndg. Rock | | | Sioux Cty. | | | Cor. Cty. | |
Total	*Ind.*	*Other*	*Total*	*Ind.*	*Other*	*Total*	*Ind.*	*Other*
8,019	4,799	3,220	3,817	2,833	984	4,202	1,966	2,236

Labor Force Participation

	Civilian Non-Institutional Population (16 and older)	*Labor Force*	*Participation Rate*
Total Reserv.	4,688	2,624	56.0%
Indian	2,402	1,136	47.3
Non-Indian	2,286	1,488	65.1

Joblessness

	Official Unemployment Rate	Alternative Measure of Econ. Hardship *Joblessness Including "Discouraged"*	Alternative Measure of Econ. Hardship *Joblessness Including "Discouraged" and "Underemployed"*
Total Reserv.	14.1%	20.3%	24.4%
Indian	28.7	38.6	43.0
Non-Indian	3.0	4.3	8.2

Source: South Dakota Department of Labor, Press Release, Pierre, S.D., May 8, 1989, p. 4.

Table 1 summarizes the major statistical findings of the study. In comparing these figures with the respective state labor department figures for Corson and Sioux counties, we can see that the Standing Rock study numbers are significantly higher.

Figures 1 and 2 graph our analysis of the breakdowns of the Standing Rock study statistics. Our purpose in representing the statistics in this way is to illustrate that although the Standing Rock study produces figures that are a more accurate reflection of Native American unemployment on the reservation, the new methodology has apparently been ignored. The DOL methodology was still used for the December 1989 report and consequently showed very low 1989 unemployment rates for the counties that constitute Standing Rock reservation. It should be acknowledged that the methodology variance was granted only in October 1989, and there may be a significant delay before the results in state

FIGURE 1

Population and Labor Force, Standing Rock Special Study, October 1988

George E. Tinker and Loring Bush

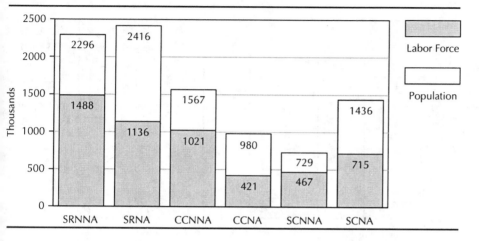

unemployment reports can be seen. However, if Corson County is taken as an example, the Labor Market Information Center reports an unemployment rate of 2.8 percent for December 1989. Figure 2 shows that this statistic, according to the Standing Rock study, represents only a fraction of the unemployed population in Corson County. Since the vast majority of unemployed in Corson County are Native Americans, the statistic functions to conceal Indian unemployment. Even if the variance does begin to rectify these severe undercounts on Standing Rock reservation in the future, it must be noted that Standing Rock is the *only* reservation in the country that has been granted this variance. It is not at all certain that such a methodology variance will be implemented for any other reservation in the United States.

If the Standing Rock study methodology is implemented for other reservations, there is still the problem of unemployment undercounts of Native Americans in urban centers. They face many of the same difficulties as the Indians on the reservations, and we have shown that they also suffer high unemployment rates. We can expect that the undercount problem will continue.

Figures 1 and 2 illustrate another point that was considered when looking at the statistics from the Navajo Nation. In Standing Rock, as on the Navajo reservation, the white sector of the work force has the lowest rate of unemployment, while the Native American sector of the work force has the highest rate. This fact begins to make explicit the complex economic, political, and social issues that have resulted in not only the high rates of Indian unemployment but also the subsequent oversight of this information in DOL methodologies. . . .

FIGURE 2

*Unemployment Rates, Standing Rock
Special Study, October 1988*

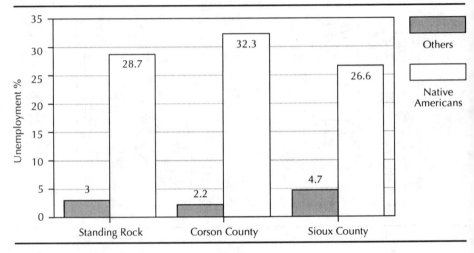

CONCLUSION

Indeed, American social structures must recognize their culpability in the code-pendent relationship in which subtle racist institutional structures use statistical devices in order to conceal massive social deficiencies in Indian communities. The political reality moves even further in blaming racial/ethnic peoples themselves for any social dysfunctionalities in their communities without attempting to put those dysfunctionalities into a broader context of oppression and social or cultural dislocation. It is an example of the victim being blamed for his or her own victimization.

The explanation of the unemployment crisis for Native Americans is found within the larger issue of corporate and institutional racism. Private enterprise alone—even if it is initiated from Native American rather than white capital—will not remove the obstacles to full Indian participation in the U.S. economy because a tribal economy will always, for the foreseeable future, be dependent on the national economy of the United States. It is at that level that institutional racism always functions implicitly and, often enough, naively to create new obstacles. If Native Americans were really welcomed into the political and economic life of the United States, they would demonstrate unemployment rates on par with that of the white population. There would be no "grants economy" to keep Indian communities dependent on the U.S. government. The future of Indian lands would be determined by the people who live on those lands.

That is not the reality today. The reality that determines public policy toward Native Americans may best be illustrated through the analogies used by two racial/ethnic individuals, one black and one Native American. The contrast between these two people—both based on similar images—explains how Native Americans perceive themselves as more excluded from mainstream American society than other racial/ethnic groups. When recently asked about white antagonism toward affirmative action, a black university student replied that the dominant culture of this society does not see affirmative action as racial/ethnic people see it. For this black citizen, affirmative action represented another trip to the rich master's "big house"—which is now the White House—in order to find opportunity in American society. In other words, not much has changed since the days of slavery. Racism still drives the American government, even in its liberal policies of affirmative action.

In testimony at hearings on Pine Ridge reservation regarding the Guaranteed Job Opportunity Program, Sandra Frazier, chairwoman of the Employment Services Department of the Cheyenne River Sioux Tribe, illustrated the overall situation of Native Americans in contemporary American society. Frazier repeated a story told by Felix Cohen, an expert on Indian law. As a rich man enjoyed a plentiful banquet at a table groaning under the weight of food and drink, he looked out the window and saw an old woman, half starved and weeping. The rich man's heart was touched with pity. Because the old woman was breaking his heart, he told his servant to chase her away. The same characterizes the treatment of Native Americans by the U.S. government. Frazier used this story to illustrate that "Many things in Indian country are like nothing else in America."

Unlike the perception of the black student, who at least felt he could go to the "big house" to address his grievances, Native Americans have been consistently "chased away" by the U.S. government and American society as a whole. While we could argue that blacks and other racial/ethnic peoples have been (grudgingly) invited to share a room in the "big house" through affirmative action, Native Americans remain uninvited, despite affirmative action provisions that include Indian communities. All racial/ethnic peoples know who still owns this "big house." They are reminded every time unemployment rates are published for their minority group. For Native Americans, there is a double insult because their unemployment rates surpass those of other racial/ethnic groups and yet remain masked by governmental jargon and methodology. Today, after more than two decades of civil rights reforms in this country, racial/ethnic peoples can only imagine no longer being shut out of the American "big house" or being relegated to the status of a guest in that house. For North American racial/ethnic peoples, and particularly for Native Americans, having their own house remains a distant hope.

Population, Economic Mobility and Income Inequality: A Portrait of Latinos in the United States, 1970–1991

After African Americans, Latinos are the largest minority group in the United States. Latinos are currently experiencing rapid population growth and socioeconomic progress. Yet, as Havidán Rodríguez points out in the following selection, Latinos have lower levels of education, lower rates of labor force participation, and higher rates of poverty than non-Latinos. And there are socioeconomic differences among the various Latino groups. Puerto Ricans, for example, experience more socioeconomic deprivation and Cubans more economic advantage than other Latino groups. Rodríguez believes that it is important for researchers to continue studying the social and economic conditions of Latinos in order to find ways to improve the group's situation in American society.

Key Concept: Latinos and the economy

INTRODUCTION

Latinos in the United States are the second largest minority group, after African Americans, and are one of the fastest growing groups (U.S. Bureau of the Census, 1985; Davis, Haub and Willette, 1983; Tienda and Angel, 1982). The 1985 Current Population Survey (CPS) reported an increase of 16% in the Latino population in the United States, from 1980 to 1985, compared to 2.4% for the non-Latino and 3.3% for the total United States population. If this rate of growth continues at present levels, Latinos will become the largest minority group in the United States in the near future.

In general, U.S. Latinos are economically handicapped when compared to the non-Latino population. They have lower levels of education and labor force participation, and higher poverty rates relative to non-Latinos (Davis, Haub and Willette, 1983; Ford Foundation, 1984). However, there are significant demographic and socioeconomic differences between the different ethnic groups clustered under the name of "Hispanics." Puerto Ricans are disproportionately concentrated in the lowest rungs of the economic ladder. Mexicans fare better than Puerto Ricans, however, both Mexicans and Puerto Ricans are at a serious economic disadvantage when compared to the Cuban population in the United States. . . .

Three important factors account for the significant growth of the Latino population: high fertility rates, immigration, and an improvement of Census coverage in 1980 relative to 1970. As I will discuss in later sections, Latinos have the highest levels of fertility in the United States when compared to non-Latinos, African Americans and the total U.S. population. Davis, Carl and Willette (1983) indicate that about two-thirds of the growth in the Hispanic population, from 1970 to 1980, was a result of Latinos' high fertility. Immigration, particularly in the case of Mexican-Americans and most importantly in the case of Central and South Americans played a significant role in their growth rates. Bean and Tienda (1987) estimate that less than half of the population increase among Mexicans was a result of measured immigration while it was the most important source for South and Central Americans. "Immigration" accounted for only 12% to 15% of the Puerto Rican intercensal growth. It is important to note that since Puerto Ricans are American citizens and have unrestricted movement from the United States mainland to Puerto Rico there are no official records of their movement between island and mainland. Most of the estimates on the contribution of "immigration" to population growth for Puerto Ricans is derived from Census and vital statistics data. . . .

Finally, the strong commitment by the Census Bureau to count every household and individual in the United States, in 1980, and improve minority coverage combined with the increasing awareness among the Latino population and their willingness to be counted, improved the Census coverage of this population in the United States. This fact also accounts for some of the increase in the Latino population from 1970 to 1980. Nevertheless, it is important to note that a non-trivial number of Latinos were not counted by the U.S. Bureau of the Census in 1980 (de la Puente, 1992; Fein, 1990). . . .

SELECTED DEMOGRAPHIC CHARACTERISTICS OF LATINOS IN THE UNITED STATES

Age

Latinos as a group are very young when compared to the rest of the United States population. In 1980, the median age (the value that shows that half of the population are under while the other half is over this age) of Latinos was 23 years compared to 25 for African Americans, 32 for non-Latino whites and 30 for the total United States population.... [T]here is much variation in the median age between Latinos in the United States. The median age for Mexicans and Puerto Ricans is approximately 22 years compared to 26 for "other Latinos" and is significantly higher for Cubans, 38 years. The relatively low age of Latinos is a result of high fertility rates and substantial immigration of young adults to the United States. However, because of their low fertility, as shown below, Cubans have a median age above that of Latinos, African Americans and non-Latino whites. It is noteworthy that the median age of all Latinos groups increased significantly from 1980 to 1991. The median age of Mexican Americans, Puerto Ricans and Cubans increased to 24.3, 26.7 and 39.3 years, respectively, in 1991) (U.S. Bureau of the Census, 1991). This has been, in part, due to declining fertility rates among the Latino population....

Marital Status

The marital status of Latinos also differs significantly according to ethnicity. Cubans are more likely to be married (58%) followed by Mexicans (56%), "other Latinos" (53%) and finally Puerto Ricans were less likely to be married (46%). Further, Puerto Ricans show the highest levels of marital dissolution when compared to other groups. When we combine individuals who indicated that they were separated or divorced, we find that 15% of Puerto Ricans fit into this category compared to 8% for Mexicans, 10% for Cubans and 11% for "other Latinos." Close to one-third of Mexicans, Puerto Ricans and "other Latinos" reported that they were single compared to one-fourth for Cubans. The higher tendency of Cubans to report that they were widowed can be attributed to their higher overall age relative to other groups.

Fertility

... Latinos as a group have significantly higher fertility than other groups in the United States. Using the number of children ever born per 1,000 women aged 15 to 44, we get an estimate of fertility for Latinos and other groups in the U.S. While this is a rough measure of fertility, it tells us the actual number of children born for women in their reproductive ages. Although the available evidence shows that fertility among Latinos in the United States is on the decline, it is still relatively high. The total number of children born to Latinas in their reproductive ages (15 to 44 years), as measured by the 1980 Census, was 1,591 compared to 1,302 for the total U.S. female population, 1,575 for Black and 1,232 for white females.

Again, there is significant variation in fertility according to ethnic group among Latinos. Mexican American females, in the 15–44 age category, reported the highest number of children born. An average of 1,715 children were born to Mexican American women compared to 1,663 for Puerto Rican, 1,355 for other Latinas and 1,068 for Cuban females. The above numbers show that the fertility levels of Cuban females are even lower than that for non-Latino white women....

The higher levels of fertility among Mexican Americans translates into larger families when compared to other groups. The average number of persons in Mexican families, in 1980, was 4.1 compared to 3.7 for Puerto Ricans and 3.4 for Cubans. The average family size declined slightly for Cubans (2.8) and Puerto Ricans (3.4) while it remained stable for Mexican families, from 1980 to 1991 (U.S. Bureau of the Census, 1991).

The Growth of Female Headed Households

The dramatic increase in the proportion of households headed by females since the mid-1960's has been of great concern to many social scientists and policy analysts. Garfinkel and McLanahan (1986) point out that in 1960 only one out of every twelve children lived in a household headed by a single woman but by 1983 more than 20% of all children in the U.S. lived in this type of family arrangement. W. J. Wilson (1985) indicates that from 1970 to 1979 the total number of families in the U.S. grew by 12%, however, the number of families headed by single females increased by 51%. A change of this magnitude has important implications for these females, their children and our society.

... [T]he percent of female headed families (with no spouse present) among Latinos in the United States increased significantly from 1970 to 1988, however, the growth during this period varied significantly according to ethnicity. The percent of female headed families increased from 13% in 1970 to 16% in 1980 for Mexican families and from 12% to 14% for Cuban families. The percent of female headed families among "other Latinos" increased from 14% in 1970 to 20% in 1980. However, the most dramatic growth of female headed families occurred among Puerto Ricans which increased from 24% in 1970 to 35% in 1980. By 1988, 44% of all Puerto Rican families were headed by females compared to 18% for Mexican, 16% for Cuban, and 25% for Other Latino families. In 1988, only 13% of non-Latino white families were headed by females. The pattern of growth of female headed families among Puerto Ricans resembles that of African Americans who, in 1988, had 43% of all their families headed by a female with no spouse present.

... As we shall see in the following section, there has been an increase in female labor force participation for all Latinos, while the participation of Cuban and Puerto Rican males declined from 1970 to 1980. This decline in labor force participation has resulted in a decline in the "marriageable pool" of males and, therefore, may have contributed to the increase in the proportion of female headed households.

The higher levels of female headed households among Puerto Ricans may be a result (and in turn may contribute to) their lower socioeconomic status relative to other Latinos. Further, Hernández (1983) shows that, from 1970 to 1976, young women were a much greater percentage of recent migrants than young men, a pattern which has become quite consistent for Puerto Ricans. One could speculate that there is a pattern of selective migration among young Puerto Rican women migrating to the U.S. in which separated or divorced women are overrepresented among the migrants. This is an area which needs to be researched. ...

SELECTED SOCIOECONOMIC CHARACTERISTICS FOR LATINOS IN THE UNITED STATES

Education

... One of the most serious problems that Latinos are currently confronting are their disproportionately high attrition rates from high school. Vélez (1989) indicates that Latinos have the highest dropout rate relative to all the other major racial and ethnic groups in the United States. Bean and Tienda show that, in 1980, 32% of United States born Puerto Ricans, aged 18–25 years, dropped out of high school without completing the degree compared to 47% for Island born Puerto Ricans. Among Latinos, this figure is only surpassed by foreign born Mexicans (59%) while 30% of native born Mexicans dropped out from high school in 1980. These figures are substantially lower for Cubans, Central and South Americans and "other Latinos" (Bean and Tienda, 1987: Table 8.9). Fernández and Vélez (1990:60) indicate that dropout rates for mainland Puerto Rican students have been reported as high as 80% in New York City while they vary from 45% to 60% in other cities of the United States. They indicate that other reports on high school attrition show similar dropout rates for Mexican Americans.

The reasons for the alarmingly high rates of dropouts among Latinos, and for Puerto Ricans and Mexicans, in particular, are many and complex. Factors such as poverty, being set back a grade or more, low academic achievement, language difficulties, grade repetition, low levels of parents education, raised in female headed households, and discrimination, among others, are important factors which may explain their high dropout rates (See Fernández and Vélez, 1990; Vélez, 1989; Bean and Tienda, 1987; Hernández, 1983; Hernández, 1976). If education is an important determinant of economic well-being, then Mexican Americans and Puerto Ricans will be at a serious economic disadvantage when compared to Cubans and "other Latinos."

Labor Force Participation and Occupation

The labor force participation rates for Mexican American males, over the age of 16, showed some improvements from 1970 to 1991. In 1970, 75% of Mexican males were in the labor force and this figure increased to 80% in 1988. "Other Latinos" showed a similar pattern to Mexican Americans and no significant differences in participation between these two groups exist. However, the labor force participation rates of Puerto Rican and Cuban males declined from 1970 to 1991. In 1991, Puerto Rican males had considerably lower participation rates than the rest of the Latino groups. Only sixty six percent of Puerto Rican males were in the labor force in 1991 compared to 73% for Cuban and 80% for Mexican and other Latino males.

Females had significantly lower participation rates than their male counterparts regardless of ethnicity. The participation rates of Mexican and other Latino females increased from 1970 to 1988 while that of Puerto Rican and Cuban females increased from 1970 to 1980 and then remained constant from

1980 to 1988. However, the labor force participation rates of Mexican females declined by approximately two percent, from 1988 to 1991, while it increased by the same amount for Puerto Rican and Cuban females. Again, Puerto Rican females are handicapped in terms of labor force participation rates relative to the other groups of Latinas. In 1991, 51% of Mexican, 55% of Cuban, and 57% of "other Latinas" were in the labor force. In sharp contrast, only 42% of Puerto Rican females were participating in the labor market. . . .

The occupation that a person holds will most definitely affect his/her economic well-being. . . . While Cubans were more likely to be concentrated in the technical, sales and administrative support occupations, Mexicans and Puerto Ricans were more likely to be in the operators, fabricators and laborers occupations. Further, about 19% of Cubans were in the managerial and professional occupations compared to 16% for "other Latinos," 12% for Puerto Ricans and only 10% for Mexican Americans. It is quite clear that Cubans and "other Latinos" occupy better occupational positions than Mexicans and Puerto Ricans.

While these occupational categories give us a general idea of where the different Latino groups are concentrated they can be misleading. Many Latinos remain employed in low-wage, low-skilled and dead-end jobs where the chances for promotion are non-existent. When compared to the total United States population, Latinos "remain clustered in low-paying blue-collar and semi-skilled jobs in fields like construction and manufacturing that suffer high seasonal or cyclical unemployment and thus earn far less and are more likely to be unemployed" (Davis, Haub and Willette, 1983:34). Even among professional workers, Hernández (1983) found that, for example, Puerto Rican young adults were employed in the least desired, low prestige level jobs.

ECONOMIC WELL-BEING

Family Income and Poverty

. . . The general pattern, from 1969 to 1979, was an increase in family income, for the exception of Puerto Ricans. From 1979 to 1987, the family income for all Latino groups and whites declined. However, the decline of family income was not equal for all groups and the levels of income differ markedly according to ethnic status.

The median family income of Mexican Americans increased from $21,564 in 1969 to $23,110 in 1979 while that of Cuban families increased from $26,418 to $28,557 during this period. Puerto Rican families not only had lower incomes than the other groups of Latinos, not to mention whites, but their income declined steadily from 1969 to 1987.

In 1987, the median family income of Mexicans was about $20,000 compared to $22,065 for "other Latinos," $27,294 for Cubans and only $15,185 for Puerto Rican families. Despite the fact that Cuban family income was significantly higher than that for other Latino groups it was considerably lower than that of whites. The median family income for whites was $32,274 in 1987. Further, while Cuban families experienced the most moderate decline in family income (a decline of $1,263), relative to the other Latino groups, from 1979 to 1987, it was much greater than that for whites (which declined by only $617).

Female headed families were confronting serious economic difficulties relative to all Latino families. In 1979, female headed families had substantially lower incomes when compared to Latino families but again, Puerto Rican female heads were the most economically disadvantaged group. In 1979, the median family income for white female heads was $18,180 compared to $12,788 for "other Latina," $15,242 for Cuban, $11,797 for Mexican and only $7,727 for Puerto Rican female heads. Further, while the family income of all these groups increased slightly, from 1969 to 1979, that of Puerto Rican female heads declined significantly.

As a result of their lower income, Puerto Rican families have the highest poverty rates when compared to other Latino groups. In 1990, 38% of Puerto Rican families had incomes below the established poverty threshold compared to 25% for Mexican, 21% for "other Latino," 14% for Cubans and only 8% for non-Latino white families. What is even more striking is that nearly two-thirds (64%) of Puerto Rican female headed families were living in poverty in 1990 compared to 46% for Mexican and other Latina female headed families. Again, not only did Puerto Ricans have the highest levels of poverty, from 1969 to 1987, but their poverty levels increased during this entire period while it increased for other groups, from 1979 to 1987. The unprecedented increase in female headed families that occurred among Puerto Ricans coupled with the decline in family income for this group has had a significant impact on the economic well-being of the Puerto Rican population. . . .

Economic Mobility

What differences in the background and circumstances of the different Latino groups have allowed some to achieve economic mobility while others have remained behind in economic progress? In particular, why have Cuban Americans achieved such rapid economic mobility resembling more closely the white population while Mexican Americans and particularly Puerto Ricans have remained concentrated in the lowest rungs of the economic ladder? Why did the economic conditions of Puerto Ricans deteriorate during the 1970's while that of the other Latino groups improved? Steinberg (1989) cites the economic conditions and opportunities available to immigrants at their time of arrival as important factors in accounting for their economic mobility. Lieberson (1980) also indicates that the educational and occupational skills that immigrants brought with them at their time of arrival to the United States plays an important role in determining their current occupational concentrations. Further, the structural changes that have occurred in the labor market have affected most dramatically some groups in particular. Following, this perspective we attempt to address why Cubans "made it" in America while Puerto Ricans and Mexican Americans did not.

Cubans have been constantly cited as the most recent ethnic success story. ... [T]heir median income is significantly higher than that of Puerto Rican families and that of all Spanish origin families. Cubans came to the United States as political refugees. They were seen as fleeing Communism and were very well received by the American government and population, at least until the Mariel boatlift. As political immigrants, Cubans received economic help from public schools, churches, civic groups but the U.S. government had the major financial responsibility in assisting Cubans. In 1961, the Migration and Refugee Assistance Act was established to give permanent authority to the Cuban Refugee program (Pedraza-Bailey, 1985:41). Pedraza-Bailey (1985) indicates that this Act provided transportation costs from Cuba, financial assistance to needy refugees, costs to reside in areas outside of Miami, employment training and other types assistance. Further, the initial Cuban immigrants arriving to the U.S., from 1959 to 1962, were primarily landowners, industrialists, managers, professionals and merchants (Portes and Bach, 1985).

The knowledge and skills that Cubans brought with them to the U.S. coupled with the social and economic support provided by the U.S. government and population provided this group with the necessary tools to function effectively and establish a stronghold in the American economy and society. Cubans were able to establish an economic and ethnic enclave in Miami which serves to provide employment opportunities for other Cuban immigrants. ...

Mexican Americans or Chicanos first became American citizens by annexation of the Southwest to the United States. At the end of the Mexican-American war in 1848, states such as Texas, California, New Mexico, Colorado and Arizona were taken over by the United States government. The Mexican population was, and continues to be, a source of cheap agricultural labor for American industrialist. Under the Bracero program, which was in effect, with interruptions, from 1942 to 1964, over 80,000 Mexicans were brought from Mexico to the United States to work in the agricultural farms of the Southwest. Today, despite efforts in the past to repatriate Mexican illegals back to their homeland, as was the case in the 1930's and "operation wetback" in the 1950's, they continue to be a source of cheap labor and are still exploited in the agricultural lands of the Southwest. Mexicans to a large extent continue to be "preferred" workers in the U.S., at least in agriculture. It must be indicated, however, that Mexican Americans are largely an urban population with only 7% reporting a farm related occupation in 1980.

Puerto Ricans, as well as Mexicans, and contrary to Cubans, were incorporated into the United States by military conquest. This fact has important implications for the economic well-being of these groups. Puerto Ricans were not very well received in the United States as was the case for Cubans. As Mexicans under the Bracero Program, Puerto Ricans were, to some extent, "preferred" workers, at least for a short period of time. There were direct recruitment efforts in Puerto Rico by U.S. companies to obtain cheap labor for the needle work industry in New York and for agricultural employment throughout the U.S. Further, when focusing on the economic well-being of Puerto Ricans, we must emphasize their deteriorating labor market conditions which has to a large extent been a result of the structural shifts that have occurred in the American economy.

When referring to metropolitan areas such as New York, where 50% of Puerto Ricans [lived] in 1980, we must take into account the pronounced tendency of companies to abandon the central cities. Puerto Ricans, as well as other people of color are vulnerable to "relocation of manufacturing industries out of central cities" (Wilson, 1984:102). Berry and Kasarda point out that there has been a continuous suburbanization of industry. They point out that, between 1947 and 1967, central cities registered a net loss of 293,307 manufacturing jobs while manufacturing employment in the suburbs increased by 3,902,326 (1977:232–233). There has also been an "industrial flight" from the cities of the snowbelt (East and Midwest) to the cities in the sunbelt (West and South) (Borman & Spring, 1984; Berry and Kasarda, 1977). In the 1970's, New York City alone, lost 600,000 manufacturing jobs, the most important single source of employment for Puerto Ricans in the United States. The suburbanization of industry, coupled with the flight of industry from snowbelt to the sunbelt, has greatly contributed to the depressed socioeconomic status of Puerto Ricans relative to other Latino groups in the United States.

Another problem that Puerto Ricans in New York experience is the increasing amount of competition for low-skilled jobs. There are increasing numbers [of] Dominican immigrants, as well as many other undocumented workers, in New York. Puerto Ricans must then compete with these recent migrants for the low-skilled jobs available. However, Puerto Ricans may be bypassed by many employers as being "too expensive." Tienda (1989) argues that Puerto Ricans have been placed at the end of the hiring queue. This may be reflected by the fact that despite their recent arrival, Dominican females, for example, in 1980 had a labor force participation rate 13 percentage points higher than that for Puerto Ricans (Mann and Salvo, 1984:18)....

Ethnic and racial discrimination in the labor market and in housing is a serious problem that mainland Puerto Ricans confront. Bean and Tienda point out that:

> ... Puerto Ricans were often relegated to the lowest levels of the labor market. They frequently experienced social deprivation in both the housing and labor markets, and they often fared as badly or worse than blacks who migrated from the North (1987:25).

The United States Commission on Civil Rights (1976) found that there were significant income differences between the Latino population and non-Hispanic whites. They indicate that these income differences are, in part, a result of discrimination which Latino workers confront. They also point out that what is true for Latinos is more pronounced for Puerto Ricans. Hernández (1983) suggests that being a Puerto Rican is in itself a negative factor in determining labor force participation in the United States.

The above information, although limited, clearly indicates that there are a variety of factors accounting for the different levels in economic well-being between Cubans, Mexicans and Puerto Ricans. The skills that Cubans brought with them to the United States along with the financial support received by the American government has put them at an economic advantage relative to Mexican Americans and Puerto Ricans. We can see that an economic hierarchy exist within the Latino population with Cubans occupying the most advantage position and Puerto Ricans experiencing severe economic difficulties. Mexican Americans have not experienced the economic mobility of Cubans but their economic status falls above that of Puerto Ricans.

It is not my intention to indicate that all Cubans have succeeded in the United States while all Puerto Ricans have not because this is clearly not the case. What should be evident is that each of these groups has its own class structure in which we can identify a low, middle and upper class. Each group has a segment of the population which is employed in professional and managerial jobs and a group of households which have a total income of $35,000 or more. Clearly, these segments of the population can be put in the category "upper class" within their particular groups. While those households with less than $10,000 of income and those employed as farm workers, laborers and in service oriented jobs could be classified as part of the lower economic class. What we should emphasize is that while many Cubans have succeeded economically a non-trivial percent have not and while some Puerto Ricans have made it up the economic ladder a disproportionately large segment of this population has not. Further, Latinos who have indeed "succeeded" in the labor market and as a result have higher incomes than their counterparts in their particular groups have not been fully incorporated into the mainstream of the American economy and society. For example, Cuban families, whose income was the highest of all Latino families, had an income which was 84% of the median family income for whites. So despite Cubans economic success they still lag behind the progress of non-Latino whites. . . .

CONCLUSIONS

. . . We have seen that Cubans are positioned in the upper levels of the economic ladder while Puerto Ricans are at a significant economic disadvantage relative to all Latino groups and Mexican-Americans fall in between these two groups. The group of "other Latinos" is also quite diverse. It appears that Central and South Americans have similar socioeconomic conditions to those of Mexican Americans while the rest of the "other Latino" population resembles the economic achievements of Cubans.

The diversity of this Latino population makes it almost impossible to talk about the demographic and socioeconomic characteristics of "Hispanics" and yet much research tends to ignore this heterogeneity. We must note that because of space limitations, this article did not focus on the socioeconomic differences between Latinos of foreign birth and those born in the United States and between those who identified themselves as African Americans, whites or other.

The available research clearly indicates that there are significant differences between Latinos born in the United States and those born outside of the U.S. (i.e., Mexico, Puerto Rico, Cuba, etc.). Those who are foreign born tend, in general, to have higher school dropout rates, lower levels education, labor force participation and economic well-being (Falcón and Hirschman, 1992;

Rodríguez, H., 1992; Bean and Tienda, 1987; Rogler and Santana-Cooney, 1984). It is quite clear that the new generations of Latinos have improved their socioeconomic well-being vis-a-vis their parent generations but it is also clear that much more progress needs to be made, particularly in the case of Puerto Ricans and Mexicans.

Much variation also exists among Latinos in terms of racial identification. In 1980, 55% of Mexicans, 48% of Puerto Ricans, 84% of Cubans and 63% of "other Latinos" identified themselves as whites. Although "other Latinos" were more likely to identify themselves as "Blacks" relative to the other Latino groups, only 4.5% did so. (Denton and Massey, 1989b:Table 1). These figures show that Latinos, and in particular Puerto Ricans and Mexicans do not place themselves in the Black-white U.S. dichotomy. Research on the effects of race on economic well-being and residential segregation shows that Latinos identified as "Blacks" tend to fare worse off than those classified as whites. Denton and Massey (1989b) indicate that the higher levels of segregation among Puerto Ricans is, in part, due to their skin color. Rodríguez, C. (1990) shows that Puerto Ricans identifying themselves as "other" in the race question in the 1980 Census, were at a significant economic disadvantage when compared to those who identified themselves as white while those indicating that they were Black were similar to white Puerto Ricans in some variables and similar to "other" Puerto Ricans in other variables. Race clearly plays a significant role in the economic well-being of Latinos, therefore, research on this area merits further consideration. . . .

Whether Latinos, as a group, will "make it" in the American society depends on a host of factors such as educational levels, household composition, employment opportunities, type and amount of income, structural changes in the American economy, levels of residential and employment segregation, and racial and ethnic discrimination, among other factors. It is, therefore, important that we as researchers continue to focus on the economic well-being of Latinos in the United States. We must examine in more detail the differences that exist between these groups and what social, cultural, demographic and economic factors account for these differences. Further, we must develop alternatives to improve the socioeconomic and political conditions of Latinos in the United States, and in particular, that of Puerto Ricans and Mexican Americans.

CHAPTER 9 The Legal Institution

9.1 ROBERT STAPLES

White Racism, Black Crime, and American Justice: An Application of the Colonial Model to Explain Crime and Race

In an attempt to understand the dilemma inequality poses for a society that espouses equal rights for all, sociologists have developed a set of conceptual approaches for the study of inequality—in particular, racial and ethnic inequality. The race and ethnic relations theory that has been most prominent within the social sciences for several decades is the *assimilation theory*. This theory has been used to examine the experiences of immigrant groups that have become part of the United States, both voluntarily and involuntarily. Studies focusing on the assimilation of European immigrants have generally lauded these people's success, while studies on non-European racial and ethnic populations have frequently found these groups to be biologically, culturally, and structurally deficient. The perceived deficiencies of racial and ethnic populations have produced a characterization of these populations that is demeaning and that reinforces negative stereotypes of racial and ethnic populations. In an attempt to redress the limitations of assimilation theory in the study of racial and ethnic populations, some scholars have turned to an *internal colonial* framework.

Robert Staples, a professor at the University of California, San Francisco, applies the internal colonial model to explain the relationships between race and crime in U.S. society. To Staples, crimes committed by Blacks are the products of their colonial relationship to the greater society, which, in turn, "is based on racial inequality and perpetuated by the political state." Staples maintains that Blacks are not protected by American law, that police brutality is a fact of daily existence in Black America, and that the cultural values of White supremacy place little significance on the lives of Blacks in U.S. society.

Key Concept: White racism, Black crime, and colonialism

*I*n the past hundred years criminologists have shown great interest in the relationship between race and crime. Various theories have been put forth to explain the association between racial membership and criminal activity. These theories have ranged from Lombroso's[1] discredited assertion that certain groups possess inherent criminal tendencies to the more widely accepted theory that certain racial groups are more commonly exposed to conditions of poverty which lead them to commit crimes more often.[2] The purpose of this paper is to examine the relationship of race and crime in a new theoretical framework which will permit a systematic analysis of racial crime within the political-economic context of American society. One function of this model will be to delineate the nature of the solution required to reduce the magnitude of crime among certain racial groups.

The approach here used to explain race and crime is the colonial model. This framework has been formulated and used in the writings of Fanon, Blauner, Carmichael and Hamilton, Memmi, and others.[3] It is particularly attributed to Fanon, whose analysis of colonial relationships in Africa has been transferred to the American pattern of racial dominance and subjugation. While there are many criminologists who will summarily dismiss this model as lacking any relevance for understanding the relationship between race and crime, it merits a hearing since many blacks, especially those presently incarcerated, give it considerable credence. In fact, it is their self-definition as political prisoners that has motivated the many prison protests that have occurred in recent years.

Basically, the colonial analogy views the black community as an underdeveloped colony whose economics and politics are controlled by leaders of the racially dominant group. Using this framework, it is useful to view race as a political and cultural identity rather than to apply any genetic definitions. Race is a political identity because it defines the way in which an individual is to be treated by the political state and the conditions of one's oppression. It is cultural in the sense that white cultural values always have ascendancy over black cultural values, thus what is "good" or "bad," "criminal" or "legitimate" behavior is always defined in terms favorable to the ruling class. The result is that crime by blacks in America is structured by their relationship to the colonial structure, which is based on racial inequality and perpetuated by the political state.

Obviously, there are some imperfections in the colonial analogy as a unitary heuristic model to explain race and crime. More theoretical and empirical research is necessary before the structural forms characteristic of classical colonialism may be mechanically applied to the complexities of crime in America. Yet, the essential features of colonialism are manifest in American society. Blacks have been, and remain, a group subjected to economic exploitation and political control; and they lack the ability to express their cultural values without incurring serious consequences. While other colonial factors such as the geographical relationship of the colonial masters to the colonized, the population ratio, and the duration of colonization may be missing, they do not profoundly affect the form or substance of black and white relations in America: white superordination and black subordination.

In using this model I am not dissuaded by the complications of class often interjected into the issue of crime and race. Domestic colonialism is as much cultural as economic. While members of the white working class are more victimized by their class location than other whites, they are not subjected to the dehumanized status of blacks of all social classes. The racist fabric of white America denies blacks a basic humanity and thus permits the violation of their right to equal justice under the law. In America the right to justice is an inalienable right; but for blacks it is still a privilege to be granted at the caprice and goodwill of whites, who control the machinery of the legal system and the agents of social control.

LAW AND ORDER

One of the key elements in securing the citizenry's obedience to a nation's laws is the belief of the citizens that the laws are fair. A prevalent view of the law among blacks is summed up in Lester's statement that "the American Black man has never known law and order except as an instrument of oppression. The law has been written by white men, for the protection of white men and their property, to be enforced by white men against Blacks in particular and poor folks in general."[4] Historically, a good case can be made for the argument that the function of law was to establish and regulate the colonial relationship of blacks and whites in the United States. Initially, the colonial system was established by laws which legitimated the subordination of the black population.

The legalization of the colonial order is best represented in the Constitution itself. While the Constitution is regarded as the bulwark of human equality and freedom, it denied the right to vote to Afro-Americans and made the political franchise an exclusive right of white property owners. In fact, blacks were defined as a source of organic property for white slave holders in the notorious 3/5 clause. This clause allowed the slaveowner to claim 3/5 constituency for each slave that he possessed. Since non-citizens are beyond the pale of legal equality, the Dred Scott decision affirmed that slaves were not citizens and could not bring suit in the courts. As the ultimate blow to the aspirations of blacks, in 1896 the Supreme Court upheld racial segregation in its "separate but equal" decision in the Plessy *v.* Ferguson case.[5]

In a contemporary sense, blacks are not protected by American law because they have no power to enforce those laws. They have no law of their own and no defense against the laws of the colonizers. Thus, the power to define what constitutes a crime is in the hands of the dominant caste and is another mechanism of racial subordination. How crime is defined reflects the relationship of the colonized to the colonizers. The ruling caste defines those acts as crimes which fit its needs and purposes and characterizes as criminals individuals who commit certain kinds of illegal acts, while other such acts are exempted from prosecution and escape public disapprobation because they are not perceived as criminal or a threat to society.

As a result of the colonial administration's power to define the nature of criminality, the white collar crimes[6] which involve millions of dollars go unpunished or lightly punished, while the crimes of the colonized involving nickels and dimes result in long jail sentences. The main executor of the colonial regime can wage a war that takes thousands of lives in direct violation of the Constitution, while the colonized are sent to the gas chambers for non-fatal crimes such as rape. It is no coincidence that the two criminal acts for which politicians wanted to preserve the death penalty were kidnapping and airline hijacking, the former a crime committed mainly against the wealthy while the latter is a political act against the state.

INTERNAL MILITARY AGENTS

In any colonial situation, there must be agents to enforce the status quo. A classical colonial world is dichotomized into two parts of society, and the policeman acts as the go-between. Fanon describes it in Colonial Africa:

> In the colonies it is the policeman and the soldier who are the official instituted go-betweens, the spokesman of the settler and his rule of oppression... By their immediate presence and their frequent and direct action, they maintain contact with the native and advise him by means of rifle-butts and napalm not to budge. It is obvious here that the agents of government speak the language of pure force. The intermediary does not lighten the oppression, nor seek to hide the domination; he shows them up and puts them into practice with the clear conscience of an upholder of the peace, yet he is the bringer of violence into the home and into the mind of the native.[7]

One could hardly find a more perfect analogy on the role of the policeman than in the findings of the United States Commission on Civil Rights in the 1960's. Police brutality was discovered to be a fact of daily existence for Afro-Americans and a primary source of abuse by whites against any challenge by blacks to the status quo. In essence:

Police misconduct often serves as the ultimate weapon for keeping the Negro in his place, for it is quite clear that when all else fails, policemen in some communities can be trusted to prevent the Negro from entering a "desegregated" school or housing project, a voting booth, or even a court of law. They may do it merely by turning their backs on private lawlessness, or by more direct involvement. Trumped up charges, dragnet roundups, illegal arrests, the "third degree" and brutal beatings are all part of the pattern of "white supremacy."[8]

In order to enforce this type of colonial rule, policemen must have certain traits. First and foremost, they must be members of the dominant racial group. Almost every major urban area has a police force that is predominantly white, although the cities themselves may contain mostly blacks. The highest ratio of black policemen to the black population is found in Philadelphia, where 29 percent of the city's population is black and 20 percent of the police force is black. The lowest is probably New Orleans, with the black population composing 41 percent of the total population and 4 percent of the police force.[9]

It is not only that the police force is composed mostly of members of the colonizers' group, but they also represent the more authoritarian and racist members of that sector. One survey disclosed that the majority of white police officers hold antiblack attitudes. In predominantly black precincts, over 75 percent of the white police expressed highly prejudiced feelings towards blacks, and only 1 percent showed sympathy toward the plight of blacks.[10] A series of public hearings on police brutality in Chicago revealed that candidates for the police department who do poorly on the psychological tests or who demonstrate personality problems while undergoing training in the police academy are assigned to "stress areas" in Chicago's black and brown ghettos.[11] The predominantly black city of Oakland, California was recruiting its police officers among men recently returned from military service in Vietnam.

Considering the characteristics of policemen assigned to the black colony, it is no surprise to find that for the years 1920–1932, of 479 blacks killed by white persons in the South, 54 percent were slain by white police officers.[12] In more recent periods cities outside the South provide interesting statistics. Seventy-five percent of the civilians killed by Chicago police in 1971 were black.[13] The state of California reports that blacks, who make up 7 percent of its population, were 48 percent of the persons killed by policemen in 1971.[14]

Even less surprising are the studies which show blacks believe that policemen are disrespectful, that police brutality exists in their areas, and that blacks are treated worse than whites by the police.[15] Besides the abuse suffered at the hands of white police officers, two basic types of complaint are the basis for these beliefs. One is that the police in black communities are more tolerant of illegal activities such as drug addiction, prostitution, and street violence than they would be in white communities. The other is that the police see as much less urgent the calls for help and complaints from black areas than from white areas.[16]

Such complaints about the police force are due to ignorance of their functional role in colonial society. The police are not placed in black communities to protect the indigenous inhabitants, but to protect the property of the colonizers who live outside those communities and to restrain any black person from breaking out of the colonial wards in the event of violence. No amount of "proper" behavior on the part of the police, therefore, nullifies the fundamental colonial machinery which imposes law and order according to the definitions of the colonizers. The law itself constitutes the basis for colonial rule; and the ideology of white supremacy shapes the police force, the courts, and the prisons as instruments of continued colonial subjugation.

CRIME BY BLACKS

The colonial character of American society tends to structure the racial pattern of crime. In the urban areas, where most blacks live, the majority of serious property crimes such as burglary, larceny (over $50), and auto thefts are committed by whites. More blacks than whites are arrested for serious crimes of violence such as murder, rape, and aggravated assaults. These crimes of violence by blacks are most often committed against other blacks.[17] The homicide rate for blacks is about ten times the rate for whites. Indeed, homicide is the second leading cause of death among black males aged 15–25, the third leading cause between 25–44.[18] In interracial crimes of violence, whites attack and assault blacks more often than blacks attack and assault whites.[19]

The above statistics follow the typical pattern in the colonial world. The violence with which the supremacy of the values of whites is affirmed and the aggressiveness which has infused the victory of these values into the ways of life and thought of the colonized mean that their challenge to the colonial world will be to claim that same violence as a means of breaking into the colonizers' forbidden quarters. According to Fanon, colonized men will initially express against their own people this aggressiveness which they have internalized. This is the period when the colonized terrorize and beat each other, while the colonizers or policemen have the right to assault the natives with impunity. This is a pattern of avoidance that allows the colonized to negate their powerlessness, to pretend that colonialism does not exist. Ultimately, this behavior leads to armed resistance against colonialism.[20]

The cultural values of white supremacy place little premium on the lives of blacks in the United States. A native's death is of little importance to the continuation of colonial rule, except that it may deprive a particular colonizer of the labor of a skilled worker. Hence, while blacks are generally given longer prison terms than whites for the same crime, they get shorter sentences for murder.[21] According to Bullock,

> These judicial responses possibly represent indulgent and non-indulgent patterns that characterize local attitudes concerning property and intra-racial morals. Since the victims of most of the Negroes committed for ... [murder] were also Negroes, local norms tolerate a less rigorous enforcement of the law; the disorder is mainly located within the Negro society. Local norms are less tolerant (in Black crimes against white property), for the motivation to protect white property and to protect "white" society against disorder is stronger than the motivation to protect "Negro" society.[22]

Colonial practices are not confined to the police. Rather, the political state, which is also dominated by whites, controls the dispensation of justice from police apprehension to prison; and these all serve the interests of the colonizers. In the courts, most judges in the state, federal, circuit, superior and supreme courts are appointed by the political state, and not elected. No black person in the United States has the power to appoint a judge to the bench. Consequently, there are almost no black judges in the South, and few in the North and West.[23] Moreover, any blacks appointed to the bench are likely to possess the values of the colonizers.

A trial by jury guarantees no more equal justice to the accused black offenders. Blacks are still systematically excluded from juries in some parts of the South, and are often underrepresented on juries in which they are allowed to serve. Sometimes they are excluded by more subtle and indirect means such as preemptory challenges by the prosecution, requirements of voter registration, property ownership, or literacy tests.[24] Despite the American creed of equal justice before the law, few black offenders before the courts will receive a neutral hearing before a jury of normal white Americans. As Fanon states, in a racist society the normal person is racist.[25]

Blacks are further victimized by the lack of adequate legal representation. Since colonial administrations allow few natives to attain professional skills and become members of the native bourgeoisie, there is a scarcity of black lawyers to represent black alleged offenders before the courts. Another feature of colonialism is the creation of dependency in the natives upon the members of the ruling group to achieve ordinary rights of citizenship. Thus, black defendants often choose white lawyers over black ones because they feel they can neutralize the impact of racism in decisions rendered by a white judge and jury. Many black defendants, of course, cannot afford an attorney and must accept a court-appointed lawyer. In federal larceny cases, 52 percent of the blacks did not have their own lawyers, as compared to 25 percent of the whites.[26]

Another disadvantage faced by black defendants is the illegitimacy of their cultural values. There are several examples of words and phrases used by blacks which have a totally different meaning in the white community. These cultural differences are particularly crucial in certain types of crimes such as assault and battery and public obscenity. But the colonial order insists that the natives' society is lacking in values, and that differences in cultural symbols, *i.e.*, language, are not recognized in a court of law. There are other linguistic barriers in the courtroom that affect black defendants. Often, they may not comprehend the legal jargon of the attorneys and give answers based on their mistaken interpretation of the language used in the courtroom.[27]

Given all these factors, black defendants are often shortchanged in the decisions of the courts and the length of their prison sentences. Most of the available data reveal that blacks usually receive longer prison terms than whites for the same criminal offenses. They are particularly discriminated against when one considers their chances of receiving probation or a suspended sentence. In larceny cases, for example, 74 percent of guilty blacks were imprisoned in state larceny cases compared to only 49 percent of guilty whites. The racial gap in larceny cases is greater than in assault convictions because larcenies by blacks are more often committed against whites, while assaults occur more frequently against other blacks. Hence, racial disparities in prison sentencing are not only related to the skin color of the alleged offender, but to that of his victim, too.[28]

It is in the area of capital punishment that the racial, and thus colonial, factors stand out. The statistics on capital punishment in the United States reveal most glaringly the double standard of justice that exists there: One for the wealthy and another for blacks and poor people. Even the former Warden of the Sing Sing prison once remarked, "Only the poor, the friendless, and the foreign born are sentenced to death and executed."[29] But it is particularly the colonial wards of America, *i.e.,* blacks, who have received the heaviest brunt of this dual standard of American justice.

For blacks in America, capital punishment is only a transfer of the functions of lynch mobs to the state authority. Under the auspices of the political state, blacks have been executed for less serious crimes and crimes less often receiving the death penalty, particularly rape, than whites. They were of a younger age than whites at the time of execution and were more often executed without appeals, regardless of their offense or age at execution. Of the 3,827 men and 32 women executed since 1930, 53 percent were black. The proportion of blacks on death row in 1972 was 52 percent. It is in the South that discrimination in capital punishment is most evident. Practically all executions for rape took place in the South. In that region, 90 percent of those executed for rape were black.[30]

Again, the colonial pattern emerges. The two things the colonizers fear most are the stealing of their possessions and the rape of their women, and they punish with special fury the crime of sexual violation of upper caste women. About 85 percent of the black rape offenders executed had white victims,[31] although the overwhelming majority of the black males' rape victims are black women.

POLITICAL PRISONERS

The combination of the colonial administration of justice and the oppression of blacks has resulted in the internment of a disproportionate number of blacks in the nation's prisons. The number of blacks in prison is three times their representation in the society at large.[32] There are actually more blacks in prison than in college. Yet, as Angela Davis has observed:

> Along with the army and the police, prisons are the most essential instruments of state power. The prospect of long prison terms is meant to preserve order; it is supposed to serve as a threat to anyone who dares disturb existing social relations, whether by failing to observe the sacred rules of property, or by consciously challenging the right of an unjust system of racism and domination to function smoothly.[33]

In recent years the number of prison protests by black prisoners have risen. Part of the reason is the prisoners' self-definition as political prisoners. Two basic types of political prisoners may be defined. One kind is the person arrested under the guise of criminal charges, but only because of the state's wish to remove the political activist as a threat to the prevailing racial conditions. Examples of this type are Angela Davis, Bobby Seale, and H. Rap Brown. The second type is more numerous and consists of those blacks who are arbitrarily arrested and then "railroaded" through the courts, where they face white politically appointed judges, all-white juries, without a lawyer, or with an appointed lawyer who suggests a guilty plea in exchange for a reduced sentence.

Since most crimes by blacks have black victims, not all black prisoners are *ipso facto* political prisoners. The incarceration of these blacks stems from the subjugated condition of black people in the United States. As Chrisman asserts, "a Black prisoner's crime may or may not have been a political action against the state, but the state's action against him is always political."[34] The basis for this judgment is that black criminals are not tried and judged by the black community itself, but that their crimes are defined and they are convicted and sentenced by the machinery of the ruling colonial order, whose interests are served by the systematic subjugation of all black people. As long as crime by blacks occurs within the context of racial subjugation and exploitation, blacks will continue to believe that their criminal acts will not be objectively and fairly treated, but rather that the treatment will be affected by the racial inequality which constitutes the essence of American colonialism.

In this paper the colonial model has been applied to explain the relationship between crime and race. While the fit between theory and empirical data is not perfect, it does point the way to reducing some of the racial inequities in American criminal justice. Among the remedies suggested by this model is community control of the police. Community control would respond to the charge that the police in black neighborhoods constitute an occupation army in their midst. Policemen would be chosen by the people in the community and required to live in their precinct. In this way, blacks would have greater assurance that the police are there to protect their interests rather than the property of whites who live outside the community.[35]

Another remedy to be considered is a trial by jury of one's peers. This means a jury whose experiences, needs, and interests are similar to those of the defendant. When this is not feasible, proportional representation of blacks on juries, in the legal staff, and on the bench might be considered. While these suggestions will not radically affect the socioeconomic conditions that generate crime, they will at least reduce the impact of domestic racism on the administration of justice to the black population.

NOTES

1. Gina Lombroso, "Ferrero," in *Criminal Man According to the Classifications of Cesare Lombroso* (New York, 1911).

2. C. F. Marvin Wolfgang and Bernard Cohen, *Crime and Race: Conceptions and Misconceptions* (New York, 1970).

3. Frantz Fanon, *The Wretched of the Earth* (New York, 1966); Robert Blauner, "Internal Colonialism and Ghetto Revolt," *Social Problems* XVI (Spring, 1969), 393–408; Stokely Carmichael and Charles Hamilton, *Black Power* (New York, 1967); Albert Memmi, *The Colonizer and the Colonized* (Boston, 1967).

4. Julius Lester, *Look Out, Whitey: Black Power's Gon' Get Your Mama* (New York, 1968), p. 23.

5. Cf. Mary Berry, *Black Resistance—White Law: A History of Constitutional Racism in America* (New York, 1971).

6. Edwin H. Sutherland, *White Collar Crime* (New York, 1949).

7. Fanon, *op. cit.*, p. 31.

8. Wallace Mendelson, *Discrimination* (Englewood Cliffs, 1962), pp. 143–44.

9. *Report of the National Advisory Commission on Civil Disorders* (New York, 1968), p. 321.

10. Albert J. Reiss, Jr., "Police Brutality—Answers to Key Questions," *Transaction*, V (July–August, 1968), 10–19.

11. Testimony of Dr. Evrum Mendelsohn of the Elmhurst Psychological Center before Congressman Ralph Metcalfe's Public Hearing on Police Brutality in Chicago, September 1, 1972.

12. Gunnar Myrdal, *An American Dilemma* (New York, 1944).

13. Testimony of a team of law students from Northwestern University at the Metcalfe hearing, August 30, 1972.

14. Report by Evelle Younger, Attorney General of the State of California, cited in *The Los Angeles Sentinel*, August 10, 1972, p. A2.

15. Report of the National Advisory Commission on Civil Disorders, *op. cit.*, p. 302.

16. *Ibid.*, p. 268.

17. United States Department of Justice, Federal Bureau of Investigation, "Crime in the United States," *Uniform Crime Reports*, 1969.

18. Lee N. Robins, "Negro Homicide Victims—Who Will They Be?" *Transaction*, V (June, 1968), p. 16.

19. Marvin Wolfgang, *Patterns in Criminal Homicide* (Philadelphia, 1958).

20. Fanon, *op. cit.*, p. 43.

21. Wolfgang, *Crime and Race, op. cit.*, p. 82.

22. Henry A. Bullock, "Significance of the Racial Factor in the Length of Prison Sentences," *The Journal of Criminal Law, Criminology and Police Science*, VII (November, 1961), 411–17.

23. United States Commission on Civil Rights Report, 1963, p. 124.

24. United States Commission on Civil Rights Report, *Justice* (Washington, D.C., 1961), p. 92.

25. Frantz Fanon, "Racism and Culture." in *Toward the African Revolution* (New York, 1967).

26. Stuart Nagel, *The Legal Process From a Behavioral Perspective* (Homewood, Illinois, 1969).

27. Daniel H. Swett, *Cross Cultural Communications in the Courtroom: Applied Linguistics in a Murder Trial*, a paper presented at the Conference on Racism and the Law (San Francisco, December, 1967), pp. 2–5.

28. Nagel, *op. cit.*

29. Cited in Hugo Bedau, *The Death Penalty in America* (New York, 1967), p. 411.

30. William J. Bowers, *Racial Discrimination in Capital Punishment: Characteristics of the Condemned* (Lexington, Massachusetts, 1972).

31. *Ibid.*

32. National Prisoner Statistics, 1971.

33. Angela Davis, "The Soledad Brothers," *The Black Scholar,* II (April–May 1971), 2–3.

34. Robert Chrisman, "Black Prisoners, White Law," *The Black Scholar,* II (April–May 1971), 45–46.

35. Cf. Arthur Waskow, "Community Control of the Police," *Transaction,* VI (December 1969), 4–5.

9.2   ADALBERTO AGUIRRE, JR., AND
DAVID V. BAKER

A Descriptive Profile of Mexican American Executions in the Southwest

Since 1976, when the United States Supreme Court reinstated capital punishment after a 10-year moratorium on the execution of capital offenders, death penalty jurisdictions have executed 23 Latinos. Southwestern states have executed most of these Latino prisoners. Sociologists know very little about the execution of Latino prisoners in the United States, however. Most social scientific research on capital punishment in the United States has focused on the highly disproportionate number of Black prisoners sentenced to death under the criminal justice system. No death penalty research has focused on Latino executions.

The following reading is from "A Descriptive Profile of Mexican American Executions in the Southwest," *The Social Science Journal* (vol. 34, no. 3, 1997). In it, Adalberto Aguirre, Jr., a professor of sociology at the University of California at Riverside, and David V. Baker, an associate professor of sociology at Riverside Community College, augment existing research on capital punishment by constructing a descriptive profile of Mexican American executions in the Southwest. Aguirre and Baker argue that this descriptive profile documents the existence of Mexican American executions as a social fact in the Southwest.

Key Concept: Mexican American executions in the United States

More than two decades ago, after an exhaustive study of criminal justice agencies and the Mexican American population in the U.S. Southwest, the U.S. Commission on Civil Rights (1970) concluded: "This report paints a bleak picture of the relationship between Mexican Americans in the Southwest and

*Adalberto
Aguirre, Jr., and
David V. Baker*

the agencies which administer justice in those states.... There is evidence of
police misconduct against Mexican Americans" (p. 87). Accordingly, Grebler et
al. (1970) in their groundbreaking study of the Mexican American population in
the United States noted the persistence of a racist perception of Mexican Americans in the Los Angeles police department vis-a-vis comments made by the
police chief regarding Mexican Americans and criminal activity: "it's because of
some of these people being not too far removed from the wild tribes of the district of the inner mountains of Mexico. I don't think you can throw the genes out
of the question when you discuss behavior patterns of people" (p. 530). Since
the publication of these two studies a substantial body of documentation has
accumulated suggesting that Mexican Americans have been, and continue to
be, oppressed by the criminal justice system in the United States (Bondavalli &
Bondavalli, 1980; Garza, 1973; Mirande, 1987; Morales, 1972; Romero & Stelzner,
1985; Trujillo, 1974).

One illustration of the relationship between Mexican Americans and the
criminal justice system in the Southwest is their *representativeness* within the
criminal justice system. *Representativeness* is used by researchers as a means
of determining the extent to which a minority population (nonwhite) is overrepresented in the criminal justice system relative to its numerical size in the
general population (Gross & Mauro, 1984; Baldus et al., 1983; Kleck, 1981). In
addition, the over-representation of a population permits researchers to examine the operation of extra-legal factors, such as biased attitudes and perceptions,
in the population's processing by the criminal justice system (Aguirre & Baker,
1990; Gross & Mauro, 1989). For the purpose of illustration, we have summarized select criminal justice statistics in Table 1 for the Mexican American
population in the Southwest. One can make the general observation from Table
1 that the Mexican American population in the Southwest is disproportionately
represented in select criminal justice categories. An exception is found in Texas
where Mexican Americans are not disproportionately represented as state and
federal prisoners. One can also observe in Table 1 that the greatest amount of
disparity is found in New Mexico, and that the least amount of disparity is
found in Texas. While it is not our intent in this article to examine the disproportionate representation of the Mexican American population in the criminal
justice system, we note that the research literature has observed that the Mexican American population is over-represented in the criminal justice system
as a result of such extra-legal factors as ethnic identity, socioeconomic status,
and English language use, (Aguirre & Baker, 1988, 1989, 1994; Bondavalli &
Bondavalli, 1980; Chang & Araujo, 1975; Holmes & Daudistel, 1984).

In general, one can make observations regarding the treatment of Mexican Americans by the criminal justice system and their representation within
the criminal justice system. However, one is limited in making observations regarding other features of the relationship between the Mexican American population and the criminal justice system. Gomez-Quinones (1994), for example,
notes that the study of the Mexican Americans as members of law enforcement agencies, especially police departments, has been ignored. Accordingly,
Aguirre and Baker (1989) have noted that the institutional analysis of Mexican
Americans in the criminal justice system has focused very little attention on the
study of executed Mexican American prisoners in the Southwest. These then are

TABLE 1

*Selected Criminal Justice Statistics for Mexican American
Population by State in the Southwest*

Criminal Justice Category	Arizona	California	Colorado	New Mexico	Texas
Mexican Americans on Probation	(a)	(a)	21%	55%	28%
Mexican American Jail Inmate Population	25%	34%	25%	54%	28%
Mexican Americans in State and Federal Facilities	26%	28%	25%	56%	22%
Mexican American Population as Percent of State's Overall Population	19%	26%	13%	38%	25%

a: not available.

Sources: U.S. Department of Justice, Bureau of Justice Statistics, *Sourcebook on Criminal Justice Statistics,* 1992 (Washington, DC; U.S. Government Printing Office, 1993); F. Schick and R. Schick, *Statistical Handbook on U.S. Hispanics* (Oryx Press, 1991).

two features of the relationship between Mexican Americans and the criminal justice system that have attracted little attention.

Our purpose in this article then is to enhance one's understanding regarding one of these two features by constructing a descriptive profile for Mexican American prisoners executed in the Southwest. On the one hand, the construction of a descriptive profile for executed Mexican American prisoners is necessary for observing the institutional interaction of Mexican Americans across all dimensions of the U. S. criminal justice system. On the other hand, the construction of a descriptive profile addresses an observation made by Romero and Stelzner (1985) that Mexican Americans are nonexistent in the study of prisoners and executions because the analysis of executions has been limited to black-white differences. Thus, the construction of a descriptive profile for Mexican American prisoners executed in the Southwest fills in a gap regarding the relationship between the Mexican American population and the criminal justice system.

MEXICAN AMERICAN EXECUTIONS IN THE SOUTHWEST

There are several major data sources on executions in the United States (Aguirre & Baker, 1994). The Espy File, however, is the most comprehensive list of confirmed executions in the United States (Schneider & Smykla, 1991). In May 1970, M. Watt Espy began collecting data on public executions from his home in Headland, Alabama. Espy's data collection project was moved to the University of Alabama Law Center in Tuscaloosa, Alabama in 1977 under the directorship

of John Ortiz Smykla and the Inter-University Consortium of Political and Social Research. Since then the University of Alabama has continued the documentation of new cases, amending cases already confirmed, and computeriza-
tion of the data.

The Espy File contains information on 14,570 executions conducted under
civil authority in the U.S. beginning with the first execution in the American
colonies of Captain John Kendall in 1608. The inventory concludes with the
electrocution of a 41-year old white man named Whitley for rape-murder in
Virginia on July 6, 1987. The Espy File contains information on the individual
prisoners executed and the circumstances surrounding the crime for which the
prisoner was executed. The data identify the name, race, age, sex, and occupation of the offender, as well as the date, place, jurisdiction, crime, and method
of execution. The Espy File consists of information on executions collected from
prison officials and state departments of corrections; contemporary newspaper coverage of crimes, trials, and executions; actual court records of trials and
various appeals; and through contacts with local historians, historical societies,
museums, archives, and county clerks.

According to the Espy File, 301 Hispanic prisoners were executed in the
United States from as early as 1783, to the close of the inventory in July 1987.
The majority of the executions (81.1%) took place in the Southwest (Arizona,
California, Colorado, New Mexico, Texas). The Espy File, however, does not
specify how prisoners were identified as Hispanic in the enumeration process.
We have discussed in previous work the conceptual limitations that arise when
Spanish-language use or Spanish surname are utilized as the primary basis of
identification in the enumeration process used to gather criminal justice statistics on Hispanics (Aguirre & Baker, 1988). Some of the conceptual limitations
that arise are the exclusion of Hispanics that do not speak Spanish or do not
have a Spanish surname (for other examples see: Aguirre, 1982, 1984; Artiz,
1986; Berkanovic, 1980; de la Puente, 1993; Kirkmanliff & Mondragon, 1991;
Macias, 1993).

For our purpose in this article we cross-referenced the prisoners identified
by race as "Hispanic" in the Espy File with the Immigration and Naturalization Service's (INS) compilation of Spanish surnames. We have utilized this
approach in previous research as a means of identifying Mexican American
prisoners in the Southwest (Aguirre & Baker, 1989). As a result of the cross-
referencing, our sample of 244 Mexican American prisoners is limited to those
with a Spanish surname and whose race is identified as "Hispanic" in the Espy
File. In addition, we have made the meta-theoretical assumption regarding our
sample that given the fact that over 65% of the Mexican American population
in the United States has resided, and continues to reside, in the Southwest one
can assume with a certain degree of confidence that the majority of "Hispanics"

executed in the Southwest are Mexican American (U. S. Bureau of the Census, 1991a, 1991b).

A DESCRIPTIVE PROFILE OF EXECUTED MEXICAN AMERICAN PRISONERS

Capital punishment has a long history in the Southwest. Deaths by hanging, firing squad, lethal gas, and electrocution are methods of execution that have been used in the Southwest. In her memoirs of life in early 1800s California, for example, Angustias de la Guerra Ord (1878) observed that lashing was often used as punishment with Mexican prisoners. From 1910 to 1916, and from 1918 to 1932, Arizona used hanging as the method of execution. Over the thirty-year period from 1933 to 1963, Arizona executed capital offenders using lethal gas. California hanged prisoners executed of capital crimes until 1937. Then, in August of that year, the gas chamber was relocated to San Quentin Prison and lethal gas was adopted as the official means of execution. Colorado hanged prisoners from 1890 to 1934, but eventually adopted lethal gas. New Mexico is the only southwestern state that used electrocution from 1933 to 1956 to put capital offenders to death. In 1960, however, New Mexico began using lethal gas. On June 19, 1969, New Mexico officially abolished the death penalty except for prisoners convicted of killing police officers or for prisoners convicted of multiple murders. Presently, Colorado, New Mexico, and Texas use lethal injection to execute prisoners. Arizona and California still use lethal gas. California, however, may soon adopt lethal injection as its official method of execution since death by lethal gas is being challenged in the courts as a cruel form of punishment.

Table 2 is a summary of the total number of Mexican American prisoners executed in the Southwest by state and decade from 1795 to 1987. Our list comprises the number of Mexican American prisoners executed under state, federal, military, and territorial authority. There were no Mexican American prisoners executed in the United States under local authority during this period. In Table 2 we identify four distinct developmental periods in the history of Mexican American executions in the Southwest. A "growth" period begins on January 10, 1795, with the execution of a prisoner surnamed Rochine by firing squad under military authority for murder in the territorial region of California. We have labeled this period "growth" because the number of Mexican American prisoners executed over this period progressively increases. The "growth" period ended with the hanging of a prisoner surnamed Juarez for murder in California on May 10, 1867. There was a total of 49 Mexican Americans executed during this period. The total accounts for 20.1% of all Mexican American prisoners executed in the Southwest.

In Table 2 we identify a period of "stability" in Mexican American executions in the Southwest from the 1880s through the 1930s. We refer to this execution phase as "stability" because the number of Mexican American executions is stable throughout the period. The hanging of a 17 year old prisoner surnamed Domingues for murder in Arizona on November 26, 1880, ushered

TABLE 2   295

Mexican American Executions in the Southwest by State and Decade, 1795–1987

Adalberto
Aguirre, Jr., and
David V. Baker

Decade	Arizona N	%	California N	%	Colorado N	%	New Mexico N	%	Texas N	%	Regional Totals N	%	Developmental Period
1790s	0	0	1	1.2	0	0	0	0	0	0	1	0.4	
1800s	0	0	1	1.2	0	0	0	0	0	0	1	0.4	
1810s	0	0	0	0	0	0	0	0	0	0	0	0	
1820s	0	0	0	0	0	0	0	0	0	0	0	0	Period
1830s	0	0	3	3.7	0	0	0	0	0	0	3	1.2	of
1840s	0	0	6	7.3	0	0	0	0	0	0	6	2.5	Growth
1850s	0	0	9	11.0	0	0	1	2.4	4	5.2	14	5.7	
1860s	0	0	4	4.9	0	0	3	7.1	1	1.3	8	3.3	
1870s	2	6.9	4	4.9	1	7.1	0	0	9	11.7	16	6.6	
1880s	2	6.9	6	7.3	3	21.5	4	9.5	9	11.7	24	9.8	Period of
1890s	0	0	4	4.9	2	14.4	12	28.6	5	6.5	23	9.4	Stability
1900s	5	17.2	4	4.9	0	0	5	11.9	10	13.0	24	9.8	
1910s	9	31.0	5	6.1	0	0	9	21.4	8	10.4	31	12.7	Peak Decade
1920s	5	17.2	11	13.4	1	7.1	6	14.3	5	6.5	28	11.5	
1930s	3	10.3	7	8.5	5	35.7	1	2.4	13	16.8	29	11.9	
1940s	1	3.5	6	7.3	0	0	1	2.4	6	7.8	14	5.7	
1950s	1	3.5	7	8.5	1	7.1	0	0	0	0	9	3.7	Period
1960s	1	3.5	4	4.9	1	7.1	0	0	1	1.3	7	2.9	of
1970s	0	0	0	0	0	0	0	0	0	0	0	0	Decline
1980s	0	0	0	0	0	0	0	0	6	7.8	6	2.5	
Totals	29	100.0	82	100.0	14	100.0	42	100.0	77	100.0	244	100.0	

in the "stability" period; and the electrocution of a 24 year old farmhand surnamed Salazar for murder in Texas on December 16, 1939, brought an end to the "stability" period. During this period there were 159 Mexican American executions, accounting for 65.1% of all Mexican American prisoners executed in the Southwest.

Except for the peak decade of the 1910s when 31 Mexican American prisoners were executed, there were about 26 Mexican American prisoners executed per decade over this sixty year period. There were 24 Mexican American executions conducted per decade from the 1880s to the 1900s, increasing to thirty-one executions in the 1910s, decreasing to twenty-eight executions in the 1920s, and again increasing to twenty-nine executions in the 1930s. Texas executed 50 Mexican American prisoners from the 1880s through the 1930s. The number of Mexican American executions in Texas during this period accounts for 64.9% of all Mexican American prisoners executed in Texas. Arizona and New Mexico, however, executed the largest percentage of their total number of Mexican American prisoners during the period with 82.6% and 88.1% respectively.

The 1910s is a "peak" execution period for Mexican American prisoners in the Southwest. Thirty-one Mexican American prisoners were executed during this period. The 31 executions account for nearly 13% of the total number of Mexican American prisoners executed in the Southwest. About half of the Mexican American executions conducted during the 1910s occurred over a two-year period from 1915 to 1916. Of the 31 Mexican American prisoners executed during the 1910s, 28 were hanged for murder, 2 were hanged for rape-murder, and 1 was hanged for robbery-murder.

During the "peak" period in Mexican American executions, New Mexico hanged six Mexican bandits (designated occupation) on two separate days in June 1916. None of the ages of these bandits are known, but their surnames were Alvarez, Castillo, Garcia, Rangel, Renteria, and Sanchez. Five of the 31 Mexican American prisoners executed during the 1910s were conducted under the territorial jurisdiction of Arizona between 1910 and 1911. A boy surnamed Sanchez was the youngest Mexican American prisoner executed in this period (1910s). Sanchez was fifteen years old at the time of his hanging in Texas. His execution date was March 3, 1915, and his occupation was noted as "jail prisoner."

A period of "decline" in the number of Mexican American executions occurred from the 1940s to the 1980s. Over this fifty year period there were 36 Mexican American prisoners executed in the Southwest. California and Texas conducted the most executions of Mexican Americans, seventeen and thirteen respectively. The number of executions performed during this period account for 14.8% of the total number of Mexican American prisoners executed in the Southwest from 1795 to 1987. A prisoner surnamed Moreno was the last Mexican American executed in this period of "decline." Moreno died from lethal injection in Texas on March 4, 1987, for murder. He was a 27 year old lawn mower repairman.

Taken together, Tables 3, 4 and 5 provide information on Mexican American executions conducted by each state in the Southwest. In Table 3 we have tabulated the year in which each state entered the union to determine the years in which Mexican American prisoners were executed under territorial authority rather than state authority. Table 3 shows that Arizona executed 29 Mexican American prisoners between 1873 and 1963. A detailed analysis of the 29 executions shows that Arizona executed 14 Mexican American prisoners under territorial jurisdiction during the 39 year pre-statehood period from 1873 to 1912. As a result, nearly half of all the executions of Mexican American prisoners in Arizona were conducted before it became a state and entered the union. Bowers (1974) reports that Arizona abolished the death penalty from 1916 to 1918. The Espy File data reveals, instead, that the period of abolition actually lasted from July 1916 to April 1920 for Mexican American prisoners. The abolition period began with the hanging of a 39 year old smelter surnamed Peralta for murder on July 7, 1916. Arizona ended its 33 month hiatus on state executions with the hanging of a 24 year old shepherd surnamed Torrez for murder on April 16, 1920. Arizona executed fifteen more Mexican American prisoners from 1921 to 1963.

By the time California entered the union in 1850, eleven Mexican American prisoners had been executed in the region. All of the executions were conducted under military jurisdiction and occurred between January 1795 and August 1847. Four of the Mexican American prisoners were executed for murder, three for robbery-murder, one for rape-murder, one for sodomy-buggery-bestiality, and two for theft-stealing. The ages of all but one, an eighteen year old, of these prisoners are unknown. Three of the Mexican American prisoners executed during this period were military personnel (soldiers) and one was a servant.

TABLE 3

Executions in the Southwest

Adalberto Aguirre, Jr., and David V. Baker

		Arizona	California	Colorado	New Mexico	Texas
Year of Statehood		1912	1850	1876	1912	1845
Period of Exeuctions		1865–1963	1778–1967	1859–1967	1851–1960	1819–1987
Period of Mexican American Executions		1873–1963	1795–1963	1879–1967	1851–1946	1850–1987
Period of Abolition		1916–1918	None	1897–1901	1969–Present	None
Number of Non Mexican American Executions	N	75	627	87	31	702
	%	72.1	88.4	86.2	42.5	90.1
Number of Mexican American Executions	N	29	82	14	42	77
	%	27.9	11.6	13.8	57.5	99
Missing Data in The Espy File on Mexican American Executions		Age=4 Occ=7	Crime=3 Age=28 Occ=45 Nam=1	Age=8 Occ=8	Crime=1 Age=39 Occ=26	Age=43 Occ=37 Name=2

California executed another 71 Mexican American prisoners after it became a state. Two of these executions were conducted under federal authority. On July 1, 1890, a man surnamed Osequeda was hanged for an unknown crime. Osequeda's age and occupation are unknown. The other federal execution of a Mexican American prisoner in California occurred on December 10, 1948, for murder. His surname was Ochoa. Ochoa was twenty-nine years old, his occupation was "criminal," and he died in the gas chamber at San Quentin prison.

Figure 1 presents the percentages of Mexican American executions in the Southwest by state between 1795 and 1987. One can observe in Figure 1 that California and Texas account for most of the Mexican American executions in the Southwest. Taken together, the 82 Mexican American prisoners executed in California, and the 77 Mexican American prisoners executed in Texas, comprise over 65% of all Mexican American prisoners executed in the Southwest. The twenty-nine executions of Mexican American prisoners conducted in Arizona comprise about 12% of all Mexican American prisoners executed in the South-

TABLE 4

*Characteristics of Mexican American Prisoners
Executed in the Southwest, 1795–1987*

State in Region	Arizona		California		Colorado		New Mexico		Texas		Regional Totals	
Category	N	%	N	%	N	%	N	%	N	%	N	%
Crime												
Murder	23	79.3	54	65.9	10	71.4	33	78.6	50	64.9	170	69.7
Rape	0	0	0	0	0	0	0	0	5	6.5	5	2.0
Robbery-Murder	6	20.7	17	20.7	2	14.3	7	16.7	11	14.3	43	17.6
Rape-Murder	0	0	4	4.9	2	14.3	1	2.4	7	9.1	13	5.3
Murder-Burglary	0	0	1	1.2	0	0	0	0	2	2.6	3	1.2
Rape-Robbery	0	0	0	0	0	0	0	0	2	2.6	2	0.9
Sodomy-Buggery-Bestiality	0	0	1	1.2	0	0	0	0	0	0	1	0.4
Theft-Steal	0	0	2	2.4	0	0	0	0	0	0	2	0.9
Unknown	0	0	3	3.7	0	0	1	2.4	0	0	4	1.6
Method												
Hanging	24	82.8	55	67.1	8	57.1	40	95.2	47	61.0	174	71.3
Lethal Gas	5	17.2	16	19.5	6	42.9	0	0	0	0	27	9.8
Firing Squad	0	0	11	13.4	0	0	0	0	0	0	11	4.5
Electrocution	0	0	0	0	0	0	2	4.8	24	31.2	26	10.6
Injection	0	0	0	0	0	0	0	0	6	7.8	6	2.5
Sex												
Male	29	100	81	98.8	14	100	41	97.6	76	98.7	241	98.8
Female	0	0	1	1.2	0	0	1	2.4	1	1.3	3	1.2
Jurisdiction												
State	15	51.7	69	84.1	14	100	18	42.9	76	98.7	192	78.7
Federal	0	0	2	2.4	0	0	0	0	1	1.3	3	1.2
Territorial	14	48.3	0	0	0	0	24	57.1	0	0	38	15.6
Military	0	0	11	13.4	0	0	0	0	0	0	11	4.5
Age												
Average Age	28.8	–	32.2	–	34.6	–	22.3	–	27.7	–	29.2	–
Unknown	4	13.8	28	34.1	8	57.1	39	92.9	43	55.8	122	50.0

west. New Mexico executed 42 Mexican American prisoners, which accounts for about 17% of all Mexican American prisoners executed in the Southwest. The 14 Mexican American prisoners executed in Colorado represent the smallest percentage, nearly 6%, of all Mexican American prisoners executed in the Southwest.

Figure 1 also shows that Mexican American executions constitute noticeable proportions of the total number of prisoners executed in Arizona and New Mexico between 1795 and 1987. Mexican American executions comprise nearly 30% of all prisoners executed in Arizona, and nearly 60% in New Mexico. Mexican American executions constitute about 12% of all prisoners executed in California, nearly 14% in Colorado, and about 10% in Texas.

CHARACTERISTICS OF EXECUTED MEXICAN AMERICAN PRISONERS

In Table 4 we present a summary of characteristics for executed Mexican American prisoners in the Southwest from 1795 to 1987. In terms of the criminal offenses for which Mexican American prisoners were executed in the Southwest, one can note in Table 4 that crimes involving murder comprise the category of offense for which nearly 94% of all Mexican American prisoners were executed. Rape and rape-robbery comprise the second category of crime for which Mexican Americans were executed. Nearly 3% of all Mexican American prisoners were executed for rape or rape-robbery. These figures are similar to the percentages of prisoners executed for similar crimes outside the Southwest. The Espy File, for example, shows that nearly 80% of all prisoners executed in the United States were executed for murder and crimes involving murder, and nearly 7% were executed for rape and crimes involving rape.

Method of Execution

In Table 4 one can note that hanging was the most frequent method of execution in the Southwest. About 71% of all Mexican American prisoners executed in the Southwest were hanged. Nearly 11% of Mexican American prisoners were executed using electrocution. These percentages are similar to the percentages found in the general population of executed prisoners in the United States. The Espy File shows, for example, that hanging has been the method of execution used to execute about 64% of all prisoners in the United States. About 30% of the executed prisoners have been electrocuted. Other methods of execution not used in the Southwest but that prevailed in other parts of the country include pressing, breaking on the wheel, burning, hung in chains, bludgeoned, and gibbeted (Aguirre & Baker, 1991). According to the Espy File, these outrageous methods of execution were most often used with African slaves.

Gender

According to Table 4, three female Mexican American prisoners were executed in the Southwest between 1795 and 1987. The first Mexican American female prisoner was hanged in July 1851 in California for murder. Her name was listed as Juanita. Here age, occupation, and the day of execution are unknown. Ten years later, under the jurisdictional authority of the New Mexico territory, a woman named Angel was hanged for murder on April 26. Her age and occupation are unknown. The last Mexican American female prisoner executed in the Southwest was hanged on November 13, 1863, for robbery-murder. Her surname is listed as Rodriquez. Her age is unknown, but her occupation was listed as innkeeper. According to the Espy File, there were 357 female prisoners executed in the United States, accounting for 2.5% of all executed prisoners. Schneider and Smykla (1991) found that the majority (87%) of female prisoners executed in the United States occurred pursuant to local authority before 1866.

Jurisdiction

Jurisdictional authority is historically important in the administration of capital punishment in the United States. The transfer of execution authority

FIGURE 1

Mexican American Executions in the Southwest by State, 1795–1987

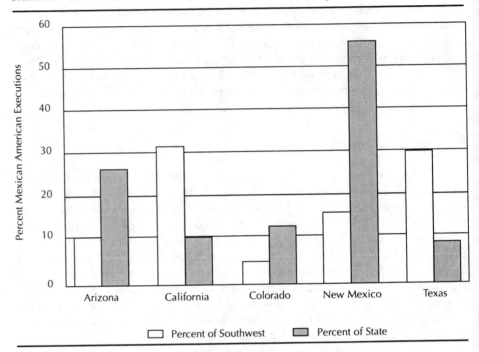

from local to state jurisdictions was a fundamental movement in the imposition of the death penalty in the United States (Bowers, 1974). States began to require that executions be conducted under state authority with the introduction of the state prison system. Although the first state imposed execution occurred as early as 1853 in the District of Columbia, states did not begin to execute capital offenders routinely until the 1890s. Local executions decreased through the decades as state executions increased. For example, according to Bowers (1974) local executions decreased from 87% of all executions in the 1890s to no executions since the 1960s. In contrast, state executions increased from 13% of all executions in the 1890s to accounting for all executions in the 1960s.

Table 4 shows that nearly 79% of all Mexican American executions in the Southwest were administered pursuant to state authority. About 16% were territorial executions. Taken together, federal and military executions constitute about 6% of all Mexican American executions in the Southwest. There were no Mexican American prisoners executed under local, Indian Tribunal, or Courts of Admiralty jurisdiction. These figures coincide with the percentages of jurisdictional authority over executions in the Espy File. For example, 87% of all executions in the United States from 1608 to 1987 were state executions. Military and Courts of Admiralty executions comprised about 8% of the executions in the U. S., federal executions about 2%, and Indian Tribunal executions about

0.3%. There was one local execution conducted in Texas on September 25, 1951, of a White restaurant owner surnamed Mitchell.

Age

In Table 4 one can note the mean age at execution of Mexican American prisoners. With half of the information on the age of Mexican American prisoners in the Southwest missing, it is difficult to accurately determine the average age of executed prisoners. For those Mexican American prisoners whose age is known, the average age at the time of execution is 29.2 years. The mean age of Mexican American prisoners executed in the Southwest is considerably lower than the mean age of all executed prisoners in the Espy File, 32.6 years.

Occupation

The Espy File identifies the occupation of prisoners executed in the United States at the time of their execution. We have tabulated occupational categories for executed Mexican American prisoners in Table 5. Table 5 shows that the occupation for half of the Mexican American prisoners executed in the Southwest is unknown. For those prisoners whose occupation is known, Table 5 shows that most Mexican American prisoners are in the following categories: laborers not involved in farm production (16.8%), farm workers (12.3%), or criminals (11.5%). About 8% of the prisoners comprised other occupational categories.

CONCLUDING REMARKS

Our purpose in this article has been to construct a descriptive profile of Mexican American prisoners executed in the Southwest. We have created a sample of Mexican American prisoners executed in the Southwest from data available in the Espy File. We have noted in our discussion regarding sample construction that conceptual limitations arise from the use of either Spanish language use or Spanish surname as a principal means of ethnic identification. We suspect that the racial category of "Hispanic" was used in the Espy File as an inclusive category for persons from Mexico, Central and Latin America. In order to enhance the specificity of our sample identification to *Mexican Americans,* we cross-referenced Spanish surname with racial identity. In addition, given that the majority of the Mexican American population in the United States has resided and continues to reside in the Southwest, we gain a degree of confidence that our constructed sample consists primarily of Mexican Americans. No doubt constraints are still present in our constructed sample. However, it is a suitable approach to the construction of a sample from a secondary data source.

The descriptive profile we have constructed in this article also addresses the lack of documentation regarding the execution of Mexican American prisoners. We have noted in this article that researchers have suggested that the

TABLE 5

*Occupation of Mexican American Prisoners
Executed in the Southwest, 1795–1987*

Occupational Group	Arizona		California		Colorado		New Mexico		Texas		Regional Totals	
	N	%	N	%	N	%	N	%	N	%	N	%
Managers	0	0	0	0	0	0	0	0	1	1.3	1	0.4
Sales Workers	0	0	0	0	1	7.1	0	0	1	1.3	2	0.8
Craft	3	10.3	1	1.2	0	0	0	0	3	3.9	7	2.9
Operatives	1	3.4	0	0	0	0	1	2.4	1	1.3	3	1.2
Service Workers	1	3.4	2	2.4	0	0	1	2.4	2	2.6	6	2.5
Laborers	10	34.4	20	24.4	2	14.2	1	2.4	8	10.4	41	16.8
Farm Workers	4	13.7	5	6.1	2	14.2	5	11.9	14	18.2	30	12.3
Criminals	3	10.3	6	7.3	1	7.1	8	19.1	10	12.3	28	11.5
Soldier	0	0	3	3.7	0	0	0	0	0	0	3	1.2
Unknown	7	24.1	45	54.9	8	47.1	26	61.9	37	48.0	123	50.4
Totals	29	100.0	82	100.0	14	100.0	42	100.0	77	100.0	244	100.0

Manager–innkeeper; *Sales Workers*–rug peddler, appliance salesman; *Craft*–carpenter, lawnmower repairman, welder, musician, plumber; *Operatives*–fork lift operator, lumbermill worker, smelterer; *Service Workers*–dishwasher, domestic servant, school guard, servant, gardner, bartender; *Laborers* (excluding farm)–boxer, laborer, painter's helper, ranch hand, railroad worker, WPA worker, construction worker, migrant worker, miner, warehouse worker; *Farm Worker*–migrant farm worker, farm hand/laborer, goat herder, shepherd, farmer, cowhand; *Criminals*–bandit, bandit leader, Mexican bandit, bootlegger, gang member, jail prisoner, parolee, convict, ex-convict, asylum escapee, criminal. Totals may not add to 100% due to rounding.

study of executed Mexican American prisoners has been ignored because the criminological literature focuses on black-white racial differences (Holmes & Daudistel, 1984; Romero & Stelzner, 1985). The descriptive profile we have constructed thus augments the research record regarding Mexican American executions. In particular, the descriptive profile documents the existence of Mexican American executions as a social fact in the Southwest.

Finally, the descriptive profile we have constructed in this article is a valuable tool for addressing other research questions. One can ask whether the execution of Mexican American prisoners in the Southwest is associated with socioeconomic factors similar to the execution of Blacks in the South (Aguirre & Baker, 1991). For example, is the flow of Mexican immigrants into the Southwest and the demand for low wage labor in the Southwest associated with temporal periods in the execution of Mexican American prisoners? Are there extra-legal factors associated with the execution of Mexican American prisoners in the Southwest? In a preliminary analysis of execution data in the Southwest, for example, Aguirre and Baker (1989) have noted that executed Mexican American prisoners had a lower rate of appeal than either black or white prisoners. They have suggested that the lower rate of appeal for Mexican American prisoners may reflect the operation of an extra-legal factor, limited ability to communicate in English with the criminal justice system. The descriptive profile constructed in this paper thus opens a window for asking questions that increase our understanding of Mexican Americans and their interaction with the criminal justice system.

9.3 MARC MAUER AND TRACY HULING

Young Black Americans and the Criminal Justice System

One illustration of the relationship between Blacks and the criminal justice system in the United states is their *representativeness* within the criminal justice system. Social researchers use *representativeness* for determining the extent to which a minority (non-White) population is overrepresented in the criminal justice system compared with its numerical size in the general population. Criminal justice statistics, for example, show that Black males are far more likely to enter the criminal justice process than White males. In addition, the overrepresentation of a population in the criminal justice system permits researchers to examine the operation of extralegal factors, such as biased attitudes and perceptions, in the population's processing by the criminal justice system.

In the following selection from the Sentencing Project report *Young Black Americans and the Criminal Justice System: Five Years Later* (October 1995), Marc Mauer and Tracy Huling suggest that housing segregation, high unemployment rates, poor schooling, and high crime rates may explain much of the Black overrepresentation in the criminal justice system.

Key Concept: African American males in the criminal justice system

*I*n 1990, The Sentencing Project released a report that documented that almost one in four (23%) African American males in the age group 20–29 was under some form of criminal justice supervision—in prison or jail, on probation or parole. That report received extensive national attention and helped to generate much dialogue and activity on the part of policymakers, community organizations, and criminal justice professionals.

Despite these efforts, many of the factors contributing to the high rates of criminal justice control for African American males remains unchanged or have worsened during the succeeding five years. Public policies ostensibly designed to control crime and drug abuse have in many respects contributed to the growing racial disparity in the criminal justice system while having little impact on the problems they were aimed to address.

The key findings of this report, as seen in Tables 1–3, are the following:

- Almost one in three (32.2%) young black men in the age group 20–29 is under criminal justice supervision on any given day—in prison or jail, on probation or parole.
- The cost of criminal justice control for these 827,440 young African American males is about $6 billion a year.
- In recent years, African American women have experienced the greatest increase in criminal justice supervision of all demographic groups, with their rate of criminal justice supervision rising by 78% from 1989–94.
- Drug policies constitute the single most significant factor contributing to the rise in criminal justice populations in recent years, with the number of incarcerated drug offenders having risen by 510% from 1983 to 1993.The number of Black (non-Hispanic) women incarcerated in state prisons for drug offenses increased more than eight-fold—828%—from 1986 to 1991.
- While African American arrest rates for violent crime—45% of arrests nationally—are disproportionate to their share of the population, this proportion has not changed significantly for twenty years. For drug offenses, though, the African American proportion of arrests increased from 24% in 1980 to 39% in 1993, well above the African American proportion of drug users nationally.
- African Americans and Hispanics constitute almost 90% of offenders sentenced to state prison for drug possession.

The criminal justice control rates documented in this report should prove even more disturbing than those revealed five years go. Combined with the potential impact of current social and criminal justice policies, they attest to the gravity of the crisis facing the African American community.

The current high rates of criminal justice control are also likely to worsen considerably over the next several years. In addition to the steady twenty-year increase in criminal justice populations, the impact of current "get tough" policies in particular suggests continuing increases in criminal justice control rates and increasing racially disparate impacts.

CRIMINAL JUSTICE CONTROL
RATES IN THE 1990S

Our 1990 report documented shockingly high rates of criminal justice control for young African American males in particular. We find that many of the contributing factors to these high rates endure or have worsened in the intervening years. As a result, they have failed to slow the increasing rate of criminal justice control for young black males and they have contributed to a dramatic

TABLE 1

1994 Criminal Justice Control Rates

*Marc Mauer
and Tracy
Huling*

Population Group 20–29	State & Federal Prisons	Jails	Probation	Parole	Total	Criminal Justice Control Rate
Males						
White	180,915	110,585	640,956	136,620	1,069,076	6.7%
Black	211,205	95,114	351,368	130,005	787,692	30.2%
Hispanic	81,391	41,641	138,703	56,412	318,147	12.3%
Females						
White	9,875	11,872	177,360	15,802	214,909	1.4%
Black	12,138	10,876	96,481	14,921	134,416	4.8%
Hispanic	3,537	4,171	36,099	6,137	49,944	2.2%

rise in the number of black women in the criminal justice system. These factors include:

- The continuing overall growth of the criminal justice system;
- The continuing disproportionate impact of the "war on drugs" on minority populations;
- The new wave of "get tough" sentencing policies and their potential impact on criminal justice populations;
- The continuing difficult circumstances of life for many young people living in low-income urban areas in particular.

1994 Criminal Justice Control Rates

The data below represent estimates of the numbers of persons in each demographic group under criminal justice control—in prison or jail, or on probation or parole—on a given day in 1994.

- As seen in Table 1, as of 1994, 30.2% of African American males in the age group 20–29 were under criminal justice control—prison, jail, probation, or parole—on any given day. This represented an increase of 31% from the figures of 1989.
- These data all examine criminal justice control rates *on any given day.* If we were able to examine the flow of people through the criminal justice system over the course of a year or ten-year period, the rates would obviously be much higher. Other researchers have attempted to calculate these rates. A 1987 study by Robert Tillman found that ⅔ of black males in California had been arrested between the ages of 18 and 29, double the rate for white males.

TABLE 2

African American Male Control Rates (Ages 20–29)

Year	Number	Control Rate
1989	609,690	23.0%
1994	787,692	30.2%
1995	827,440	32.2%

- These figures only reflect arrest rates through the early 1980s, well before the dramatic rise in drug arrests and criminal justice populations overall. More recently, researchers at Northwestern University have estimated that it is possible that $1/3$–$2/3$ of the 100,000 poorest black male three-year olds of today will eventually end up in prison.

1995 Criminal Justice Control Rate for African American Males

Using the annual rate of increase for criminal justice populations overall from 1989 to 1994 as a basis, we have calculated the estimated rate of control of young black males for 1995 as well. As seen in Table 2, these estimates suggest that almost one in three young black men is now under criminal justice supervision on any given day. Based on average costs for various components of the criminal justice system, we estimate that the cost of criminal justice control for these 827,440 males is about $6 billion a year.

Changes in Criminal Justice Control Rates, 1989–1994

As seen in Table 3, the largest increase of the demographic groups studied in this period is for black women whose numbers increased from 78,417 in 1989 to 134,416 by 1994 and whose rate of criminal justice control increased by 78% during this period. We believe that much of this increase is due to the impact of the "war on drugs..."

THE OVERREPRESENTATION OF YOUNG BLACK MALES IN THE CRIMINAL JUSTICE SYSTEM

We have documented the dramatically high rates of criminal justice control for young black men. In many respects it would be quite surprising if these rates were not high, given the social and economic circumstances and crime rates in their communities.

The growth of the criminal justice system in the past twenty years has coincided with a host of economic disruptions and changes in social policy

TABLE 3

Changes in Criminal Justice Control Rates: 1989–1994 (Ages 20–29)

*Marc Mauer
and Tracy
Huling*

Population Group	1989 Control Rate	1994 Control Rate	% Increase
Males			
White	6.2%	6.7%	8%
Black	23.0%	30.2%	31%
Hispanic	10.4%	12.3%	18%
Females			
White	1.0%	1.4%	40%
Black	2.7%	4.8%	78%
Hispanic	1.8%	2.2%	18%

that have had profound effects on income distribution, employment and family structure. Since the 1970s, many urban areas have witnessed the decline of manufacturing, the expansion of low-wage service industries and the loss of a significant part of the middle class tax base. Real wages have declined for most Americans during this period, with a widening of the gap between rich and poor beginning in the 1980s. For black male high school dropouts in their twenties, annual earnings fell by a full 50 percent from 1973 to 1989. Social service benefits such as mental health services and other supports have generally declined while the social problems that they address have been exacerbated.

The impact of these changes on the African American community has resulted from the intersection of race and class effects. Since African Americans are disproportionately represented in low-income urban communities, the effects of these social ills are intensified. As Douglas Massey and Nancy Denton have illustrated, the persistence of housing segregation exacerbates the difficult life circumstances of these communities, contributing to extremely high rates of unemployment, poor schooling, and high crime rates.

Over the years many researchers have examined the extent to which racial disparity within the criminal justice system can be explained by higher crime rates among blacks or other relevant factors. Historically, there can be little doubt about the prominent role played by race in criminal justice processing, given the history of lynching in the South, the development of chain gangs, and the well-documented racial patterns involved in the imposition of the death penalty.

More recently, though, researchers have found that the evidence on these issues is mixed. While some studies have documented specific cases of racially unwarranted outcomes, much research has concluded that, with one significant exception, race plays a relatively minor role in sentencing and incarceration. Michael Tonry's review, for example, concludes that "for nearly a decade there has been a near consensus among scholars and policy analysts that most of the black punishment disproportions result not from racial bias or discrimination within the system but from patterns of black offending and of blacks' criminal records." Similarly, Alfred Blumstein's research has concluded that 76 percent of the racial disparity in prison populations is explained by higher rates of offending among blacks for serious offenses.

But both authors find, as Tonry indicates, that "Drug law enforcement is the conspicuous exception. Blacks are arrested and confined in numbers grossly out of line with their use or sale of drugs." Blumstein concludes that for drug offenses, fully half of the racial disproportions in prison are not explained by higher arrest rates.

While scholars will continue to study the relative influence of race within the criminal justice system, several key issues should not go unaddressed in explaining these disparities. First, as noted above, it is difficult to isolate the relative influence of race and class in public policy and decisionmaking. That is, to the extent that African Americans are overrepresented in the criminal justice system, to what degree is this a function of their being disproportionately low-income?

In its comprehensive examination of the problem of violence, the National Research Council reviewed existing studies of homicide victimization and class. The Council found that among low-income populations blacks had much higher rates of homicide victimization than whites but that among higher income groups, there was essentially no difference. The Council suggests that the more concentrated effects of inner-city poverty may contribute to a more serious breakdown of family and community support than in other low-income neighborhoods.

Studies of sentencing practices reveal that the current offense and the offender's prior record are the most significant factors determining a prison sentence. But if low-income youth are more subject to policy scrutiny and have fewer counseling and treatment resources available to them than middle class adolescents, their youthful criminal activities will more likely result in a criminal record that will affect their chances of going to prison later on.

The most prominent example of the intersection of race and class in criminal justice processing, of course, is the O. J. Simpson case. Regardless of where one stands on his guilt or innocence, what is clear is that a wealthy and famous African American was able to assemble a very formidable defense. This is contrasted with the typical scene in almost every courthouse in cities across the country, where young African American and Hispanic males are daily processed through the justice system with very limited resources devoted to their cases.

Comparing sentencing policies in the U.S. with those of other nations sheds light on this issue as well. Although it is difficult to make comparisons across cultures, a number of studies have concluded that American sentencing policies tend to be harsher than those of many European nations, particularly regarding the length of sentence imposed for various crimes. Given the relatively greater homogeneity of many European countries one can ask whether policymakers and the public in these nations are less willing to lock up their fellow citizens for long periods of time since they view their societies as more cohesive....

IMPACT OF HIGH RATES OF CONTROL ON THE AFRICAN AMERICAN COMMUNITY

The high rate of incarceration of African American males raises concerns about its impact not only on the individuals who are incarcerated, but on their communities, as well. As increasing numbers of young black men are arrested and incarcerated, their life prospects are seriously diminished. Their possibilities for gainful employment are reduced, thereby making them less attractive as marriage partners and unable to provide for children they father. This in turn contributes to the deepening of poverty in low-income communities.

The large scale rates of incarceration may contribute to the destruction of the community fabric in other ways as well. As prison becomes a common experience for young males, its stigmatizing effect is diminished. Further, gang or crime group affiliations on the outside may be reinforced within the prison only to emerge stronger as the individuals are released back to the community. With so few males in underclass communities having stable ties to the labor market, the ubiquitous ex-offenders and gang members may become the community's role models.

The cumulative impact of these high rates of incarceration has been to postpone the time at which large numbers of African American males start careers and families. While we should not ignore the fact that these men have committed crimes that led to their imprisonment, current crime control policies may actually be increasing the severity of the problem, particularly when other options for responding to crime exist. . . .

PROJECTIONS FOR THE FUTURE

The criminal justice system has experienced unprecedented growth for more than twenty years. Since 1973, the number of inmates in prisons and jails nationally has quadrupled, and the United States is now second in the world only to Russia in its rate of incarceration. Probation and parole populations have increased dramatically as well, rising by 173% in the period 1980–94.

These dramatic increases, along with the fiscal and human costs entailed, might make one think that the end of this cycle might be in sight. A look at recent policy changes, though, shows that, if anything, these problems may be exacerbated in coming years.

In recent years, the federal government and many states have adopted a variety of harsh sentencing policies. Among the most prominent of these have been the "Three Strikes and You're Out" policies, adopted by the federal system and fourteen states. These laws generally provide for a sentence of life without parole upon a third conviction for a violent felony.

While it is too early to assess the full consequences of these laws, it is already clear that there will be a broad variation in their impact on prison populations. In Washington state, for example, the first state to adopt such a policy in 1993, fewer than two dozen offenders were sentenced under its provisions during the first year of implementation.

In California, though, the law has already had a substantial impact on courts, jails and prisons during its first year of operation. The California law, the broadest of any state, requires a sentence of 25 years to life for an offender with two prior violent felony convictions who commits *any* third subsequent felony. Thus, in the well-publicized case of Jerry Williams, his third "strike" for stealing a slice of pizza from children at a boardwalk brought the same sentence as would a rape or armed robbery. The California Legislative Analyst's Office has estimated that the state prison population will rise from 125,000 in 1994 to 211,000 by 1999, largely as a result of the "Three Strikes" law.

Other policy changes are expected to have similarly large impacts. In Virginia, for example, parole has been abolished and violent offenders are now expected to serve up to 500% more time in prison than in the past. The combined impact of this policy along with other changes is projected to almost double the prison population from 27,000 in 1995 to 51,000 by 2005.

A 1995 survey of corrections officials by *Corrections Compendium* confirmed this anticipated rise in the prison population. State corrections officials estimated that their 1994 inmate populations would rise 51% by the year 2000.

The rise in prison populations is likely to be exacerbated as well by the impact of federal crime legislation passed by Congress in 1994 and another bill proposed in 1995. Under the prison funding provisions of these bills, "Truth in Sentencing" grants will be made available to states that enact sentencing policies that require violent offenders to serve 85% of their sentence before release. Currently, violent offenders serve an average of 48% of their sentence. One analysis of the 1995 legislation estimated that for every dollar states receive under the six-year funding cycle of the bill, they would spend $2–7 due to higher costs of incarceration.

An additional sobering factor that does not portend well for controlling the growth of the criminal justice system regards the demographics of crime. Since young males are responsible for a disproportionate amount of crime, the age distribution of the population has a significant effect on overall crime rates. Over the course of the next decade, the number of 15–19 year olds in the population will increase by 25%; for Hispanics, there will be a 47% rise in this group. Unless we see substantial changes both in criminal justice and social policy, we can anticipate increases in crime generated by the rise in the numbers of young males.

Disturbing as these anticipated increases appear, even more so is the potential impact on African American and Hispanic communities. A number of factors suggest that the rise in criminal justice populations may affect minority communities even more so than the population as a whole. For example, the initial impact of the "Three Strikes" law in California appears to be having a disproportionate impact on African Americans. An analysis of the first six months experience with the law in Los Angeles County found that African Americans constituted 57% of the third "strike" cases charged, compared to 31% of all felony cases.

As we have also seen, the impact of the "war on drugs" has fallen disproportionately on low-income African Americans. To the extent that current policies remain in place, change in these disparities in the coming years is unlikely.

Race and Ethnicity in Popular Culture and Community

On the Internet . . .

Sites appropriate to Part Four

The Center for Equal Opportunity, a nonprofit research institution, is a project of the Equal Opportunity Foundation. It sponsors conferences, supports research, and publishes policy briefs and monographs on issues related to race, ethnicity, assimilation, and public policy. The site includes information on racial preferences, immigration and assimilation, and multicultural education.

    http://www.ceousa.org/

This DePaul University site pursues the preservation, enrichment, and transmission of knowledge and cultures across a broad scope of academic disciplines and human endeavors. It includes resources on race, gender, religion, ethnicity, sexual orientation, size/weight, age, and disability. You can also submit questions to the Diversity Advice column.

    http://diversity.depaul.edu/forum.html

This site is an excellent resource of race, ethnic, and multicultural links. Over 80 sites are referenced, including minority and diversity links, African American resources, Asian American resources, Latin American resources, and Native American resources.

    http://mel.lib.mi.us/social/
      SOC-cultures.html

10.1 ROBERT STAPLES AND TERRY JONES

Culture, Ideology and Black Television Images

Since its inception in the late 1930s, television has portrayed minorities as culturally inferior and nonthreatening to White middle-class society. Such television shows as *Amos 'n' Andy, The Jeffersons, Chico and the Man,* and *The Lone Ranger* have consigned minorities to stereotypical roles. Even *The Cosby Show,* while effectively breaking long-accepted stereotypes of African Americans, failed to address issues of poverty and racism. In the present selection, Robert Staples and Terry Jones argue that American television continues to glorify White culture and to perpetuate the racial ideology that minority group members are second-class citizens.

Staples is a professor of sociology at the University of California, San Francisco, and the author of *The World of Black Singles: Changing Patterns of Male-Female Relations* (Greenwood Press, 1981). Jones is an associate dean and a professor of sociology at California State University, Hayward. His work has appeared in such journals as *The Western Journal of Black Studies* and *The Black Scholar.*

Key Concept: the mass media and racial ideology

THE LOOKING GLASS SELF

With the coming of television and the electronic revolution, the concern over the level and quality of black participation in the film and video industry has significantly escalated. From an early concern about getting blacks on television, that concern has expanded to include the quality of that participation. While the number of blacks has increased since they first began to appear on television in the late 1940s and early 1950s, the quality of their portrayals has been uneven.

The decade of the 1980s found elusive anything approaching a decent portrayal of black life and culture on television. The people who control what is shown on TV seem to believe that whites feel most comfortable with blacks playing the roles of fools, maids, funny men, and small time hustlers, and are most uncomfortable with blacks in romantic roles. For example, a recent survey of ABC television programming revealed that blacks are generally stereotyped, with 49 percent of all blacks playing roles of criminals, servants, entertainers, or athletes. Rarely are blacks portrayed a loving, sexual, sensitive, or cerebral people.

According to a recent A.C. Nielson survey, blacks watch television an average of 10 percent more than whites. Other Nielson Index figures indicate that by the time the average child has graduated from high school he will have viewed 15,000 hours of television. Since a good percentage of this 15,000 hours of viewing shows black people in a negatively, distorted light, it may not be unreasonable to argue that with all its promise, television serves no greater purpose than to create a false sense of superiority on the part of white people and a false sense of inferiority on the part of blacks.

In the pages that follow we will provide a historical overview of blacks in television, discuss the significance of black roles in television, examine white cultural ideology as it relates to black roles, and explore the impact television has on black culture.

TELEVISION: PROMISE AND REALITY

Television came on the American scene in the 1950s with great promise for what it could do to promote world harmony, peace, understanding, and goodwill. In his award winning book *Blacks and White TV, Afro-Americans in Television since 1948,* J. Fred MacDonald captures the optimism of both blacks and whites for the potential of television as a great unifier. He writes:

> Television had the potential to reverse centuries of unjust ridicule and misinformation. In terms of utilization of black professional talent, and in the portrayal of Afro-American characters, TV as a new medium had the capability of ensuring a fair and equitable future.

Since television was controlled by the same groups that controlled radio, i.e., ABC, CBS, and NBC, this optimism may have been somewhat naive, given their track records in the portrayal of blacks. Radio had a long history of confining black talent to demeaning roles. To obtain steady employment on radio or in film, blacks were relegated to roles of Uncle Toms, Aunt Jemimahs, or dancing dandies and these roles worked to foster the image of blacks as loyal, child-like and semi-human. Television, the medium, may have been new, but those

who controlled it were products of a racist society and, as such, found themselves trapped by the cultural, political, economic, and social ideology of that
same society. It would be unreasonable to expect that the product of television
would somehow escape the human limitation of its managers, producers, and
advertisers.

Blacks were there in the beginning of television and, while there was great hope
for progress in race relations through television, actual practice fell far short of
this dream. In the early days of television, blacks were more likely to appear
on television in some musical context and usually as a guest, not a regular. In
addition to the dancing and singing black guests who appeared on television,
the next most popular format for the black entertainer was that of subservient
clown. In short, blacks were allowed to appear on television as long as their
roles fostered the traditional stereotypes of blacks as happy, carefree, musical
and lazy. Fitting this mood almost perfectly were such television characters as
Rochester on the *Jack Benny Show,* Louise the maid on *The Danny Thomas Show*
and Willi on the *Trouble With Father Show* of the early 1950s. These roles had
previously been made famous on radio by such people as Eddie "Rochester"
Anderson, Butterfly McQueen, Ruby Dandridge and Lillian Randolph.

When the promise of television settled into its reality, the demeaning
stereotypes of black characterizations became commonplace. Despite the efforts of such personalities as Ed Sullivan, Steve Allen, Arthur Godfrey, and
Milton Berle to showcase blacks in a positive and non-stereotypical light, the
die had been cast, and the black stereotype had won out over multidimensional
black humanity. Two of the most notable examples of the stereotyping of blacks
are found in the *Amos and Andy Show* and *The Little Rascals,* a successful television attempt to revise the film shorts of the *Our Gang* series of the 1920s and
1930s.

RACIST STEREOTYPES

While there are many examples of television's insensitivity to the need for honest and realistic portrayals of black characters, one very good example of this
phenomena is that of the *Little Rascals* series. The intent of *Our Gang*, as the
original 221 film episodes were known, was to capture the innocence of "just
plain kids" in a film series. Though the series may have partially accomplished
that goal, it also perpetuated racial stereotypes through the characters of Sun-
shine Sammy, Stymie, and Buckwheat. The series was laced with examples of
these black characters acting out negative stereotypes. Examples include rolling
their eyes, being frightened to the point that their hair would stand on end, and
uttering lines almost always meant to demean. In short, the black characters
on the *Little Rascals* almost invariably were cast in a way as to make fun of,
ridicule, or demean black people. Many whites may have found some joy in
these portrayals, but most blacks found them to be highly offensive.

However, it wasn't until the 1970s that civil rights groups were able to have an impact on the *Little Rascals* series. King Productions, who produced the series for television, realizing that the growing minority opposition to the *Little Rascals* might drive it off television, invested a great deal of time and money to re-edit the series. According to Maltin and Bann, Kind World Productions removed the racial and other gags that could be interpreted as being in bad taste. Maltin and Bann also note that:

> Some twenty-minute episodes were cut by as much as ten minutes, while others ("Little Daddy," "The Kid From Borneo," "A Tough Winter," "Lazy Days," "Little Sinner," "A Lad as a Lamp," "Moon and Groan, Inc.," "Big Ears") were eliminated from the TV package altogether.

The *Little Rascals*, shown at prime time for children, (Weekdays between 3:00 to 5:00 and Saturdays), has been a living monument to the film industry's inability or unwillingness to portray black characters as whole human beings.

In 1951 television unveiled the *Amos 'n' Andy* show to the American public. What many thought to be black characters were actually white. In fact, for radio and stage productions, using white actors to "imitate" blacks was a common occurrence. In the case of the *Amos 'n' Andy* show, its stars were Freeman Gosden and Charles Correll, two white radio men who perpetuated white stereotypes of blacks through "talking black." According to historians W. Augustus Law and Virgil Clift, the *Amos 'n' Andy* show, in spite of its stereotyped imagery, became a favorite of both black and white audiences during the 1920s and 1930s.

When the *Amos 'n' Andy* show was being prepared for national television, Gordon and Correll decided to use black actors to continue the stereotyped characters in the show. In spite of NAACP protests the show premiered in June 1951 on CBS television. MacDonald vividly reminds us that:

> The roles they sought to cast were classical minstrel figures. *Amos Jones* (played by Alvin Childress) was a low key, compliant Uncle Tom. He and his wife, Ruby, were an unhumorous twosome who tried to bring reason and level-headedness to bear upon rascalish Harlem friends. *Andy*, whose full name was Andrew Hogg Brown, was an easy going dimwit.... In *George "Kingfish" Stevens*, the show presented the stereotyped scheming "coon" character, whose chicanery left his pals distrustful, and the audience laughing. Added to the three mainstays were Kingfish's shrewd wife, *Saphire Stevens* and domineering mother-in-law, *Mama*, a feeble minded janitor, *Lightenin*, and a thoroughly disreputable lawyer, *Algonquin J. Calhoun*.

In effect, the *Amos 'n' Andy* television show brought the image of the old minstrel stereotype of blacks as slow, footshuffling, fun-loving, slightly dishonest people from the radio to television for all the world to see. Protests against the show (produced from 1951–1953) began even before the first television broadcast and continued until CBS agreed to withdraw it from circulation in 1966. While there were many defenders of the *Amos 'n' Andy* show, the critics, both black and white, objected to the program because of the way it negatively stereotyped black Americans and black American life.

The *Little Rascals* and the *Amos 'n' Andy* show were not the only programs with black characters during the early days of television but, some argue, the stereotypes they presented represented the worst of the lot. In continuing with the pattern of stereotyping blacks, ABC was the first network to star a black actress in her own regular television show. *Beulah*, starring Ethel Waters and later Louise Beavers, first broadcast in 1950 and while favorably received by the general public, was not devoid of stereotypes. *Beulah* was a maid for a white family and, as such, carried out the stereotype of the black woman as "mammie." She was warm, loving, caring, funny, and very dedicated to her white employer and their children.

In 1956, the *Nat King Cole Show* premiered on NBC. For the first time, on national television, a black man had his own show and was not portrayed as a clown. From the beginning the show met with problems and never really did well in the ratings. By 1957 the show died for lack of a sponsor. The speculation was that the American public was not yet ready for a black performer in other than a stereotyped role and that corporate sponsors were reluctant to back such a show out of fear of offending white audiences.

It took until 1965, but Bill Cosby, in the adventure series *I Spy*, demonstrated that the American public would accept a black actor in a non-stereotyped role. *I Spy*, starring Bill Cosby and Robert Culp, was televised on NBC from 1965 to 1968 and showed the black male in a rather positive manner. Cosby was the first black to star in a network series, and also the first black to win two Emmy Awards for best actor in a running series and the first to star in a series where race was not the control force. Though very successful, *I Spy* was not without its stereotypes. For example, Bill Cosby was cast as the trainer for a world class tennis player and rarely got romantically involved. Occasionally there was the illusion of romance when black guest starlets such as Pam Grier and Denise Nichols would appear on the show.

By the late 1960s with the civil rights movement in full swing, blacks were becoming commonplace on American television. Though their percentages on television never matched their percentages in the American population, there was the establishment of a definite black presence on American television. In addition to the above mentioned shows, Diahann Carroll, Teresa Graves, Leslie Uggams and Flip Wilson were given their own series. Couple this with such shows as *Room 222*, *Mission Impossible*, and *Beretta*, all of which had regular black supporting actors, and it began to appear that blacks were making progress in the television industry.

However, that progress was more apparent than real. The early 1970s was a period in which the white oligarchy regained the ideological initiative as a result of the waning of the civil rights movement. Bill Cosby's role in *I Spy* was that of a government spy, thus lending credence to espionage as a legitimate institution. Moreover, a disproportionate number of black television roles were as policemen, which had the effect of inculcating respect for law and order in order to counter black militancy in the streets. Thus, the trend toward the black situation comedies, which trivialized black oppression, were concomitant with the election of Richard Nixon, the white backlash, the macho white supremacy of Clint Eastwood and the emergence of Archie Bunker, all used as an antidote to the black movement.

During this same time-frame, black athletes became stars of television documentary events—the sports contest. Still, the impact of black domination in the sports arena was counteracted by the racist interpretation of their performance by an all-white reporting corps. Black excellence on the field was interpreted as a function of genetically endowed skills while white athletes were heralded as leaders, hard working and of stern moral character. This ebb and flow of black portrayals might be seen as a struggle for the hearts and minds of white America in response to the dynamics of the black community.

By the early 1970s American fell in love with the situation comedy and such shows as *Maude, All In The Family*, and the *Mary Tyler Moore Show*. Following close behind these shows were such programs as *That's My Mama, Good Times, Different Strokes*, and *What's Happening*. These shows either had all black casts or blacks in central roles, and they relied very heavily on a "black humor" that came dangerously close to being as demeaning and stereotypical, as the *Amos 'n' Andy* show. In fact, some argued that they were every bit as demeaning as *Amos 'n' Andy*.

But in the 1980s, continuing in this trend of stereotyping blacks on television, the networks brought us *Give Me a Break*, with Nell the live-in housekeeper and the *A-Team* with the very muscular Mr. T. The role of Nell is little more than that of a sophisticated mammy of earlier TV days, and the *A-Team's* Mr. T. casts a black male in the role of a super masculine menial, a brainless eunuch who is no real threat to the white male.

What appears to have happened, as we move into the latter part of the 20th century, is that we have gone full circle in terms of the roles blacks play on TV. From blacks in stereotyped, demeaning minstrel-like roles, to some attempt to portray blacks with some dignity and depth in the late 1950s and 1960s, back to the stereotypes and minstrel-like portrayals of the 1950s.

THE BILL COSBY SHOW

In this cyclical trajectory of black television history, there has been one significant exception. *The Bill Cosby Show*, the number one television show in America in 1984–85 was seen by some 30 million people a week. The show is about a middle class black family and that family's experiences. The show is a move away from stereotyping blacks. There is no ghetto, the family lives in a fashionable New York neighborhood, the father is in the home, and there are no drug deals or killings. *The Bill Cosby Show* has been an exceptional show and demonstrates that the American public will watch a television show about unstereotyped black Americans. On this point, Cosby notes:

> This is a major, major step, not just for American people but for those who control what goes on the air. The truth is in the numbers, and this helps straighten out nonbelievers concerning what an American audience will watch.

It is difficult to assess why the show is so popular, beyond the fact that Bill Cosby is an extraordinary talent. Some argue that the show is popular because of the universal appeal of the situation in which the family finds itself. It is a show featuring black people, but it is not a black show. Everyone can relate to the predicaments Dr. and Ms. Huxtable encounter with their five children. While critics argue that it is not black enough, does not deal with racism and poverty, or make a social statement, few can argue that it is not a move away from the demeaning stereotyping of black Americans.

CULTURE AND STEREOTYPES

In spite of *The Bill Cosby Show*, television has not been kind to black America. Its continual portrayal of black people in demeaning roles has had a negative impact on both black and white America. In order to understand white America's need to denigrate black America, it is necessary to examine white cultural ideology and its relationship to the television industry.

It is important to recognize that we live in a highly ethnocentric and racist society. Two Americas, if you will, one black and the other white. The social distance between the races results in distinct cultural differences between blacks and whites in America. Culture play a significant role in our perception of others and the world around us. Since we are influenced in our perception of others by our culture, it would appear that the greater the distance between cultures, the greater the room for misinterpretation, distortions, or negative perceptions to develop.

In short, one's culture is pretty much like road signs, or guides, or anchors; it helps to keep one on course. We rely heavily on these signs, guides, or anchors and in our daily lives use them to make our way. Usually, in a subconscious way, we judge other situations, other groups, and other individuals by these guides.

If there were equal power amongst the races these misperceptions would be unfortunate, sometimes painful, but in general they would probably balance out in some rough way. But the powerful, mostly whites in the United States, are so engrossed in their power and perpetuating it, that their perception of others, especially minorities is severely distorted. Karl Mannheim once noted:

> The ruling groups in their thinking become so intensely interest bound to a situation that they are simply no longer able to see certain facts which would undermine its sense of domination.

The mass media, especially television, has helped to perpetuate this ignorance and distortion. Harold Cruse, in *The Crisis of the Negro Intellectual observes that:*

> The mass media would seriously distort the Negro Cultural Image; make the Negro style banal and trivial, thus ripe for low level entertainment values; low originality; and intensify the cultural exploitation already at work.

Some of these distortions are out of ignorance based on cultural distance and difference. Others, no doubt, are based on ethnocentrism and racism and the need to maintain control and keep a social distance between the races.

Ralph Ellison makes this point another way when he states that white social scientists have generally accepted the stereotype of the black community, or Harlem, as "piss in the halls and blood on the stairs." While such stereotypes may hold some element of truth, they significantly oversimplify the richness and diversity of black life.

TELEVISION AND WHITE SUPREMACY

Television, controlled by American advertisers, regulated by the Federal Communications Commission, and influenced by the American public has chosen to adapt a white American cultural ideology based on the glorification of white norms, mores, and values. This ideology glorifies whiteness and demeans blackness by establishing, maintaining, and refining a society based on race and racial privilege. In television programming this is evident in the historical portrayal of blacks and other minorities in a patronizing, demeaning, childlike and stereotyped way. Television, then, like radio, and even newspapers support this white cultural ideology that works to maintain a status quo for black Americans as second class citizens.

The situation is no better for other minority groups. No lead character of any of the top entertainment shows is Hispanic, only three of the 264 speaking roles in the last year were played by Hispanic, and two-thirds of the Hispanic characters were cast as criminals. It was even worse for Asians in that none of the 173 major roles cast last year were portrayed by an Asian actor.

At work here is a not so subtle attempt to reinforce white domination through the medium of television. Prime time television watchers get a distorted view of the real world. More specifically, television is damaging to black children in that most of the people they see doing interesting and important things, are whites and, when black people are seen, it is likely to be in a stereotyped supportive role. The area of sex and romance, in particular, have been forbidden territory for the black actor. Until the... addition of Billie Dee Williams and Diahann Carroll on *Dynasty*, blacks have been virtually cast as sexual eunuchs on television. This absence of a love life for the black actor is another of the missing pieces of a fully developed role for blacks in television....

TELEVISION AS BUSINESS

It is incumbent upon us to remember that television is more than just fun and entertainment. It is big business....

Where there are large sums of money at stake, people tend to want an atmosphere of predictability and stability. Since television has become a vehicle for the generation of these large sums through advertising, it tends to be a rather timid, conservative and inoffensive medium. Advertisers, either directly or indirectly, influence the information presented in the media their dollars underwrite. The advertisers, in trying to match their products to programs the public will find satisfying, are quite conscious of public opinion, or at least they attempt to be. In the early days of television Ed Sullivan, Steve Allen, and Milton Berle were subjected to this type of pressure. MacDonald has noted that television producers were especially wary of their Southern audiences. Television executives, not wanting to alienate their southern white audiences, tried to avoid programs that cast black people in too favorable a light. While present day television executives have, no doubt, become more sophisticated over the years, they are still concerned about what television viewing audiences will find acceptable.

Most networks use some manner of marketing or survey research to determine just what the American public will find acceptable. Using a slightly different twist, networks, also want to make sure they present what they think the audience wants. The CBS network, at one time, used a British based company, TAPE Ltd. to evaluate television movies, with the thought that they knew just what the American public would find acceptable. One example of their conclusions was revealed in a *National Leader* article in October, 1982:

> It was revealed that TAPE uses a formula that deducts points for ideas whose central characters are Negroes, Jews, Italians, Mexicans, etc. . . . Thomas McManus, North American sales representative of TAPE, stated that if networks wanted to reach a mass audience, then they would need to take into consideration the fact that the mass audience is a white audience.

The conventional wisdom, supported by such information provided by companies like TAPE, has it that television and its advertisers, in attempting to sell to national markets should attempt to avoid themes that focus on minorities and certain controversial subjects.

Many years ago sociologist W.I. Thomas talked about the "self-fulfilling prophecy" or the Thomas theorem which in short states that "if men define situations as real, they are real in their consequences." It follows that if television executives are convinced that whites will not accept blacks on television, or will accept them only in certain stereotyped situations, blacks will routinely be denied opportunities for other kinds of roles, no matter what their qualifications.

In essence, the definition that whites impose on blacks has powerful social consequences because whites are in a position to translate the definition into reality. *The Bill Cosby Show*, with its all black cast, has challenged the traditional wisdom that a white audience will not buy a black show in which the characters are not placed in stereotyped roles. Is this the beginning of a breakthrough in television, or is it only an aberration? Only time will tell.

THE IMPACT OF TELEVISION ON BLACKS

It is difficult to make an overall assessment of the impact of television on blacks. The constant bombardment of white cultural ideology through television is bound to have had some impact. As has been noted, blacks watch more television than whites. The meaning of their greater television viewing habits has yet to be determined. Television is such a new force in our socialization process that we are still trying to measure its effect.

What is clear, however, is that 98 percent of all homes have television sets, and the average home watches six hours of television a day. Furthermore, by the time the average American child reaches eighteen years of age he has: watched 22,000 hours of TV, as compared to 11,000 hours of school; and seen 350,000 commercials.

The significance of such television viewing habits are summarized by Tony Brown:

1. Blacks are more likely than whites to use TV as a source of information when buying a product;
2. Blacks most often turn to TV rather than newspapers or other people for news of the black community;
3. Black adults prefer programs which feature blacks;
4. Blacks perceive TV as a representative of real life more than whites;
5. Black children learn aggressive behavior from TV role models and they are more likely to imitate a white role model than a black one;
6. Black adolescents are more likely than whites to use TV to learn how to behave with the opposite sex, to develop codes of social conduct.

Richard L. Allen, a researcher on minorities' use of television, takes exception with some of these findings. It is his belief that blacks do not watch television passively, that they tend to be critical of the programs they watch. From their perspective, blacks do not helplessly soak up all that is put before them and become puppets of white cultural ideology. They filter what they view, accepting some, intellectually filter out some other, and possibly accept still some other as just fun with no socially redeeming value.

Clearly television has certain negative impacts on the present conditions of 1980s black American. The greater frequency of television viewership, in part, is due to the high rate of unemployment among black males. According to Joe and Yu, about 46 percent of black males between the ages of 16-64, are not in the labor force. It is black males who form most of the black television audience since black women are least likely, of all groups, to watch television. The frequent television viewership of black males may have as one of its consequences the high illiteracy rate of that same group. People who watch television constantly are not developing or cultivating reading skills. Among black males the national illiteracy rate is 44 percent. That fact renders them largely ineffectual in the expanding sectors of the economy: service and information processing.

INDOCTRINATION BY TELEVISION

Television fare has no socially redeeming value, while inculcating negative social values in impressionable black youth. Because half of black families are headed by a single parent, many of them suffering from role overload, television often serves the role of custodian and socializer of black children.

What black children learn from television is that many people, primarily whites, live much better than they do. Television shows such as *Dallas* and *Dynasty* illuminate the opulence of America's bourgeoisie. Thus, they acquire the desire for material goods without the means (legitimate means, that is) for achieving them. However, the abundance of crime and violence on television shows teaches them there are illegitimate means for achieving the same goals. Since these same shows do not convey the consequences of criminal behavior, or transmit any sense of morality, black youth reaches the conclusion that it is morally acceptable and effective, to rob and murder people. Certainly, television must share some of the responsibility for the petty thefts, rapes and murders perpetrated by the television generation against the black community. . . .

CONCLUSION

The role of blacks in the media is a complex one. While constantly being told that blacks are not saleable to the white audience in music, films and television, the facts tell a different story. While *The Bill Cosby Show* is ranked number one among all shows in 1985, at least three other black shows held that ranking in the 1970s. The black shows have generally had higher ratings as a genre than comparable white television shows because they have attracted a vast white audience and keep a loyal black viewership. In fact, the most watched television program of all times, *Roots*, had a black theme and starred black actors.

The same is true of movies. Sidney Poitier was a number one box office star in the 1960s and Richard Pryor and Eddie Murphy attained the same ranking in the 1980s. In 1983, black actors starred in three of the six biggest hits of that year. While blacks were assumed to be successful only in sidekick roles, Eddie Murphy's break with tradition in the film, *Beverly Hills Cop* made it the most financially successful non-summer movie in film history. It should be noted that almost every film critic credited Murphy's comedic ingenuity for the movie's success. Popular music is certainly no exception to the rule of black acceptability to white audiences. The largest selling record album of all time was made by a black performer, *Michael Jackson's Thriller*. Ranked first and second among best selling record albums in 1984 were works by Lionel Richie and Prince, both black.

Being an entertainer has been one of the few accessible means of attaining success for American blacks. With the exception of sports, blacks have more significant participation in this area of the white world than any other. It is practically the only path to financial success for young blacks. In an article on young black millionaires in *Ebony*, almost all of them were athletes or entertainers. While blacks bring a certain creativity to the arts based on the expressive orientation of their culture, it is also the only area they were allowed access to, restricted as it is, in American society. The white world would accept them as entertainers when they could not be businessmen, political leaders, scholars, or even athletes.

Only through the gatekeeping role of white media leaders has the dominance of blacks in the entertainment complex been prevented. The entertainment industry is a multi-billion dollar field and black participation has been limited. Black successes in each medium have rarely been followed by other black successes because the media gatekeepers have practiced tokenism in the entertainment world, as they have in other sectors of the society. Black entertainers often rise to the top of the field because so few are permitted access or exposure to white audiences they command more attention when they do so. Only a few are selected for such exposure and most mediums remain dominated by white artists. Radio does it by playing only the songs of a few black artists. The movies accomplish it by consigning black actors to sidekick roles while the white male actor is the main hero who romances the white female lead. Television allows more access but restricts most blacks to demeaning comedies that eventually become the same, and tiring to the viewing audience.

While this pattern reinforces the cultural ideology of white supremacy by retaining most positive values for members of the white group, we should not be deluded into thinking the media operates that positively for whites. The entertainment complex is selling a fantasy for the mass public that obscures class inequalities in the economic substructure of American society. Most of the media reflects bourgeois values. Rarely are the lives of most working class Americans, white or black, reflected accurately in films or television. Instead, we are shown the lives, loves, and problems of the bourgeoisie and taught to identify with their lifestyles.

As a result of the fame that comes to actors and actresses portraying these roles, a whole industry develops around providing vicarious thrills by showing glimpses into their intimate lives and affluence. Radio serves the same function of perpetuating false class consciousness by providing its listeners with a steady diet of songs of romantic fantasy, bitter and unrequited love, while most couples lead lives of quiet desperation. The ultimate fantasy is fed to an unsuspecting white public, which is led to believe that the world they live in is habited by other whites who remain in firm control of the destiny of other races. It is a fantasy that even white cultural ideology cannot prevent from its inevitable collision with social reality.

10.2 RALPH C. GOMES AND
LINDA FAYE WILLIAMS

Race and Crime: The Role of the Media in Perpetuating Racism and Classism in America

The American news media are extremely selective as to what is reported to the public. The race and class backgrounds of the victims of criminal activity and their victimizers often determine how the media will report the crimes. Some serious types of criminality found among corporations and the wealthy are frequently not perceived as criminal by the media, the justice system, or society. While street crime is often sensationalized by the media, corporate crimes such as bribery, embezzlement, illegal kickbacks, occupational safety violations, the promotion and sale of unsafe consumer goods, and environmental poisoning are rarely portrayed by the media as crimes. Also, non-Whites are most often portrayed in the media as the victimizers and Whites as the victims. Here the media helps to perpetuate the common fear that young Black males have natural criminal tendencies.

The causes of poverty are also depicted by the media as the result of cultural deficiencies by impoverished persons rather than the inherent contradictions of corporate capitalism. By focusing more attention on the victimization of the wealthy than of the poor, the American media has created a societal impression that persons with middle-class backgrounds are more often the victims of crime.

In the present selection, social researchers Ralph C. Gomes and Linda Faye Williams contend that by inconsistently reporting crime, the American news media perpetuate racism and classism in the United States. The authors challenge the accuracy of the media's portrayal of the interrelationship between race and crime. Then, using a race/class conceptual framework, Gomes and Williams examine the differences in how crimes are reported in the context of the nature of race and racism in the United States and the role of the press in reproducing the racial order.

Key Concept: the role of the media in perpetuating racism and classism in American society

As far back as the formation of the National Association for the Advancement of Colored People (NAACP) in 1909, African Americans and their white allies announced that they would concentrate on an educational campaign to improve African American images in society, and particularly in the media. From the NAACP's perspective, white newspapers (as well as advertisements, films, and other media forms) promoted the view that African Americans were innately inferior. Officials of the NAACP attempted to enlighten white America through massive educational efforts aimed at depicting African Americans in a realistic and non-stereotypical manner. They sought to change public opinion of African Americans through lobbying and disseminating publications of their own (especially *Crisis,* the official organ of the NAACP), and through press releases aimed at garnering more favorable coverage of African Americans in the nation's news.

Almost sixty years after the formation of the NAACP, however, the Kerner Commission concluded that the press was still a source of "ignorance" about African Americans. Today, the dawn of the 1990s, African Americans continue to protest the images portrayed of them in the press. This article focuses on the controversy between African Americans and news organizations over the portrayal of African Americans in relation to crime. One especially egregious case of negative crime coverage involving an African American suspect is used to exemplify this phenomenon. This case is examined in the context of (1) the nature and functions of racism and classism in the United States; and (2) the role of the press in reproducing racial order in America. Conclusions are drawn regarding both standard press practices and differential press treatment of African Americans compared to whites, and the way in which they lead to distortions in coverage of African Americans vis-a-vis crime. Several recommendations are made to correct this situation.

THE STUART MURDER CASE, BOSTON

In October 1989, Charles Stuart, a Boston fur salesman earning over $100,000 a year, claimed that he had been shot and his wife (an attorney) and unborn child had been murdered by a lone African American male assailant as they left a birthing class. Both local and national coverage was awash with stories of the gruesome murder. The presumed circumstances as reported in the press generated sympathy for the middle-class Stuarts and a disgust for residents of Mission Hill, an African American neighborhood where the crime allegedly occurred. The press incessantly raised questions about the nature of a community that could produce a person who could commit such a vicious crime. Images of a community run "wild," of a side of town populated with animalistic people became common fodder in press coverage of the crime. Simultaneously, the Stuarts were presented as "the Camelot couple," Their image in the broadcast and print media was of good, decent, hard-working, young Americans with a future and an exceptionally happy marriage, while collectively, the residents of Mission Hill were depicted as the opposite.

Within a matter of weeks, an African American man was arrested. He became the widely publicized suspect. Press coverage focused on his previous arrests and convictions; even his report card from high school was published in an article that concluded the man was not only mentally deficient, but also monstrous. On the other hand, the press did not question Charles Stuart's character or his account of the crime, nor did it temper its conclusions about the African American man arrested. Subsequently, Charles Stuart identified his purported assailant from a police line-up. With that, caution in press coverage (if there had been any at all), was completely thrown to the wind. As a result, instead of reporting that the police had named a suspect, the press simply pointed to the arrested African American man as the killer.

Meanwhile, Boston's Mayor Ray Flynn reacted by assigning more police officers to the Mission Hill district than had ever been assigned to any Boston community. Several elected officials went as far as to call for reinstituting the death penalty in reaction to the crime. White suburbanites, wringing their hands and shaking their heads, vowed not to come into the city again.

Then came a stunning turn of events. A couple of months after the murder, Matthew Stuart, Charles Stuart's brother, came forward and convincingly implicated Charles Stuart in the murder of his wife and unborn baby, as well as shooting himself. Matthew Stuart also claimed to be an unwitting accomplice to the crime. The motive, according to newspaper accounts after Matthew's revelations, was profit from Carol Stuart's life insurance policies coupled with infatuation with a younger woman. In the aftermath of Matthew's statements, his brother committed suicide, taking with him the full answer for why he had acted so heinously.

Now that it was clear that an entire community had been shamelessly and wrongfully treated in the press, Boston's predominantly African American Roxbury section erupted in anger. Roxbury, especially its Mission Hill community, had not only been subjected to intense and harsh scrutiny by the press; it was also the object of indiscriminate police harassment, the most prevalent of which included "stop and search" procedures. Several prominent leaders in Boston's African American community concluded that Stuart, the police, elected officials, and the press had acted wrongly in convicting an innocent man and perpetrating malicious stereotypes of African American Bostonians as a whole. In the fractious aftermath, there were calls in the African American community for a boycott of Boston's two major newspapers, *The Boston Globe*, and *The Boston Herald*. Additionally, there were demands for apologies from the print and broadcast media, the city's mayor, and other elected and appointed officials. No such apologies were forthcoming. Indeed, from the mayor's office to law enforcement officials to the press, no one admitted doing much of anything wrong. Only one reporter attempted to rewrite history by claiming to have always been skeptical of Charles Stuart's and the police account. However, there was absolutely no evidence of such skepticism in her printed stories.

Several key questions about crime and the press coverage of African Americans flow from the Stuart case. First, how was Stuart able to convince the press and the general public of his version of events, especially given well-established findings that most women victims are murdered by their lovers or husbands? Would the press have handled the story differently if Stuart had been African American and poor instead of white and relatively affluent? Why has the press continued to maintain its innocence in the way it covered the case? What does it say about the likelihood of news organizations learning any lessons from the way the case was covered? What can African Americans and news organizations do to more accurately and objectively cover African America? To begin to answer these questions, the next section places Charles Stuart's hoax and the negative coverage of an African American man and his community in the perspective of literature on race and crime.

CONTROVERSY OVER THE SUPPOSED SYMBIOSIS OF RACE AND CRIME

Stuart's understanding of the potency of blaming an African American suspect was grounded in a long history of media popularization of the validity of the relationship between race and crime. It is a widely held view among African Americans that African American victims of crime are often not covered adequately in press accounts; in contrast African American perpetrators of crime tend to receive exaggerated coverage, especially when the victim is white. Holding this view more than fifty years ago, Langston Hughes's fictional character Jesse B. Simple declared: "The only time colored folk is front page news is when there's been a lynching or boycott or a whole bunch of us have been butchered or is arrested. Then they announce it."

Twenty years later, Pulitzer Prize winner Seymour Hersh drew a similar real life conclusion. As a cub reporter in Chicago, Hersh stumbled onto what he thought was a big story. A man in an African American neighborhood had murdered five people and then killed himself. Hersh phoned a report to his newsroom, but the veteran deskman who answered was not impressed. As Hersh reported it, the deskman said, "Ah, my good Mr. Hersh, could it be that these unfortunate victims are of the American Negro persuasion?" Hersh answered that they were African American, and he was instructed to "cheapen it up." The story was granted only one or two paragraphs in the local newspapers.

Today, many if not most members of minority groups in the United States still agree with Hughes's fictional account and Hersh's real life conclusions regarding news coverage of people of color. Minorities often see the mainstream press in the United States as omitting them altogether or presenting negative news stories about them without countervailing stories focusing on positive aspects of minority life. Instead of being considered full-fledged members of society, people of color are viewed as "them," that is, people who have problems or cause problems for "us." As a result, minorities have often criticized the media's over-reliance upon official sources, to the exclusion of minority viewpoints, as well as the less favorable treatment of minority news items compared to items about whites in comparable situations. This is nowhere more evident than in reports on crime and violence.

As a reaction to their perceptions of negative stereotyping vis-à-vis crime, African Americans protested against newspapers in Baltimore, Chicago, Detroit, New York, Washington, D.C. and a host of other cities during the 1980s.

In almost every city with a large African American population, there have been emotionally charged meetings with white editors over negatively biased coverage of the African American community. One poignant example of these protests occurred at *The Washington Post* in 1987. African American picketers spent every Sunday for three months protesting the profile of an African American rap singer, who was a murder suspect, as the lead article in the premier issue of the *Post's* newly refashioned Sunday magazine. They also protested a column in the same issue written by a liberal columnist that supported jewelry store owners who refused to allow young African American men into their stores, fearing they might be robbed.

For the most part, the literature on the coverage of African Americans in the press supports these concerns and protests. As early as 1936, George Simpson discussed the largely invisible position of African Americans in the white press except for their stereotypical portrayals as the perpetrators of violent crimes. Later, the Kerner Commission criticized the news media's focus on the African American criminal as contributing to racism. A number of critical conclusions have been developed in research on crime coverage in recent years. First, crimes that attract media attention are not representative of the actual mix of crimes in society, according to Shelly and Askins. Second, crime news may make people excessively fearful of being victimized by crime according to Einstedel, Salomone, and Schnieder. Third, according to Pritchard, all other things being equal, the critical factor influencing crime coverage is the race of the suspect. Fourth, according to Jamieson, African Americans are featured in news stories about crime in numbers that are exceptionally disproportionate to the percentages of such crimes they commit.

In short, a number of studies have concluded that the press focuses on crimes in a way that distorts the true picture of African Americans as perpetrators and as victims of crimes. In this context, it should be clear that differential press coverage of African Americans and their communities, as well as protests in Boston's African American neighborhoods against unfair portrayals of Mission Hill and poor African American Bostonians, and the resultant call for a boycott of the *Globe* and *Herald* newspapers are nothing new. What is new is that rarely, if ever, has the supposed symbiosis of race and crime in the American psyche been so speedily and starkly revealed to be a horrific lie—a lie in this instance built upon a concoction of a white killer or killers who banked on racism to do for him or them just what it did. The police, elected officials, the press, and concomitantly, the overwhelming majority of the public became handmaidens for concealing a crime.

Still, it must be admitted that Charles Stuart's lie could not have been so widely or easily accepted if a link between race and crime had not already been so deeply imbedded in the American mind. One crime could not have so easily set off racial tensions were they not already there. These tensions did not originate with skillful use of the politics of fear by now President Bush in his exploitation of the Willie Horton case in 1988. Rather, racial tension has a long history with its basis on the functional utility of racial and class discrimination in the American economy....

MANIFESTATIONS OF RACE/CLASS DISCRIMINATION IN AMERICAN SOCIETY

Without pretending to be exhaustive, it is now possible to give some illustrations of race/class discrimination and exploitation in the United States. The point here is not to provide new facts, but rather to provide examples of the effects of the race/class dialectic.

Discrimination in the Dual Labor Market

Sociologist Edna Bonacich outlined the dual labor market model in which minorities, in general, and African Americans, in particular, worked primarily in the irregular economy (manual jobs). Bonacich stated:

> A racial division of labor continues to be very evident in this society. Despite the movement of a small number of people of color... Anyone who keeps their eyes open for one minute will see it. Who makes the beds in the hotels? Who cleans the floors in the middle class houses? Who collects the garbage? Who empties the bedpans in hospitals? Who does most of the minimum wage jobs?
>
> The exploited labor of these millions of workers fills the coppers [sic] of the wealthy, virtually all of whom are white. Wealth is continuously drained from black and Latino and Native American communities through the hard labor and lack of remuneration of their people. The huge wealth of America's white-owned corporations rests on the backs of the hard labor of workers, many of whom are people of color.

Elliot Liebow's study of working African American men portrayed a similar plight for the African American.

Discrimination in the Criminal Justice System

In the criminal justice system, African Americans account for about 50 percent of the prison inmates. This percentage constitutes about four times the African American representation in the general population. Explaining the condition for African American males, a study by the Sentencing Project, a non-profit organization in Washington, D.C. found:

> Nearly one-quarter of American black men in their 20's are behind bars or on probation or parole—the highest percentage ever... The shocking figure—610,000 black men from age 20–29 easily tops the 436,000 young black males in higher education (on the other hand). One in 16 whites and one in 10 Hispanics are behind bars or on probation or parole.

Commenting on the court system in the United States, Anthony Lester, a British lawyer states:

TABLE 1

Ethnic Representation in the American Elite

*Ralph C. Gomes
and Linda Faye
Williams*

Institutions	Wasps	Other Protestants	Irish Catholics	Other Catholics	Jews	Minorities	Probably Wasps	N
Overall Elite	43.0%	19.5%	8.5%	8.7%	11.3%	3.9%	5.0%	(539)
Business	57.3%	22.1%	5.3%	6.1%	6.9%	0.0%	2.3%	(131)
Labor	23.9%	15.2%	37.0%	13.0%	4.3%	2.2%	4.3%	(46)
Political Parties	44.0%	18.0%	14.0%	4.0%	8.0%	4.0%	8.0%	(50)
Voluntary Organization	32.7%	13.5%	1.9%	7.7%	17.3%	19.2%	7.7%	(52)
Mass Media	37.1%	11.3%	4.8%	9.7%	25.8%	0.0%	11.3%	(62)
Congress	53.4%	19.0%	6.9%	8.6%	3.4%	3.4%	5.2%	(58)
Political Appointees	39.4%	28.8%	1.5%	13.6%	10.6%	3.0%	3.0%	(66)
Civil Servants	35.8%	22.6%	9.4%	9.4%	15.1%	3.8%	3.8%	(53)

Source: Richard D. Alba and Gwen Moore, "Ethnicity in American Elite," *American Sociological Review* 47 (June 1982): 377.

Southern officials admitted to me that there are four standards of justice. First, where white is against white, there is equal protection of the law. Second, where Negro is against Negro, the common complaint is that Southern courts and police are too lenient. One senior official explained to me that Negroes are primitive and emotional like children or animals, with little sense of right or wrong. If a Negro commits a crime against another Negro, he will usually receive a far lighter punishment than a white against a white. Third, where a white commits a crime against a Negro, he will be punished lightly if at all, and the Negro complainant may expect reprisals... Fourth, where a Negro commits a crime against a white, retribution is swift and severe.

Discrimination in the Elite Structure

Moving to positions of prestige and decision-making, sociologists Richard D. Alba and Gwen Moore in their study of "top office holders" (decision-making authority) showed the race/class discrimination in American institutions. Table 1 indicates that the dominant race/class group [White Anglo-Saxon Protestants (WASPS)] accounts for 43 to 48 percent of all elites, while minorities account for only 3.9 percent. In the area of mass media, WASPS account for 37 to 48 percent of elites, followed by Jews, 25.8 percent, and there is no representation of minorities.

Due to their numbers and positions, WASPS exert an inordinate amount of power and control over material production and wealth. Furthermore, due to their position and overrepresentation in the media, they have control over mental production as well. Although today the situation is improving, the racial disparity remains. The data also show that overall minorities are underrepresented in all areas of the elite structure with one exception, voluntary institutions....

RACE, CLASS AND THE ROLE OF THE MEDIA

... More than twenty years ago, the Kerner Commission pointed out the media's inordinate influence on the socialization of children and adults in the United States. More importantly, the Commission clearly implicated the media in not just the *reflection* of racism, but also the *production* and *reproduction* of racism. Even today, there have been few full studies of the role of the media, particularly the news media, in reproducing and perpetuating the race/class hierarchy.

Part of the problem is the paucity of African American journalists. Only about 4 percent of the reporters on daily newspapers are African Americans. Far fewer are editors and managers. African American representation in broadcast media and as owners is even lower. Compounding the problem of underrepresentation is the lack of knowledge of the African American community demonstrated by the present media intelligentsia. The lack of contact with African Americans and knowledge about African Americans on the part of white reporters and decision-makers in the media often leads to, at best, insensitivity when they report on the African American community and, at worst, "downright" racism.

The central problem is that this insensitivity and/or racism is spread since many people form their views based on media accounts. To paraphrase David Colby and Timothy Cook, generally, the media helps to determine which matters, such as drug abuse or crime, become defined as public events or as epidemics. "Since the reach, scope, and gravity of problems cannot be fully judged in one's immediate environment, the media construct the public reality that is distinct from the private worlds that we otherwise inhabit and provide resources for discourse in public matters.

Colby and Cook concluded that the media's identification and definition of public problems work, not only on mass audiences, but also on policy-makers:

> Policy-makers are highly attentive to news coverage. They are more likely to respond to highly salient issues, even when they might provoke considerable conflict but largely in the context of the initial frame that the media have provided.... By their ability to transform occurrences into news, the media exert power.... After all, one dimension of power can be construed as the ability to have one's account become the perceived reality of others.

Thus, it is important for "reality" as presented by the press to be balanced and objective. This may hardly ever be the case, however, for the news industry is part of the hegemonic portrayal of reality in the United States. Indeed, the media is enveloped in a reality that flows from an economic base of racist functionality to an ideology of racial division. Thus, it is actually not surprising that the media does very little to change the hegemony of racist and classist ideology and much to reproduce it or even to invent it.

CONCLUSION

Some form of protest of stereotypical coverage of African Americans in the media should be part of the African American agenda. The news media is too important a component to ignore. It shapes the understanding of experiences, events, and the social order for Americans of all races. The media does not passively report information regarding race, ethnicity and class, nor does it simply reflect the ethnocentric consensus. Instead, the media interprets and helps to construct and reproduce these racist understandings. Especially because various groups and classes of Americans live in somewhat separate societies, much of what Americans think they know about others outside their racial and linguistic communities and income groups is derived from the news media. Media reportage, then, can promote attitudes of acceptance or of hostility and fear. It can expose problems and present suggested solutions or it can ignore uncomfortable situations until they explode. In covering the Stuart case, Boston's media made all the latter choices from October through December 1989. By its refusal to admit making big mistakes, the Boston media continues to be part of the problem rather than the solution.

In addition to building a protest strategy, African American communication researchers need to develop an audience model that is sensitive to the African American subculture. More research should be conducted, both about the effects of the mass media on African Americans and about the substance of news coverage vis-à-vis race. Researchers should continue monitoring the employment of African Americans in the media. African American colleges and universities must increase the number of African Americans trained for employment in news organizations. In addition, African Americans must include in their demands the hiring and promotion of well-trained African Americans. At the same time, African Americans must monitor the substance of their media coverage regardless of the race of the reporter or decision-maker. The ultimate goal is improved coverage of African Americans. Thus, reporters of all races and backgrounds must be better trained. Eliminating ethnocentrism in coverage of African Americans both in the United States and abroad must be a realizable goal.

Finally, many other groups are inaccurately portrayed in the press. These include other minorities such as Latinos and Asians, as well as poor whites. A growing amount of distrust and even hostility toward the press's ignorance is coupled with distortion of these groups' experiences. Recognizing this, these groups should form coalitions to work on issues of press coverage as well as underrepresentation among media personnel.

The decade of the 1990s could be a decade for finally beginning to turn around the stereotypical coverage of African Americans vis-à-vis crime and other matters. Conversely, it could continue the long news media tradition of negative portrayals in the press of African American individuals and their communities. Behind the determination of which kind of decade is ultimately registered lies a struggle on many fronts. A direct assault on unbalanced, inaccurate coverage of African Americans must be waged in concert with the larger struggle to improve their status on economic, social, and political fronts. Fundamental change in the media's role of reproducing racial and class orders in America will fully be made only when the economic order, so well served by racial oppression and class exploitation (which first produced it), is transformed.

10.3 RICHARD E. LAPCHICK AND DAVID STUCKEY

Professional Sports: The Racial Report Card

Professional athletics is commonly viewed as one of the few parts of the occupational structure that are particularly open to non-Whites. In 1991, for instance, Blacks accounted for nearly three-quarters of professional basketball players, nearly one-fifth of baseball players, and over two-thirds of football players. Yet, even here, patterns of racial discrimination are evident.

In this selection, Richard E. Lapchick and David Stuckey examine the positions of blacks in the three major sports in which blacks are most prominent. The authors explain that the hiring of athletes, coaching staff, and front office workers, as well as salary allocation are problematic in terms of racial parity.

Key Concept: race and professional sports

*N*ortheastern University's Center for the Study of Sport in Society, which has monitored the issue of race in sport since opening in 1984, today issued its second Racial Report Card designed to evaluate the racial factor in the National Basketball Association, the National Football League and Major League Baseball, the three major sports in which blacks compete most regularly.

The NBA once again achieved an overall grade of "A" while the NFL held at a "C+" and Major League Baseball fell to a "C." The greatest problem areas remain front office management hiring practices and head coach or manager positions in both the NFL and Major League Baseball where barely passing grades were achieved.

In 1987, Al Campanis said blacks simply don't have the "necessities" to lead in sports; in 1988, Jimmy "The Greek" Snyder informed us that blacks were created differently than whites; in 1989, Roger Stanton wrote that white football players' IQs would be higher than blacks 100 percent of the time; in 1990, Hal Thompson told us that blacks weren't members of the club at Shoal Creek because "that's not done in Birmingham."

So the question becomes how good are the options for the black athlete in football, baseball and basketball? Is he treated equally in each sport? Is he viewed as the equal of his white counterparts by coaches, the front office and the fans? Is he paid the same? Are the stereotypes applied to him earlier in his career still assumed by whites? Is he limited to playing certain positions because of positional segregation (stacking)? Does his fame endure after his playing career? Will he become a coach in the pros or join the front office of his team?

The 1990 Racial Report card was decidely upbeat but the 1991 version [see Table 1] is less optimistic due to either stagnation or decline in key indicators aside from on the field play.

SPORT VERSUS SOCIETY

When compared to society-wide data compiled from various sources, blacks in all three sports are doing well.

Racial minorities, especially blacks, continue to see a deterioration, vis-à-vis whites in several key areas: per-capita income, employment, percentage living in poverty, perceptions of whites toward blacks, college education and health factors.

According to the Census Bureau, the median income for white families rose from $32,713 in 1970 to $35,980 in 1989—a 10% increase; black median income barely changed, from $20,067 in 1970 to $20,210 in 1989.

According to the Joint Center for Political and Economic Studies, nearly half of all black children live in poverty today compared to 14.1% of white children.

According to a survey done by the National Opinion Research Center, more than half of all whites believe blacks are less hardworking, more violence prone, less intelligent, less patriotic, and live off welfare.

Police seem to sometimes act on stereotypical assumptions about blacks. While only 15% of drug users are black, 41% of those arrested for drugs are black.

Black males between 15–24 are 1% of the population but represent 13.7% of murder victims.

The number of black men in college is declining.

Blacks have a much higher incidence of heart disease, stroke, breast cancer and diabetes.

Given [these] discouraging data, across nearly all relevant indicators, the Center does not wish to present contradictory messages regarding the relative prospects of mobility in professional sports. Thus, while the sportsworld has made improvements, the number of blacks benefitting from this is minuscule compared to the general population. The disheartening socio-economic indicators for the larger society must not be looked upon as further evidence for the irrational pursuit of 10,000-to-1 odds of a high-school athlete becoming a professional athlete. The black high-school athlete still has a better chance of becoming an attorney or a doctor than a professional player....

TABLE 1

1991 Racial Report Card

Subject: Professional Sports vs. Society	NBA	NFL	MLB	Society
Overall Grade	A	C+	C	D+
Improvement	A	B+	C	D
Overall GPA	3.8	2.5	2.1	1.5
Improve GPA	3.8	3.0	2.0	1.0
based on a 5.0 scale for A+; 4.0 for B+; 3.0 for B; 2.5 for C+; 2.0 for C; 1.5 for D+ and 1.0 for D				
Player				
Opportunities	A+	A	C	D–
Improvement	Same	A+	C+	D–
*Commissioner's				
Leadership	A+	A	C+	D+
Improvement	Same	A+	C+	C+
Player's Salaries	N/A	B	A	D+
Improvement	N/A	C+	A+	D+
Stacking	N/A	D+	D+	D+
Improvement	N/A	C+	B	D+
Subject: Hiring Practices–Front Office				
*Management	B	D+	D	D
Improvement	B+	C	D	C
Support Staff	B	C+	B	C
Improvement	C+	B+	B	C+
Subject: Hiring Practices–Coaches				
*Head Coach or Manager	B+	D+	C	N/A
Improvement	Same	Same	Same	N/A
Assistant Coaches	B+	B	N/A	N/A
Improvement	B	B–	N/A	N/A

*given double weight in overall grades

THE COMMISSIONERS

NFL Commissioner Paul Tagliabue took a leadership role in the racial issue in 1990–91.

He took the lead in removing the Super Bowl from Phoenix after Arizona voters refused to make Martin Luther King's birthday an official holiday.

The decision was a very controversial one in Arizona where many felt the NFL created a backlash that resulted in the defeat of the legislation. However, Commissioner Tagliabue's intervention marked the first time that an NFL Commissioner became actively involved in a racial issue. He had already created the Players Advisory Council which, among other things, is charged with the responsibility of developing career planning programs to smooth the transition into private life for professional football players. Tagliabue also helped make hiring minorities a priority in the World League of American Football to prepare minority coaches and front office employees for future positions in the NFL. This is discussed later in the Report Card.

Perhaps the biggest indicator of Commissioner Tagliabue's commitment was demonstrated by the appointment of blacks in three key posts: Dr. Lawrence Brown became the NFL Drug Advisor; Reggie Roberts was appointed Director of Information for the National Football Conference; and Harold Henderson was named Executive Vice President-Labor Relations for the NFL. Henderson became the highest ranking black in the history of the NFL.

The racial issue was hardly mentioned in the nearly four years since Al Campanis brought the reality of racism to baseball's front burner in his widely noted appearance on *Nightline*. However, a June 6 1991 *Nightline* updated the situation and served to bring attention to the issue again.

Commissioner Fay Vincent's public statements seemed to indicate a desire to follow the late Bart Giamatti's progressive leadership. However, his statements were not reflected by the record.

David Stern still has the best record of all the commissioners. His leadership has been consistent and NBA policies encouraging high level positions for minorities reflected those policies.

Blacks Playing Professional Sport

The integration of baseball, basketball, and football over the past four decades has been remarkable. There is no other area of the economy, with the exception of entertainment, where blacks play such a significant role. While opportunities for blacks in society seemed to be rolling back in the 1990s, blacks made up the majority of players in the NBA and NFL. As a result of their presence declining during the 1980s in favor of Hispanic-American and Latin players, black players continued to represent a minority of total players in Major League Baseball. That decline seemed to stop in 1991, when the number of blacks in Major League Baseball rose from 17% to 18%, marking the first increase in recent years. The percentage of Latins (11%) remained the same while the percentage of Hispanic-Americans rose to 3% and that of whites declined from 70% to 68%.

The percentage of blacks in the NBA dropped slightly to 72% and increased to 61% in the NFL.

COACHING POSITIONS

[The] year 1991 marked the first time in history of pro sports that there was black head coach in all three sports for two consecutive years. The firing of Frank Robinson was "balanced" when Kansas City hired Hal McRae early in the 1991 season. McRae and Cito Gaston (Toronto) are the only two black baseball managers.

... [T]he percentage of blacks (6%) and Hispanics (13%) holding Major League jobs as manager, trainer, scout, coach or instructors has not changed between the 1989 and 1990 seasons.

The NBA has regularly had blacks leading teams since the 1970s and it remains the best by far of all pro sports at offering blacks accessibility in the coaching arena after their playing days are over.

The percentage of blacks in NBA head coaching positions remained the same since last year's Report Card. There have been six head coaches in each of the last two years. In 1990–91 they were Lenny Wilkins (Cavaliers), K. C. Jones (Supersonics), Don Chaney (Rockets), Stu Jackson (partial season with the Knicks), Gene Littles (Hornets) and Wes Unseld (Bullets).

Twelve of the 58 (21%) assistant coaches were black in 1990–91.... [T]he percentage of black assistants... dropped slightly in 1990–91.

The NFL, which has historically had the poorest record in hiring blacks in head coaching positions, announced that its new World League of American Football could serve as a training ground for black coaches. Commissioner Tagliabue also created a special program to train black college coaches.

Of the 10 head coaching positions in the WLAF, none were held by blacks. Thirteen of the 44 (30%) assistant coaches in the WLAF were black, a full 15% above the NFL's average. Three blacks—Darrell "Pop" Jackson (New York), George Warhop (London) and Johnnie Walton (Raleigh)—served as coordinators. Fifty-seven percent of the players in the WLAF were black.

Art Shell of the Los Angeles Raiders remained the only black head coach in the NFL in 1990.

Like the NBA, the percentage of blacks as assistant coaches in the NFL dropped slightly in 1990. In the 1989 study, 17% (50 out of 247) of the assistants were black. In 1990, there were 50 black assistants listed for the 308 positions (16%). How the promise of the WLAF and the college program will translate into NFL jobs remains to be seen.

THE FRONT OFFICE

The year 1990–91 seemed to be one in which gains by minorities in front offices leveled off, or, in the case of the NBA, increased slightly.

Neither baseball nor the NFL has ever had a black general manager, while the NBA had five. Elgin Baylor (Clippers), Wayne Embry (Cavaliers), Willis Reed (Nets), Bill McKinney (Timberwolves) and Bernie Bickerstaff (Nuggets) heading the operations of their franchises in 1990–91. This represented a remarkable 40% increase from 1989–90. Other blacks holding top management positions at the start of the season included Wes Unseld (Bullets) and Al Attles (Warriors).

Susan O'Malley was named President of the Washington Bullets, the first woman to hold this position in any sport.

... Minority advancement continues to take place in the NBA front offices. Blacks now hold 9% (vs. 7% in 1989–90) of front office management positions. Women now occupy 32% of all NBA front office positions (management and staff). Blacks hold 10% of NBA support staff positions, down from 16% in 1989–90.

An overview of NFL front office personnel has shown only slight improvement in recent years. Of the 235 management positions listed in the NFL media guides, 14 were held by blacks. That represented 6 percent, down from 1989's 7 percent. According to an NFL source, overall minority employment in the NFL dropped from 246 in 1989 to 244 in 1990 (14.9% to 14.7%).

Men who moved near the top last year included: Rod Graves, Assistant Director of Player Personnel-Chicago Bears; Patric Forte, Vice President for Administration-New England Patriots; Dick Daniels, Assistant General Manager-San Diego Chargers; and Bab Wallace, Assistant to the President and General Counsel-Philadelphia Eagles.

According to the NFL, 79 minorities have either been hired or promoted to the National Football League during the past three years. This number represents 32% of the total minority force. (NFL statistics are more expansive than those reflected in the Report since the NFL's records include blacks and other minorities.) The key appointments of Dr. Lawrence Brown, Reggie Roberts and Harold Henderson as noted in the section on "Commissioners" was a major step forward for the League office itself.

There was improvement below the management level. Blacks occupied 71 of the 826 support staff positions, representing a significant increase to 9% of the total (7% in 1989). The NFL official told the *CSSS Digest* that minority employment has had "modest, positive results." ...

It is ironic that the issue of front office hiring practices is where all the concern began and it is in this area where progress is slowest. There can be little doubt that the decline of public pressure over the last two years has reduced the "need" for baseball to increase the number of minorities in the front office.

SALARIES AND ENDORSEMENTS

For the black superstars, life is secure. Their salaries are equal to white stars. According to *The Sports Marketing Letter*, 1991 saw both Magic Johnson and Bo Jackson join Michael Jordan among the top ten endorsement earners in 1991. Jordan topped the list with an estimated $11 million. It was the first time that

Jordan wasn't the only black in the top 10, and showed positive movement since eight of the 10 most popular athletes in America were black.

Richard E. Lapchick and David Stuckey

It is more difficult to tell if better chances for minority endorsements apply across the board since companies rarely release the value of the endorsement packages.

Historically, information to compare salaries between blacks and whites has been very difficult to obtain. In the early 1980s, whatever information that was obtained showed whites consistently outearning blacks.

Data have been easier to obtain in recent years for the NFL and Major League Baseball.

In the 1990 NFL season, white salaries once again topped black salaries. According to the salaries published in *USA Today*, the NFL average for all players was $298,000. The average black player's salary was $287,000, compared to $313,000 for whites.

Most of this is explained by the salaries of quarterbacks, the highest paid position and one where whites outnumber blacks by nearly 10 to 1. In fact, if the salaries for quarterbacks were deleted the average salary for blacks ($281,000) would be greater than that for whites ($269,000).

This represented a reversal from the 1990 Report Card when average salaries of blacks topped those of whites (according to a *USA Today* survey) by $253,916 for blacks vs. $236,516 for whites (based on 1988 data).

There was a most dramatic development in Major League Baseball, where both black and Latin players topped whites in average salary for the first time. In 1991 whites made an average of $867,476 while blacks made $1,051,696. Latin players averaged $873,581 while Hispanic-American players remained at the rear making $552,887.

There is no doubt that pros today, black and white, are nearing salary equity in a stratospheric salary range that almost anyone else in society would envy. Therein, of course, lies the draw of the unrealistic dream of so many young athletes who think they can achieve the same status.

POSITIONAL SEGREGATION IN THE NFL AND MLB

Historically, much has been said about stacking (positional segregation) in professional football.

Is it a factor now in the NFL? Using the twenty-eight NFL 1990 team media guides, the statistics are overwhelming. On offense, 93 percent of the quarterbacks were white (versus 99 percent in 1983); 87 percent of the centers, 76 percent of the offensive guards, and 71 percent of the tackles were white (versus 97, 77 and 68 percent respectively in 1983).

Sociologist Jonathan Brower did a survey of coaches and asked them how they would characterize the three positions dominated by whites. They used the following words: intelligence, leadership, emotional control, decision making, and technique. Are coaches stereotyping positions they think only whites can handle?

The fact that Doug Williams led the Washington Redskins to the Super Bowl victory, coupled with the tremendous recent success of star quarterbacks like Warren Moon and Randall Cunningham and the emergence of others like Rodney Peete and Andre Ware in 1990, showed that there could be rapid progress in eliminating positional segregation at the club level. The wealth of fine black college quarterbacks should also hasten this.

But a note of caution to temper this optimism is sounded by the story of Rodney Peete. Prior to the 1989 draft, Peete was rated by most scouting combines as among the top three quarterbacks available. Charges of racism flared when he was picked in the sixth round and was the ninth quarterback chosen! Mike Wilbon of the *Washington Post* wrote that "The fact that eight other quarterbacks were chosen before Peete says one thing to me about NFL people and what they're looking for in a quarterback. If he's white and can stand up straight, he's a better prospect than a black quarterback with various and obvious talents."

Chosen by the Detroit Lions, Peete started some games as a rookie in 1989 and won the starting job in 1990 with Andre Ware behind him. The story recalled an earlier era when Warren Moon, who remained one of the NFL's highest paid players in 1990, was not even chosen in the draft and had to prove himself in Canada. Talent may not be totally blind to color.

The fact that the Redskins decided to go with younger quarterbacks one year after Williams' Super Bowl triumph and not one team was willing to pick up Doug Williams would have to be another reason to temper the optimism on a trend toward black quarterbacks in the NFL.

In spite of the cautionary notes it no longer seems impossible for a black to make it at quarterback in the NFL. However, it is still unlikely as the 93 percent white figure shows.

As another example, in 1990 90 percent of the running backs and 86 percent of the wide receivers were black (up from 88% and 77% respectively in 1983).

The defensive position that shows the most meaningful statistical difference by race is at cornerback. Ninety-six percent of the cornerbacks were black in 1990 (up from 92 percent in 1983).

The words used by the coaches for the positions of running back, wide receiver, and defensive back were: strength, quickness, and instinct. All three are black-dominated positions.

There were no black coaches in the NFL until Art Shell became the Raiders coach in 1989. If the white coaches hold traditional racial beliefs, then player assignments would easily be made according to race....

Baseball has its own positional segregation. The pitcher and the catcher are central to every play of the game. Of the 69 catchers listed in the New York Times 1991 opening day rosters, cross-referenced in the *1991 Who's Who in Baseball*, only one was black. Ten percent were Latins and Hispanics combined. Only thirteen (4 percent) of the 306 pitchers were black, down from 7 percent in 1983! Another 10 percent were Latins or Hispanics, up from 7.5% in 1983. It is not surprising that these pivotal "thinking positions" were held mostly by whites.

What was surprising was who was playing second base, shortstop, and third base. All three are also considered to be thinking positions. In 1991, blacks make up 22 percent of second basemen, 19 percent of shortstops, and 20 percent of third basemen (versus 21, 11, and 9 percent in 1983). These increases, which put blacks nearly on par with their overall percentage in the league, may be indicating a significant shift away from positional segregation in baseball. However, like the positive developments in football at quarterback, it is too soon to tell what the long term effects will be.

More cautionary notes: first basemen and outfielders mainly react to other players. Outfielders need quickness and instinct. Not as much skill and training is considered necessary to hold these positions as others. Seventy-six percent of all blacks listed as offensive players were either first basemen or outfielders. While the percent of blacks in the outfield decreased to 51 percent from 1983 when it was 65 percent, there was a slight increase at first base (20 percent in 1991 from 19 percent in 1983). In spite of being outnumbered in the league by more than five to one, blacks have a numerical superiority over whites in the outfield (81 to 56).

According to *Who's Who in Baseball* for 1983 and 1991 and the Opening Day rosters of 1991, the positional breakdown is as follows in Table 2.

As can be seen, the number of Hispanics and Latins have had major increases at first base (7 to 17 percent), second base (14 to 27 percent) and shortstop (16 to 34 percent). The decrease in the number of blacks in the league overall has more than been made up by the number of Hispanic and Latin ballplayers.

It is no small irony that after Jackie Robinson blacks were let into sports largely to increase attendance. Their numbers in baseball have decreased over the past 10 years. Is it because it is perceived that too many blacks will hurt attendance? Shouldn't baseball have learned something from the NBA and NFL in this regard? Are more Hispanics and Latins playing now to promote baseball in those virtually untapped markets? Will the door swing closed on them sometime in the future?

CONCLUSION

While a sense of despair and hopelessness permeates many urban communities because of a general deterioration of life conditions, all three pro sports did better than society. However, in the key areas of employment in coaching and front offices in both the NFL and Major League Baseball minorities seemed to be losing ground.

The NBA remained at the top while the NFL showed improvement in the Commissioner's leadership, player opportunities, opportunities for black quarterback, and management and support staff hiring. Nonetheless, the greatest room for improvement was in on-the-field and front office hiring practices. Baseball improved in player opportunities, salary equity and in stacking. It still needed the greatest amount of improvement in front office hiring.

TABLE 2

Stacking in Major League Baseball

Position	Whites by Percentage		Blacks by Percentage		Latins and Hispanics by Percentage	
	1983	1991	1983	1991	1983	1991
Pitcher	86	86	7	4	7	10
Catcher	93	88	0	1	7	11
1B	55	63	38	20	7	17
2B	65	51	21	22	14	27
3B	82	76	5	21	13	13
SS	73	47	11	19	16	34
OF	45	35	46	51	9	13

Compiled by Northeastern University's Center for the Study of Sport in Society from 1983 and 1991 opening day rosters and *1991 Who's Who in Baseball*.

There was less of a feeling of hope expressed in baseball and football that the 1990s would bring steady improvement. It would seem that public pressure, especially from the civil rights groups, might be necessary to affect sweeping changes.

Whether sport can lead the way to improved race relations remains a question that is unanswered in the early 1990s.

CHAPTER 11 The Race and Ethnic Community

11.1 RICHARD DELGADO

Words That Wound

The occurrence of bias-motivated violence has become so pervasive in recent years that the U.S. criminal justice system now recognizes it as a new category of violent personal crime—*hate crime*. Most hate crimes involve intimidation, vandalism, and assaults, but many hate crimes involve murder, attempted murder, and attempted rape. National figures on hate crimes show that in 1995 some 8,610 persons victimized 9,372 persons because of their race, ethnicity, religion, or sexual orientation. However, criminal justice statistics are extremely limited with regard to how much hate crime exists in U.S. society because they do not include figures on hate literature and rallies, graffiti in public places, name-calling, and epithets not associated with assaults and other threats. A major problem with fighting hate crime in the United States is getting law enforcement officers to recognize and understand what is a hate crime. Many victims fail to report hate crimes because they fear reprisal from police officers and other government agencies.

In the following selection from "Words That Wound: A Tort Action for Racial Insults, Epithets, and Name-Calling," *Harvard Civil Rights–Civil Liberties Law Review* (vol. 17, 1982) is by Richard Delgado, a professor of law at the University of Colorado at Boulder whose work on critical race theory and the effects of racist speech has led to a new way of thinking about civil rights. In it, he suggests that one way to satisfy the social need for legal redress for victims of racial insults, epithets, and name-calling is to seek a tort remedy in civil court.

Key Concept: tort action for racial insults, epithets, and name-calling

PSYCHOLOGICAL, SOCIOLOGICAL, AND POLITICAL EFFECTS OF RACIAL INSULTS

American society remains deeply afflicted by racism. Long before slavery became the mainstay of the plantation society of the antebellum South, Anglo-Saxon attitudes of racial superiority left their stamp on the developing culture of colonial America. Today, over a century after the abolition of slavery, many citizens suffer from discriminatory attitudes and practices, infecting our economic system, our cultural and political institutions, and the daily interactions of individuals. The idea that color is a badge of inferiority and a justification for the denial of opportunity and equal treatment is deeply ingrained.

The racial insult remains one of the most pervasive channels through which discriminatory attitudes are imparted. Such language injures the dignity and self-regard of the person to whom it is addressed, communicating the message that distinctions of race are distinctions of merit, dignity, status, and personhood. Not only does the listener learn and internalize the messages contained in racial insults, these messages color our society's institutions and are transmitted to succeeding generations.

THE HARMS OF RACISM

The psychological harms caused by racial stigmatization are often much more severe than those created by other stereotyping actions. Unlike many characteristics upon which stigmatization may be based, membership in a racial minority can be considered neither self-induced, like alcoholism or prostitution, nor alterable. Race-based stigmatization is, therefore, "one of the most fruitful causes of human misery. Poverty can be eliminated—but skin color cannot." The plight of members of racial minorities may be compared with that of persons with physical disfigurements; the point has been made that

> [a] rebuff due to one's color puts [the victim] in very much the situation of the very ugly person or one suffering from a loathsome disease. The suffering... may be aggravated by a consciousness of incurability and even blameworthiness, a self-reproaching which tends to leave the individual still more aware of his loneliness and unwantedness.

The psychological impact of this type of verbal abuse has been described in various ways. Kenneth Clark has observed, "Human beings... whose daily experience tells them that almost nowhere in society are they respected and granted the ordinary dignity and courtesy accorded to others will, as a matter of course, begin to doubt their own worth." Minorities may come to believe the frequent accusations that they are lazy, ignorant, dirty, and superstitious. "The accumulation of negative images... present[s] them with one massive and destructive choice: either to hate one's self, as culture so systematically demand[s], or to have no self at all, to be nothing."

The psychological responses to such stigmatization consist of feelings of humiliation, isolation, and self-hatred. Consequently, it is neither unusual nor abnormal for stigmatized individuals to feel ambivalent about their self-worth and identity. This ambivalence arises from the stigmatized individual's awareness that others perceive him or her as falling short of societal standards, standards which the individual has adopted. Stigmatized individuals thus often are hypersensitive and anticipate pain at the prospect of contact with "normals."

It is no surprise, then, that racial stigmatization injures its victims' relationships with others. Racial tags deny minority individuals the possibility of neutral behavior in cross-racial contacts, thereby impairing the victims' capacity to form close interracial relationships. Moreover, the psychological responses of self-hatred and self-doubt unquestionably affect even the victims' relationships with members of their own group.

The psychological effects of racism may also result in mental illness and psychosomatic disease. The affected person may react by seeking escape through alcohol, drugs, or other kinds of anti-social behavior. The rates of narcotic use and admission to public psychiatric hospitals are much higher in minority communities than in society as a whole.

The achievement of high socioeconomic status does not diminish the psychological harms caused by prejudice. The effort to achieve success in business and managerial careers exacts a psychological toll even among exceptionally ambitious and upwardly mobile members of minority groups. Furthermore, those who succeed "do not enjoy the full benefits of their professional status within their organizations, because of inconsistent treatment by others resulting in continual psychological stress, strain, and frustration." As a result, the incidence of severe psychological impairment caused by the environmental stress of prejudice and discrimination is not lower among minority group members of high socioeconomic status.

One of the most troubling effects of racial stigmatization is that it may affect parenting practices among minority group members, thereby perpetuating a tradition of failure. A recent study of minority mothers found that many denied the real significance of color in their lives, yet were morbidly sensitive to matters of race. Some, as a defense against aggression, identified excessively with whites, accepting whiteness as superior. Most had negative expectations concerning life's chances. Such self-conscious, hypersensitive parents, preoccupied with the ambiguity of their own social position, are unlikely to raise confident, achievement-oriented, and emotionally stable children.

In addition to these long-term psychological harms of racial labeling, the stresses of racial abuse may have physical consequences. There is evidence that high blood pressure is associated with inhibited, constrained, or restricted anger, and not with genetic factors, and that insults produce elevation in blood pressure. American blacks have higher blood pressure levels and higher morbidity and mortality rates from hypertension, hypertensive disease, and stroke than do white counterparts. Further, there exists a strong correlation between degree of darkness of skin for blacks and level of stress felt, a correlation that may be caused by the greater discrimination experienced by dark-skinned blacks.

In addition to such emotional and physical consequences, racial stigmatization may damage a victim's pecuniary interests. The psychological injuries severely handicap the victim's pursuit of a career. The person who is timid, withdrawn, bitter, hypertense, or psychotic will almost certainly fare poorly in employment settings. An experiment in which blacks and whites of similar aptitudes and capacities were put into a competitive situation found that the blacks exhibited defeatism, half-hearted competitiveness, and "high expectancies of failure." For many minority group members, the equalization of such quantifiable variables as salary and entry level would be an insufficient antidote to defeatist attitudes because the psychological price of attempting to compete is unaffordable; they are "programmed for failure." Additionally, career options for the victims of racism are closed off by institutional racism—the subtle and unconscious racism in schools, hiring decisions, and the other practices which determine the distribution of social benefits and responsibilities.

Unlike most of the actions for which tort law provides redress to the victim, racial labeling and racial insults directly harm the perpetrator. Bigotry harms the individuals who harbor it by reinforcing rigid thinking, thereby dulling their moral and social senses and possibly leading to a "mildly . . . paranoid" mentality. There is little evidence that racial slurs serve as a "safety valve" for anxiety which would otherwise be expressed in violence.

Racism and racial stigmatization harm not only the victim and the perpetrator of individual racist acts but also society as a whole. Racism is a breach of the ideal of egalitarianism, that "all men are created equal" and each person is an equal moral agent, an ideal that is a cornerstone of the American moral and legal system. A society in which some members regularly are subjected to degradation because of their race hardly exemplifies this ideal. The failure of the legal system to redress the harms of racism, and of racial insults, conveys to all the lesson that egalitarianism is not a fundamental principle; the law, through inaction, implicitly teaches that respect for individuals is of little importance. Moreover, unredressed breaches of the egalitarian ideal may demoralize all those who prefer to live in a truly equal society, making them unwilling participants in the perpetuation of racism and racial inequality.

To the extent that racism contributes to a class system, society has a paramount interest in controlling or suppressing it. Racism injures the career prospects, social mobility, and interracial contacts of minority group members. This, in turn, impedes assimilation into the economic, social, and political mainstream of society and ensures that the victims of racism are seen and see themselves as outsiders. Indeed, racism can be seen as a force used by the majority to preserve an economically advantageous position for themselves. But when individuals cannot or choose not to contribute their talents to a social system because they are demoralized or angry, or when they are actively prevented by racist institutions from fully contributing their talents, society as a whole loses.

Finally, and perhaps most disturbingly, racism and racial labeling have an even greater impact on children than on adults. The effects of racial labeling are discernible early in life; at a young age, minority children exhibit self-hatred because of their color, and majority children learn to associate dark skin with undesirability and ugliness. A few examples readily reveal the psychological damage of racial stigmatization on children. When presented with otherwise identical dolls, a black child preferred the light-skinned one as a friend; she said that the dark-skinned one looked dirty or "not nice." Another child hated her skin color so intensely that she "vigorously lathered her arms and face with soap in an effort to wash away the dirt." She told the experimenter, "This morning I scrubbed and scrubbed and it came almost white." When asked about making a little girl out of clay, a black child said that the group should use the white clay rather than the brown "because it will make a better girl." When asked to describe dolls which had the physical characteristics of black people, young children chose adjectives such as "rough, funny, stupid, silly, smelly, stinky, dirty." Three-fourths of a group of four-year-old black children favored white play companions; over half felt themselves inferior to whites. Some engaged in denial or falsification.

THE HARMS OF RACIAL INSULTS

Immediate mental or emotional distress is the most obvious direct harm caused by a racial insult. Without question, mere words, whether racial or otherwise, can cause mental, emotional, or even physical harm to their target, especially if delivered in front of others or by a person in a position of authority. Racial insults, relying as they do on the unalterable fact of the victim's race and on the history of slavery and race discrimination in this country, have an even greater potential for harm than other insults.

Although the emotional damage caused is variable and depends on many factors, only one of which is the outrageousness of the insult, a racial insult is always a dignitary affront, a direct violation of the victim's right to be treated respectfully. Our moral and legal systems recognize the principle that individuals are entitled to treatment that does not denigrate their humanity through disrespect for their privacy or moral worth. This ideal has a high place in our traditions, finding expression in such principles as universal suffrage, the prohibition against cruel and unusual punishment, the protection of the fourth amendment against unreasonable searches, and the abolition of slavery. A racial insult is a serious transgression of this principle because it derogates by race, a characteristic central to one's self-image.

The wrong of this dignitary affront consists of the expression of a judgment that the victim of the racial slur is entitled to less than that to which all other citizens are entitled. Verbal tags provide a convenient means of categorization so that individuals may be treated as members of a class and assumed to share all the negative attitudes imputed to the class. Racial insults also serve to keep the victim compliant. Such dignitary affronts are certainly no less harmful than others recognized by the law. Clearly, a society whose public law recognizes harm in the stigma of separate but equal schooling and the potential offensiveness of the required display of a state motto on automobile license plates, and whose private law sees actionable conduct in an unwanted kiss or the forcible removal of a person's hat, should also recognize the dignitary harm inflicted by a racial insult.

The need for legal redress for victims also is underscored by the fact that racial insults are intentional acts. The intentionality of racial insults is obvious: what other purpose could the insult serve? There can be little doubt that the dignitary affront of racial insults, except perhaps those that are overheard, is intentional and therefore most reprehensible. Most people today know that certain words are offensive and only calculated to wound. No other use remains for such words as "nigger," "wop," "spick," or "kike."

In addition to the harms of immediate emotional distress and infringement of dignity, racial insults inflict psychological harm upon the victim. Racial slurs may cause long-term emotional pain because they draw upon and intensify the effects of the stigmatization, labeling, and disrespectful treatment that the victim has previously undergone. Social scientists who have studied the effects of racism have found that speech that communicates low regard for an individual because of race "tends to create in the victim those very traits of 'inferiority' that it ascribes to him." Moreover, "even in the absence of more objective forms of discrimination—poor schools, menial jobs, and substandard housing —traditional stereotypes about the low ability and apathy of Negroes and other minorities can operate as 'self-fulfilling prophecies.' " These stereotypes, portraying members of a minority group as stupid, lazy, dirty, or untrustworthy, are often communicated either explicitly or implicitly through racial insults.

Because they constantly hear racist messages, minority children, not surprisingly, come to question their competence, intelligence, and worth. Much of the blame for the formation of these attitudes lies squarely on value-laden words, epithets, and racial names. These are the materials out of which each child "grows his own set of thoughts and feelings about race." If the majority "defines them and their parents as no good, inadequate, dirty, incompetent, and stupid," the child will find it difficult not to accept those judgments.

Victims of racial invective have few means of coping with the harms caused by the insults. Physical attacks are of course forbidden. "More speech" frequently is useless because it may provoke only further abuse or because the insulter is in a position of authority over the victim. Complaints to civil rights organizations also are meaningless unless they are followed by action to punish the offender. Adoption of a "they're well meaning but ignorant" attitude is another impotent response in light of the insidious psychological harms of racial slurs. When victimized by racist language, victims must be able to threaten and institute legal action, thereby relieving the sense of helplessness that leads to psychological harm and communicating to the perpetrator and to society that such abuse will not be tolerated, either by its victims or by the courts.

Minority children possess even fewer means for coping with racial insults than do adults. "A child who finds himself rejected and attacked ... is not likely to develop dignity and poise. . . . On the contrary he develops defenses. Like a dwarf in a world of menacing giants, he cannot fight on equal terms." The child who is the victim of belittlement can react with only two unsuccessful strategies, hostility or passivity. Aggressive reactions can lead to consequences that reinforce the harm caused by the insults; children who behave aggressively in school are marked by their teachers as troublemakers, adding to the children's alienation and sense of rejection. Seemingly passive reactions have no better results; children who are passive toward their insulters turn the aggressive response on themselves; robbed of confidence and motivation, these children withdraw into moroseness, fantasy, and fear.

It is, of course, impossible to predict the degree of deterrence a cause of action in tort would create. However, as Professor van den Berghe has written, "for most people living in racist societies racial prejudice is merely a special kind of convenient rationalization for rewarding behavior." In other words, in racist societies "most members of the dominant group will exhibit both prejudice and discrimination," but only in conforming to social norms. Thus, "[W]hen social pressures and rewards for racism are absent, racial bigotry is more likely to be restricted to people for whom prejudice fulfills a psychological 'need.' In such a tolerant milieu prejudiced persons may even refrain from discriminating behavior to escape social disapproval." Increasing the cost of racial insults thus would certainly decrease their frequency. Laws will never prevent violations altogether, but they will deter "whoever is deterrable."

Because most citizens comply with legal rules, and this compliance in turn "reinforce[s] their own sentiments toward conformity," a tort action for racial insults would discourage such harmful activity through the teaching function of the law. The establishment of a legal norm "creates a public conscience and a standard for expected behavior that check overt signs of prejudice." Legislation aims first at controlling only the acts that express undesired attitudes. But "when expression changes, thoughts too in the long run are likely to fall into line." "Laws . . . restrain the middle range of mortals who need them as a mentor in molding their habits." Thus, "If we create institutional arrangements in which exploitative behaviors are no longer reinforced, we will then succeed in changing attitudes [that underlie these behaviors]." Because racial attitudes of white Americans "typically follow rather than precede actual institutional [or legal] alteration," a tort for racial slurs is a promising vehicle for the eradication of racism.

Race and Environmental Justice in the United States

Many people would agree that environmental pollution is one of America's most critical national dilemmas. Toxic chemicals, air and water pollution, and waste disposal continue to threaten not only the environment but the lives of people as well. In the present selection, Robert D. Bullard explains that environmental pollution does not threaten all people equally —it has a disproportionate impact on the nation's poor, persons of lower socioeconomic status, and racial and ethnic minorities. Bullard refers to this phenomenon as "environmental racism."

Bullard is a professor of sociology at the University of California, Riverside. His publications include *Unequal Protection: Environmental Justice and Communities of Color* (Sierra Club Books, 1994).

Key Concept: environmental racism

No segment of American society should have a monopoly on a clean environment. Nevertheless, some communities are forced to bear the brunt of this nation's pollution problem. Industrial toxins, polluted air and drinking water, and the siting of municipal landfills, lead smelters, incinerators, and hazardous waste facilities have had a disproportionate impact upon people of color, working class communities, and the poor.

Ecological inequities in the United States result from a number of factors, including the distribution of wealth, housing and real estate practices, and land use planning. Taken together, these factors give rise to what can be called "environmental racism": practices that place African Americans, Latinos, and Native Americans at greater health and environmental risk than the rest of society. This paper analyzes the causes and impacts of environmental inequities in the United States. Part I examines the links between institutional racism and ecological disparities. Part II focuses on how institutional racism affects government practices in the siting of municipal and hazardous waste disposal facilities. Part III surveys the efforts of people of color to achieve environmental justice in the United States.

I. RACISM AND ENVIRONMENTAL INEQUITY

Despite attempts made by the U.S. government to level the playing field, African American, Latino, and Native American communities have borne a disproportionate share of environmental and health risks. While both class and race determine the distribution of environmental hazards, racial minorities are more likely to be exposed to environmental threats than are whites of the same social class. Race is a powerful predictor of many environmental hazards, including the distribution of air pollution, the location of municipal solid waste facilities, the location of abandoned toxic waste sites, toxic fish consumption, and lead poisoning in children.

Lead poisoning, for example, affects between three and four million children, most of whom are African Americans and Latinos living in urban areas. A 1988 study by the federal Agency for Toxic Substances and Disease Registry found that among children five years old and younger living in urban areas of more than one million people, the percentage of African Americans with excessive levels of lead in their blood far exceeds the percentage of whites with excessive levels. In families earning less than $6,000 per year, 68% of African American children have lead poisoning, compared with 36% of white children. In families with annual incomes exceeding $15,000, more than 38% of African American children suffer from lead poisoning, compared with 12% of white children. Thus, even when income is held constant, African American children are two to three times more likely than white children to suffer from lead poisoning.

Lead poisoning is a preventable disease that then Secretary of Health and Human Services Louis Sullivan has called the "number one environmental threat to the health of children in the United States." Yet very little has been done to eliminate this preventable disease because the groups most affected by it are underrepresented in the public and private institutions best positioned to address the problem. The underrepresentation of people of color in government, law, and business is partially a manifestation of deeply rooted institutional racism. Racism has long been a "conspicuous part of the American sociopolitical system and, as a result, black people in particular, and ethnic and racial minority groups of color, find themselves at a disadvantage in contemporary society." This continues to be the case. Because a range of environmental decisions—from the prevention of lead poisoning to the siting of waste facilities—involve complex interactions among governmental, legal, and commercial actors, institutional racism leads to environmental racism. As a result, whites have maintained their quality of life at the expense of people of color. Minorities remain vulnerable to decisions that adversely affect the economic vitality of their neighborhoods, the quality of their schools, and the likelihood of exposure to environmental toxins.

Communities of color have been systematically targeted for the siting of noxious facilities such as sewer treatment plants, garbage dumps, landfills, incinerators, hazardous waste disposal sites, lead smelters, and other risky technologies, thereby exacerbating existing inequities. African Americans are especially hard hit by environmental racism, as they are by other forms of institutionalized discrimination. No matter what their education, occupation, or income level, African Americans suffer from less effective educational systems, lower quality housing, more dilapidated neighborhoods, increased mortality rates, and greater environmental threats than do whites. African American communities have long struggled to get paved streets, sidewalks, running water and sewer lines, street lights, and fire and police stations. They have also protested inadequate garbage collection and the construction of freeways through their neighborhoods. Nevertheless, many such protests have gone unheeded because African Americans are underrepresented in key decision-making positions.

The environmental problems facing communities of color are exacerbated by other institutional barriers, such as housing discrimination and de facto residential segregation, that make it difficult for African Americans and Latinos to buy their way out of health-threatening physical environments. Government policies and the practices of the banking and housing industries have created communities that segregate African Americans, and to a lesser extent, Latinos and other minorities, from whites.

Millions of African Americans and Latinos today live in geographically isolated, economically depressed, and polluted urban neighborhoods. In the heavily populated South Coast air basin of Los Angeles, "71% of African Americans and 50% of Latinos reside in the areas with the most polluted air, while only 34% of . . . whites do." Similarly, most of Richmond, California's African Americans live next to the city's petrochemical corridor—a cluster of some 350 industrial facilities that handle hazardous waste. Although only half of the city's 80,000 people are African Americans, African Americans make up 72–94% of the population in the fourteen Richmond neighborhoods closest to this corridor.

In short, all communities are not created equal. Housing and development policies limit social mobility, diminish job opportunities, and decrease environmental choices for millions of Americans. As one scholar has put it, these policies create an American apartheid that, "while lacking overt legal sanction, comes closest to the system even now being reformed in the land of its invention."

Why do some communities get dumped on while others do not? Although waste generation correlates directly with per capita income, few garbage dumps and toxic waste facilities are actually built in the suburbs. Following the NIMBY principle—"not in my backyard"—white homeowners have repeatedly mobilized against and defeated proposed sitings of so-called "locally unwanted land uses" (LULUs)—such as garbage dumps, landfills, incinerators, sewer treatment plants, garbage transfer stations, and recycling centers—in their neighborhoods. Many have used the same approach to defeat proposed sitings of prisons, drug treatment units, low-income public housing, and homeless shelters in their communities. By contrast, it has been difficult for millions of African Americans in segregated neighborhoods to say "not in my backyard" when they do not even own backyards. Whereas two-thirds of all Americans own their homes, only about 44% of African Americans do. And while 74% of middle-class whites own their own homes, only about 59% of middle-class African Americans do.

An individual's ability to leave a health-threatening physical environment is usually directly correlated with affluence. However, racial barriers, such as the prejudice of sellers, impede the ability of affluent African Americans to leave environmentally hazardous neighborhoods. Affluent African Americans (those with incomes of $50,000 or more) are as residentially segregated as African Americans on welfare. Blacks and whites do not have the same opportunities to vote with their feet and escape unhealthy physical environments. When coupled with the fact that federal, state, and local policies on economic development and the environment rarely reflect equity concerns, the inability to escape environmental hazards often leaves minority communities unprotected.

II. THE NATION'S DUMPING GROUNDS

Few national studies have focused on the socio-demographic characteristics of populations living near toxic waste sites. The first such private study was conducted by the United Church of Christ Commission for Racial Justice, a church-based civil rights organization. Its report, *Toxic Wastes and Race*, identified race as a more accurate predictor than income, home ownership rates, and property values of the location of abandoned toxic waste sites. The study also found that: (1) 60% of African Americans live in communities with at least one abandoned toxic waste site; (2) of the five largest commercial hazardous waste landfills, three, which by themselves account for 40% of the nation's total estimated landfill capacity, are located in predominately African American or Latino communities; and (3) African Americans are heavily overrepresented in the populations of those cities with the largest number of abandoned toxic waste sites—Memphis, St. Louis, Houston, Cleveland, Chicago, and Atlanta.

Like landfills, hazardous waste incinerators tend to be located in communities with large minority populations, low incomes, and low property values. A 1990 Greenpeace report, *Playing with Fire*, found that (1) the minority portion of the population in communities with existing incinerators is 89% higher than the national average; (2) communities where incinerators are proposed have minority populations 60% higher than the national average; (3) average income in communities with existing incinerators is 15% below the national average, (4) property values in communities with incinerators are 38% lower than the national average; and (5) average property values in communities where incinerators are proposed are 35% lower than the national average.

Environmental inequities are particularly acute in areas with strained race relations. In the southern United States, pro-business attitudes, lax enforcement of environmental regulations, and discriminatory industrial practices have combined to create exploitative development policies. Waste facility siting in Houston provides one disturbing illustration of these trends. Known as the "golden buckle of the Sunbelt," Houston experienced unparalleled economic and population growth in the 1970s. That growth resulted in a garbage crisis, and the city's African American neighborhoods suffered the consequences of Houston's increased demand for municipal solid waste facilities. From the early

1920s to the late 1970s, all five of Houston's city-owned municipal landfills and six of its eight garbage incinerators were located in black neighborhoods. Of the remaining facilities, one was located in a Latino neighborhood and another in an industrial park near a predominantly white neighborhood. No city-owned landfill was sited in a low- or middle-income white Houston neighborhood during this period.

From 1970 to 1978, three of the four privately-owned landfills used to dispose of Houston's garbage were located in two African American neighborhoods, Almeda Plaza and Northwood Manor. The fourth privately-owned landfill was located in an industrial area south of the racially mixed Chattwood subdivision. A large industrial park served as a buffer between the landfill and the residential area. Since the landfill site opened, the sector of Houston in which the Chattwood subdivision lies has undergone a dramatic racial transformation: between 1970 and 1980, its African American population grew from 40% to 70%. Overall, although African Americans made up only 28% of Houston's population during these years, 82% of the public and private municipal landfill sites were located in black neighborhoods.

Nevertheless, some minority communities have challenged attempts to site garbage dumps in their neighborhoods. In the early 1970s, for example, demonstrations by local residents pressured city officials to close a garbage dump in Trinity Gardens, a predominantly black neighborhood in Houston. In 1979, residents of Northwood Manor challenged local city officials, the state, and the waste disposal giant Browning-Ferris Industries (a company headquartered in Houston) for selecting their community to host a municipal landfill. The residents cited significant statistical evidence that indicated a history of locating municipal waste disposal facilities in Houston's African American neighborhoods. They also formed the Northeast Community Action Group (NECAG) and filed one of the first class action lawsuits challenging the siting of a waste facility as a violation of civil rights. In this case, *Bean v. Southwestern Waste Management Corp.*, a federal judge failed to find discrimination.

The *Bean* case is not unique. As recently as 1991, a biracial community group known as Residents Involved in Saving the Environment (RISE) charged the King and Queen County (Virginia) Board of Supervisors with racial discrimination in its selection of a primarily African American community as the site of a 420-acre regional landfill. In June 1991, a U.S. district judge for the Eastern District of Virginia ruled in *R.I.S.E. v. Kay* that the siting did not violate the equal protection clause of the Fourteenth Amendment, even though the county had placed all three of its landfills in predominantly black communities. While acknowledging that the placement of landfills in the county—which is 50% black and 50% white—from 1969 to 1991 had a disproportionate impact on black residents, the court found no constitutional violation.

African Americans are not the only group affected by environmental racism. Latinos and Native Americans are harmed as well. For example, Chemical Waste Management, Inc., the world's largest waste disposal company, selected Kettleman City, California, as a site for a proposed hazardous waste incinerator. Kettleman City is a small farmworker community of nearly 1,200 residents, 40% of whom speak only Spanish. Yet Kings County, where Kettleman City is located, conducted public hearings and prepared environmental impact reports and other written materials in English only. In 1991, local residents filed a class action lawsuit challenging the impact report, the exclusive use of English to communicate risks to local residents, and Chemical Waste Management's operation of hazardous waste incinerators in predominantly minority communities. In January 1992, a California Superior Court judge overturned the Kings County Board of Supervisors' approval of the incinerator because of its impact on air quality in the agriculture-rich Central Valley. The judge ruled that the county's environmental impact report was inadequate and that the county had not involved local residents in the decision because it had failed to provide Spanish translations of material about the project.

Native American lands pose a special case for environmental protection. Few reservations have environmental regulations or waste management infrastructures equivalent to those of the state or federal governments. As federal and state environmental regulations have become more stringent in recent years, Native American reservations have become prime targets of waste disposal firms. The special quasi-sovereign status of Indian nations, which are subject to federal but not most state regulations, affords disposal companies an opportunity to skirt many state-level environmental regulations. As a result, Native American lands from New York to California are threatened environmentally. More than three dozen reservations have been targeted for landfills and incinerators. Economic conditions on reservations—such as poverty, high unemployment, and few business development opportunities—make reservations especially vulnerable to garbage imperialism, particularly when government and industry promote the construction of a waste facility as economic development. This particular tactic succeeded in southern California where the Campo Indians agreed in 1990 to host a hazardous waste facility.

Other Native American communities have had greater success in blocking garbage imperialism. By now, nearly all of the proposals for siting waste facilities on Native American lands have been defeated or are under review. In 1991, the Choctaws in Philadelphia, Mississippi defeated a plan to locate a 466-acre hazardous waste landfill on their lands. In the same year, a Connecticut company that had never before operated a municipal landfill proposed building a 6,000 acre landfill on Sioux lands in South Dakota. The project, later attacked in an article entitled *Dances with Garbage,* was thwarted by a grassroots group known as the Good Road Coalition, which led to a recall election of the Tribal Council government and the proposal's rejection.

III. THE ENVIRONMENTAL JUSTICE MOVEMENT

A. The Environmental and Civil Rights Movements

The resistance of communities to environmental inequities is not a new development. However, while earlier protests were largely ignored by policy-makers, environmentalists, and the media, present-day efforts have been legitimized by the convergence of the environmental and social justice movements.

Much early activism took place before the first Earth Day in 1970. In 1967, for example, the drowning of an eight-year-old African American girl at a garbage dump—located next door to an elementary school in the middle of an African American neighborhood—triggered a campus riot at the predominantly African American Texas Southern University. The student protest escalated into a serious disorder, in which students hurled rocks and bottles at police. Gunshots were fired and a police officer was killed by a ricocheting bullet. Nearly 500 students were cleared from the dormitories, and many of the protest's leaders were arrested. This incident was one of the first instances when civil rights activists, perhaps inadvertently, protested against environmental racism.

Despite such events, it was not until the early 1980s that a national movement for environmental justice developed in several mainstream civil rights organizations. A series of protests in 1982 in Warren County, North Carolina, a rural, predominantly African American county selected as the burial site for 30,000 cubic yards of soil contaminated with highly toxic PCBs (polychlorinated biphenyls), provided the catalyst for that development.

A number of national African American civil rights groups, including the United Church of Christ Commission for Racial Justice, the Southern Christian Leadership Conference, and the Congressional Black Caucus, led the protest in Warren. Civil rights activists, government officials, religious leaders, and local residents marched in protest against "Hunt's Dump," a PCB landfill nicknamed for then Governor Jim Hunt. More than 500 protesters were jailed. Although the demonstrations were unsuccessful in halting the landfill construction, the protests marked the first time African Americans mobilized in such broad opposition to what they defined as environmental racism.

The demonstrations also prompted District of Columbia Delegate Walter Fauntroy, who was chairman of the Congressional Black Caucus and an active participant in the protests, to initiate the 1983 U.S. General Accounting Office (GAO) study of hazardous waste landfill siting in EPA Region IV, which includes Alabama, Florida, Georgia, Kentucky, Mississippi, North Carolina, South Carolina, and Tennessee. The GAO study found a strong correlation between the location of offsite hazardous waste landfills and the racial and socioeconomic makeup of surrounding communities. African Americans made up the majority of the population in three of the four communities in Region IV that the study identified as containing offsite hazardous waste landfills. Although African Americans made up only one-fifth of the region's total population, they represented three-fourths of the population in communities with offsite landfills. Nearly a decade later, these ecological imbalances have not been reversed. African Americans still make up about one-fifth of the population in Region IV, but the two operating offsite hazardous waste landfills in the region are located in zip codes where African Americans make up the majority of the population.

Pressure from grassroots groups, academicians, and environmental justice activists regarding environmental issues ranging from lead pollution to the siting of landfills and incinerators also prompted the EPA to take several positive steps in addressing the equity question. The agency established an internal Work Group on Environmental Equity, which issued a two-volume final report in June 1992, and created an Office of Environmental Equity and an Environmental Equity Cluster. However, grassroots groups have not waited for the EPA or local governments to solve environmental problems in their communities. Many groups, like those in Los Angeles and Dallas, have succeeded in forcing changes in government policy. The following sections examine these efforts.

B. Case Study: Los Angeles

With a population of 3.5 million, Los Angeles is the nation's second largest city. It is one of the most culturally and ethnically diverse cities in the United States. Latinos, Asians, and Pacific Islanders, African Americans, and Native Americans now constitute 63% of its population.

Eight of ten African Americans in Los Angeles and about half of the city's Latinos live in segregated neighborhoods. One such neighborhood, South Central Los Angeles, is over 52% African American and 44% Latino and suffers from years of systematic neglect, infrastructure decay, high unemployment, and poverty. A recent article in the *San Francisco Examiner* described the zip code in which South Central Los Angeles lies as the "dirtiest in the state." The one-square-mile area is saturated with abandoned toxic waste sites, freeways, smokestacks, and waste-water pipes from polluting industries. In 1989 alone, some 18 industrial firms discharged more than 33 million pounds of waste chemicals into its environment.

Los Angeles' growing population has created a mounting waste problem. In 1979, under a grant from the EPA, the city developed a plan to build three waste-to-energy incinerators. The mayor and city council appointed several advisory councils and committees between 1981 and 1984 to coordinate the project, known as the Los Angeles City Energy Recovery project or LANCER.

The city council selected South Central Los Angeles as the site for the first of the three incinerators, LANCER 1, designed to handle 1600 tons of waste per day. Proponents of LANCER 1 attempted to hasten the project's implementation in order to help ensure that the other two proposed incinerators, LANCER 2 and 3, would also be authorized. LANCER 2 and 3 were planned for the wealthier and mostly white neighborhoods of Westside and San Fernando Valley; thus, proponents felt that if LANCER 1 were up and running, officials would be hard-pressed to justify canceling plans for LANCER 2 and 3 on health and environmental grounds without encountering charges of racism. The city involved residents in the decision-making process on LANCER 1 only after the city council had approved the final environmental impact report. Although LANCER 1 had been in the works for more than six years, neighborhood residents were not informed about the city-sponsored project until August 1985.

After discovering that the incinerator was to be constructed in their community, six African American women organized community residents into a group called Concerned Citizens of South Central Los Angeles. Concerned Citizens successfully formed a coalition against LANCER 1 that included several national and grassroots environmental groups. Greenpeace was the first national environmental group to join Concerned Citizens; other groups that later joined the fight included Citizens for a Better Environment, National Health Law Program, and the Center for Law in Public Interest. Concerned Citizens also forged alliances with two "slow-growth" groups from Westside: Not Yet New York, a coalition of environmentalists and homeowners, and an anti-incineration group called California Alliance in Defense of Residential Environments (CADRE). Concerned Citizens and its allies conducted an intense campaign to persuade Mayor Tom Bradley to reconsider his support for the LANCER project. In 1987, Mayor Bradley and the Los Angeles City Council killed the project, on which the city had already spent $12 million dollars....

C. Case Study: Dallas

With just under one million people, 30% of whom are African Americans, Dallas is the seventh-largest city in the United States. Over the years, the city's minority neighborhoods have suffered the consequences of lead smelters operating in their communities. All three of the lead smelters in Dallas are located in predominantly African American and Latino neighborhoods.

One of the city's oldest lead smelters, located in the West Dallas neighborhood, dates back to the 1930s. Of West Dallas's 13,161 residents, more than 85% are African Americans. The lead smelter is located next door to an elementary school and across the street from the West Dallas Boys' Club. A 3,500-unit public housing project is located just 50 feet downwind from the lead smelter's property line.

During the peak period of its operation in the mid-1960s, the plant employed more than 400 people, few of whom lived in the West Dallas neighborhood. The smelter pumped more than 269 tons of lead particles into the West Dallas air each year; these particles were blown by prevailing winds through the doors and windows of nearby residents, and onto West Dallas's streets, ballparks, and playgrounds.

Dallas officials knew as early as 1972 that lead was finding its way into the bloodstreams of children living in two predominantly African American and Latino neighborhoods containing lead smelters, West Dallas and East Oak Cliff. On average, these children suffered a 36% increase in blood lead level. Residents of the neighborhood and environmental groups urged the city to restrict lead emissions and to conduct a large-scale screening program to determine the extent of the public health problem, but the city failed to take immediate action. In 1981, after nearly five decades of complaining to city officials, local residents formed the West Dallas Neighborhood Committee on Lead Contamination. Staff from Common Ground Community Economic Development Corporation, a grassroots self-help and anti-discrimination group, assisted the West Dallas residents in voicing their concerns by testifying at hearings, producing reports, and providing general technical assistance. The city finally took action after a series of articles on lead appeared in the local Dallas newspapers. The articles triggered public outrage, several class-action lawsuits, and legal action by the Texas attorney general. Public pressure forced the city to appoint a task force to study the lead problem, angering West Dallas residents who had demanded more immediate action.

In June 1983 the West Dallas plaintiffs—40 property owners and 370 children, most of whom were poor black residents of the West Dallas public housing project—reached an out-of-court settlement for over $45 million. The agreement was one of the largest community lead contamination settlements ever negotiated. RSR Corporation, which operated the lead smelter, agreed to institute a soil cleanup program in West Dallas, a blood-testing program for children and pregnant women, and to install new anti-pollution equipment. However, the settlement did not require the smelter to close.

RSR never installed the pollution control equipment at the smelter. In May 1984, the Dallas Board of Adjustments, a city agency responsible for monitoring land-use violations, requested that the city attorney order the smelter permanently closed, charging that the facility violated the city's zoning code. Four months later, the Board succeeded in closing the smelter permanently. RSR completed a superficial cleanup of the area in 1984. Ultimately, it was discovered that the lead smelter had operated for almost fifty years without the necessary use permits. Despite repeated health citations, fines, and citizen complaints against the smelter, Dallas was clearly lax in its enforcement of health and land use regulations in the African American community that had involuntarily hosted the smelter.

A comprehensive cleanup of the West Dallas neighborhood finally began in December 1991, nearly twenty years after the first documentation of the lead problem in the neighborhood. An estimated 30,000 to 40,000 cubic yards of lead-tainted soil will eventually be removed from several West Dallas sites, including school property, the West Dallas Boys Club, and the yards of 140 private homes. The cleanup will cost the U.S. EPA about $4 million. However, the threat to communities of color is not over. One proposal considered by city officials called for dumping the lead-tainted soil at a landfill in Monroe, Louisiana, a community that is 60% African American.

IV. CONCLUSION

The burdens of industrial expansion are not shared equally by all members of U.S. society. Low-income and minority communities have borne a disproportionate share of the nation's environmental problems. These communities have had little success in blocking unwanted waste facilities and other polluting industries. Since the early 1980s, however, an environmental justice movement linking environmental groups and civil rights activists has gained strength. These alliances have successfully defeated several government initiatives that would have placed a disproportionate burden on communities of color. In addition, the environmental justice movement has had limited success in broader attacks upon environmental inequities. For example, the Commission for Racial Justice was a major force behind the Environmental Justice Act, a legislative initiative introduced by Congressman John Lewis and Senator Albert Gore in 1992 that will have to be reintroduced since its Senate sponsor has become Vice-President.

Still, legal challenges to environmental injustices have not yet achieved the desired outcome—the elimination of environmental decisions, policies, and practices that have a disparate impact on low-income and minority communities. Although waste facility siting practices that disproportionately affect minority communities may be insensitive and unjust, they are not illegal. This makes the task of grassroots groups that continue to challenge siting disparities all the more difficult.

Communities that suffer from the worst pollution also suffer from acute unemployment, poverty, and business disinvestment. Federal, state, and local governments can address these problems by providing small and minority businesses with incentives to explore the pollution prevention and hazard abatement field as a form of economic development. Lead abatement is one area in which training and jobs could be offered to communities threatened by both poverty and pollution.

Because of the inherent inequities associated with waste facility siting, the federal government should place a moratorium on the construction of new commercial, municipal, and hazardous waste incinerators in communities already saturated with environmental problems. State and federal permitting strategies must be altered to reflect equity concerns. Clearly, current environmental regulations and protectionist devices such as zoning, deed restrictions, and other land-use controls have not had the same impact on all segments of society. To correct this problem, governments should supplement standard technical requirements with fair share plans that take into account the sociodemographic, economic, and cultural factors of impacted communities.

The EPA must take the lead in assuring the protection of all Americans. No segment of society should become a dumping ground because of the race, ethnicity, or economic vulnerability of its members. Legislative initiatives are needed at local, state, national, and international levels to assure the integration of social concerns into all environmental regulations. All communities—black or white, rich or poor—deserve protection from environmental degradation. If the United States is to achieve environmental equity, the environment in urban ghettos, barrios, reservations, and rural poverty pockets must receive the same protection as the environment in suburban regions. Moreover, the domestic policy of dumping on the poor and communities of color in the United States should not be exported abroad by dumping on the poor and communities of color in Third World nations.

The Future of Race and Ethnic Relations in the United States

On the Internet . . .

Sites appropriate to Part Five

JustCause works to discourage racism, prejudice, and homophobia through the use of media campaigns that promote tolerance and diversity. In addition, JustCause works behind the scenes to monitor legislation and news events that are important to our everyday lives. It also offers suggestions as to what can be done on an individual level to discourage hate and prejudice.

http://www.webcom.com/~justcaus/

The National Conference is a human relations organization dedicated to fighting bias, bigotry, and racism in America. This site provides information on National Conference public policy statements and links to other human relations, civil rights, human rights, and education organizations.

http://members.aol.com/NatlConf/index.html

The Toronto Coalition Against Racism is a coalition of over 50 community-based antiracist and social justice organizations. It unites many individuals and communities in a common struggle against racism and fascism. Its aim is to build a broad, mass-action coalition that will represent and be led by communities that are targeted by racism and fascism.

http://www.ryerson.ca/~melbirt/tcar/

Future
Prospects

12.1 DERRICK BELL

Racism Will Always Be With Us

Racism is an integral part of America's cultural fabric. It is a major social malady that deeply affects the stability of the nation. Some social critics argue that racism is indispensable to the American political and economic structure. In the present selection, for example, Derrick Bell asserts that racism is inevitable in American society, where majority rule can effectively maintain control of an ideological framework that defines minorities as expendable. He shows that by compromising minority interests in favor of protecting White interests, the ruling class is able to retain political and economic control in society.

Bell is a professor of law at Harvard University and a former deputy director for civil rights in the Department of Health, Education, and Welfare. His many publications include *And We Are Not Saved: The Elusive Quest for Racial Justice* (Basic Books, 1989).

Key Concept: the inevitability of racism

*R*acism, like death, will always be with us. It is a permanent fixture of American society, and its effect—if not its form—has been fairly consistent in the US for 350 years.

There is an allegorical story in my upcoming book called "The Space Traders," which takes place in the year 2000 and involves an alien people who come to Earth and offer the US gold to pay off all its debts, chemicals to clean up its environment, and inexpensive, safe nuclear fuel to satisfy its energy needs. All the aliens want in return is an agreement that they can go back to their home star with America's black population in tow. Whites can't see these aliens; they can only hear them. But blacks, who can see them perfectly well and who establish that they hold an uncanny resemblance to Ku Klux Klansmen, respond incredulously to the Administration: "What are you doing? Just tell them 'No!' " There are many twists and turns in the story but finally there is a national referendum and by about 70 to 30 percent, the majority votes for the trade.

"The Space Traders" story is futuristic but it is based on fact. In the history of the US, whenever there is a serious difference between contending groups of whites and compromise can be reached by sacrificing the rights of blacks, that is what happens. There were no aliens offering gold when the Constitution was written but there were a good many powerful men who threatened to walk out of the Constitutional Convention and so sacrifice the unity of the nation if blacks were endowed with human qualities, much less rights. There were Northerners who hated slavery but Southerners who said, "either protect slavery or there will be no new federal government." Slavery was protected.

THE THEORY OF MORAL RELATIVITY   In 1830, Alexis de Tocqueville wrote: "I do not believe that the white and black races will ever live in any country upon an equal footing. But I believe the difficulty to be still greater in the US than elsewhere. An isolated individual may surmount the prejudices of the religion of his country or his race but a whole people cannot rise, at it were, above itself. A despot who should subject the American and his former slaves to the same yoke might perhaps succeed in co-mingling the races but as long as the American democracy remains at the head of affairs, no one will undertake so difficult a task and it may be foreseen that the freer, that is the more democratic the white population of the US becomes, the more isolated it will remain."

Indeed, the Framers of the Constitution were afraid of majoritarian government; and in *The Federalist*, James Madison urged a large, diverse electorate composed of many factions as the best defense against majority tyranny. Madison's approach is viable as long as coalition building occurs freely across racial lines, but when issues come to be seen across the fault line of race, minorities always pay the highest price.

The fact of contemporary American politics is that ours is a majoritarian system, divided along racial lines and whites tend to oppose those policies blacks support: Affirmative action and civil rights legislation are only the most obvious examples.

One effect of race-based politics is that ideas of justice, equality and morality become infinitely manipulatable based on one's racial perspective—who is doing what to whom, when, where and under what circumstances.

An example: The attack by Los Angeles police on Rodney King last spring shocked the US not because *any* act of police brutality is, in and of itself, immoral and illegal but because we saw it on television and we could no longer avoid the issue. However, the fact of the matter is that the Los Angeles police force has a decades-old reputation—and out-of-court settlements to victims to substantiate the reputation—of brutality toward minorities.

Blacks saw the King beating as a pattern in practice—a graphic comment on the quality of their citizenship. Yet, until a video was made of this brutality in action, most people were willing to look the other way as long as these policemen protected their car stereos and their homes.

Most whites would not vote for police to beat black heads. But if there are police who say that the only way they can do their job and protect property is if they can beat black heads, compromises—meaning the sacrifice of civil rights —will be made.

THE PRINCIPLE OF INTEREST CONVERGENCE   If the first principle of political physics is compromise—with blacks always being compromised first— the second principle is that no law is passed that benefits blacks unless that law benefits or at least does no harm to the interests of whites—a principle I call "interest convergence."

The 1954 *Brown v. Board of Education* is a perfect example of interest convergence. I often cite the NAACP and government briefs in the *Brown* case, both of which maintain that abandonment of state-supported segregation would be a crucial asset as we compete with communist countries for the hearts and minds of Third World people just emerging from long years of colonialism. Certainly, it would have been harder to convince the Third World of our superiority if we had continued to have official apartheid built right into the Constitution or its interpretation.

Though Dr. W. E. B. DuBois did not endear himself to civil rights advocates with the following statement, years after the *Brown* decision he observed that "no such decision would have been possible without the world pressure of communism," which he felt rendered it "simply impossible for the US to continue to lead a "Free World" with race segregation kept legal over a third of its territory." In *Parting the Waters*, Taylor Branch notes that the Voice of America immediately translated Justice Warren's opinion into 34 languages for overseas broadcast, while some domestic media outlets fell silent and Universal Newsreels never even mentioned the most important Supreme Court decision of the century.

But the Court, after handing down *Brown* in 1954 then said, "Come back next year and we will tell you how to go about implementing the desegregation ruling." And what they said the next year was that they were going to implement *Brown* very, very slowly. But for the protests, the bus boycott in Montgomery in 1959, the sit-ins that started in 1960, who knows what would have happened to *Brown*.

As it was, *Brown* dealt with the effects of segregation but didn't address its causes. Indeed, *Brown* is an amazing piece of legal writing in that there is an acknowledgement of serious harm but no admission of wrong doing. Segregation just floated down out of the sky; it is bad; we don't know how it got started; we have got to end it. As if racism was an anachronism that could be picked out of society like so many weeds.

Had the Court been serious about the equal educational opportunity *Brown* promised, as well as concerned about white opposition to actual desegregation, it might have approached the issue from the victim's perspective and issued the following orders in *Brown*—orders which would have given priority to desegregating not the students but the money and the control:

1. Even though we encourage voluntary desegregation, we will not order racially integrated assignments of students or staff for ten years.
2. Even though "separate but equal" no longer meets the constitutional equal-protection standard, we will require immediate equalization of all facilities and resources.
3. Blacks must be represented on school boards and other policy-making bodies in proportions equal to those of black students in each school district.

The third point would have been intended to give blacks meaningful access to decision making—a prerequisite to full equality still unattained in many predominantly black school systems. For example, an "equal representation" rule might have helped protect the thousands of black teachers and principals who were dismissed by school systems during the desegregation process.

Had this been the approach, however the Court never would have reached a unanimous decision. In fact, it probably would not even have gotten a majority to go along with the school desegregation plan.

So, instead, Brown essentially equated integration with the effective education black children need. And because Brown did not have the power to regulate the behavior of white parents who could afford to move to the suburbs or send their children to private schools, or to redistribute taxes so that a district's tax base would not destine poor areas to inferior educational facilities, 36 years after *Brown* the schools are resegregated and black children continue to receive an inferior education in substandard facilities.

RACE AS METAPHOR   Racism, however, is merely a metaphor for what happens to the vast majority of Americans—white, black or brown—on a much larger scale. I am always amazed that problems of race I see dramatically in regard to blacks are present, although less dramatically, for whites also. Rhetoric about equality and justice aside, the failure of these ideals to translate into reality in any meaningful way go well beyond race.

But the "race question" is an extremely powerful diversion. Twenty years ago, economist Robert Heilbroner argued that the reason the US lagged so far behind countries in Northern Europe on issues of housing, prison reform, social security and health care—even though Northern Europe was much less rich than the US—was because those countries were homogeneous and people were able to perceive that, "there but for the grace of God go I."

In our heterogeneous country, it is very easy for those opposed to these programs to argue against them on the basis that prison reform will only coddle the black prisoner; that affirmative action gives jobs to reward lazy minorities who would rather stand on the corner than study; that welfare is being abused by lazy, pathological, drug-abusing black women. The US is able to distance the suffering and relative disadvantage of many whites by arguing that people of color disproportionately and unfairly benefit from social welfare programs. . . .

George Bush used Willie Horton, a black felon, in a national television campaign to scare voters away from his opponent. [North Carolina Senator] Jesse Helms appealed to white voters by showing white hands tearing up a rejection slip, the message being: Blacks, through affirmative action, are stealing your jobs. These two men, who should have been excoriated, were hailed— and elected—though they merely utilized a modern version of a tried-and-true coalition-building tactic: playing to white fears of loss—job, position, prestige, safety—to blacks.

These are only two examples of the fact that those who wish to protect their place within the economic and political status quo need only remind voters that they must stand together against blacks who, through affirmative action or crime, pose a major threat to them all. Racism is a very effective organizing tool.

THE PERKS OF RACISM   Tocqueville understood in 1830, and Yale professor Edmond Morgan confirmed in his book *American Slavery, American Freedom,* what most of us today refuse to acknowledge: that there is a significant connection between democracy and discrimination. Both men understood quite clearly that the presence of a class at the bottom in slavery meant that those on top were able to preach the apostrophes of freedom to poor and working-class whites, urge them to vote and be a part of the system, while denying them any real opportunities. We have had variations of this theme ever since.

Except for a few brilliant exceptions such as Tocqueville or Thomas Jefferson, who, considering the evil of slavery, wrote: "I tremble for my country when I reflect that God is just," racism is rarely acknowledged in its then-currently-functioning form. During slavery, there were arguments about how enslavement actually helped slaves. Variations on this argument were used during the days of "separate but equal." We hear more of the same today, except the arguments are negative: Affirmative action actually hurts the self-esteem of blacks; civil rights legislation hurts small businesses.

I have come to the conclusion, after many years, that my obligation is not to overcome racism but to recognize and oppose it. Just as death is inevitable, racism is intractable. It is the failure to develop a realistic perspective on the problem that stymies progress and makes setbacks very discouraging.

We must advocate an infusion of tragedy into our American culture, an understanding of our past and the limits of our shared future.

Certainly, there is tragedy in America vis-à-vis blacks. In failing to acknowledge this we invite side shows: We argue about who is to blame rather than what is to be done; we fight to desegregate the schools, rather than to educate our children; we argue about why Vietnamese immigrant children succeed while blacks remain behind, rather than demanding that all children be well-educated.

This said, the likelihood of getting any unanimous agreement on policies is very poor. However, strategy and tactics are less important than having a sense of what we are fighting. We must first understand the peculiar hold racism has on American society. Then, after we have some understanding, we must use whatever tools we have available to loosen its hold on our lives.

Combating Racism

Many researchers agree that any attempts to eliminate racism from the American social system must entail a strategy for altering the institutional structures that promote and legitimate racism. Christopher Bates Doob presents this argument in this selection. According to Doob, resolutions to the problem of racism that are economically and socially painless will have no lasting effects. Only by eliminating inner-city ghettos, more rigorously applying and enforcing affirmative action policies, and implementing grassroots programs, for example, can the U.S. social system hope to correct structural racial oppression.

Key Concept: the elimination of racism

*P*ublic-service announcements, sermons, and classroom lectures often stress that racism is wrong. But in spite of many notable efforts to condemn racism, the impact is limited. The problem is that such efforts do not alter structures supporting the problem.

Public officials often either fail to appreciate or simply deny that reality. When a major racial incident occurs in a city or at a college or university, authorities are likely to call meetings and create task forces, which issue reports but make few meaningful changes.

Nor can one hold the mayor of a city or the president of a college or university mainly responsible for failing to eliminate racism. As we have seen throughout this book, racism permeates American society: The steps to restrict it significantly go well beyond the capacities of political or university officials. Let's consider what needs to be done.

... Stephen Steinberg (1989) contended that an effective policy to eradicate the historical impact of racism must address fundamental problems. The following discussion includes several of Steinberg's issues, along with an additional point:

First, there must be a national commitment to eliminating ghettos. Poverty inherited from the days of slavery along with discrimination in housing have produced and maintained ghettos, and ghetto residence restricts a person's educational and occupational opportunities. Yet on television news and in textbooks, ghettos are discussed with the same neutrality shown to suburbs. That shouldn't be: Ghettos are among the most stark representations of ... the restriction of racial minorities' physical movement.

Steinberg pointed out that to implement such a multibillion-dollar program effectively, organizers would need to keep a vigilant watch on its activities, making certain that it did not become simply another scandal-ridden opportunity for construction, real-estate, and political interests. In addition, it would be essential to enlist the participation of local individuals and groups, whose perspective on ghetto dwellers' needs and interests emerge out of daily experience, not from some removed, possibly misguided, or even racist viewpoint.

We should consider one cautionary idea. A clear distinction exists between eliminating negative aspects of ghetto life and destroying vital if poor inner-city communities. Herbert Gans (1962) and Jane Jacobs (1961) produced classic studies stressing that most city planners tend to view poor, urban neighborhoods negatively, simply assuming that they are destructive to their residents and the city at large. As a result their orders are to bulldoze indiscriminately, with the frequent tragic result that vital communities developed over long periods of time are destroyed. Eliminating ghettos, in short, should not mean destroying vital communities. Before determining appropriate alterations, each area must be examined carefully to assess its strengths and weaknesses.

A second issue in Steinberg's discussion is that affirmative action needs continued support and growth.... Historically racial minorities were restricted in education and work, limited to training and jobs that would directly benefit white controllers. Affirmative-action programs attempt to address historical wrongs.

Consider some impressive successes. American Telephone and Telegraph Company, one of the largest private employers in the United States, established an agreement in 1973 with the Equal Employment Opportunities Commission to redress past discriminatory hiring practices. By 1982 the percentage of minority craft workers had increased from 8.4 percent to 14 percent of the work force, and among management the proportion of minority-group members had risen from 4.6 percent to 13.1 percent. Between 1962 and 1968, the number of black employees at IBM rose nearly tenfold—from 750 to 7251—and then in 1980 more than doubled to 16,546. Under threat of court orders, government agencies have aggressively pursued affirmative-action policies, and the results have been decisive. One result has been that since the late 1960s, the number of black police officers has increased by 20,000 (Steinberg, 1989).

The opening years of the affirmative-action period yielded modest results. In general, research found that between 1966 and 1973, companies forced to establish affirmative-action programs because they were doing business with the federal government increased their percentage of black workers more than companies not required to meet affirmative-action standards. Between 1974 and 1980, the number of African-Americans receiving jobs because of affirmative action increased even more than in the previous seven-year period; in addition, at this time as a result of affirmative action, blacks were often able to obtain better paying, more prestigious positions (Jaynes and Williams, 1989: 316–317; Leonard, 1985). Reviewing investigations on the topic, a team of researchers concluded that "affirmative action seems to have effected educational and occupational gains for women and for racial minorities" (Crosby and Clayton, 1990: 65).

A criticism frequently directed against affirmative action is that it has promoted racial minorities' opportunities for white-collar positions and ignored their involvement in blue-collar jobs. But this has not been the case. The focus of many affirmative-action initiatives has been law enforcement, construction work, and craft and production positions in large companies.

Another criticism is that giving minority-group members a hand up undermines their morale and self-confidence. Certainly each affirmative-action program needs to be examined and reexamined for its impact on participants, and if clear indications of destructive effect appear, then alterations are necessary. Often, however, this position claiming favoritism toward minorities simply serves to praise the value of individualism while conveniently forgetting structural factors underlying racism and poverty. A significantly greater concern seems to be that the vicious cycle of poverty enveloping so many minority-group members continues to expand. To prevent that, affirmative action must proceed with all deliberate speed.

With the groundwork for affirmative action now established, it appears just and reasonable to extend its programs into all educational and work areas. Inevitably resistance will continue, but if this society truly is dedicated to the elimination of racism, this policy must persist.

A third issue also relates to jobs and additionally involves immigration policy. In the past quarter-century, this nation has lost 3 million industrial jobs and also absorbed over 11 million legal immigrants, along with countless millions of illegal arrivals. Frequently immigrants have taken jobs for which Americans, particularly minority Americans could be trained.

Consider the area of nursing. To meet a critical shortage of nurses, the United States has been importing tens of thousands of foreign nurses. At the same time, nursing schools throughout the country have been closed. A program oriented to the needs and interests of American minorities would emphasize that the nursing shortage could be met with a radically different approach —expand nursing schools, publicize and promote the opportunities for nursing throughout the public-school system, especially in areas where there are large numbers of minority students, and, ultimately, stop importing large numbers of foreign nurses (Steinberg, 1989: 51–54)....

Even specialists on racial issues find themselves contributing to racism. Stephen Steinberg raised this point with his analysis of the term "underclass," which became popular in the early 1980s. The term focuses on individuals' and groups' failures to attain conventional rewards, thus keeping them "under" the established class system. It is a vague term, lumping together diverse ethnic and racial groups and failing to single out specific conditions, especially racism for racial minorities, that have played a crucial role in limiting their opportunities (Steinberg, 1989: 43–44). This term has racist, blame-the-victim overtones, implying minorities' cultural inferiority; and it is used widely. That is because even experts on race relations sometimes fail to see that their analysis of racial situations is simplistic....

It is hardly surprising that in a society where norms supporting racial conflict and separation prevail, race relations in high schools will mirror the larger social pattern.

In 1988 in a high school in Ann Arbor, Michigan, a science teacher reprimanded several African-American students for their "rowdy behavior." In the course of his reprimand, he asked, "Do you want to grow up to be dumb niggers?" The question launched a controversy that involved public confrontations between parents, teachers, and administrators. But throughout all this activity, student input was not sought.

A number of local high-school students decided to become involved. They initiated a survey, assessing students' feelings about racism in the Ann Arbor high schools and took several actions based on their findings. Two of the students—Shael Polakow-Suransky and Neda Ulaby—wrote up the highlights in an article.

In October 1987 these students took over a largely dormant organization called Student Advocates to the School Board (SASB). Members convened a meeting of students from each of Ann Arbor's four high schools. Representatives of all three racial groups in the schools—African-Americans, Asian-Americans, and whites—participated. In the first meeting, students discussed their personal experiences and began to develop a group approach. In subsequent meetings SASB students conducted brainstorming sessions in which they reworked questions for their survey until reaching a consensus. Ultimately, SASB members realized, they would need their administrators' approval for the final questionnaire, but they were determined to keep the survey's development a wholly student effort.

By January the students completed a working copy of the questionnaire. English-class members in one of the larger high schools served as guinea pigs, and as a result of this initial testing, some questions were reworded and the survey was shortened.

The district administration agreed to print up the questionnaires, and 3500 copies of the three-page instrument were produced. Two thousand and six students (57.4 percent of those surveyed) filled it out. Those who didn't either were absent the day the survey was given, or teachers in a given class chose not to administer it. Responses to demographic questions indicated that those who answered the questionnaire provided a racial and social-class cross-section of the district.

When asked about segregation at school, most students indicated that it occurred both academically and socially and that minorities often felt that they were objects of discrimination. One respondent indicated that because of segregated classes, minorities don't consider whites to be peers. Another student claimed that segregation was voluntary, with each racial group claiming to be superior. Ninety-two percent of the students indicated that social segregation existed to some degree, but most felt that it was not bad and, in fact, was natural.

Reading the questionnaire commentaries on segregation, the researchers were impressed by clear linguistic indications of racial segregation. Polakow-Suransky and Ulaby indicated that the pronouns *we* and *us* were often opposed to the pronouns *they* and *them*, producing psychological barriers between student racial groups.

Tracking was another topic in the questionnaire. When asked to choose from a list of alternatives one or more reasons why minority-group students were more likely to be tracked into lower classes, 52 percent said it was because minority-group students had lower scores on standardized achievement tests, 51 percent indicated it was because they didn't try as hard, 46 percent said it was because they had been labeled troublemakers, and 44 percent concluded it was because of their grades from elementary and junior high school. Often students were unaware that because of institutional racism, many members of racial minorities had suffered educational disadvantages since early childhood, making their likelihood of ending up in lower classes much greater than it would be for whites. Some students did recognize the destructive, self-fulfilling impact of tracking. One wrote, "If you've been treated like a dumb black child all your life, you begin to actually believe it."

Many students had strong emotional responses to members of other racial groups. Some whites felt that blacks engaged in reverse discrimination—that black organizations were segregationist and represented just another form of racism. Frequently whites were deeply resentful of the anger and bitterness encountered in daily interactions with African-American students. Some white students felt that teachers set lower standards for black students and that blacks took advantage of minority status when pursuing college admissions and scholarships. On the other hand, African-American students felt that they often encountered racism, and that little effort occurred to right wrongs of historical oppression. In addition, student responses indicated that highly negative stereotypes of black students continued to thrive in the Ann Arbor high schools.

SASB members analyzed their data and wrote up a report, which they presented to the school board. They included a list of recommendations, such as developing workshops and class discussions about the race-related issues contained in the survey; reevaluating local policies on tracking, with the aim of eliminating the practice; requiring all students to take a course exposing them to issues involving American racial oppression; and creating a task force both to evaluate the entire high-school curriculum from a multicultural perspective and to develop guidelines for handling racial incidents in the high schools.

In the next several months, SASB students organized follow-up activities for the last weeks before the end of the school year. They felt that for the first time, they were beginning to confront structures supporting racism and racial isolation. At that point students started to encounter resistance from school administrators. Two school principals backed out of earlier commitments to support students' efforts. Polakow-Suransky and Ulaby indicated that they were unhappy to discover that "the resistance to change at this level was more powerful than the district's stated policy of pursuing excellence and equity" (Polakow-Suransky and Ulaby, 1990: 606).

However, SASB members were able to schedule successful class discussions and workshops in the two smaller high schools, and they presented a proposal to the school board asking that each school be required to spend 15 hours the following year on multicultural educational activities.

During the next spring semester, SASB members decided to pursue a suggestion repeatedly made in students' questionnaires—follow up on younger students. They designed a curriculum, using simulated games, cooperative learning activities, and group discussions in which sixth graders would interact with high-school students. The SASB efforts received sufficient administrative support to make it likely that by the middle of the 1990–1991 school year, five middle schools would be participating in it.

Two years later it was difficult to gauge the impact students' efforts to dismantle racist structures produced on the Ann Arbor high schools. Currently the history curriculum is being reevaluated with the intent to present a multicultural perspective. In the 1989–1990 school year, there was a new required course on human behavior, containing a large component on racism. Members of the student group met with counselors to discuss ways of dealing with tracking, but little change has occurred in that area.

Looking back on a couple years of hard work, Polakow-Suransky and Ulaby indicated that SASB efforts had made a difference but that schools, like all American organizations, are conservative and will only change slowly. The authors concluded that the impact of racism is so pervasive in people's thoughts and actions that the struggle to find new ways to eliminate it must be unrelenting.

This group of high-school students produced impressive results. What steps would be necessary to implement such a program at your college? It might be interesting and productive to discuss this issue in class.

CONCLUSION

In the years ahead, Americans will be forced to make tough decisions about race. What programs will most effectively curtail or eliminate the legacy of racism?... Certainly it is fitting to do everything to be humane—to give all citizens an opportunity to participate fully in the bounty of our great nation.

But the issue goes beyond such altruism. It has become painfully apparent that a great shadow has spread across our society—fear of the ever-expanding violence of primarily minority citizens who have been denied access to valued opportunities and rewards. It is now painfully apparent that no token measures are going to buy them off. If the United States doesn't make a frontal attack on the combined forces of racism and poverty, then those formidable foes are going to grow in strength and in the terror they produce. Reviewing race relations in the 1990s, sociologist Lewis Killian concluded that new taxes and a more equitable distribution of wealth are necessary. He warned that without such measures "the new enemy will be our own underclass" (Killian, 1990: 13).

At the moment American culture is a racist culture. This condition is undeniable, regrettable, but potentially changeable. Collectively Americans should do what those addicted to alcohol and hard drugs are required to do: Look hard and long at themselves and face their problem head on, in this case saying, "We are racist." A heartfelt realization can be a first step toward effective action.

Chapter 12
Future
Prospects

Crosby, Faye, and Susan Clayton. 1990. "Affirmative Action and the Issue of Expectancies." *Journal of Social Issues* 46: 61–79.

Gans, Herbert J. 1962. *The Urban Villagers*. New York: Free Press.

Jacobs, Jane. 1961. *The Death and Life of Great American Cities*. New York: Vintage Books.

Jaynes, Gerald David, and Robin M. Williams, Jr. (eds.). 1989. *A Common Destiny: Blacks and American Society*. Washington, DC: National Academy Press.

Killian, Lewis M. 1990. "Race Relations and the Nineties: Where Are the Dreams of the Sixties?" *Social Forces* 69 (September): 1–13.

Leonard, Jonathan. 1985. "The Effectiveness of Equal Employment and Affirmative Action Regulation." Report to the Subcommittee on Civil and Constitutional Rights of the Judiciary Committee, U.S. Congress. Berkeley, CA: School of Business Administration, University of California, Berkeley.

Polakow-Suransky, Shael, and Neda Ulaby. 1990. "Students Take Action to Combat Racism." *Phi Delta Kappan* 71 (April): 601–606.

Steinberg, Stephen. 1989. "The Underclass: A Class of Color Blindness." *New Politics* 2 (Summer): 42–60.

12.3 MICHAEL A. OLIVAS

The Chronicles, My Grandfather's Stories, and Immigration Law

In professor of law Derrick Bell's fictional story "The Chronicle of the Space Traders," aliens from a far-off star land at the beachhead of the Atlantic coast of the United States. The Space Traders offer to the people of the United States "gold, to bail out the almost bankrupt federal, state, and local governments; special chemicals capable of unpolluting the environment, which was becoming daily more toxic, and restoring it to the pristine state it had been before Western explorers set foot on it; and a totally safe nuclear engine and fuel, to relieve the nation's all-but-depleted supply of fossil fuel." All the Space Traders want in return is "to take back to their home star all the African Americans who lived in the United States."

Michael A. Olivas is a professor of law at the University of Houston Law School and director of the Institute of Higher Education Law and Governance. In the following selection from "The Chronicles, My Grandfather's Stories, and Immigration Law: The Slave Traders Chronicle as Racial History," *St. Louis University Law Journal* (vol. 34, 1990), Olivas contends that the conquest, exploitation, colonialization, enslavement, and immigration of American racial history illustrates poignantly the reality of the Space Traders' story.

Key Concept: racial history

*T*he funny thing about stories is that everyone has one. My grandfather had them, with plenty to spare. When I was very young, he would regale me with stories, usually about politics, baseball, and honor. These were his themes, the subject matter he carved out for himself and his grandchildren. As the oldest grandson and his first godchild, I held a special place of responsibility and affection. In Mexican families, this patrimony handed to young boys is one remnant of older times that is fading, like the use of Spanish in the home, posadas at Christmas, or the deference accorded all elders.

In Sabino Olivas' world, there were three verities, ones that he adhered to his entire life: political and personal loyalties are paramount; children should work hard and respect their elders; and people should conduct their lives with honor. Of course, each of these themes had a canon of stories designed, like parables, to illustrate the larger theme, and, like the Bible, to be interlocking, cross referenced, and synoptic. That is, they could be embellished in the retelling, but they had to conform to the general themes of loyalty, hard work, and honor.

Several examples will illustrate the overarching theoretical construction of my grandfather's worldview and show how, for him, everything was connected, and profound. Like other folklorists and storytellers, he employed mythic heroes or imbued people he knew with heroic dimensions. This is an important part of capturing the imagination of young children, for the mythopoeic technique overemphasizes characteristics and allows listeners to fill in the gaps by actively inviting them to rewrite the story and remember it in their own terms. As a result, as my family grew (I am the oldest of ten), I would hear these taproot stories retold both by my grandfather to the other kids and by my brothers and sisters to others. The core of the story would be intact, transformed by the teller's accumulated sense of the story line and its application.

One of the earliest stories was about New Mexico's United States Senator Bronson Cutting, and how he had died in a plane crash after attempting to help Northern New Mexico Hispanics regain land snatched from them by greedy developers. Growing up near Tierra Amarilla, New Mexico, as he did, my grandfather was heir to a longstanding oral tradition of defining one's status by land ownership. To this day, land ownership in Northern New Mexico is a tangle of aboriginal Indian rights, Spanish land grants, Anglo and Mexican greed, treaties, and developer domination. Most outsiders (that is, anyone south of Sante Fe) know this issue only by having seen *The Milagro Beanfield War*, the Robert Redford movie based on John Nichols' book. But my grandfather's story was that sinister forces had somehow tampered with Senator Cutting's plane because he was a man of the people, aligned against wealthy interests. Senator Cutting, I was led to believe as I anchored the story with my own points of reference, was more like Jimmy Stewart in *Mr. Smith Goes to Washington* than like the Claude Rains character, who would lie to get his own greedy way.

Of course, as I grew older, I learned that the true story was not exactly as my grandfather had told it. Land ownership in New Mexico is complicated; the Senator had his faults; and my grandfather ran afoul of Cutting's political enemy, Senator Dennis Chavez. But the story still held its sway over me.

His other favorite story, which included a strong admonition to me, was about how he and other Hispanics had been treated in Texas on their way to World War I. A trainload of soldiers from Arizona and Northern New Mexico, predominantly of Mexican origin (both New Mexico and Arizona had only recently become states), were going to training camp in Ft. Hays, Kansas. Their train stopped in a town near Amarillo, Texas, and all the men poured out to eat at a restaurant, one that catered to train travelers. But only to some. A sign prominently proclaimed, "No colateds or Mexicans allowed," and word spread among them that this admissions policy was taken seriously.

My grandfather, who until this time had never been outside the Territory or the State of New Mexico (after 1912), was not used to this kind of indignity. After all, he was from a state where Hispanics and Indians constituted a majority of the population, especially in the North, and it was his first face-to-face encounter with racism, Texas style. Shamefacedly, the New Mexicans ate the food that Anglo soldiers bought and brought to the train, but he never forgot the humiliation and anger he felt that day. Sixty-five years later, when he told me this story, he remembered clearly how most of the men died in France or elsewhere in Europe, defending a country that never fully accorded them their rights.

The longer, fuller version, replete with wonderful details of how at training camp they had ridden sawhorses with saddles, always ended with the anthem, "Ten cuidado con los Tejanos, porque son todos desgraciados y no tienen verguenza" (Be careful with Texans because they are all sons-of-bitches and have no shame). To be a *sin verguenza*—shameless, or without honor—was my grandfather's cruelest condemnation, reserved for faithless husbands, reprobates, lying grandchildren, and Anglo Texans.

These stories, which always had admonitions about honorable behavior, always had a moral to them, with implications for grandchildren. Thus, I was admonished to vote Democrat (because of FDR and the Catholic JFK), to support the National League (because the Brooklyn Dodgers had first hired Black players and because the relocated Los Angeles Dodgers had a farm team in Albuquerque), and to honor my elders (for example, by using the more formal *usted* instead of the informal *tu*).

People react to Derrick Bell and his storytelling in predictably diverse ways. People of color, particularly progressive minority scholars, have been drawn to his work. The old guard has been predictably scornful, as in Lino Graglia's dyspeptic assessment: "There can be no sin for which reading Professor Derrick Bell is not, for me, adequate punishment.... [The Chronicles are] wails of embittered, hate-filled self-pity...."

My objection, if that is the proper word, to the *Chronicle of the Space Traders* is not that it is too fantastic or unlikely to occur, but rather the opposite: This scenario has occurred, and more than once in our nation's history. Not only have Blacks been enslaved, as the *Chronicle* sorrowfully notes, but other racial groups have been conquered and removed, imported for their labor and not allowed to participate in the society they built, or expelled when their labor was no longer considered necessary.

Consider the immigration history and political economy of three groups whose United States history predates the prophecy for the year 2000: Cherokee removal and the Trail of Tears; Chinese laborers and the Chinese Exclusion Laws; and Mexicans in the Bracero Program and Operation Wetback. These three racial groups share different histories of conquest, exploitation, and legal disadvantage; but even a brief summary of their treatment in United States law shows commonalities of racial animus, legal infirmity, and majority domination of legal institutions guised as "political questions." I could have also chosen the national origins or labor histories of other Indian tribes, the Filipinos, the Native Hawaiians, the Japanese, the Guamese, the Puerto Ricans, or the Vietnamese, in other words, the distinct racial groups whose conquest, colonization, enslavement, or immigration histories mark them as candidates for the Space Traders' evil exchange.

CHEROKEE REMOVAL AND THE TRAIL OF TEARS

Although the Cherokees were, in the early 1800s, the largest tribe in what was the Southeastern United States, genocidal wars, abrogated treaties, and Anglo land settlement practices had reduced them to 15,000 by 1838, predominantly in Georgia, Tennessee, North Carolina, and Alabama. During the 1838–1839 forced march to the "Indian Territory" of what is now Oklahoma, a quarter of the Cherokees died on the "Trail of Tears," the long march of the Cherokees, Seminoles, Creeks, Choctaws, and Chickasaw. Gold had been discovered on Indian land in Georgia. The newly confederated states of the United States did not want sovereign Indian nations coexisting in their jurisdiction; and President Andrew Jackson, engaged in a bitter struggle with Chief Justice John Marshall, saw the removal of the Indians as a means to his own political ends.

Not only were the tribes removed from their ancestral homelands, guaranteed to them by treaties, at forced gunpoint, but there were other elements that foreshadowed Bell's *Chronicles*. The Cherokees had sought to integrate themselves into their conquerors' social and legal systems; they engaged as sovereigns to negotiate formally and lawfully their place in the United States polity; and they litigated their grievances in Federal courts to no avail. Like the fictional Blacks in the *Chronicles*, they too appealed to the kindness of strangers. One authoritative account of this shameful occasion noted:

> [M]any Cherokees continued to hold to their hope even while soldiers drove them from their homes into the stockades and on to the Trail of Tears. Some refused to believe that the American people would allow this to happen. Until the very end, the Cherokees spoke out supporting their rights to resist removal and to continue to live in the ancestral homelands.

In order to coexist with their conquerors, the Cherokees had adopted Anglo ways, developing their own alphabet, bilingual (English-Cherokee) newspapers, a court system, and a written constitution. They entered into a series of treaties that ceded dominion to the United States, but that preserved a substantial measure of self determination and autonomy. Beginning in 1802 with the Georgia Compact, however, white landowners and officials variously entered into and repudiated treaties and other agreements with Indian tribes. By 1830, the Indian Removal Act had been passed by Congress, and the stage was set for *Cherokee Nation v. Georgia* and *Worcester v. Georgia*. In *Cherokee Nation,*

Justice Marshall held that the Cherokee were a "domestic dependent nation[,]" and thus the Supreme Court did not have original jurisdiction; he invited another "proper case with proper parties" to determine the "mere question of right."[sic].

The "proper party" presented itself the following year, in *Worcester v. Georgia*, and Chief Justice Marshall held for the Cherokees. Marshall found that each Indian tribe was

> a distinct community, occupying its own territory, with boundaries accurately described, in which the laws of a state can have no force, and which the citizens of [a state] have no right to enter, but with the assent of the [Indians] themselves, or in conformity with treaties, and with the acts of Congress.

Despite this first clarification of Indian sovereignty and the early example of preemption, the state of Georgia refused to obey the Court's order, and President Jackson refused to enforce the Cherokees' victory. Georgia, contemptuous of the Court's authority, in what it contended was its own affairs, did not even argue its side before the Court.

The Cherokees' victory was Pyrrhic, for even their supporters, such as Daniel Webster, turned their attention away from enforcement of *Worcester* to the Nullification Crisis, which threatened the very existence of the Union. The case of *Worcester* was resolved by a pardon, technically mooting the Cherokees' victory. The "greater good" of the Union thus sacrificed Cherokee rights at the altar of political expediency, foreshadowing Blacks' sacrifice during the Civil War, Japanese rights sacrificed during World War II, Mexicans' rights sacrificed during Operation Wetback, and Black rights extinguished in the year 2000 for the Space Traders.

CHINESE EXCLUSION

No racial group has been singled out for separate, racist treatment in United States immigration law more than have the Chinese. A full political analysis of immigration treaties, statutes, cases, and practices reveals an unapologetic, variegated racial character that today distinctly disadvantages Latin Americans. But peculiar racial antipathy has been specifically reserved for Asians, particularly the Chinese. While Chinese laborers were not enslaved in exactly the same fashion that Blacks had been, they were imported under a series of formal and informal labor contracting devices. These were designed to provide cheap, exploitable raw labor for the United States railroad industry, a labor force that would have few legal or social rights. Immigration law developments in the 1800s, particularly the last third of the century, were dominated by racial devices employed to control the Chinese laborers and deny them formal rights. These formal legal devices included treaties, statutes, and cases.

Anti-Chinese animus was particularly virulent in California, where a series of substantive and petty nuisance state ordinances were aimed at the Chinese. These ordinances provided for arbitrary inspections of Chinese laundries, special tax levies, inspections and admission regulations for aliens entering California ports, mandated grooming standards for prisoners that prohibited pigtails, and a variety of other regulations designed to harass and discriminate against the laborers. Many of these statutes were enacted in defiance of the preemptive role of the federal government in immigration policymaking, and would not have survived the United States–China Burlingame Treaty, adopted in 1868.

Although many of these statutes were struck down and Reconstruction legislation was worded to specify certain protections to immigrants, by 1880 the Burlingame Treaty had been amended to restrict the immigration of Chinese laborers. Congress enacted the Chinese Exclusion Act in 1882, and even harsher legislation in 1884. By 1888, Congress reached the point of no return. Another harsher act was passed which virtually prohibited Chinese from entering or reentering the United States, while the Burlingame Treaty was altered again, ratcheting even further the mechanisms aimed at the Chinese.

In a series of important cases, the United States Supreme Court refused to strike down these federal laws and treaties, on political question grounds. In one of these cases, the Court stated:

> The power of exclusion of foreigners being an incident of sovereignty belonging to the government of the United States, as a part of those sovereign powers delegated by the Constitution, the right to its exercise at any time when, in the judgment of the government, the interests of the country require it, cannot be granted away or restrained on behalf of any one.... If there be any just ground of complaint on the part of China [or the Chinese immigrants], it must be made to the political department of our government, which is alone competent to act upon the subject.

Although the aliens, like the Cherokees before them, prevailed in some of the most egregious instances, the racist tide had undeniably turned. In 1892, Congress extended the amended Burlingame Treaty for an additional ten years, and added a provision for removing, through deportation, those Chinese who had managed to dodge the earlier bullets. An extraordinary provision suspended deportation for those Chinese laborers who could qualify (through a special hardship exemption) and could furnish "one credible white witness" on their behalf.

In 1893, this proviso was tested by the luckless Fong Yue Ting, who foolishly produced only another Chinese witness to stay his own deportation. The United States Supreme Court upheld his expulsion, on political question grounds. The majority opinion speculated that the Chinese would not be truthful, noting that Chinese testimony in similar situations "was attended with great embarrassment, from the suspicious nature, in many instances, of the testimony offered to establish the residence of the parties, arising from the loose notions entertained by the witness of the obligations of an oath." As my grandfather would have said, they obviously had no shame and were probably *sin verguenzas*.

Congress enacted additional extensions of the Chinese exclusion statutes and treaties until 1943. When the immigration laws began to become more codified, each iteration formally included specific reference to the dreaded and unpopular Chinese. Thus, the Immigration Acts of 1917, 1921, and 1924 all contain references that single out this group. If the Space Traders had landed in the late 1800s or early 1900s and demanded the Chinese in exchange for gold, antitoxins, and other considerations, there is little doubt but that the States, Congress, and the United States Supreme Court would have acquiesced.

MEXICANS, THE BRACERO PROGRAM, AND OPERATION WETBACK

Nineteenth century Chinese labor history in the United States is one of building railroads; that of Mexicans and Mexican Americans is agricultural labor, picking perishable crops. In the Southwestern and Western United States, Mexicans picked half of the cotton and nearly 75 percent of the fruits and vegetables by the 1920s. By 1930, half of the sugar beet workers were Mexican, and 80 percent of the farmhands in Southern California were Mexican. As fields became increasingly mechanized, it was Anglo workers who rode the machines, consigning Mexicans to stoop-labor and hand cultivation. One observer noted: "The consensus of opinion of ranchers large and small . . . is that only the small minority of Mexicans are fitted for these types of labor [i.e., mechanized agricultural jobs] at the present time."

Most crucial to the agricultural growers was the need for a reserve labor pool of workers who could be imported for their work, displaced when not needed, and kept in subordinate status so they could not afford to organize collectively or protest their conditions. Mexicans filled this bill perfectly, especially in the early twentieth century Southwest, where Mexican poverty and the Revolution forced rural Mexicans to come to the United States for work. This migration was facilitated by United States growers' agents, who recruited widely in Mexican villages, by the building of railroads (by Mexicans, not Chinese) from the interior of Mexico to El Paso, and by labor shortages in the United States during World War I.

Another means of controlling the spigot of Mexican farm workers was the use of immigration laws. Early labor restrictions through federal immigration law (and state law, as in California) had been aimed at Chinese workers, as outlined in the previous section. When agricultural interests pressured Congress to allow Mexican temporary workers during 1917–1921, the head tax (then set at $8.00), literacy requirements, public charge provisions, and Alien Contract Labor Law provisions were waived. By 1929, with a surplus of "native" United States workers facing the Depression, the supply of Mexicans was turned off by reimposing the immigration requirements.

While United States nativists were pointing to the evils and inferiority of Southern European immigrants, Mexicans were characterized as a docile, exploitable, deportable labor force. As one commentator noted:

> Mexican laborers, by accepting these undesirable tasks, enabled [Southwestern] agriculture and industry to flourish, thereby creating effective opportunities for

[white] American workers in the higher job levels.... The representatives of [United States] economic interests showed the basic reason for their support of Mexican immigration[;] employers of the Southwest favored unlimited Mexican immigration because it provided them with a source of cheap labor which would be exploited to the fullest possible extent.

To effectuate control over the Southern border, the Border Patrol was created in 1924, while the Department of Labor and the Immigration Bureau began a procedure in 1925 to regulate Mexican immigration by restricting the flow to workers already employed or promised positions.

During the Depression, two means were used to control Mexican workers: mass deportations and repatriations. Los Angeles was targeted for massive deportations for persons with Spanish-sounding names or Mexican features who could not produce formal papers, and over 80,000 Mexicans were deported from 1929–1935. Many of these persons had the legal right to be in the country, or had been born citizens but simply could not prove their status; of course, many of these workers had been eagerly sought for perishable crops. In addition, over one-half million Mexicans were also "voluntarily" repatriated by choosing to go to Mexico rather than remain in the United States, possibly subject to formal deportation.

By 1940, the cycle had turned: labor shortages and World War II had created the need for more agricultural workers, and growers convinced the United States government to enter into a large scale contract-labor scheme, the Bracero Program. Originally begun in 1942 under an Executive Order, the program brokered laborers under contracts between the United States and Mexico. Between 1942 and 1951, over one-half million "braceros" were hired under the program. Public funds were used to seek and register workers in Mexico who, after their labor had been performed, were returned to Mexico until the crops were ready to be picked again. This program was cynically employed to create a reserve pool of temporary laborers who had few rights and no vesting of equities.

By 1946, the circulation of bracero labor, both in its certification and its deportation mechanism, had become hopelessly confused. It became impossible to separate Mexican Americans from deportable Mexicans. Many United States citizens were mistakenly "repatriated" to Mexico, including men with Mexican features who had never been to Mexico. Thus, a system of "drying out wetbacks" was instituted. This modest legalization process gave some Mexican braceros an opportunity to regularize their immigration status and remain in the United States while they worked as braceros.

In 1950, under these various mechanisms, 20,000 new braceros were certified, 97,000 agricultural workers were dehydrated, and 480,000 old braceros were deported back to Mexico. In 1954, over one million braceros were deported under the terms of "Operation Wetback," a "Special Mobile Force" of the Border Patrol. The program included massive roundups and deportations, factory and field raids, a relentless media campaign designed to characterize the mop-up operation as a national security necessity, and a tightening up of the border to deter undocumented immigration.

CONCLUSION AND MY
GRANDFATHER'S MEMORIES

In two of his books based on folktales from Tierra Amarilla, New Mexico, the writer Sabine Ulibarri has re-created the Hispano-Indian world of rural, northern New Mexico. In *Cuentos de Tierra Amarilla (Tales from Tierra Amarilla),* he collects a variety of wonderful tales, rooted in this isolated town that time has not changed, even today. My grandfather enjoyed this book, which I read to him in his final years, 1981 and 1982. But his favorite (and mine) was Ulibarri's masterwork, *Mi Abuela Fumaba Puros (My Grandmother Smoked Puros* [Cigars]), in which an old woman lights cigars in her house to remind her of her dead husband.

My grandfather loved this story, not only because it was by his more famous *tocayo,* but because it was at once outlandish ("mujeres en Nuevo Mexico no fumaban puros"—that is, women in New Mexico did not smoke cigars) and yet very real. Smells were very real to him, evocative of earlier events and cuentos, the way that tea and madeleines unlocked Proust's prodigious memory. Biscochitos evoked holidays, and empanadas Christmas. Had he outlived my grandmother, he would have had mementos in the house, perhaps prune pies or apricot jam.

My grandfather's world, with the exception of his World War I sortie in Texas and abroad, was small but not narrow. He lived by a code of behavior, one he passed to his more fortunate children (only one of whom still lives in New Mexico—my father) and grandchildren (most of whom no longer live in New Mexico). But for me, no longer in New Mexico, reading Derrick Bell's Chronicles is like talking to my grandfather or reading Sabine Ulibarri; the stories are at once outlandish, yet very real.

Folklore and corridos have always held a powerful place in Mexican society. Fiction has always held a powerful place in the human experience, and the Chronicles will inform racial jurisprudence and civil rights scholarship in the United States in ways not yet evident. Critical minority renderings of United States racial history, immigration practices, and labor economy can have equally compelling results, however, recounting what actually happened in all the sordid details. If Derrick Bell's work forces us to engage these unsavory practices, he will have performed an even greater service than that already attributed to him in this forum and elsewhere. He will have caused us to examine our grandfathers' stories and lives.

It is 1990. As a deterrent to Central American refugees and as "bait" to attract their families already in the United States, the INS began in the 1980s to incarcerate undocumented adults and unaccompanied minors in border camps. One, near Brownsville, Texas, was once used as a United States Department of Agriculture pesticide storage facility. The INS has defied court orders to improve conditions in the camps, and by 1990 hundreds of alien children were being held without health, educational, and legal services. Haitian boat persons were being interdicted at sea, given "hearings" on the boats, and repatriated to Haiti; by 1990, only six of 20,000 interdicted Haitians had been granted asylum. The INS had begun a media campaign to justify its extraordinary practices on land and on sea. The cycle of United States immigration history continued, and all was ready for the Space Traders.

ACKNOWLEDGMENTS

1.1 From Michael Omi and Howard Winant, *Racial Formations in the United States from the 1960s to the 1980s* (Routledge, Kegan & Paul, 1986). Copyright © 1986 by Michael Omi and Howard Winant. Reprinted by permission of Routledge, Inc.

1.2 From Beth B. Hess, Elizabeth W. Markson, and Peter J. Stein, "Racial and Ethnic Minorities: An Overview," in Beth B. Hess, Elizabeth W. Markson, and Peter J. Stein, *Sociology* (Macmillan, 1985). Copyright © 1985 by Macmillan Publishing Company, a division of Simon & Schuster, Inc. Reprinted by permission. References omitted.

1.3 From John Hope Franklin, "Ethnicity in American Life: The Historical Perspective," in John Hope Franklin, ed., *Race and History: Selected Essays, 1938–1988* (Louisiana State University Press, 1989). Copyright © 1989 by Louisiana State University Press. Reprinted by permission.

2.1 From Robert K. Merton, "Discrimination and the American Creed," in Robert M. MacIver, ed., *Discrimination and National Welfare* (Harper & Row, 1949). Copyright © 1949 by The Institute for Religious and Social Studies. Reprinted by permission of HarperCollins Publishers, Inc.

2.2 From William Julius Wilson, "The Declining Significance of Race," *Society* (January/February 1978). Copyright © 1978 by William Julius Wilson. Reprinted by permission of Chicago University Press.

2.3 From Joe R. Feagin, "The Continuing Significance of Race: Antiblack Discrimination in Public Places," *American Sociological Review*, vol. 56 (February 1991). Copyright © 1991 by The American Sociological Association. Reprinted by permission.

3.1 From Louis L. Knowles and Kenneth Prewitt, "Institutional and Ideological Roots of Racism," in Louis L. Knowles and Kenneth Prewitt, eds., *Institutional Racism in America* (Prentice Hall, 1969). Copyright © 1969 by Prentice Hall, a division of Simon & Schuster, Inc. Reprinted by permission.

3.2 From Elizabeth Martínez, "Beyond Black/White: The Racisms of Our Time," *Social Justice*, vol. 20, nos. 1–2 (1993). Copyright © 1993 by *Social Justice*. Reprinted by permission.

3.3 From Nancy Stein, "Affirmative Action and the Persistence of Racism," *Social Justice*, vol. 22, no. 3 (Fall 1995), pp. 28–43. Copyright © 1995 by *Social Justice*. Reprinted by permission. References omitted.

4.1 From Milton M. Gordon, "Assimilation in America: Theory and Reality," *Daedalus*, vol. 90, no. 2 (Spring 1961). Copyright © 1961 by *Daedalus*, a journal of The American Academy of Arts and Sciences. Reprinted by permission.

4.2 From Ruth W. Grant and Marion Orr, "Language, Race and Politics: From 'Black' to 'African-American,'" *Politics and Society* (June 1996), pp. 137–149. Copyright © 1996 by Sage Publications, Inc. Reprinted by permission.

4.3 From Lewis M. Killian, "Race Relations and the Nineties: Where Are the Dreams of the Sixties?" *Social Forces*, vol. 69, no. 1 (September 1990). Copyright © 1990 by University of North Carolina Press. Reprinted by permission. References omitted.

5.1 From William Ryan, *Blaming the Victim* (Pantheon Books, 1971). Copyright © 1971 by Pantheon Books, a division of Random House, Inc. Reprinted by permission.

5.2 From Edna Bonacich, "Inequality in America: The Failure of the American System for People of Color," *Sociological Spectrum,* vol. 9, no. 1 (1989), pp. 77–101. Copyright © 1989 by Taylor & Francis, Inc., Washington, DC. Reprinted by permission.

5.3 From Leslie Inniss and Joe R. Feagin, "The Black 'Underclass' Ideology in Race Relations Analysis," *Social Justice,* vol. 16, no. 4 (Winter 1989), pp. 13–32. Copyright © 1989 by *Social Justice.* Reprinted by permission. References omitted.

6.1 From Noel Jacob Kent, "The New Campus Racism: What's Going On?" *Thought and Action* (1997). Copyright © 1997 by *Thought and Action.* Reprinted by permission. Notes and references omitted.

6.2 From Bobby Wright and William G. Tierney, "American Indians in Higher Education: A History of Cultural Conflict," *Change,* vol. 23, no. 2 (March/April 1991). Copyright © 1991 by The Helen Dwight Reid Educational Foundation. Reprinted by permission of Heldref Publications, 1319 18th St., NW, Washington, DC 20036-1802.

6.3 From Jonathan Kozol, *Savage Inequalities: Children in America's Schools* (Crown Publishers, 1991). Copyright © 1991 by Jonathan Kozol. Reprinted by permission of Crown Publishers, Inc.

7.1 From Leobardo F. Estrada, F. Chris García, Reynaldo Flores Macías, and Lionel Maldonado, "Chicanos in the United States: A History of Exploitation and Resistance," *Daedalus,* vol. 110, no. 2 (Spring 1981). Copyright © 1981 by *Daedalus,* a journal of The American Academy of Arts and Sciences. Reprinted by permission. Some notes omitted. This essay is a joint effort by the authors. The listing of names in no way indicates the extent of contribution. Rather, all four authors contributed equally.

7.2 From Su Sun Bai, "Affirmative Pursuit of Political Equality for Asian Pacific Americans: Reclaiming the Voting Rights Act," *University of Pennsylvania Law Review,* vol. 139 (1991), pp. 731+. Copyright © 1991 by *University of Pennsylvania Law Review.* Reprinted by permission. Notes omitted.

7.3 Adapted from Frank Harold Wilson, "Housing and Black Americans: The Persistent Significance of Race," in William Velez, ed., *Race and Ethnicity in the United States* (General Hall, 1997). Copyright © 1997 by General Hall, Inc. Reprinted by permission. References omitted.

8.1 From Reynolds Farley, "Blacks, Hispanics, and White Ethnic Groups: Are Blacks Uniquely Disadvantaged?" *American Economic Review,* vol. 80, no. 2 (May 1980). Copyright © 1980 by The American Economic Association. Reprinted by permission.

8.2 From George E. Tinker and Loring Bush, "Native American Unemployment: Statistical Games and Coverups," in George W. Shepherd, Jr., and David Penna, eds., *Racism and the Underclass: State Policy and Discrimination Against Minorities* (Greenwood Press, 1991). Copyright © 1991 by Greenwood Press, an imprint of Greenwood Publishing Group, Inc., Westport, CT. Reprinted by permission. Notes omitted.

8.3 From Havidán Rodríguez, "Population, Economic Mobility and Income Inequality: A Portrait of Latinos in the United States, 1970–1991," *Latino Studies Journal,* vol. 3, no. 2 (May 1992). Copyright © 1992 by Havidán Rodríguez. Reprinted by permission. References omitted.

9.1 From Robert Staples, "White Racism, Black Crime, and American Justice: An Application of the Colonial Model to Explain Crime and Race," *Phylon,* vol. 36

388

Acknowledgments

(1972). Copyright © 1972 by Clark Atlanta University, Atlanta, GA. Reprinted by permission.

9.2 From Adalberto Aguirre, Jr., and David V. Baker, "A Descriptive Profile of Mexican American Executions in the Southwest," *The Social Science Journal*, vol. 34, no. 3 (1997), pp. 389–401. Copyright © 1997 by JAI Press, Inc. Reprinted by permission. Notes and references omitted.

9.3 From Marc Mauer and Tracy Huling, *Young Black Americans and the Criminal Justice System: Five Years Later* (The Sentencing Project, 1995), pp. 396–404. Copyright © 1995 by The Sentencing Project. Reprinted by permission.

10.1 From Robert Staples and Terry Jones, "Culture, Ideology and Black Television Images," *The Black Scholar* (May/June 1985). Copyright © 1985 by *The Black Scholar*. Reprinted by permission. References omitted.

10.2 From Ralph C. Gomes and Linda Faye Williams, "Race and Crime: The Role of the Media in Perpetuating Racism and Classism in America," *The Urban League Review*, vol. 14, no. 1 (1990). Copyright © 1990 by Transaction Publishers, Inc. Reprinted by permission. Notes omitted.

10.3 From Richard E. Lapchick and David Stuckey, "Professional Sports: The Racial Report Card," *Center for the Study of Sports in Society Digest*, vol. 3 (1991). Copyright © 1991 by The Center for the Study of Sports in Society, Northeastern University. Reprinted by permission.

11.1 From Richard Delgado, "Words That Wound: A Tort Action for Racial Insults, Epithets, and Name-Calling," *Harvard Civil Rights–Civil Liberties Law Review*, vol. 133 (1982), pp. 159–165. Copyright © 1982 by the President and Fellows of Harvard College. Reprinted by permission. Notes omitted.

11.2 From Robert D. Bullard, "Race and Environmental Justice in the United States," *Yale Journal of International Law* (vol. 18, 1993). Copyright © 1993 by *Yale Journal of International Law*. Reprinted by permission. Notes omitted.

12.1 From Derrick Bell, "Racism Will Always Be With Us," *New Perspectives Quarterly* (vol. 8, 1991). Copyright © 1991 by *New Perspectives Quarterly*. Reprinted by permission.

12.2 From Christopher Bates Doob, *Racism: An American Cauldron* (HarperCollins, 1993). Copyright © 1993 by HarperCollins College Publishers, Inc. Reprinted by permission.

12.3 From Michael A. Olivas, "The Chronicles, My Grandfather's Stories, and Immigration Law: The Slave Traders Chronicle as Racial History," *St. Louis University Law Journal*, vol. 425 (1990), pp. 9–17. Copyright © 1990 by *St. Louis University Law Journal*. Reprinted by permission. Notes omitted.

Index